Do You Love Me?

R. D. LAING

DO YOU
LOVE
ME?

*An Entertainment in
Conversation and Verse*

Pantheon Books, *New York*

Library of Congress Cataloging in Publication Data
Laing, Ronald David.
Do You Love Me?
  I. Title.
PR6062.A36D6   822'.9'14   76-9983
ISBN 0-394-40017-8

Manufactured in the United States of America

FIRST EDITION

Contents

Do You Love Me?

One

1

Return of the prodigal I

MOTHER	he's come back to see you
SON	hullo dad
FATHER	hello (*pause*) Who are you?
SON	I'm your son dad
FATHER	O you're my *son*
SON	yes dad
FATHER	and what's your name?
SON	Peter
FATHER	you're my son Peter
SON	yes dad
FATHER	you're my son Peter
SON	yes dad I'm your son Peter
FATHER	you used to live with my wife
	I never thought I would see you again
SON	well here I am dad
FATHER	very nice to see you again Peter
SON	very nice to see you again dad
FATHER	and are you married Peter?
SON	yes dad
FATHER	and have you any children?
SON	yes dad
FATHER	and what have you been up to?
SON	I've been traveling around
FATHER	and have you been successful?
SON	yes so far touch wood
FATHER	that's wonderful that's wonderful
	and are you married Peter?

SON	yes dad
FATHER	and have you any children?
SON	yes dad
FATHER	and what do you do?
SON	I'm a musician
FATHER	Peter was always interested in music
SON	yes
FATHER	are you staying long?
SON	I have to leave in a few minutes
FATHER	well I'm very glad to see you Peter
SON	very glad to see you dad

        (*pause*)

SON	how have *you* been keeping?
FATHER	I don't want her to die before me
MOTHER	you shouldn't say that

        (*pause*)

FATHER	you're a magician
SON	yes
FATHER	my son Peter's a musician do you know him?
SON	I'm not sure
FATHER	he travels around a lot he's married he's successful he's got children are you sure you don't know him?
SON	I *am* him
FATHER	O you *are* him
SON	I'm your son Peter
FATHER	You're my son Peter I never thought I would see you again Peter that's wonderful do you hear that he's my son Peter
SON	you've got a son called Peter?
FATHER	that's my boy
SON	what do you think of Peter dad?

MOTHER   that's enough!
SON   why?
MOTHER   you've already gone too far
SON   be quiet   It's all right
MOTHER   you were always like that
SON   don't interfere
MOTHER   it's my business
SON   what do you think of Peter?
FATHER   (*laughing*) he's a bit of a rascal
MOTHER   (*puts palm across father's mouth with out-
         stretched arm and keeps it there, addressing
         son*)
         there will be no more of this nonsense
SON   (*removes mother's hand from father's mouth
         with slow steady application of force. She re-
         sists silently with all her power, till her two
         hands are placed across her lap*)
         it's all right   (*kisses her*)   I promise
         I have to go now anyway
         (*turns to father*)
         I'm Peter   I have to go now dad
FATHER   well I'm very glad to see you Peter
         I never thought I would see you again
SON   goodbye dad
         very glad to see you again
FATHER   goodbye Peter   Wonderful
SON   goodbye mum
         (*kisses*)
MOTHER   don't be so long next time
SON   I won't
         (*kisses*)

2

Mutterings

1 I couldn't believe it I just couldn't believe it just could not
believe it I I I just couldn't believe it couldn't believe it
couldn't believe it I just couldn't believe couldn't believe
it couldn't believe it I I just I just couldn't I just
couldn't believe it could not believe it I couldn't believe
it couldn't believe it couldn't believe it

2 do y'know what I mean you know y'know what I mean
it's sort of it's well it's it's well it's you know what I
mean y'know you just cant have any idea yknow what I
mean yknow its its well its not like anything really you
know what I mean its nothing really dyou know what
I mean I cant stand it

3 What am I going on about anyway? Whats the problem?
Is there a problem? Thats the problem. Maybe. Maybe
not. But anyway. Why do I think there may be a
problem if there is no problem and why do I think there
may be no problem if there is? Anyway. Whether there
is or there isnt a problem its a problem how much time to
spend figuring out if there is or there isnt anyway
what difference does it make anyway if there is or is
not a problem what *is* a problem is a problem anyway

4 no thinking no no thinking no no no *no* thinking
no no no no no no thinking no forgetting no recall
no action no no action *do* nothing don't
do nothing don't do anything what is not allowed is
forbidden

5 My neck is on the guillotine the blade comes down
   my head goes this way the rest goes that
   which side will I be on?

3

Have you a corkscrew?

Little old shop, evening, December
YOUNG MAN, *overcoat, bottle of red wine in*
hand, enters from front door
OLD MAN *enters from back of shop to behind*
counter

OLD MAN	Good morning
YOUNG MAN	(*pause, then abruptly*) Good morning ...
OLD MAN	Yes?
YOUNG MAN	Yes. Sorry. Have you a corkscrew please?
OLD MAN	Why?
YOUNG MAN	(*pause, then abruptly*) I want to open this bottle
OLD MAN	(*quickly, and as though that explains it*) Oh I see (*pause*)
YOUNG MAN	Well?
OLD MAN	(*pleasantly and patiently*) What?
YOUNG MAN	Have you a corkscrew?
OLD MAN	No
YOUNG MAN	Well tha—
OLD MAN	(*interrupts*) I'm sorry. I haven't
YOUNG MAN	Well th—
OLD MAN	(*interrupts*) No I'm very sorry I haven't (*pause*) Have you tried elsewhere?
YOUNG MAN	Yes I have
OLD MAN	Did they have one?
YOUNG MAN	No they didn't
OLD MAN	Did you try up the road?
YOUNG MAN	Yes I did

OLD MAN	Did they have one?
YOUNG MAN	No they did not
OLD MAN	It's no use trying up the road, they never have anything
YOUNG MAN	Well th—
OLD MAN	(*interrupts*) Have you tried *down* the road?
YOUNG MAN	No I have not
OLD MAN	(*with sudden finality*) Try down the road!
YOUNG MAN	Yes well thanks. I shall. Yes thank you very much
OLD MAN	Not at all. My pleasure. Goodday
YOUNG MAN	Goodday

4

I've lost it

Lost what?

Have you seen it?

Seen what?

My face

No

5

DOCTOR   How are you?

The patient points to a tracheotomy tube in his neck

DOCTOR   I'm sorry

Realizing the patient can't speak
the doctor takes a pad and pencil and writes
                HOW ARE YOU?
and hands pad and pencil to the patient for his reply

The patient takes the pad and pencil and writes
                I'M NOT DEAF

6

Red spiders did you say?

With green eyes

When did it start?

When I left her

Still going on?

They stopped some months ago
now it's vampires seven feet across with green eyes
close together. One nearly got me the other day

How?

I was off guard, I was in the bath just relaxing
into some nice black Nepalese. One of them came at me

What happened?

It had breached my psychic defense shield. It got
to a foot of my throat

And?

I stopped it by mind control but it was close

You can't be too careful

Too true

Are you seeing her again?

Tomorrow

Best of luck

7

You're jewish aren't you?

Yes

You don't look jewish, you know what I mean

No

You're not *orthodox*, are you, or anything like that?

O no

There's not anti-semitism here, you know, so you shouldn't have any problems, you know what I mean

Good good

No you shouldn't have any problems (*pause*) you're sure you're not orthodox?

O no I'm a psychoanalyst

O yes of course of course no you shouldn't have any problems just say you're presbyterian you know what I mean

8
Return of the prodigal II

Father!
Bastard!
Father!
Bastard!
Barnacle Bill's my father
I'm Barnacle Bill
Father!
Bastard!

Two

9

Fable 1

Jack and Jill are married and love each other
Jack from time to time thinks Jill has affairs
with Tom, Dick, or Harry, but he is wrong

Jack's best friend is John
John's wife leaves him, and Jack invites John
to stay with him and Jill

While Jill is consoling John, John fucks Jill
Jill thus discovers that Jack can't trust John

Enraged at John's betrayal of Jack
Jill tells Jack he can't trust John, but not why
Jack feels Jill is jealous of John and him and is trying
to break up their friendship

Jack leaves Jill

Jack and John go off together

10
Fable II

Jack and Jill are married, in love, and have children

Jack thinks Jill is having an affair with Tom, his best friend
he confides in Jane, Jill's best friend, who confirms his suspicions

So does Tom

Jill denies everything
Jack can no longer believe her
he leaves Jill and the children
and goes to live with Jane

Jill goes to live with Tom

Actually, it was Jane and Tom who were the secret lovers: a fact Jack and Jill never knew

11
Fable III

Jack, Dick, and Tom are best friends
Jill, Jane, and Joan are best friends

Jack and Jill fall in love
Dick and Jane fall in love

Jack and Joan fall in love
Tom falls in love with Joan
Joan falls out of love with Jack and into love with Tom
Jane falls in love with Tom
Tom falls out of love with Joan and into love with Jane
Jack falls out of love with Joan and into love with Jane

Jane has Jack, Dick, and Tom

Joan kills herself

Jane falls out of love with Tom
and into love with Dick again

Jack falls out of love with Jane
and into love with Jill again

Dick and Jill do not know about
Jack and Jane, Jack and Joan,
Tom and Jane, Tom and Joan

Tom does not know about Jack and Jane

Three

12

You never look at me

He puts on some music
After a little

SHE How about some music?

He takes record off, and puts on another
She takes that one off and puts on another
After a little

SHE Do you like it?

HE Not particularly
     (*pause*) but I don't mind it (*pause*)
     no one's dancing

She puts on another

HE Couldn't you put on something a bit
     more personal?

She takes it off and puts on another without comment
They sit in silence till the end of side I

SHE I don't know what to put on now

HE Don't put on anything then

SHE But I would like *some*thing

HE Then put on something you know and like

SHE Do you know this one?

HE No. Do you?

SHE No

She puts it on
After a bit

HE Why can't you put on something we both
     know and like or *you* at least know and

like? I don't like our home being invaded
by a crowd of complete strangers

SHE   I quite like it

HE   I don't

She takes it off. Puts on the first one she had on

SHE   I know and like this

He takes it off. Puts on another

HE   I *love* this one

He turns the volume up

SHE   Would you mind turning it down a bit, please?

He turns it down

SHE   Can I change it? No. I'll wait

HE   I think I'm entitled to one side

She turns it down a bit more

HE   I can't hear it now. (*pause*) Mind if I turn it up
      a little?

SHE   No

He turns it up a little

SHE   You never look at me

HE   I beg your pardon

SHE   I'm not going to shout

He turns it down

SHE   You never look at me

He turns it up again

13
Not tonight Josephine

HE   what do you want?

SHE   make love to me

HE   you are a
placenta that sucks me dry and poisons me
a womb that suffocates and crushes me
an umbilical cord that stings and strangles me
your vagina is the entry to hell
not tonight Josephine

SHE   you would put anyone off

HE   put out the light

SHE   you have put it out yourself

14
Not tonight Oedipus

HE   how about it?

SHE   not like that

HE   I fancy you more than you fancy me

SHE   that's because you are emotionally blocked

HE   how do you make that out?

SHE   you can't stand your feelings
so you put them all into your penis

HE   you have less time for me
than I have have for you

SHE   you mean you want to fuck me more often
than I want to be fucked

HE   I like looking into your eyes

SHE   emotionally mature people do not seem
to need to look into one another's eyes
as long and as often as you seem to need
to look into mine

HE   your face is beautiful in the firelight

SHE   no doubt I remind you of your mother

HE   mummy!

SHE   not tonight Oedipus

15
Kisses

SHE   you were going to ask me what I wanted for
a birthday present

HE   O yes. I forgot. What would you like?

SHE   guess

HE   the head of John the Baptist

SHE   don't be frivolous

HE   what then?

SHE   a divorce

HE   it's too expensive

SHE   O darling please

HE   I'll see what I can do but I can't
promise

SHE   promise you'll do your best

HE   promise

SHE   kisses

HE   kisses

16
I can't hear you

HE   I can't hear you

SHE   you're not listening

HE   I'm trying

SHE   I love you for *trying*

HE   I was trying to acknowledge I heard you

SHE   I detest being acknowledged

HE   all right

SHE   it's not all right

HE   what's not?

SHE   you're not listening

HE   you're not communicating

SHE   the dumb speaking to the deaf

HE   there we are

SHE   don't do that

HE   am I not allowed to agree with you?

SHE   it's not funny

HE   I never said it was

17
It's difficult

HE	it's difficult
SHE	difficult
HE	difficult to stop
SHE	very difficult
HE	especially
SHE	yes
HE	when
SHE	quite
HE	it's difficult
SHE	let's stop it
	(*pause*)
HE	stopped
SHE	stopped
	(*pause*)
	(*almost simultaneously*)
SHE	oh
HE	it's started again
SHE	let's stop it
HE	how?
SHE	stopped
	(*pause*)
SHE	(*talking about it*)
	it is difficult
HE	what *is* it?
	(*pause*)
SHE	it's started again
HE	stopped
	(*pause*)

SHE ⎫ you're at it again
HE ⎬ you're at it again
    ⎭ (*pause*)
SHE ⎫ difficult
HE ⎬ it is difficult

18
Stop it

SHE   stop it

HE   you stop it

SHE   I can't stop what I'm not doing

HE   you started it

SHE   and you stop it

HE   I can't stop what I'm not doing

SHE   you think you're going to get away with it

HE   get away with what?

SHE   you're not going to wriggle out of it this time

HE   wriggle out of what?

SHE   don't kid you're daft

HE   I'm not doing anything of the kind

SHE   come off it

HE   I'm not on it

SHE   cut it out

HE   cut what out?

SHE   will you stop it

HE   stop what?

SHE   that

HE   what?

SHE   you know perfectly well

HE   I'm afraid I don't

SHE   I'm afraid I don't

HE   I'm going to sleep

SHE   you've never woken up

19

Where does it all come from?

SHE where does it all come from?

HE all what come from?

SHE all that shit you keep pouring over me all the time

HE count your blessings

SHE I'm counting my toes

HE the Lord giveth the Lord taketh away

SHE you should have told me

HE what?

SHE that I was living with the Lord God Almighty

HE what's the matter now?

SHE you obviously think you're the Lord God
Almighty

HE can't you moderate your language?

SHE Lord Muck that's what you are
Lord Muck

HE I am not the Lord God Almighty
and I am not Lord Muck

SHE really?

HE yes really

SHE you're such a liar

20

You think you're going to get away with it

SHE   you think you're going to get away with it

HE   get away with what?

SHE   you hate women, you destroy women. Look at all the women you've destroyed

HE   look at them?

SHE   take a good look at them

HE   I've no particular desire to

SHE   well?

HE   well what?

SHE   you're not going to do that to me

HE   do what to you?

SHE   what you've done to them

HE   what have I done to them?

SHE   look at them

HE   well

SHE   you've cut them up and stuffed the pieces and you have them here plastered all around us. You're not going to cut me up and stuff me like that

HE   really, I can't see anything

SHE   I can *smell* it

HE   your nose is too near your arse

21
Well then

SHE	well then
HE	well then what?
SHE	you know
HE	I know what?
SHE	you know perfectly well
HE	no I do not know perfectly well
SHE	come on
HE	you come on
SHE	come off it
HE	you come off it
SHE	you give it up
HE	you started it
SHE	it's you that's keeping it going
HE	what going?
SHE	you're still at it
HE	at what?
SHE	you know perfectly well
HE	I'm not going into that again
SHE	you've never gone into anything
HE	look who's talking
SHE	I'm looking

22
You're such a fuckin liar

SHE	well then?
HE	well then what?
SHE	you did didn't you?
HE	what are you talking about?
SHE	you know perfectly well what I'm talking about
HE	if you're still on about that I've said all I am going to say
SHE	you did didn't you?
HE	I've already told you
SHE	you did didn't you?
HE	I'm not going to be interrogated
SHE	just tell me the truth
HE	I've told you
SHE	who was it?
HE	no one
SHE	you're such a liar
HE	you said you weren't jealous
SHE	don't change the subject
HE	what are you going on about? I've already told you
SHE	I'm not jealous I only have to know
HE	why have you such a suspicious mind?
SHE	I know who it was
HE	you've made up your mind. There's nothing more I can say
SHE	you think you're going to get away with it
HE	there's nothing to get away with
SHE	you did I know you did
HE	no
SHE	you might as well admit it
HE	there's nothing to admit
SHE	she told me herself

HE	I know you are making that up
SHE	she came and told me herself
HE	why do you have to resort to such lies?
SHE	I'm not going to let you destroy my sense of reality along with everything else
HE	you are paranoid
SHE	you're not going to get away with it
HE	you fancy her yourself
SHE	no
HE	you're an unconscious lesbian
SHE	no
HE	you should see a psychiatrist
SHE	don't fob me off
HE	you're obsessed
SHE	you did I know you did (*pause*) I'll phone her up right now (*pause*) you did (*pause*)
HE	once
SHE	you're such a liar
HE	I didn't enjoy it
SHE	O you're such a fuckin liar

23
Darling please forgive me

HE   darling please forgive me

SHE   I've forgiven you for everything already

HE   please forgive me one more time

SHE   there's nothing more to forgive

HE   don't despair darling

SHE   no?

HE   darling please forgive me

SHE   I've forgiven you so much I'm exhausted please

HE   but darling I can't come if you don't forgive me

SHE   try going then

HE   but darling if you don't forgive me I *have* to again so you'll forgive me again

SHE   I'll never forgive you

HE   you're so arrogant

SHE   I'll never forgive you for anything any more

HE   but you can't *help* it darling

SHE   no?

HE   you can't keep it up don't worry it'll be all right

SHE   I mean it

HE   I'll give you something else to forgive

SHE   not for my sake please

HE   not at all. I like helping along your spiritual development

24
Shut up

SHE   it's the same thing

HE   no it is not

SHE   yes it is

HE   let's not go through all that again

SHE   right

HE   why do you always have the last word?

SHE   you have it

HE   thank you
       (*pause*)

SHE   don't mention it

HE   why can't you shut up?

SHE   why can't *you* shut up?

HE   shut up

SHE   you shut up
       (*both together*)

HE } shut up
SHE } shut up

25

never saw it
never heard it
never smelt it, touched it, tasted it
never felt it
never heard it mentioned
never had any idea of it
never dreamt of it
never wanted it
never missed it
never lost it
never found it

26

Why did the peacock scream?
  in order to hear himself

why did the peacock scream?
  because he couldn't see himself

Four

27

I can't help it

SHE	I can't help it
HE	can't help what?
SHE	getting into this
HE	getting into what?
SHE	if I could say I wouldn't be in it
HE	what's it like?
SHE	it's terrible
HE	in what way?
SHE	I can't say. That's why it's so terrible
HE	try harder
SHE	I'm doing my best
HE	your best is not good enough however
SHE	I know
HE	you're very blasé about it
SHE	I'm desperate
HE	where were we?
SHE	I don't know
HE	what do you mean you don't know?
SHE	what do you mean what do I mean?
HE	what were you saying?
SHE	I was saying I can't help it
HE	can't help what?
SHE	getting into this
HE	this what?
SHE	what we are in now
HE	what are you talking about?

SHE	(*silence*)
HE	you must have been talking about something
SHE	I can't say
HE	what do you mean you can't say?
SHE	I can't say
HE	can't say what?
SHE	you know perfectly well
HE	I do not
SHE	don't you?
HE	why don't you stop it?
SHE	stop what?
HE	being difficult
SHE	I'm doing my best
HE	your best is not good enough however
SHE	I'm trying
HE	try to answer my question then
SHE	what question?
HE	why are you so difficult?
SHE	I'm not difficult
HE	that's what you're like
SHE	that's not what I'm like
HE	that's how you are
SHE	no that's not how I am
HE	yes it is
SHE	no it's not
HE	you can't help it?
SHE	I can't help it
HE	yes you can
SHE	no I can't
HE	and you're not being difficult?
SHE	no
HE	what are you then?

SHE	I don't know
HE	you are what you are
SHE	I'm not what I am
HE	accept yourself
SHE	I am not what I am
HE	what are you then?
SHE	(*silence*)
HE	there you are then
SHE	(*silence*)
HE	you're yourself
SHE	I'm not myself
HE	why are you so difficult?
SHE	I'm not difficult
HE	stop playing games with me
SHE	I can't help it
HE	just give it up
SHE	give what up?
HE	all that
SHE	all what?
HE	you know
SHE	I don't know
HE	why can't you be less self-centered?
SHE	I've lost myself
HE	you think about yourself too much
SHE	I can't help it
HE	you're self-contradictory
SHE	I can't help it
HE	why don't you let me help you?
SHE	how?
HE	by being less difficult
SHE	how?
HE	answer my question
SHE	what was your question?

HE	I'm asking the questions not answering them for the moment
SHE	what was your question then?
HE	why are you so difficult?
SHE	I'm not difficult
HE	what were you complaining about then?
SHE	I wasn't complaining
HE	why do you contradict me all the time?
SHE	I don't contradict you all the time
HE	what were you doing just now?
SHE	I disagreed with you
HE	you feel you must compete with me
SHE	I'm not trying to compete with you
HE	it's not a question of winning
SHE	I never said it was
HE	and you call that not being difficult?
SHE	yes
HE	and you're not playing games?
SHE	no
HE	what are you going on about then?
SHE	I wasn't going on about anything
HE	you must have been going on about something
SHE	I just wish I could get out of this
HE	what are you really complaining about?
SHE	I'm not complaining
HE	have you a bad memory?
SHE	no
HE	why can't you remember then?
SHE	remember what?
HE	you've lost your memory again
SHE	I have not
HE	you can't see how difficult you're being?

SHE	no
HE	can't you see I'm trying to help you?
SHE	yes I can see you're trying to help me
HE	why don't you let me help you then?
SHE	I never asked you to help me
HE	can't you see you can't get out of this yourself?
SHE	that's what I'm saying
HE	why won't you let me help you then?
SHE	your help is like salt water to a drowning man
HE	there you are
SHE	no I'm not
HE	why are you like you are?
SHE	I'm not like I am
HE	what are you like then?
SHE	nothing
HE	you're impossible
SHE	I can't help it
HE	can't help what?
SHE	getting into this
HE	what are you complaining about?
SHE	I'm not complaining
HE	you have a bad memory?
SHE	no
HE	why can't you remember then?
SHE	remember what?
HE	how long you've had it
SHE	had what?
HE	your complaint
SHE	I am not complaining
HE	what are you doing then?
SHE	I was saying I can't help it
HE	I believe you can
SHE	I can't

HE	it's the word of hope
SHE	it's hopeless
HE	do not despair
SHE	I can't help it
HE	can't help what?
SHE	getting into this
HE	getting into what?
SHE	into this
HE	and what is this?
SHE	this *(pause)* this
HE	you are not making any sense
SHE	I know
HE	why do you go on like this then?
SHE	I wish I could stop
HE	why don't you stop then?
SHE	I can't help it
HE	you wouldn't go on like this if you were yourself
SHE	I wish we could stop getting into this
HE	into what?
SHE	into this
HE	and what is this?
SHE	this *(pause)* this
HE	try to be more explicit
SHE	I'm being as explicit as I can
HE	what are you going on about?
SHE	I'm not going on about anything
HE	what are you up to?
SHE	I'm not up to anything
HE	what are you saying then?
SHE	I've said it before
HE	say it again
SHE	I've said it for the umpteenth time
HE	what is it?
SHE	I wish I could get out of this

HE	out of what?
SHE	what we're in now
HE	what's that?
SHE	it's endless
HE	can't you see I'm trying to help you?
SHE	O my god
HE	what's the matter?
SHE	you
HE	there you go again
SHE	leave me alone
HE	I'm not molesting you
SHE	O yes yes yes you are
HE	you know you know that's not true
SHE	I don't think I'm going to be able to control myself much longer
HE	what do you suppose you will do?
SHE	when?
HE	when you give it up
SHE	what up?
HE	this up
SHE	and what is this?
HE	what you're doing
SHE	I wish I wasn't here
HE	you feel suicidal?
SHE	I don't seem to be able to help it
HE	you are denying your responsibility
SHE	I can't tell you anything
HE	try to be less global
SHE	that's what I mean
HE	for instance
SHE	it's like talking to a wall or an empty space
HE	you cannot admit my existence as another human person like yourself

SHE	there's no one there
HE	I feel that
SHE	feel what?
HE	you're not there
SHE	what's the use?
HE	you're depressed
SHE	I'm desperate
HE	because you can't allow me to help you
SHE	how?
HE	you need my help to help you realize you need it
SHE	please stop trying to help me
HE	I can't help it
SHE	can't help what?
HE	there's nothing much to be done I'm afraid
SHE	done about what?
HE	you
SHE	I didn't ask you to do anything about me
HE	what were you asking then?
SHE	I wasn't asking anything
HE	why are you here then?
SHE	I was saying I couldn't help always coming back to the same place
HE	what are you complaining about?
SHE	I'm just saying that each moment with you is better than the next
HE	you are pushing your feelings away now
SHE	I don't feel that
HE	I'm sorry, I forgot, you can't help it
SHE	this is awful
HE	you can't feel anything?
SHE	please don't try to make me feel something

HE	I know you don't really mean that
SHE	really I don't want to feel anything
HE	are you a robot?
SHE	please (*stretches out her hand*) I'm not a robot
HE	I'm not wasting my precious time on a filthy robot
SHE	I'm not a robot
HE	stop acting like one then
SHE	I can't help it
HE	maybe you can't
SHE	I wouldn't be here if I could help it
HE	I'm trying to help
SHE	don't take offense
HE	don't flatter yourself
SHE	I tried not to
HE	not to what?
SHE	not to offend you
HE	you haven't offended me
SHE	I feel I have
HE	you are at the stage of infantile omnipotence
SHE	have I offended you?
HE	how?
SHE	I can't say
HE	what can't you say?
SHE	how I have offended you
HE	you feel you have offended me?
SHE	yes
HE	you felt you offended me just now?
SHE	I'm not sure
HE	perhaps it was your imagination?
SHE	perhaps
HE	perhaps it wasn't?

SHE	it wasn't my imagination?
HE	you're at it again
SHE	how?
HE	you're at it now
SHE	what?
HE	you know perfectly well
SHE	no I do not
HE	here and now
SHE	I don't know what you are talking about
HE	will you stop it?
SHE	stop what?
HE	what you're doing this very instant
SHE	living
HE	do you call what you're doing living?
SHE	I'm doing my best
HE	your best is not good enough however
SHE	I can't help it
HE	can't help what?

Five

28

Take this pill
to help you not to shout
it takes away the life
you're better off without

29

The trouble with you
's you've lost a screw

I'm sorry it's you
but there's nothing to do

There'll be no abatements
there are no replacements

don't make a to-do
just say toodle-oo

I'm sorry I can't help you
you'd cost too much to redo

you'll have to be abolished
report to be demolished

30

Is he trying to amuse me
to confound and confuse me?
Does he bring me home flowers
in order to use me?

I tell her I love her
because I hate her
I'm nice to her now
to do her in later.

Does he kiss me and pet me
just to perplex me?
If I cut my throat
will he aid and abet me?

After she's gone
I'll quickly forget her
go on the prowl
and find something better.

31

She's nasty to me
so I'm nasty to her

she follows me
so I follow her

32
They say that good intentions
pave the road to hell
if a thing is not worth doing
it's not worth doing well

33

I dreamt I was a butterfly
dreaming it was me
it looked into a mirror
there was nothing there to see

"You lie!"
        I cried

It woke
        I died

34

Sometimes I come
sometimes I go
but which is which
I don't know

sometimes I am
sometimes I'm not
but which is which
I forgot

35
I dreamt I was a dead rat
in a city sewer
I started to rust
and turned to dust
until I was no more

36

Why is there she?
why is there me?

why why why why why why why why why

I can't even see
why a flea
is so wee

let alone
where I'll be
when I die

Why is there she?
why is there *he*?

why why why why why why why why why

I can't even see
where it goes
when I pee

let alone
where I'll be
when I die

37

Mummy'll scream
if you have a wet dream

Do not let frustration
lead to masturbation

Little Billy
plays with his willy
that's why he's silly

38

Hello *(casually)*
Yes it is *(absently)*
No *(uncuriously)*
Really *(with some surprise)*
Whose was it *(out of politeness)*?
Mine *(incredulously)*!
When *(challengingly)*?
Really *(interestedly)*
A hha *(reminiscently)*
Mmmm *(musingly)*
You should have told me *(ironically)*
A pity I couldn't have had it for you *(gleefully)*
There it is *(grimly)*
Give me a ring sometime *(dutifully)*
You could always have another *(brutally)*
C'est la vie *(consolingly)*
Goodbye *(sincerely)*

Six

39

Where's the pleasure?
where's the fun?

is this only
one long bum run?

is what seemed joy
one more decoy?

where's the delight
I took in your sight?

is there a morning
to follow this night?

40

The die is cast
you're breathing your last
no more will you roam

your breath has a smell
that's straight from hell
you've found your Home Sweet Home

41

You can rant and rave
I won't be your slave
or another gap to fill in

it's none too soon
for a new spittoon
and something else to shit in

42

Why do you lie in bed
soft in the head
on a cold and frosty morning?

the other side of light
isn't very bright
I didn't heed the gypsy's warning

43

Do I hurt you
when I touch you?

was that a shiver
or a quiver?

tell me where
you're there

taunt me
haunt me
as long as you want me

44
You'll cry
when I die

you'll yawn
when I'm gone

you'll be bored
unadored

45

Cross your fingers
tell me your woes
there are lies that linger
cross your nose
If Cain were able
he would give you a rose

46

Was that a kiss?
or a hiss
from the abyss?

47

I liked to eat mice
that was then
I was ten
now it's men
they're not as nice

48
I could tell
       from your eyes
you fell
       from the skies

  out of the blue
  there were you

but I knew it wasn't true
and away
       you flew

Seven

49

Daisy, Daisy
what are we going to do?
I'm half crazy
I'm in love and in hate with you

although I'm so contrary
at least I'm not a fairy

'twould break my heart
if we should part
it's already divided in two

50

You're gonna get it
you're gonna live to regret it
        if only you'll marry me
        if only you'll marry me

You won't forget me in a hurry
I'll make you sorry, make you worry
        if only you'll marry me
        if only you'll marry me

I'll squash you like a fly
make you squish and squirm and fry
        if only you'll marry me
        if only you'll marry me

I'll mate you and bait you
and settle down to hate you
        if only you'll marry me
        if only you'll marry me

We'll live a life of misery
        if only you'll marry me

51

You were a nice little gay thing
a bird that only could sing
but joy began to cloy
for you were not a boy
some bell just wouldn't ring

you were a pretty safe plaything
a bee without any sting

I took my chances
with other romances

we had a fight
I proved I was right

you were second best
but now you've left

I'm a yoyo without a string

52
Song of the false guru's wife

If only it were as easy
as they try to make it sound
I'd always be chirpy and cheery
    and whirl round and round and round
    and whirl round and round and round

    But

    his Chakras are filled up with sawdust
    his Kundalini is coiled up in glue
    his third eye is stuffed with broken glass
    and I don't know what to do

When I'm washing the dishes
when I take out the children to play
I often feel I'd rather be dead
    if things go on this way
    if things go on this way

    For

    his Chakras are filled with sawdust
    his Kundalini is coiled up in glue
    his third eye is stuffed with broken glass
    and I don't know what to do

When I open my eyes in the morning
when I shut them tight at night
there he's sneering and jeering and leering
    and from him comes a foul white light
    and from him comes a foul white light

    For

    his Chakras are filled up with sawdust
    his Kundalini is coiled up in glue

his third eye is stuffed with broken glass
and I don't know what to do

His veins are clogged with mercury
I'm certain it's not right
the bells of hell shall ring his knell
for in his heart is night
for in his heart is night

For

his Chakras are filled up with sawdust
his Kundalini is coiled up in glue
his third eye is stuffed with broken glass
and I don't know what to do

53

I swooned for the moon
                    but didn't get it

I peed in the sea
                    but didn't wet it

I poked the sun with a pole
                    but only made a hole

but

though I may be dim
if the sea tries to swim
                    I'll net it

I swallowed the stars
                    but still was hollow

I turned back the years
                    there's still tomorrow

I've offered God a role
but He's out of my control

I'm a pig in a poke
an awfully bad joke
                    I can't follow

54

I was discontented
with girls that were rented
so I invented my own

I could switch her on
I could switch her off

she used to make me feel
I was quite a toff
          but now it's my night to moan

she was mainly plastic
her arteries were elastic
and her voice was electronic monotone

she had a lovely hole
that was easy to control

I tried to fondle her
in case I'd grow fond of her
          but now it's my night to moan

I was her maker
and I could break her
if she didn't answer the telephone

one day I broke her heart
but I'd lost the spare part

that's when she packed up
and then I cracked up
          so now it's my night to moan

55

As I was going along a road
I met a man, a bull, a god

He whisked me off to heaven
to be his concubine
but madame didn't like it
so now I'm worse than swine

He promised me the earth
gave me a present of the sky
he offered me a moonbeam
to wear if I was shy

He said I was a treasure
money couldn't buy
he knew just how to make me laugh
just when he'd made me cry

He taught me not to worry
to forget it when he came
he thought it would be better
if I didn't give the baby his name

56

In days of old
when knights were bold
and women were just being invented

they locked up their wives
and fled for their lives
but never were contented

now times have changed
and those knights of yore
have no more armored plating

it's wipe your bum
before you come
and no more masturbating

still happy days will come again
we're meant for more than mating

but now we must
bite the dust

can't keep the ladies waiting

yes
happy days will come again
of that you can be sure

when women were women
and men were men
and we had pure manure

57

I went down to St. James's infirmary
to see my love dying there
I went down to St. James's infirmary
my own true love was dying there

It was the first thing in the morning
both the moon and the sun were there
it was the first thing in the morning
she left me gazing at her dead stare

It was down at St. James's infirmary
who knows if it's fair
they wouldn't let me kiss her
they said she wasn't there

They took her own sweet body
they stuffed her own sweet nose
they tied her toes together
they wouldn't let me have her clothes

Maybe I don't see it
but they didn't seem to care
that my own true love had left me
standing helpless there

58

Refugees from the sixth dimension
take care when you mention
what's past recollection

the womb
's a tomb
death
's our first breath

out of the furnace
into the mire
out of the frying pan
into the fire

you may regret it
or, better, forget it
or tell a faded story
sans glory

but if you confess it
if you try to tell them
what they do not want to know

they'll pickle you in piddle
frizzle you in drizzle
fry you in snow

because they're wetter
doesn't mean you're better

to be emphatic
is not to be dogmatic

to be skeptic
is not to be erratic

one man's jubilation
's another's lamentation

your hallucination
's beyond their station

Eight

59

Now
if not forever
is
sometimes
better than never

60

Is there a unicorn in your eyes?
tell no lies

did the swordfish
pierce the moon?
answer soon

61

When I try
from Zen sickness to fly

I'm sometimes low
and I'm sometimes high

sometimes I'm in
sometimes I'm out

sometimes I sing
and sometimes I SHOUT

sometimes I just laze around
sometimes I go underground

but

nevertheless
I must confess
it all seems less
than second best

without the one for whom I care
to pick my nose
and pull my hair

62

Love is like the falling snow
once it comes it has to go

never say so, it's a lie
love's forever, 'tis time must fly

Nine

63

I mean to scream

I die forlorn
I was not born

I deny
I'm a butterfly

I'm a blot
I am not

I'm a fight no one fought
I'm a cold no one caught

I'm
the
Self-Appointed
Lord's
Anointed

I'm a turd
I'm absurd

I'm a twinkling light
in someone else's night

I'm an insoluble riddle
I'm a hole with no middle

I'm going to hell
to yell
and smell

I fiddle
when I piddle

I'm a nitwit
I'm a titbit

I'm a kinkie
like a pinkie

I'm a flower with no name
I grow all the same

I'm a piece of fluff
in the huff

Never learned the game
I left before I came

I mean
to
scream

I'm a dot
God forgot

I'm past mending
I'm a happy ending

Ten

64

Do you love me?

SHE	do you love me?
HE	yes I love you
SHE	best of all?
HE	yes best of all
SHE	more than the whole world?
HE	yes more than the whole world
SHE	do you like me?
HE	yes I like you
SHE	do you like being near me?
HE	yes I like being near you
SHE	do you like to look at me?
HE	yes I like to look at you
SHE	do you think I'm stupid?
HE	no I don't think you're stupid
SHE	do you think I'm attractive?
HE	yes I think you're attractive
SHE	do I bore you?
HE	no you don't bore me
SHE	do you like my eyebrows?
HE	yes I like your eyebrows
SHE	very much?
HE	very much
SHE	which one do you like the most?
HE	if I say one the other will be jealous
SHE	you have to say
HE	they are both exquisite
SHE	honest?

HE	honest
SHE	have I got nice eyelashes?
HE	yes nice nice eyelashes
SHE	do you like to smell me?
HE	yes I like to smell you
SHE	do you like my perfume?
HE	yes I like your perfume
SHE	do you think I've good taste?
HE	yes I think you have good taste
SHE	do you think I'm talented?
HE	yes I think you're talented
SHE	you don't think I'm lazy?
HE	no I don't think you're lazy
SHE	do you like to touch me?
HE	yes I like to touch you
SHE	do you think I'm funny?
HE	only in a nice way
SHE	are you laughing at me?
HE	no I'm not laughing at you
SHE	do you really love me?
HE	yes I really love you
SHE	say "I love you"
HE	I love you
SHE	do you want to hug me?
HE	yes I want to hug you, and cuddle you, and bill and coo with you
SHE	is it all right?
HE	yes it's all right
SHE	swear you'll never leave me?
HE	I swear I'll never ever leave you, cross my heart and hope to die if I tell a lie *(pause)*
SHE	do you *really* love me?

About the Author

R. D. Laing studied medicine at Glasgow University. He was a psychiatrist in the British army and a physician at the Glasgow Royal Mental Hospital, and taught at the University of Glasgow. Subsequently, he joined the Tavistock Clinic and was later appointed Director of the Langham Clinic in London. From 1961 to 1967 he undertook research into families, and he is now in private practice as a psychoanalyst.

Since 1964, Dr. Laing has been President of the Philadelphia Association in London. This organization is mainly concerned with setting up households as places of sanctuary, asylum, refuge, and dwelling, where people may live, unmolested by "treatment," who are in extreme mental distress.

He is the author of numerous articles and reviews. His other books are *The Divided Self*, *Self and Others*, *Reason and Violence* (with David Cooper), *Sanity, Madness and the Family*, Vol. 1: *The Families of Schizophrenics* (with Aaron Esterson), *Interpersonal Perception: A Theory and a Method of Research* (with H. Phillipson and A. R. Lee), *The Politics of Experience*, *The Politics of the Family*, *Knots*, and *The Facts of Life*.

Academic
Rewards
in Higher
Education

Academic Rewards in Higher Education

Edited by

Darrell R. Lewis
Professor of Economic Education
University of Minnesota

and

William E. Becker, Jr.
Associate Professor of Economics
Indiana University

Ballinger Publishing Company • Cambridge, Massachusetts
A Subsidiary of Harper & Row, Publishers, Inc.

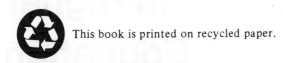
International Standard Book Number: 0–88410–189–4

Library of Congress Catalog Card Number: 79–11692

Printed in the United States of America

Library of Congress Cataloging in Publication Data

Main entry under title:

Academic rewards in higher education.

The product of a colloquium series in higher education held at the University of Minnesota in the fall and winter of 1977–78.
Bibliography: p.
1. Education, Higher—United States—Congresses. 2. Education, Higher—Economic aspects—United States—Congresses. 3. Academic achievement—Congresses. 4. Rewards and punishments in education—Congresses. I. Lewis, Darrell R. II. Becker, William E.
LB2301.A13   378.73   79–11692
ISBN 0–88410–189–4

✳

Contents

List of Tables

List of Figures

Contributors

Helen S. Astin, professor of higher education, University of California, Los Angeles

Alan E. Bayer, professor of sociology, Florida State University

William E. Becker, Jr., associate professor of economics, Indiana University

James P. Begin, professor of industrial relations, Rutgers University

Howard R. Bowen, professor of economics, Claremont Graduate School

Sanford M. Dornbusch, professor of sociology and education, Stanford University

Kenneth R. Doyle, Jr., research associate of educational psychology, University of Minnesota

Richard B. Freeman, professor of economics, Harvard University

George E. Johnson, professor of economics, University of Michigan

Theodore E. Kellogg, professor of educational psychology, University of Minnesota

Wayne R. Kirschling, director for basic studies, National Center for Higher Education Management Systems

Darrell R. Lewis, associate dean and professor of economic education, University of Minnesota

Wilbert J. McKeachie, professor of psychology, University of Michigan

Frank P. Stafford, professor of economics, University of Michigan

Howard P. Tuckman, professor of economics, Florida State University

Preface

The development of *Academic Rewards in Higher Education* arose from a concern that we had about the lack of understanding that many faculty members and administrators have about how faculty are both motivated and rewarded within American higher education. Knowledge about what motivates faculty to become effective scholars is of critical importance for rational decisionmaking in higher education today. Unfortunately, while many groups have given considerable attention to the status of academia and academics, little disciplined inquiry has been directed to the issues surrounding faculty motivation and rewards. Of the many prescriptive essays on this subject in the popular literature of higher education, few acknowledge a solid theoretical or empirical base. Of the many administrative decisions being made daily on these issues, few are fully informed.

In the organization and governance of American higher education, both faculty and administrators share, either formally or informally, in the decisions concerning academic productivity, especially as they relate to teaching and research programs, personnel decisions, and rewards. In most four year institutions the academic department or school is an especially important unit. Departments or schools are generally organized according to academic disciplines or common professional concerns. Within such units, faculty in their teaching and research tend to operate much like individual entrepreneurs, but they also have a strong self-interest in the successful operation and long-term future of their own respective units. Their stated aims, of course, are the common form of collegial self-governance and a desire for excellence.

In a very real sense, the faculty of most higher education institutions are the institutions. Not only do faculty salaries comprise over 80 percent of most collegiate budgets, but the very reputation and success of an institution depends largely on the teaching and research ability and productivity of the faculty. Consequently, trustees and administrators generally allow a considerable amount of independence to their faculty in teaching and research activities. It is also generally recognized that a successful administration attempts to work closely with the faculty in the definition and attainment of the educational objectives of the institution. Less clearly understood, however, is the role that reward systems play in all of this. It is not at all clear what forms and amounts of rewards (or negative sanctions) might most efficiently enhance the aims of the institution or which screening procedures and criteria might most facilitate academic productivity. The influence of academic reward systems on faculty behavior and academic productivity is one of the most important and sensitive questions facing both faculty and administrative decision-makers in higher education today. Yet a theoretical and empirical understanding of the academic reward structure is often lacking.

In partial response to these concerns, we developed a colloquium series in higher education at the University of Minnesota in the fall and winter of 1977–1978 in order to systematically address the topics and issues surrounding academic rewards. We reviewed the literature, developed the topical outline, consulted with our colleagues both in the related disciplines and in the field of higher education, contacted the speakers and authors, conducted the colloquium series with faculty and graduate students in higher education, and subsequently edited this publication as the collective product of the colloquium.

In the development of the colloquium series, special assistance and support was provided by the Center for Educational Development, Center for Economic Education, Teacher Center, Graduate Program in Higher Education, and the College of Education's Office of the Dean. The faculty and graduate students in an adjunct seminar (Educ 8–229; Issues in Higher Education) were especially helpful in assisting the authors in developing their topics and papers. Throughout this project, the advice and assistance from a number of key people at the University of Minnesota were essential to whatever success it enjoyed. Such a list must include Mary Corcoran, Theodore Kellogg, and Robert Keller, all professors in higher education, and Marcia Finke, our efficient secretary.

In *Academic Rewards in Higher Education*, we have brought together a group of scholars who have individually made significant

contributions to the field of higher education. Each chapter author was chosen because he or she was the best person available to address the issues and problems of that part of the book. Each author drew heavily from his or her own work, was nationally known in the field or specialty, and understood the purposes and context of the colloquium series and this publication.

The chapters in the first part of *Academic Rewards in Higher Education* concentrate on theoretical views of faculty behavior in academic labor markets. Individual perspectives are taken from the three social sciences of psychology, economics, and sociology in an attempt to assess what motivates faculty behavior. Attention is given to the views of faculty as individuals who (1) pursue self-determined internal targets as performance goals, (2) optimize internal goals subject to external monetary rewards, and (3) respond to authority vis-à-vis rules and externally determined performance criteria.

The second part presents a conceptual understanding of academic labor markets in higher education. The economic determinants of the supply of and demand for faculty are discussed in the context of employment conditions. Emphasis is given to institutional characteristics of academia and to an empirical model of the demand for faculty.

Part Three addresses some of the conceptual problems in measuring academic labor productivity. Attention is given to the problems inherent in measuring both individual and institutional outcomes. Problems of joint product involving teaching, research, and service as interactive outcomes of higher education are of special concern. The use of student evaluations as cues for determining faculty rewards is also explored.

The chapters in the fourth part focus on the empirical aspects of current reward structures in American higher education. Although all forms of faculty reward structures are reviewed, primary attention is given to salaries. The historical status of salaries in higher education is presented, sex differences in academic rewards are examined, and the effects of such institutional policies as collective bargaining are explored. The authors in this part of the book, wherever possible, single out policy alternatives that flow from their data and analysis.

The fifth, and concluding, part of the book reviews a number of the external pressures that currently confront higher education. Suggestions are given for the use of reward system policies and strategies that follow from the preceding chapters of the book.

Although the major focus of most of the chapters in this book is on the major institutions (universities) of American higher education, much of what is discussed applies to many of the other higher edu-

cation institutions as well. In considering the problems of applying reward systems across higher education, we are cognizant of the fact that a mixed situation exists in terms of the academic aspirations, motivations, and reputations of individual faculty in the 2,500 institutions of higher education in this country. However, there are many similarities, and we are confident that many of the policy inferences drawn from the chapters of this volume may be generalized to much of higher education today.

Minneapolis
September 1978

Darrell R. Lewis
William E. Becker, Jr.

Part I

What Motivates
Academic Behavior?

The three chapters of Part One serve as an introduction and concentrate on theoretical views of faculty behavior in American higher education. Separate perspectives are given from the three social sciences of psychology, economics, and sociology in assessing what motivates faculty behavior. Attention is given to the views of faculty as individuals who (1) pursue self-determined internal targets as performance goals in Chapter 1, (2) optimize internal goals subject to external monetary rewards in Chapter 2, and (3) respond to authority vis-à-vis rules and externally determined performance criteria in Chapter 3.

Chapter 1

Perspectives from Psychology: Financial Incentives are Ineffective for Faculty

Wilbert J. McKeachie

INTRODUCTION

What motivates professors to do a good job? By and large, faculty members work hard, put in long hours, and are productive researchers and teachers (Mueller & French, 1970). What is it that maintains this motivation throughout careers lasting approximately forty years? What can one do if one wants to influence faculty behavior?[1]

When college and university administrators think about changing faculty behavior, they are likely to rely upon overly simplistic views of motivation, such as the traditional views that people work for money and that one can change behavior by offering more money for those things that one wants done and by taking away money for doing those things one does not want done. Therefore, if one wishes better teaching, one pays higher salaries to good teachers and omits salary increases for those who are doing poor teaching.

This view of motivation has persisted because there is some truth in it. People often are motivated by money, and faculty members are not immune to the glitter of gold. Nevertheless, this purely materialistic view of human motivation is now known to be true only under limited circumstances and only for certain people. Moreover, use of this method of influencing behavior is likely, in the long run, to produce results contrary to those desired. If one is to be effective in changing faculty behavior, one must recognize that motivation is much more complex than a simple materialistic view; in fact, it is much more complex than a reward-punishment view.

In this chapter I shall try to bring together two streams of current research and theory. One of these is motivation theory in psychology; the other, the accumulating research on faculty characteristics and satisfaction.

CONTEMPORARY MOTIVATION THEORY

For a number of years, evidence has been accumulating that simple reward and punishment views of human motivation are inadequate. Individuals persist in doing things that are punished, and rewards sometimes weaken rather than strengthen the tendency to continue a behavior.

How can such behavior be accounted for? One element of such an account is a cognitive one. In order to understand human behavior, one must understand the way in which individuals think about rewards and punishments. For example, suppose a faculty member is not working hard and, as a consequence, receives low salary increases for several years. Will such a policy result in his changing the inadequate performance that has been punished? The answer may depend upon how he interprets the situation. In my own experience, faculty members in such a situation are likely to feel resentment about the way in which they have been treated. Since they are appreciated inadequately, they work less. Thus, punishment has not had the effect intended.

On the reward side, suppose that a college establishes an award for good teaching. Certain individuals may feel that they have an opportunity to win such an award and exert effort to gain the kind of student or colleague approbation that will increase the likelihood of getting the award. In this case the award has been interpreted as a goal. But what happens once the goal has been attained? Sometimes pride, the discovery of other satisfactions in good teaching, or other motives will maintain the level of effort, but there is a real danger that someone whose motivation was primarily materialist will now turn to other activities that bring such rewards.

In other cases, a reward may fail in its effect because the interpretation of the individual may be different from that intended by those giving the reward. Thus, praise by a department chairman may sometimes be interpreted as indicating that the chairman has such a low opinion of one's ability that she or he praises even routine performance. Modern motivation uses "expectancy," rather than "reward" or "reinforcement," as a key concept. Rewards may influence behavior, but their effect depends upon their influence upon the individual's expectations. Research studies have demonstrated that when

you are rewarded for something that you previously did for fun, you are less likely to choose that activity when the rewards cease. You have come to expect that you should be paid. Thus, extrinsic rewards may actually diminish motivation rather than increase it.

If extrinsic rewards and punishments are not effective in increasing motivation, then what is? The answer lies in those satisfactions that are inherent in the activities upon which you wish faculty members to spend more time. Let us first make a simple distinction between three kinds of motives.

First are the external rewards and punishments, such as salary, promotions, awards, or dismissal. Because these rewards and punishments can be controlled by administrators, they are the ones most likely to be used when administrators want change. We have already seen that these often do not work as they are supposed to. I shall subsequently have more to say about their appropriate use.

A second class of motives involves satisfactions that are related to motives in the individual that may or may not be satisfied by the activity desired. One may, for example, be respected by one's colleagues for excellence in teaching, but such respect is not intrinsic in teaching. Similarly, desire for status may be satisfied in relationships with students, but status is not an intrinsic satisfaction of all styles of teaching.

A third class of motives includes those whose satisfaction is intrinsic to the task. Intellectual curiosity, stimulation by students, close interpersonal relationships with students—these are some of the motivational elements intrinsic to teaching. As contrasted with the other classes of motives, intrinsic satisfactions come during the activity; other kinds of satisfactions come afterwards.

MOTIVES FOR TEACHING AND RESEARCH

Faculty members typically work longer hours than individuals in occupations in which money is the chief incentive (fifty-six hours a week in the sample of French, Tupper, & Mueller, 1965). They do this because they enjoy their work, not because they are trying to earn more money or striving for goals outside their work. In analyzing a problem of lack of energy or of failure to allocate enough energy or time to a particular activity, one needs to think about those characteristics of the work one wants done that are fun—that will arouse interest or that will spark curiosity. One needs to think about those aspects of the task that will lead a person to look forward to a day of work on Saturday even though the department chairman won't ever know about it.

RESEARCH ON FACULTY MOTIVATION

Faculty members do research, but not many do research on faculty members. Nevertheless, there have been several substantial studies of college faculties. Several studies have asked faculty members about the sources of satisfaction and dissatisfaction in their work. Gustad (1960) carried out a questionnaire and interview study intended to find out why people choose to be college teachers. He characterized college teachers as valuing responsibility, achievement, and hard work but as being differentiated from other groups of middle class origin by their preference for independent, intellectually stimulating activities. Gustad found strong identification with the scholarly discipline among his sample. Faculty members look for acceptance in their discipline nationally, but they enjoy teaching and would like it to be valued more highly than it is perceived to be.

When asked about what was most rewarding, Gustad's faculty members listed research first, stimulation from colleagues second, and salary third. Gustad found, as have other studies, that salary is much more important to those with low salaries than to those with high salaries. Beyond a certain level of subsistence or comfort, salary is not rated as an important reward.

Some differences between the three fields studied were found. Students were perceived as more rewarding by English and psychology professors than by chemists. And Gustad found that most professors thought their own job to be as close to the ideal as realistically possible. If there were to be changes, they would prefer more upper level teaching and higher salaries, but in general they were satisfied. National surveys suggest that most Americans feel that their occupations are underpaid and that university professors feel less undercompensated than other groups.

Eckert and Stecklein (1961) studied the job satisfactions of Minnesota college teachers. Like Gustad, they found that the intellectual interest and social significance of their work outweighed recognition, prestige, and salary as sources of satisfaction. Leading the list of satisfactions was association with college students, but intellectually stimulating colleagues, observing student growth, and the opportunity to study and learn also ranked high.

The most frequent source of dissatisfaction for Minnesota college teachers in the last 1950s was a low salary—mentioned by almost half of those queried. Paradoxically, the general perception that college teachers are not highly paid may mean that faculty members are less likely to be affected by salary levels than are individuals in other professions. My rationale for this hypothesis is that vocational choice

studies suggest that young people strongly motivated for money are likely to choose careers in medicine, business, or other areas that promise high income. Thus, those most motivated by financial rewards are not likely to be found on college faculties. The next highest source of dissatisfaction, in the Minnesota study, mentioned by 14 percent, was "too much red tape." Ninety-two percent were satisfied with their choice of college teaching as a career.

Some recent data on faculty motivation come from a large national research study on job demands and worker health comparing job stresses on workers in twenty-three different jobs (Caplan et al., 1975). In these comparisons with other occupations, professors report a good fit between the complexity of their occupations and their desire for complexity. They also report good fit between their desired responsibility for other persons and the characteristics of their work. Appropriately, professors and air traffic controllers report the least boredom on their jobs, and professors and physicians report the least overall dissatisfactions with their jobs. Another indicator of freedom from stress is that professors are among the lowest groups in incidence of cardiovascular and respiratory diseases. All in all, the data suggest that of all the occupations studied, professors find the most intrinsic satisfactions in their work. They have satisfying feelings of using their ability and of responsibility for others. They receive support from their colleagues and their families. Those professors who enter administration are subject to higher stress and after five years show a higher mortality rate from heart attacks. Individuals who work for money and prestige are more likely to have heart attacks than those finding intrinsic satisfactions in their work.

In an earlier study, French, Tupper, and Mueller (1965)[2] found that faculty members rated freedom, interpersonal relations, the nature of the work, and teaching as the greatest satisfactions of their work. Interestingly, as contrasted with the 1950s, by the mid–1960s, dissatisfaction with salary was very rare.

Thus, the data from all studies are in good agreement about the major sources of work satisfaction for faculty members. In all studies, intrinsic satisfactions are reported to be much more important than extrinsic rewards. While one cannot accept self-report data as unbiased, the French studies, providing evidence from wives, physiological measures, and comparisons of self-report data from faculty with self-reports from other vocational groups, give some confidence that faculty members truly are a favored group in terms of enjoyment of their work.

One of the things that faculty members find satisfying is their freedom and autonomy. French, Tupper, and Mueller (1965), Eckert and

Stecklein (1961), Gustad (1960), and Petz and Andres (1966) all report this as a major source of faculty satisfaction and show that desire for self-direction is particularly strong among the most productive scholars. Clearly, "academic freedom" is more than a slogan to academics. They not only see this as fundamental for the quality of education, but it relates to their own need to determine what they shall say.

A second major source of satisfaction for faculty members is intellectual interchange (Gustad, 1960; Eckert & Stecklein, 1961). Faculty members satisfy this need not only through discussions with their colleagues but through work with graduate students and through teaching discussion classes and seminars.

A third faculty satisfaction is association with college students and the opportunity to contribute to student development (Eckert & Stecklein, 1961). Wilson, Woods, and Gaff (1974) show that interactions with students outside of class are relatively infrequent and varied a good deal depending upon the individual faculty member's theory of education. However, such interaction enhanced faculty members' enjoyment of teaching. The studies also agree in finding that faculty members like teaching. Those in research-oriented universities also enjoy research, but even in these institutions, faculty members would like more time for teaching.

While the general picture of faculty motivation is positive, there are frustrations and dissatisfactions, such as "red tape," committee work, constraints on teaching; large classes, poor classrooms, or teaching assignments in disliked courses; and the necessity for assistant professors in large universities to do the type of research that will result in quick publications. When faculty report their satisfactions, they emphasize those related to intrinsic motivation; when they report dissatisfactions, they emphasize extrinsic factors such as working conditions and administrative policies (Aebi, 1972).

Other satisfactions may not come out in interview studies because they are considered less estimable. For example, few faculty members would proclaim that they like to talk and to have a captive audience listening, taking notes, and sometimes even admiring the lecturer. Yet most faculty members could identify colleagues whom they see as characterized by such motivation.

THE ACHIEVEMENT MOTIVE

We have discussed both the intrinsic motivation involved in teaching and the external incentives of money and promotion. But this does not exhaust the range of motives that influence faculty behavior.

Faculty members, like other human beings, learn powerful motives that vary in individual strength but characterize most of us and that may be satisfied by teaching or research. These motives include need for achievement, need for affiliation, need for power, desire for personal growth, need for recogntion, and other needs common in our society. Individuals differ both in the strength of such needs and in the ways in which they are satisfied. For some faculty members the locus of satisfactions is on the local campus; for others, the important reference groups are colleagues in the discipline throughout the world.

The research literature on need for achievement is voluminous, and we know a good deal about how need for achievement and fear of failure affect behavior (see Atkinson, 1977). The individual high in need for achievement likes activities that require skill and are challenging. He or she will work hard and long at challenging tasks, but will not waste time on the impossible, nor on boring, simple tasks. Teaching can be challenging, but in many universities the arena for satisfying achievement needs is research. Here standards are relatively widely shared, and one's achievements can be evaluated by oneself and others.

The failure-oriented individual, on the other hand, avoids situations in which his or her competence can be evaluated. Given a choice, such individuals select activities so easy that there is little risk of failure or so difficult that there is little chance of success (and thus little opprobrium for failure). One might think of the really poor teacher as falling in this latter group, spending time on research, committee work, or other activities to the exclusion of teaching and, when teaching, doing it in the most conventional, routine way, where there is little risk of spectacular failure.

Individuals low in need for achievement are likely to be attracted by extrinsic factors such as salary, tenure, vacations, and fringe benefits. Since these factors are not usually emphasized as much in faculty recruitment as in other vocations, such individuals are probably not as prevalent in academia as in other vocations. College teaching has provided opportunity for achievement and social service for intelligent individuals from families of teachers and ministers (Gustad, 1960); also, college faculty members typically are selected on the basis of a record of academic achievement and have a good deal of opportunity for independent achievement. Thus, we would expect to find many individuals with high need for achievement among college faculty members. Caplan et al. (1975) found that professors who have moved into administrative roles were particularly high in achievement orientation.

A career as a professor thus has many elements attractive to individuals of high achievement motivation, although the security of academic life might also attract individuals not high in achievement motivation. In any case, one would expect that a faculty to include a number of individuals high in need for achievement. Such individuals are more likely to be motivated by challenges with moderate possibilities of success than by tasks well within their range of competence. Similarly, individuals characterized by such motives as need for affiliation can be motivated by opportunities to work with like-minded colleagues—for to motivate faculty, one needs to consider both ways of changing the situation to increase intrinsic rewards and ways of appealing to important individual motives.

MOTIVATION OVER THE LIFE SPAN DEVELOPMENT OF PROFESSORS

Up to this point we have talked about the general motives of faculty members as if faculty members were much alike. There are common characteristics, and faculty members do tend to be alike in many ways, but to any inhabitant of academe, the impressive thing is the diversity of professors. Not only do they come in all sexes, shapes, and sizes, they disagree on almost any issue that comes up. Thus, almost any human motive can be identified as important for some faculty members.

Moreover, motives important for a particular faculty member at one time may not be important at another time. In life span development theory, two major competing points of view are those of the stage theorists and the status theorists (Brim, 1976). While I believe neither theory to be true, there is some truth in each, and some consideration of both provides a useful set of hypotheses in thinking about faculty motivation. Moreover, both theories agree in noting that adults change over their adult years in motivation and in other important ways. To think of an adult as a constant unchanging entity is likely to be very misleading.

Levinson's Theory of Stages of Adult Development

The stage approach to life span development[3] is based upon the notion that the course of life follows a certain inevitable progression of stages—one following another in inalternable sequence. While the needs and problems of one stage are influenced by the ways in which the needs of preceding stages were handled, the stages are relatively

universal and closely linked to age. Thus Levinson et al. (1976: 21–25) describe the midlife transition thus:

> Since the course and outcome of this key event take several (perhaps three to six) years to unfold, many men at around 40 seem to be living, as one of our subjects put it, in a state of suspended animation. During the course of waiting, the next period gets under way.
>
> The next period we call the Mid-life Transition (MLT). A *developmental transition*, as we use the term, is a turning point or boundary region between two periods of greater stability. A transition may go relatively smoothly or may involve considerable turmoil. The Mid-Life Transition occurs whether the individual succeeds or fails in his search for affirmation by society. At 38 he thinks that if he gains the deserved success, he'll be all set. The answer is, he will not. He is going to have a transition whether he is affirmed or not; it is only the form that varies.
>
> The central issue is not whether he succeeds or fails in achieving his goals. The issue, rather, is what to do with the *experience of disparity* between what he has gained in an inner sense from living within a particular structure and what he wants for himself. The sense of disparity between "what I've reached at this point" and "what it is I really want" instigates a soul-searching for "what it is I really want."
>
> We shall note briefly some of the major issues within the Mid-Life Transition: (a) The sense of *bodily decline* and the more vivid recognition of one's *mortality*. This brings the necessity to confront one's mortality and to deal in a new way with wounds to one's omnipotence fantasies, to overcome illusions and self-deceptions which relate to one's sense of omnipotence. It also brings greater freedom in experiencing and thinking about one's own and other's deaths, and greater compassion in responding to another's distress and decline, deformity, death, loss and bereavement.
> (b) The sense of *aging*, which means to be old rather than young.

Levinson's studies of young and middle-aged men in New Haven included ten biology professors, but his reports do not indicate how the faculty members differed from the other men in his sample.

Levinson's theory suggests that in the midtwenties, when most academic careers begin, men are characterized by motivation to arrive at a definition of themselves as adults and to fashion an initial life structure. Life at this stage is a time of exploration and testing choices. Such a young faculty member is likely to respond well to opportunities to develop competence and to explore new faculty roles. In the early stages of a career, a young person is helped by a mentor—an older person near enough in age and attitudes to be a peer but experienced enough to guide, support, encourage, and criticize the developing young academician.

At around age thirty, the individual enters a transitional period in which he faces the question, Shall I make a deeper commitment to this job and this pattern of life or should I change before it is too late? Faculty members in this transitional period might well be characterized by inconsistency in their responses to administrative pressures.

Levinson describes the next period as "Settling Down." This period, running from the early to late thirties, involves concern with stability and security but also with "making it." This is the period in which promotion to tenure is motivationally important.

Around age thirty-five to thirty-nine comes a period that Levinson calls "BOOM"—Becoming One's Own Man. During this period the individual feels oppressed and constrained by the persons and groups who have authority over him. This is a period in which the individual is especially motivated for autonomy and for recognition. A full professorship before age forty may be one key goal affirming the faculty member's worth and his sense that he is on the right track. The data of Petz and Andres (1966) indicate that this is a period when faculty members need to stand on their own feet independent of mentors or senior scholars. For faculty members in large universities, this is a period when research and teaching converge. Teaching assignments are likely to be in one's area of specialization, and scholarly and teaching motives support one another. Research can be oriented toward longer term goals rather than immediate publication.

But the BOOM period is followed by the "midlife transition" that we have already discussed. Levinson's description of this period as transitional is supported by the data of Petz and Andres (1966). In this period motivation is affected by one's questioning about the relationship between one's life structure and one's self: I've made full professor. Is that all there is? Or, My promotion has been held back. Is it really worth striving for? What do I really want from life?

During the midlife transition, the opportunity to shift from an emphasis upon research to a career as a teacher or administrator may be attractive, and the intrinsic satisfactions of closer relationships with students may be particularly important. Continued productivity in research depends upon security and self-confidence (Petz & Andres, 1966).

The midlife transition is followed in Levinson's theory by "restabilization"—a period of shaping a new life structure for the years of middle adulthood.

The Role and Status Change Theory
of Adult Development

As contrasted with the notion that there are stages in life associated with particular ages, role and status change theory says that change in motivation over the life span is dependent upon change in the individual's sociological situations. Everyone occupies a variety of positions in society. One may be, for example, a male, a husband, an assistant professor, a Presbyterian, an American Indian, a Democrat, and many other things. Each role has certain implications for one's status within one or another group. In addition, there are norms about the behavior expected of individuals acting in that role. An adult experiences a predictable sequence of change in positions in social institutions such as education, the family, work, and so forth. Transitions from one role to another result in changes in motivation and other aspects of personality. Thus, the transition from the role of graduate student to that of faculty member involves changes both in one's self-concept and in expectations about appropriate behavior. Faculty members not only go through the life stages and crises of other human beings in our society, but there are also certain stages of life in academia that are common to most faculty members. Life before attaining tenure may be different from life after achieving tenure; achieving full professor status marks another change in status.

Unfortunately, the data on faculty motivation over the span of the entire academic career are very sparse. Petz and Andres (1966) report some age trends in their studies of scientists and engineers, but there are few other studies that are directly relevant.

Implications of Life Span Development Theory
for Understanding Faculty Motivation

Even though we may doubt that all forty to forty-five year old faculty members are going through midlife transition or that promotion to tenure or to full professor inevitably delineates significant changes in motivation, are there implications of the life span development theories for understanding faculty motivation? In terms of motivation theory, individuals at different periods of life assign different values to potential satisfactions and have different expectations about the probability of achieving the satisfaction.

For example, we have seen that Levinson (1976) would predict that faculty members of the same age would be likely to be at the same stage of development and that in attempting to motivate faculty for teaching or other activities, one would need to take account of the age of those one wishes to involve. Individuals at age forty to forty-five might be particularly attracted by a new role, while those

in their thirties would be likely to be motivated by opportunities to increase their competence of their status within the college. The full professor in her or his late forties is likely to be loyal to the college, less confident of the possibility of great changes for the better, but willing to take responsibilities necessary for the institution. In terms of Levinson's theory, such individuals may enjoy acting as and be valuable as mentors to younger faculty. Assuming that the individual has come through the midlife transition successfully, this is a period in which high levels of energy and satisfaction can be gained from one's work, and Petz and Andres (1966) found that among faculty researchers, scientific productivity rises in the fifties after a drop in the late forties.

The status theorists would see the assistant professor in the first post-doctoral job as strongly affected by the degree to which status differentiation between ranks is emphasized. At this level, promotion and salary policies might be particularly relevant to motivation. At most institutions, however, full professors have privileges and responsibilities beyond those of younger faculty members. Thus, full professors, the motive of commitment to the excellence of the college may be a powerful inducement to assume new responsibilities or to take on a new role.

For those faculty members whose careers have emphasized scholarly research, the years of the forties and early fifties may represent a peak in terms of status and recognition. As we saw earlier, scientific contributions peak in the early forties, fall in the mid-forties, and peak again in the fifties (Petz & Andres, 1966). For the established senior professor, service on national committees, requests to write chapters in invited symposia, or invitations to deliver addresses may take time formerly devoted to research and teaching. To the professor who finds adulation and applause when addressing students at other universities, it may be discomfiting to return home to an environment where he is taken for granted by those who have known him long enough not to feel that they need to tell him how great he is. Rather than a sabbatical away from their home campus, such individuals need a sabbatical from outside commitments.

Aging scholars are helped to remain productive if diversity is maintained and periodic changes in role encouraged rather than following the normal path of increased specialization (Petz & Andres, 1966). Studies of aging indicate that most of our stereotypes about decline of ability in aging are not true. In fact, relative to other groups, college professors are likely to maintain intellectual ability or to improve in old age. Because of the intrinsic satisfactions in academic work and strong commitment to their college, many older professors

would continue to be productive members of the academic community if retirement policies permitted them to continue to work. Rather simple changes in organizational arrangements could command substantial wisdom and energy from older faculty members even with decreasing salaries (McKeachie, 1977).

While theories of life span development imply regularities in the lives of faculty members, they should not be taken to mean that faculty members of a given age or status are the same. As I indicated earlier, I do not believe that either a stage theory or a status theory is complete in itself. There are biological changes associated with aging that are inevitable, even though there are great individual differences in the rate of change of such things as endocrine secretions, vision, strength, and so forth; there are role expectations associated with such things as faculty status, parenthood, membership in a research group, and being the child of an aged parent. There are trends in personality so that patterns established in childhood and adolescence may wax and wane in later life; there are changes occurring from the accumulation of experience. All of these and other factors influence the changing motives of the faculty member over her or his career. In fact, we know even less about the careers of academic women than we do about academic men. It is probably safe to assume in this era of our society that they are different, but one hopes that research will soon tell us how and why.[4] The main point is that individuals differ, that the hierarchical order of individual motives changes, and that in many ways, differences between individuals increase as they get older.

CHANGING FACULTY BEHAVIOR

Can faculty behavior be changed? The answer lies not in manipulation of extrinsic rewards such as prizes and honors, although these should not be dismissed. Rather, the answer lies in examining the characteristics of desired faculty activities that can bring satisfaction and in creating situations in which those satisfactions can be found more readily. For example, satisfactions of teaching that come from observing students learn, from the stimulus of new ideas, and from other elements in the teaching situation are more likely to be achieved with small classes than with large classes. If administrators are really serious about better teaching, they need to find methods in which faculty members can have greater opportunities to feel that classes have gone well, to know students as individuals, to follow the development of students for periods of time long enough to see changes, and to interact with students in ways that are intellectually

and emotionally rewarding. While this implies opportunities to teach small classes, it does not imply that all classes need to be small classes. Administrative and organizational arrangements that permit faculty members to follow students over a period longer than one semester and to have at least a portion of instructional time in small group settings can be devised without significant budget increases.

One of the implications of our emphasis upon individual differences in faculty motivation is that one may produce gains in motivation by better matches between people and tasks. Too often we assume that all faculty members should be teacher-researchers, equally competent to teach both introductory and advanced graduate level courses. In fact, some faculty members enjoy, and do well, with large introductory courses, while others should never be permitted near a freshman. Supporting individuals for excellent performance in jobs they like is one way of maximizing productivity.

Faculty members recognize that changing institutional conditions require different allocations of faculty work. For many, the role changes involved can be potential sources of new satisfactions. Suppose, for example, that one wishes faculty members to change from being predominantly involved in graduate instruction to undergraduate teaching. Some faculty members will welcome the change, if they are encouraged and given the resources needed. Since one of the attractions in teaching is that of creating and developing intellectual ideas and interpreting one's field to those who are less expert, one is more likely to attract more faculty members by involving them in planning a new way of introducing students to the field than by simply closing graduate courses and announcing that faculty members will be required to teach undergraduate courses. The very fact that a requirement is imposed implies that the task is an onerous and unrewarding one. If you want to improve classroom teaching, think about how to make classrooms places where students and teachers like to be. One should think about the physical setting of the classroom, the interpersonal relationships between students and teachers, the support and interest of colleagues, and those factors that contribute to a sense of competence as a teacher.

Similarly, if we want faculty members to be more active researchers, we need to examine the satisfactions that are intrinsic to research activities, such as the challenge of new ideas and untested hypotheses or the pleasure of expertness and of doing something that very few others are able to do. These are important in maintaining faculty enthusiasm and energy for research.

The faculty member's delight in problem solving, new ideas, and rationality may even account for the willingness of faculty members to serve on endless committees and to consult with various public

groups who present problems upon which faculty members have expertise. Obviously, some faculty consult for money, but the majority are involved in much problem solving and advice giving in which their compensation is minimal.

From our analysis of contemporary motivation and life span theories, the role of salary and promotion policies becomes more comprehensible. Salary and promotion are part of a social system in which salary is not so much important for what the money will buy as for what it symbolizes about what is valued by one's colleagues and one's college. Being promoted indicates that one has achieved competence in the eyes of respected peers. According to life span theories, these indicators should be particularly important in the early years of one's career.

However, heavy emphasis upon such incentives may paradoxically result in poorer, rather than better, university teaching. If individuals publish research papers or spend time on teaching because they see this as important to promotion, what happens once the promotion has been achieved? Presumably, the administration must administer an unending series of promotions and pay increases in order to maintain motivation. Otherwise the individual will look for other activities that are rewarded. For systems emphasizing extrinsic rewards, the fact that most faculty members of the past decade have attained the full professor rank before age forty means that one must devise superranks, named chairs, or other ways of providing further goals.

What one is looking for in making a decision about awarding tenure is predictors about the contribution that can be expected from the individual for the rest of his or her career as a faculty member. Thus, one wants to promote people who are enthralled by their research, who enjoy teaching, who have such enthusiasm for their work that the external rewards are incidental indicators of recognition rather than goals in themselves. During my career as a department chairman, the individuals not recommended for promotion probably averaged more publications than those who were promoted; often our decision not to promote was influenced by a certain shared sense that the faculty member was working more for promotion and recognition than from a sense of curiosity about the research problem. Such judgments are obviously risky ones to make, and we may well have made mistakes. Nevertheless, I believe it to be important that the promotion to tenure should be regarded as a prediction of the future based on past performance, rather than as a reward for past achievement.

Promotions and salaries are not irrelevant. Since they do symbolize the value placed on one's activities, good teachers whose salaries and promotions lag are likely to feel unappreciated and unaccepted

by their peers. Sometimes one's growing sense of alienation, the feeling that one is not respected by one's colleagues, can lead to bitterness, corroding the satisfactions of teaching and research and leading to a slow dying on the vine. Thus, I am not arguing against high salaries for effective teachers, but against stressing salaries as a goal or incentive to motivate teaching or other desired activities, such as chairing a department or serving as a counselor.

Moreover, one should recognize that the level of salary per se is of little motivational consequence. According to the cognitive view—a view supported by much research in industry—salary is a relative term. One interprets one's salary raise in relation to past raises and in relation to the salaries and raises of one's peers. I was a department chairman during the 1960s, a period when faculty salaries were rising rapidly. I was able to give large salary increases to many faculty members. Part of my education in faculty motivation came from finding that a faculty member who received an unusually large raise one year was disappointed if his raise the next year was smaller and that a faculty member receiving a large increase was not likely to be grateful if he found that a peer received a larger raise.

As one would expect from the cognitive theory of motivation, the role of awards for excellence in teaching depends not upon the amount of money associated with the award but upon faculty perceptions of the award. Is it regarded as tokenism—a hypocritical attempt to cover up real deficiencies in support for teaching? Is the selection of the awardees regarded as a political process designed to see that the awards are spread around to schools or departments whose deans or department heads are powerful and given to those who conform and knuckle under? Clearly, such interpretations give the awards a much different meaning from that in which the awardees are genuinely respected and honored by their students and peers.

While I have stressed the importance of intrinsic rather than extrinsic motivation, there is one reward within the control of the administrator that may be worthy of serious consideration. Time, as Kenneth Eble (1972) points out, is highly valued by faculty members. Typically, universities have given sabbaticals or released time for various scholarly projects, but it is less common to give time for remaking a course or developing a new teaching skill. If better teaching is desired, such arrangements are among the important resources of the administrator.

What about academic deadwood? What can be done to motivate the faculty member who is going to seed? In the first place, I doubt that as much academic deadwood exists as there is talk about it among those who would like to fire faculty in order to save money

or to create new slots for their institutions. Almost everyone knows one or more professors who have failed to live up to their earlier promise as scholars; some of these individuals have chosen forms of teaching, counseling, or administration service that are as valuable to higher education as the careers of their more scholarly colleagues. One person's deadwood may be another person's most valued mentor.

But what about those few who are themselves dispirited and are aware of their marginal status in the groves of academe. Our theory suggests that the reasons for such a status may vary greatly from individual to individual. For some who have felt rejected, an opportunity to try a new, needed, respected role may be invigorating. Perhaps you would not want to risk such a person in a department chairmanship, but the associate chairmanship, if it is more than scut work, might revive long dormant talent and energy. An invitation to work with a new research or teaching team might also be invigorating. One needs to remember that most faculty members are proud individuals and that pride is a powerful motive that may inhibit admission of problems but may motivate hard work when one accepts a job that demands high ability. From the standpoint of motivation theory, a change in roles creates new expectations not only from others but also by the person himself.

The reaction of a faculty member who has failed to do a good job is affected by his interpretation of the causes for his failure. If he perceives his failure as due to his own lack of ability, he is likely to give up. On the other hand, if failure is attributed to a lack of effort, the individual is likely to try again with increased effort. Thus, the department chairman attempting to motivate a faculty member to renewed efforts needs to reassure the individual about his ability and encourage attribution to interference from other activities. According to cognitive theory, the effort needs to be directed toward changing the faculty member's cognitions, and one way of doing this is by putting the person in a role in which new behavior is required. But it is important that the individual not fail in the new role. All too often, we forget that new teaching, research, or service roles may require skills that not every faculty member possesses. Thus, a plan for reassignment needs to include an analysis of the skills required and an opportunity to develop those skills. Fortunately, most campuses now have available centers that provide opportunities for learning new teaching skills, and summer institutes or sabbaticals can be used to catch up on new research skills. While it may not be easy to help a professor see the value of using such opportunities, once he or she is embarked, an increasing sense of competence and some initial

success should maintain effort. If singling a faculty member out for special training seems likely to confirm his self-perceptions of inadequacy, it may be possible to arrange training for the entire department or some subgroup.

To sum up, faculty members are intelligent, thoughtful human beings, who share the motives of other human beings, but who are fortunate enough to have chosen a vocation in which the greatest satisfactions are intrinsic to the work. Attempts to influence faculty behavior by extrinsic rewards and punishments are less likely to achieve better teaching and research than attention to methods of enhancing the intrinsic rewards.

NOTES TO CHAPTER 1

1. In preparing this chapter, the author benefited from discussions with John R.P. French, Donald R. Brown, Edward L. Walker, Warren Norman, N.R.F. Maier, Orville Brim, Edward Lawler, Stanford Erickson, William Morse, Jan Lawrence, and other colleagues. My own experience has been in a large state university; further, most of those who have written about faculty have been professors in large universities. The perspective perforce is likely to be biased toward faculty in such universities. While there are probably more similarities than differences between faculty members in large universities and those in community colleges, liberal arts colleges, and other types of institutions, there nevertheless are likely to be important differences. I trust that the reader will be mindful of these at points where my discourse is provincial.

2. The French et al. study used an interesting additional source of data. Wives of faculty members were questioned. They reported that their husbands typically spend weekends working and that their chief form of relaxation is reading, thus supporting the self-report data.

3. Levinson's theory is now becoming well-known through the popularity of Gail Sheehy's *Passages* (1976). Hodgkinson (1974) has discussed its applicability to faculty.

4. Sheehy (1976) offers some interesting speculations about adult development in women.

Chapter 2

Perspectives from Economics: The Economic Consequences of Changing Faculty Reward Structures

William E. Becker, Jr.

Concern over faculty collective bargaining, as opposed to salary assignment based on individual merits, has resulted in several studies on the effects of unionization on faculty behavior. Pressure for the application of equal pay regulation, instead of comparison of individuals, has also led to numerous studies on the faculty behavioral effects of affirmative action. Similarly, desire for a community of scholars, in contrast to a system of competition between scholars, has fostered many studies on faculty response to teaching and research evaluations. The minute one considers any form of evaluation, questions also arise as to the effects of external pecuniary versus internal psychic rewards on faculty productivity.

As Howard Tuckman (1976: 40) points out, there has been little serious effort in any studies of professorial behavior to construct formal mathematical faculty behavior models along the optimization lines favored by many economists. Without such modeling, however, one can only speculate on the faculty productivity consequences of changing the university methods and procedures for determining faculty rewards and incentives.

In this study, a formal, constrained utility optimization model is presented as the behavior model of a university professor. As in Becker (1975), it is assumed that faculty time is a variable input to various academic output. Academic outputs generate both personal satisfaction and income. Following Stiglitz's (1975) theory of screening and income assignment, however, it is assumed that academic outputs may not be precisely measurable by the university.[1] The ac-

curacy of university measurement determines the extent to which individual faculty members receive the value of their output.

Where there is little screening and high error in the measurement of individual faculty productivity, all faculty are shown to receive the same basic salary regardless of their actual contribution to the university. In essence, inaccurate screening results in the high performers sharing their productivity with the low performers, as is the case in any egalitarian pay system. If screening is accurate, individuals receive the value of their output.

A change in the intensity of screening given faculty output is shown to have differing effects depending on the faculty member's position in the output distribution. Only for high producers will a change in the measurement accuracy associated with an academic output necessarily result in like changes in faculty desire to produce that output. It is also shown that changes in the pecuniary return to a given academic output will only produce like changes in the professor's desire to produce that output if the screening methods are highly accurate. Regardless of the accuracy of screening, attempts to employ internal rewards aimed at changing the satisfaction derived from a given academic output are shown to yield indeterminant results.

PROFESSORIAL BEHAVIOR AND INSTITUTIONAL ARRANGEMENTS

It is assumed that a professor is an individual who not only derives satisfaction (or utility) from consumption activity, but also acquires satisfaction from the professional activities of teaching and research. The professorial utility function is therefore written as:

$$U(Q_1, Q_2, Q_3) \qquad (2-1)$$

where Q_i, $i = 1, 2, 3$ are, respectively, teaching output, research output, and consumption. An increase in Q_i will raise the professor's satisfaction derived from this output; U rises as Q_i rises. However, for our purposes here, this incremental benefit can be assumed to decrease as the professor's output level rises. The professor is assumed to know the exact quality and quantity of his or her professional output.[2] Consumption, on the other hand, is at least partially dependent on the university's measurement of the professor's professional output.[3]

The professor must produce professional output through the input of time. The amount of time spent in teaching activity affects pro-

duction of Q_1; time devoted to research activity affects the production of Q_2. However, time spent in research activity may enhance teaching quality since it allows the professor to share disciplinary experiences with students. The time spent in discipline-based teaching may also sharpen the quality of the professor's research.[4] The professor's production process, represented for simplicity as linear in time, is therefore given by:

$$Q_i = \sum_{j=1}^{2} a_{ij} T_j, \ i = 1, 2 \qquad (2\text{--}2)$$

where the T_js, $j = 1, 2$ are, respectively, time spent in teaching and research activity. The technology coefficients, for a fixed capital stock (both human and physical), are assumed to be nonnegative.

In the case of consumption, the professor needs income to purchase market goods. He also needs leisure consumption time to acquire and enjoy goods purchased. The consumption production function is therefore written as:

$$Q_3 = bY + a_{33} T_3 \qquad (2\text{--}3)$$

where Y is university-determined income and T_3 is time spent in leisure consumption activity. The technology coefficients b and a_{33} are assumed to be positive.

It is assumed that the professor obtains personal income from the university on the basis of teaching and research output. Likewise, the university generates its revenue on the basis of total institutional outputs of teaching and research. As suggested by Ferber (1974: 69), Garbarino (1974: 309–32), Freeman (1975a: 103–104), and others, however, there are distinct features in the internal labor market policy of universities. Faculty payment policies within a university may tend to produce the same basic salary for professors of similar rank, experience, and academic credentials regardless of field of specialization and actual contribution to the employing institution.[5] This tendency toward equalization of faculty salaries can be attributed to two related factors.

First, universities affirm an intellectual value structure that presupposes little or no inherent superiority of knowledge in various fields. According to this price scheme, faculty may be judged by their intellectual quality and scholarly output, but differences in the market price of output (which are substantial between and within department disciplines) tend to be ignored as much as possible in determining the value of faculty output.[6] In other words, in establishing

faculty salaries, the university attempts to place dollar-valued weights on teaching output and on research output that are roughtly the same for all fields within and possibly between departments. Therefore, assuming that the university assigns a single nonnegative dollar value weight W_1 for teaching output and a single weight W_2 for research output may not be an overly great simplification of reality.

Second, job content, experience, or task traits, rather than quality of individual performance, may be controlling factors in judging faculty scholarly output. Variation in the quality of intellectual performance and creativity at required tasks may be ignored by the university in judging faculty. This may be the case because:

- The rating of faculty is believed to involve an excessive amount of uncertainty (Eble, 1972: 54−72);

- The rating of faculty is considered inappropriate within a "group of Socratic scholars" (Arrowsmith, 1967);

- The rating of faculty requires the application of arbitrary assessments of externalities and interdependencies between individuals (Freeman, 1975: 103);

- The rating of faculty increases the workload of faculty or administrator evaluators and may be inherently subjective (Howard Tuckman, 1976: 53);

- The rating of faculty seems to conflict with the application of the Equal Pay Act (Lester, 1974: 121−35); or

- The rating of faculty is viewed as inconsistent with the philosophy of collective bargaining (Garbarino, 1974: 304−31).

Academic egalitarianism, whatever the reason or form, results in individuals of similar experience, academic rank, and/or task assignment being labeled equally productive even though their actual contribution to the university's output may differ.[7] Such incorrect labeling results in the high performers in a given group of scholars sharing their productivity and creativity with the less able.

The extent to which individuals share productivity because of incorrect labeling is a function of the university's screening process applied to teaching and research output. To see this, consider an example in which the number of students enrolled in undergraduate honors thesis seminars is believed to net the university, after all non-faculty expenses, W dollars per student thesis completed.

In the extreme case, where the university employs no screening of faculty thesis contribution, all professors must be labeled as equally

productive. With the exception of the truly average professors, all faculty are incorrectly labeled. To exhaust the university product, all faculty would receive the mean of total faculty product, regardless of actual contribution to student thesis.[8] The high producers in the group subsidize the low producers.

If after a somewhat intensive review of recorded thesis advising, the university decides that there are three identifiable ranges of thesis contribution, then a low, medium, and high labeling is possible. The university can now pay each professor the mean product value for the group to which he or she is assigned. However, all professors receiving one of these labels need not be equally productive. Some may be at the high end of the productivity range within each of the three separate groupings and some may be at the low end. Those at the high and low ends of each group range are mislabeled and incorrectly paid, but not as badly as when there was no screening. Through yet more intensive screening, the university could continue to reduce the measurement error and, at least conceptually, get to the point of perfect labeling of all professors.

In general, a university's screening process of intensity k_1 for teaching and k_2 for research output can be thought of as a point estimate of a professor's productivity. Let $e_i(Q_i, \hat{Q}_i, k_i)$ be the probability that a professor of productivity Q_i is labeled $\hat{Q}_i$ in a university screening of intensity k_i. As k_i is increased, the probability of correct labeling in the ith output also rises.

The twofold egalitarian nature of the internal university reward structure (where superiority of knowledge is not recognized and faculty may be incorrectly labeled) is captured by assuming income sharing between faculty given the same output label. In such a reward system, all faculty whose ith productivity is labeled or estimated to be $\hat{Q}_i$ will receive an income for this output equal to their mean product value—that is,

$$Y_i(W_i, k_i, \hat{Q}_i) = W_i \int Q_i e_i(Q_i, \hat{Q}_i, k_i) h(Q_i) dQ_i \qquad (2-4)$$

$$\div \int e_i(Q_i, \hat{Q}_i, k_i) h(Q_i) dQ_i$$

where $h(Q_i)$ is the unimodal density function of Q_i—namely, the fraction of faculty who actually have output Q_i. The slope of $h(Q_i)$ at output level Q_i is given by $h'(Q_i) = \partial h(Q_i)/\partial Q_i$.

Multiplying both the numerator and the denominator of equation (2-4) by the number of professors in the university would show the numerator to be the total product value of all those labeled $\hat{Q}_i$ and

the denominator to be the number of faculty so labeled. A professor whose true productivity is Q_i will have an expected income from this output given by:

$$Y_i(W_i, k_i, Q_i) = \int Y_i(W_i, k_i, \hat{Q}_i) e_i(Q_i, \hat{Q}_i, k_i) d\hat{Q}_i. \qquad (2-5)$$

The income consequence of any imprecise, yet somewhat accurate, assessment of a professor's position in the distribution of outputs can be established by considering a screening process in which:

$$e_i(Q_i, \hat{Q}_i, k_i) = f_i(Q_i - \hat{Q}_i, k_i) = f_i(\epsilon_i, k_i) \qquad (2-6)$$

and the measurement error ϵ_i has a mean of zero, has a variance represented by $g_i(k_i)$, and is independent of output levels and other measurement errors. In addition, the variance of measurement error is assumed to be negatively related to screening intensity—that is, $\partial g_i(k_i)/\partial k_i = g_i'(k_i) < 0$.

The assumption of a fairly accurate screening system as given in equation (2-6) implies that equation (2-4) and (2-5) can be approximated, summing over both outputs, as[9]:

$$Y(W, k, \hat{Q}) \simeq \sum_{i=1}^{2} W_i [\hat{Q}_i + h_i'(\hat{Q}_i) g_i(k_i)/h_i(\hat{Q}_i)] \qquad (2-7)$$

and

$$Y(W, k, Q) \simeq \sum_{i=1}^{2} W_i [Q_i + h_i'(Q_i) g_i(k_i)/h_i(Q_i)]. \qquad (2-8)$$

Equation (2-8) demonstrates that if the university screening of faculty is perfect, $g_i(k_i) = 0$ and $\hat{Q}_i = Q_i$, a professor can expect to receive his or her own product value $W_i Q_i$. If screening is not perfect, $g_i(k_i) > 0$, a professor below the mode, $h_i'(Q_i) > 0$, can expect to receive more than under perfect screening; a professor above the mode, $h_i'(Q_i) < 0$, can expect to receive less.[10] This is a consequence of faculty being grouped, within a given range of error, with some colleagues who are better, but underrated, and some who are worse, but overrated. Below the modal output faculty tend to be grouped with more who are better than worse; above the modal output the reverse is true.

The professor's decisionmaking framework can now be described by the algebraic expressions given above. The professor attempts to maximize utility, (2-1), subject to the production functions (2-2)

and (2−3), expected income (2−8), and the total time available, T, in the period under consideration—that is,

$$T = \sum_{i=1}^{3} T_i .$$ (2−9)

In this decision framework, the professor is free to invest time in research and training. Increase in activities, via the production functions represented in equation (2−2), raises the professor's level of satisfaction through the utility function equation (2−1). The change in income resulting from increased output depends on the professor's position in the given output distribution and on the university's accuracy in measuring productivity, as given in equation (2−8). If an increase in output results in an increase in expected income, then the professor's level of satisfaction via increased consumption in equation (2−3) is possible.

The time constraint, however, limits the level of satisfaction obtainable. An increase in the time invested in professional activity, while raising academic output and expected income, forces a reduction in the time spent in consumption activity. A possible resulting reduction in consumption lowers the professor's level of satisfaction.

The equilibrium of teaching, research, and consumption outputs depends upon the marginal rate of substitution in the utility function and production functions and on the income determination function. It also depends on the distribution of the two professional outputs, the faculty member's position in those distributions, and the variance connected with output measurement utilized by the university.

EQUILIBRIUM OUTPUT OF TEACHING, RESEARCH AND CONSUMPTION

To solve for the equilibrium level of Q_i, the decision framework is simplified to an objective function involving only one constraint. Since the utility function is defined in output space while the time constraint is not, the time constraint must be mapped into output space. This is possible, since expected income can be expressed in terms of time spent in professional activities. Substituting equation (2−2) into equation (2−8) transforms the income determination function into time space.

$$Y(W, k, Q) = \sum_{j=1}^{2} [(\sum_{i=1}^{2} W_i\, a_{ij}\, T_j) + W_j\, h_j'\, g_j / h_j] .$$ (2−10)

Substituting equation (2–10) into equation (2–3) eliminates income from the equational system and permits expression of the three production functions in matrix form where Q_1, Q_2, and Q_3 can be seen as direct functions of T_1, T_2, and T_3 for a given distribution of faculty output and variance in measuring output:

$$q = \begin{bmatrix} Q_1 \\ Q_2 \\ Q_3^* \end{bmatrix} = \begin{bmatrix} a_{11} & a_{12} & 0 \\ a_{21} & a_{22} & 0 \\ a_{31} & a_{32} & a_{33} \end{bmatrix} \cdot \begin{bmatrix} T_1 \\ T_2 \\ T_3 \end{bmatrix} = \theta \cdot t \qquad (2\text{–}11)$$

where

$$a_{3j} = b \sum_{i=1}^{2} W_i a_{ij}, \, j = 1, 2,$$

$$Q_3^* = Q_3 - b \sum_{j=1}^{2} W_j h_j' g_j / h_j \, .$$

Multiplying both sides of production system (2–11) by the inverse of θ and then substituting into equation (2–9) gives the time constraint in output space:

$$T = \sum_{i=1}^{3} \pi_i Q_i \qquad (2\text{–}12)$$

where

$$\pi_1 = \frac{a_{22} - a_{21}}{a_{22} a_{11} - a_{12} a_{21}} - \frac{bW_1}{a_{33}} \, ,$$

$$\pi_2 = \frac{a_{11} - a_{12}}{a_{22} a_{11} - a_{12} a_{21}} - \frac{bW_2}{a_{33}} \, ,$$

$$\pi_3 = \frac{1}{a_{33}} \left(1 - \frac{b}{Q_3} \sum_{i=1}^{2} W_i h_i' g_i / h_i \right) \, .$$

All three πs are expressed in terms of the time per unit of output. They can be thought of as shadow prices of respective academic outputs. A sufficient condition for $\pi_3 > 0$ is that $h_i' < 0$—a condition met if the professor is above the mode output for Q_i, $i = 1, 2$. A

necessary condition for $\pi_i > 0$, $i = 1, 2$, is that the technology matrix represented by equation (2−2) has dominant diagonal elements.

The professor's decisionmaking framework is now summarized in the objective function:

$$U(Q_1, Q_2, Q_3) + \lambda (T - \sum_{i=1}^{3} \pi_i Q_i) . \qquad (2-13)$$

Equation (2−13) conceptually defines the equilibrium level of teaching, research, and consumption desired and produceable by the professor.[11] For any given level of consumption, the equilibrium level of teaching and research defined by equation (2−13) is represented in Figure 2−1 as point A. The indifference curve labeled $U_0 U_0$ represents alternative combinations of teaching and research output that will give the professor identical internal satisfaction as specified in equation (2−1). Indifference curves $U_1 U_1$ and $U_2 U_2$ represent ever

Figure 2−1. Equilibrium Teaching and Research Output.

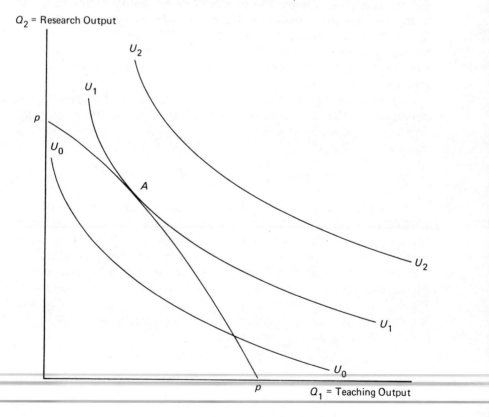

increasing levels of satisfaction from given amounts of teaching and research output. The production constraint, curve *pp*, gives alternative combinations of teaching and research that can be produced given the nonleisure time available, income weights for teaching and research, and the professor's ability to produce these outputs. It is a simple graphing of equation (2–12). Point *A* represents the highest level of personal satisfaction the professor can achieve given his or her production constraint.

SCREENING INTENSITY CHANGES AND THE REWARD STRUCTURE

Eble (1972: 58) speculated that the mere act of improving the system of evaluating teaching, increased screening through the use of student evaluations, and peer visitation of classes, for example, would lead to improved undergraduate instruction. On the other hand, Lester (1974: 130–31) speculated that the application of equal pay regulation would destroy university methods of screening faculty and thus threaten the productivity of faculty. While Eble and Lester provide little analytical basis for their assertions, the feasibility of their conclusions can be explored in this professorial behavior model by simply assessing how the production constraint and indifference mapping in Figure 2–1 change given an increase in the screening of teaching.[12]

The production constraint defined in the second expression of equation (2–13) and represented in Figure 2–1 can be written for any level of consumption as:

$$Q_2 = \frac{T - \pi_3 Q_3}{\pi_2} - \frac{\pi_1}{\pi_2} Q_1 . \tag{2-14}$$

If screening of teaching and research were perfect, π_3 would not depend on levels of Q_1 or Q_2 and equation (2–14) would be represented by the straight dotted line as in Figure 2–2. Where teaching is measured with error, and even if research is measured with precision, π_3 rises as the professor moves from the modal teaching output to higher teaching levels. As the professor moves from the modal teaching output to lower teaching levels, π_3 falls. This can be seen by noting that in this case π_3 is written in equation (2–12) as

$$\pi_3 = \frac{1}{a_{33}} \left(1 - \frac{b}{Q_3} W_1 h'_1 g_1 / h_1 \right) .$$

Figure 2-2. Change in Equilibrium Resulting from Screening: Faculty Below the Modal Teaching Output.

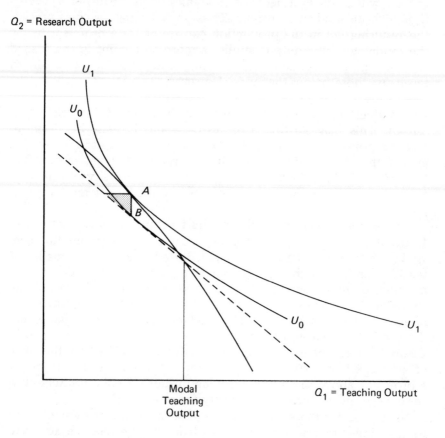

If screening of teaching is perfect, then $g_1 = 0$ and $\pi_3 = 1/a_{33}$. If teaching screening is not perfect, at the modal output h_1' is zero, so π_3 is still $1/a_{33}$. At higher outputs, however, h_1' is less than zero, implying $\pi_3 > 1/a_{33}$; at lower levels, h_1' is greater than zero, giving $\pi_3 < 1/a_{33}$. Thus, the existence of imprecise screening gives rise to the curved production constraint represented in Figure 2-2. As screening becomes more precise, this curved line moves closer to the straight dotted line. In other words, for a given level of consumption, an increase in screening causes $T - \pi_3 Q_3$ to rise if the professor is above the modal teaching output; $T - \pi_3 Q_3$ will fall if he or she is below the mode.

The effect of an increase in screening intensity will depend upon the professor's position in the output distribution. Assuming that

both teaching and research are "normal goods," then a decrease (increase) in time available for such activity—namely, $T - \pi_3 \, Q_3$ falls (rises)—will result in a decrease (increase) in the professor's production of both academic outputs. Thus, as screening becomes precise, the resulting fall in the production constraint for a professor below the modal teaching output implies a move to a point in the shaded area of Figure 2-2. Increased screening tends to reduce the desire to teach for those below the mode. However, the price of teaching relative to research is less along the dotted straight line production constraint than for the curved production constraint below the modal output. This suggests that a professor would increase his desire to teach; a point such as B is possible, but so is any point in the shaded area if this "price effect" does not overpower the earlier "production effect." The effect of an increase in the intensity of screening teaching is indeterminant for those below the modal teaching output.[13]

For an individual above the modal teaching output, as shown in Figure 2-3, an increase in screening implies that the production constraint shifts up toward the straight dotted line. Here normality of teaching and research implies that any point in the shaded area is possible. Increased screening tends to increase the professor's desire to teach. In addition, the fact that the price of teaching relative to research is less along the straight production constraint suggests that the desire to teach is further advanced, so that a point such as B in Figure 2-3 is possible. Both the production effort and the price effort work in the same direction to increase the level of teaching for a professor above the model teaching output. (Similar results follow for changes in the screening intensity for research.)

Next consider the effort of an increase in the income weight given to teaching. First, assume that both teaching and research are accurately screened. Once again, assume the professor is initially at equilibrium at point A in Figure 2-4. As can be seen in equation (2-12), an increase in the income weight W_1 implies a reduction in the shadow price π_1. Thus, the production constraint pp shifts to position pq in Figure 2-4. The normality assumption implies that any point in the shaded area is a possible new equilibrium point. The fact that the price of teaching relative to research is now less also implies that a point such as B is possible. Both the production effect and the price effect resulting from an increase in the income weight given teaching lead to an increase in the equilibrium teaching output of the professor. This is true at least in this case of accurate screening. (Similar results follow for research.)

Figure 2–3. Change in Equilibrium Resulting from Screening: Faculty Above the Modal Teaching Output.

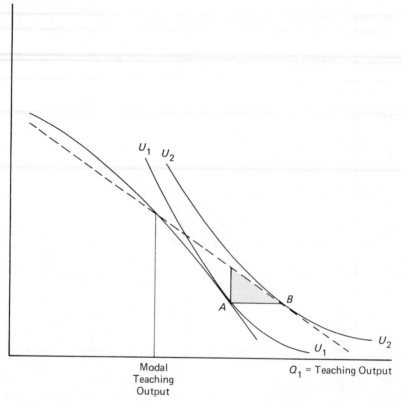

If the teaching screening mechanisms are inaccurate, then π_3 as well as π_1 are affected by a change in W_1. A rise in W_1 lowers π_1 and raises π_3 if the professor is above the modal teaching output and lowers π_3 if below. As was shown earlier, such changes in π_3 tend to raise the price of teaching relative to research for those both above and below the teaching model. Thus, where screening of teaching is imprecise, there is an indirect price effect generated by a change in the income weight given teaching that works through π_3 and tends to negate the direct price effect of a fall in the π_1/π_2 ratio. Thus, the effect of a change in the income weight given teaching is indeterminant if screening is less than accurate. (Similar results follow for research.)

Finally, consider the effect of attempts to change the professor's ability to convert time spent in teaching to teaching output. Such

Figure 2–4.   Change in Equilibrium Given a Change in the Shadow Price of Teaching.

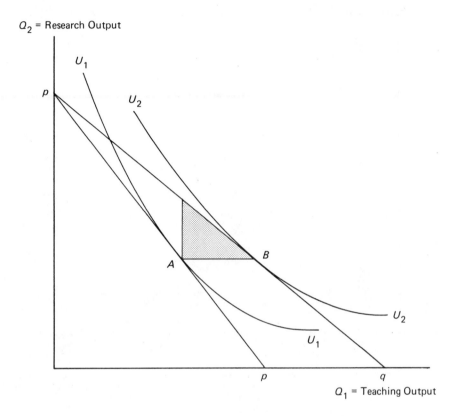

Q_2 = Research Output

Q_1 = Teaching Output

internal rewards have been proposed by McKeachie, Dornbusch, and many others. For example, providing additional graders, secretaries, or better classrooms would raise a_{11} and thus lead to more teaching output for the same time input.[14] However, the professor might elect to provide the same teaching output with less teaching time input required; the saving in time could go to leisure.

- To assess the effect of an increase in a_{11}, first note that in equation (2–12), a rise in a_{11} results in a decrease in the shadow price of teaching π_1. The effect of this is again represented in Figure 2–4, where screening is assumed perfect, by a shifting of the production constraint pp to the position given by pq. The attainable area brought about by the production constraint shift is again given by the shaded area. In addition, the price effect could enable the professor to get to a point such as B. However, the shadow price of research is also

Figure 2–5. Change in Equilibrium Given a Change in the Shadow Price of Resources.

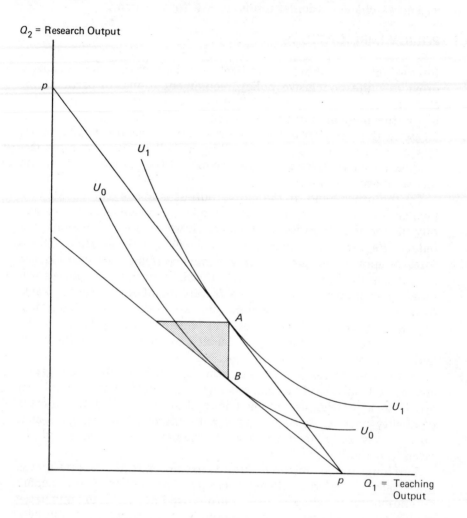

changed by a rise in the technology coefficient, a_{11}; π_2 rises. The effect of this price change is given in Figure 2–5. There the production constraint shift implies a reduction in teaching output as given by the shaded area. The fact that teaching is again relatively less expressive does imply that a point such as B is possible. But the combined effects of a rise in π_2 and a fall in π_1 leave the final equilibrium point indeterminant; teaching output could rise or fall as a result of increasing the professor's ability to convert time spent in teaching

into teaching output. This indeterminancy is simply magnified if one considers the case of less than precise screening where π_3 changes as π_1 and π_2 change. (Similar results follow for research.)

POLICY IMPLICATIONS

Interestingly, the above theoretical model of professional behavior provides quite conclusive policy recommendations. In particular, if a given academic output distribution yields a modal output value below the median output, an increase in screening will yield an increase in the given output for the majority of faculty. Furthermore, this increased screening will probably be well received by most faculty, as all those above the mode can expect to gain income from the increased accountability.[15]

On the other hand, if the modal output is above the median output, an increase in screening may or may not result in an increase in output for the majority of faculty. However, more screening will reduce the variance in measurement in salary determination. Therefore, an appropriate increase in screening combined with subsequent increases in the income determination weight given to the output will raise the level of output that every faculty member is willing and able to produce. Without the matching increase in the income determination weight, however, the increase in screening will probably not be well received by the majority of faculty, as they are below the mode and will thus expect to lose income.

In the case of research, the existing screening methods are generally agreed upon and considered highly accurate. For example, an article in a prestigious, refereed journal is accepted as an indicator of quality output. As such, a university interested in raising research output may only need to raise the income determination weight given to research.

Teaching, unlike research output, has no existing measure that is universally accepted as highly accurate. An increase in the income determination weight given this output need not result in an increase in this output. Unless accurate methods of screening are established, there may be no way, other than stipulating minimal time commitment regulations, to affect this output. Only if a university is able to adopt student evaluations, standardized student learning measures, or some other proxy index of teaching output can the reward structure be used to cause an increase in every faculty member's desire to increase productivity in teaching.

It may be very appealing to an administrator to avoid the hassle of dealing with individual faculty members over money. Furthermore,

the use of such external rewards, in contrast to the use of internal reward, may be viewed as being in opposition to the ethics of academe. Unfortunately, attempts to raise professorial output by directly affecting the way a professor converts time into academic output can not be shown to have predictable results. An attempt to raise teaching output by providing the professor with additional teaching aids may simply result in the professor producing the same teaching output with less time input; the time saving may be invested in leisure or other pursuits. This indeterminancy for changes in the technology available to the professor does not depend on the level of screening employed or the professor's position in the output distribution. Even if screening is perfect, the effect of attempts to directly change professorial productivity in a given activity is indeterminant.

Finally, the introduction of a faculty union that generates pressures for less "invidious comparisons" and more "homogenization" of various subdivisions of the university may produce parity of faculty pay. However, it will also cause those above the modal output levels to reduce their productivity as the recognition of their individual output is mitigated. Similarly, the application of the Equal Pay Act will tend to reduce the performance of the high producers. Any university action resulting in reduced academic screening will have a direct negative effect on the output of high producers. More importantly, reduced screening renders impotent the university's power to increase faculty output through changes in the income weighting given to teaching and research.

NOTES TO CHAPTER 2

1. University is used here as a generic term representing a college, department, or other academic unit that may make salary decisions.

2. The restriction to only two professional outputs is not essential to this analysis. Different forms of faculty output can be separated out, and one can consider the disaggregation of time spent in each activity as the appropriate time input.

Needham (1975) and Becker (1975) provide constructive criticism of the elementary, two dimensional indifference curve analysis of faculty behavior as presented by McKenzie (1972). The appropriateness of deterministic multidimensional mathematical modeling was also overlooked by authors such as Hansen and Kelley (1973) and Kipps (1975).

While Needham demonstrates the importance of time constraints and effort related income determination, he does not establish second order conditions for constrained utility maximization. In addition, he does not acknowledge the fact that time spent in one activity need not be proportionately related to the output; he does not specify a production process relating outputs to multiple time inputs.

3. It is assumed that the professor is risk neutral in regard to measurement error.

4. For example, in the foreword to Michael Evan's (1969) macrotheory text, Lawrence Klein cites the importance of creative research as an input to quality teaching. Martin Bronfenbrenner (1971), in the preface of his authoritative book on income distribution, acknowledges the importance of teaching as an input to research.

5. For example, Freeman (1975a: 105) found that the interfield coefficients of variation are far lower in academic than in industry or government pay structures.

6. Many studies, such as Howard Tuckman (1976: 57) and Katz (1973: 472), show a statistically significant contribution for different disciplines to faculty salary after controlling for teaching, research, and other specific faculty and university output measures. These regression studies typically do not include discipline-output interaction terms. They at least implicitly assume that the contribution of professorial output to salary are independent of field specialization. Furthermore, the fixed difference in salary that they attribute to the discipline of the professor typically amounts to less than $3,000 per year. Howard Tuckman (1976: 65–78) provides an interesting analysis of how the return to professorial output may differ between broadly defined disciplines.

7. For example, student credit hours generated by a faculty member are seldom used in determining the faculty members salary while they do generate, via some formula, revenue for the department or university as a whole. The individual contributions of scholars of jointly authored articles or the contribution of those recognized by an author for providing constructive suggestions in preparing an article are seldom recognized.

8. The university, by definition, is a nonprofit entity that cannot have a surplus or a deficit.

9. Using a Taylor expansion it can be shown that $h_i(Q_i + \epsilon_i) \simeq h_i(Q_i) + h'_i(Q_i)\epsilon_i$.

10. An error in measurement problem, $g_i \neq 0$, is typically acknowledged but ignored in empirical estimation of faculty salary–academic output regressions of the type given in equations (2–7) and (2–8); see, for example, Siegfried and White (1973), Katz (1973), Koch and Chizmar (1973), or Tuckman and Leahey (1975).

11. The mathematically inclined reader may wish to note that differentiating equation (2–13) with respect to Q_i, $i = 1, 2, 3$ gives the first order conditions:

$$\frac{\partial U}{\partial Q_i} - \lambda \left[\pi_i - \frac{h''_i h_i - h'^2_i}{a_{33} h^2_i} g_i b W_i \right] = 0, \quad i = 1, 2,$$

$$\frac{\partial U}{\partial Q_3} - \lambda \frac{1}{a_{33}} = 0 \ ,$$

$$T - \sum_{i=1}^{3} \pi_i Q_i = 0 \ .$$

12. The total effect of a change in screening intensity and income weights is established through a full differentiation of the first order equational system given in note 11. Such a mathematical analysis is provided in Becker (forthcoming). The graphical analyses presented here are intended to be descriptive of the more general mathematical results.

13. One might argue that this analysis ignores the "market" for given faculty skills. However, as cited earlier, the academic labor market, relative to industry or government, is insensitive to market prices for given faculty services. Furthermore, a professor's teaching output contribution is at best known by the employing institution. There is no widely used national information source or market for faculty teaching output. In the case of research, a high-producing professor's work is widely known. During "research boom periods," such as the 1960s, or within "research boom areas," such as the natural sciences in the late 1950s, a university has to condition its policies on the marketability of high research producers who are being screened by the market itself. During "slack periods" or within "slack areas" even the marketability of the high research producers is restricted.

14. The total effect of a change in technology coefficients is established through a full differentiation of the first order equational system given in note 11. Such a mathematical analysis is provided in Becker (1975).

15. Whether an increase in screening is well received depends on the initial screening accuracy. In the extreme case, where no screening is employed, the median person receives the average income. If the mean is above the median, gross income may first fall and then rise as the screening becomes more accurate (Stiglitz, 1975: 297).

Chapter 3

Perspectives from Sociology: Organizational Evaluation of Faculty Performances

Sanford M. Dornbusch

An optimist is a person who believes this is the best of all possible worlds. A pessimist is a person who agrees.

In discussing the evaluation of faculty in American colleges and universities, this chapter draws on a theory of evaluation and authority developed by the author and his collaborator, Richard Scott (Dornbusch & Scott, 1975). We do not wear rose-colored glasses in applying our theory, which at many points states the bases for instability and conflict in authority systems. American colleges and universities are complex organizations that provide diverse data leading to both euphoria and despair.

Higher educational institutions are professional bureaucracies, a mixed form of organization that combines two very different bases for coordinated activity on complex tasks. As professionals, the members of faculties are trained to develop internal skills and standards that can handle active (relatively unpredictable) tasks. Their professional training sets them apart, and according to the usual theory, only fellow professionals can appropriately evaluate their performances.

Simultaneously, they practice in a formal organization marked by a hierarchy of offices. Rights and duties are assigned to occupants of offices rather than to specific persons in terms of their personal characteristics. Each of several occupants of a position in a formal organization exercises the same authorized power over the occupants of a counterposition. Deans have rights and duties with respect to professors; professors have rights and duties with respect to students.

The perspective of this chapter has a long tradition and yet is unusual. The focus is on authorized power that is defined by two criteria: (1) B's evaluators, if aware that B was attempting to exercise control over C, would not evaluate B negatively for making the attempt; and (2) the evaluators of C and of all other participants whose compliance is necessary to support B's attempt to control C's performance, if aware of noncompliance, would evaluate negatively those not complying.

SCOPE OF THE THEORY

To fall within the scope of the theory (Dornbusch & Scott, 1975), organizational arrangements must satisfy several conditions. The organization must distribute sanctions (rewards and penalties) on the basis of evaluations of participants. These evaluations must be based on performance of organizational tasks. The evaluators must themselves be subject to evaluation for their performance of control tasks by participants other than those they are attempting to control. Finally, participants must care about the organizational rewards and penalties whose distribution is influenced by evaluations. Participants' concern about those sanctions makes evaluations important to them and provides a basis for controlling their performances.

These scope conditions need not apply to entire organizations; they can characterize specific arrangements within organizations. For example, an organization that determines salaries exclusively on the basis of seniority is outside the scope of the theory with regard to salary-related behavior. If, however, that same organization distributes promotions, vacations, thick rugs, or pleasant assignments on the basis of evaluations of performance, and if these sanctions are valued by participants, then all behavior related to these sanctions and evaluations falls within the scope of the predictions. The scope of the theory is sufficiently broad to apply to most organizational arrangements.

Scope Condition 1. The distribution of organizational sanctions to participants depends on evaluations made of participants.

Scope Condition 2. Evaluators who influence the distribution of organizational sanctions attempt to base their evaluations on the performance of organizational tasks by participants.

Scope Condition 3. Evaluators who influence the distribution of organizational sanctions to participants are themselves evaluated on their performance of the control task.

Scope Condition 4. The set of participants attempting to control the evaluator differs from the set of participants whom the evaluator is attempting to control.

Scope Condition 5. Participants consider important those organizational sanctions whose distribution depends on evaluations of their performances.

The emphasis in most empirical research on formal organizations, including educational institutions, has been on norms enforced by the subordinate group—that is, on endorsed as opposed to authorized power—and while the distinction between formal and informal authority is often noted, most research has studied informal rather than formal authority systems. Thus, the perspective of this chapter takes one relatively unpopular perspective and seeks to show that we can learn a lot about faculties and their activities by using it systematically.

Evaluation is a pervasive and fundamental social process. Everyone evaluates everyone else a great deal of the time. A cat may evaluate a king. We need to differentiate those evaluations that participants consider important from those they may safely ignore.

> Individual participants ultimately decide which evaluations and evaluators are important to them, but organizations attempt to influence participants as they make this decision. Most organizations specify in advance that a group of participants will evaluate other participants. To ensure that the evaluations of members of this group will be deemed important, they are allowed to influence the distribution or organizational sanctions to back up their evaluations. Participants whose evaluations are perceived as determining the distribution of organizational sanctions are termed *organizational evaluators.* (Dornbusch & Scott, 1975: 94)

It is asserted that participants will place more importance on those evaluations that influence more important sanctions or have more influence on sanctions. These linkages are expected to apply not only to evaluations but also to evaluators and tasks. Thus, the theory attempts to explain why participants in organizations care more about certain evaluations, evaluators, and tasks. An organization helps participants to decide which of many evaluations to attend to by its use of rewards and penalties.

> Organizational evaluators ... vary in importance to participants.... We will consistently employ the term *influence* to refer to the amount of control which evaluators have over the distribution of organizational sanctions. And we will employ the term *central* to refer to those evaluations

which are believed by participants to affect the distribution of those organizational sanctions they consider of value. In some cases, no sanctions of value to a given participant will be controlled by the organization. Usually, however, organizations will control at least some sanctions valued by participants. We would expect that the more the participant values the sanctions controlled by the organization, and the more influence an organizational evaluator has on the distribution of these sanctions, the more importance the participant will attach to the evaluations made by that organizational evaluator. (Dornbusch & Scott, 1975: 94—95)

There are other bases for an evaluator being viewed as important, but we will continue to stress only evaluators who control the distribution of organizational rewards and penalties. One other basis for the importance of evaluations to a performer is his or her commitment to certain goals or subgoals of the organization, so that he or she may value evaluation because of concern for the quality of the work rather than because of a link between evaluations and organizational sanctions.

Professional participants are often highly motivated to carry out their tasks, as we have noted, but the views of professionals as to which tasks are important or what constitutes proper procedure may differ in important ways from those of their organizational superiors. The most important evaluators for such professionals may be those who share a commitment to the same goals and who possess similar kinds of skills. Such persons are as likely to be located outside the employing organization as within it and, even if inside, may not hold high positions in the power structure of the organization. In such situations, the organizational evaluators may not be the most important evaluators. Hence, the organization may exercise relatively weak control over the task performances of such professional participants. To the extent that the goals pursued by professionals coincide with those set by an organization, the organization's lack of control may not be a problem; the organization can rely on professional evaluators to maintain performance standards. Problems arise, however, when professional and organizational objectives diverge. In such cases, organizational representatives may be unable to exercise effective control over professional participants.

In sum, high commitment to work goals causes participants to consider important the evaluations of persons capable of making soundly based evaluations with respect to these goals, even when these individuals have little or no influence on the distribution of organizational sanctions. (Dornbusch & Scott, 1975: 96).

A second basis for the importance of nonorganizational evaluators is their impact on the relative status of a person in informal groups composed of fellow workers. A third basis for regarding some evalu-

ations as important may be their relevance for one's self-conception. The evaluation process has been shown to be crucial to the development and maintenance of the self-conception (Mead, 1934; Miyamoto & Dornbusch, 1956).

While participants may consider evaluators important for these reasons, we will focus only on evaluators authorized to distribute organizational rewards and penalties. Their evaluations are supported by the sanctioning power of the organization and will be important to most participants simply because of their influence on the distribution of organizational rewards and penalties.

The previous principles assert that each participant places importance on evaluations, tasks, and evaluators to the extent that they influence sanctions. But given that evaluations are important, what can participants do to affect them? If evaluations reflect the performer's level and direction of effort, then, by exerting effort, performers can affect the level of their evaluations. By "level and direction of effort" we refer to such matters as how long, how hard, and in which direction the performer works. By "level of evaluation" we refer to the score given a performer by an organizational evaluator on a scale that permits interpretation of higher or lower quality as assessed by some standard.

Assuming that effort by performers does affect their evaluations in this manner, our principles assert that their efforts will be directed toward affecting those evaluations, pleasing those evaluators, and performing those tasks that are perceived to be more central and influential.

Definition. Performers believe that effort affects evaluations to the extent that they perceive that the direction and level of their effort on a task positively relate to the level of evaluations they receive.

To the extent that performers believe that effort affects evaluations, they exert more effort to affect evaluations:

1. That they consider more important, because they are given by evaluators they consider more important and are of tasks they consider more important.

2. That are more central, because they are given by evaluators whose evaluations are more central and are of tasks whose evaluations are more central.

3. That are more influential, because they are given by evaluators whose evaluations are more influential and are of tasks whose evaluations are more influential.

The next principles begin by restating the major assertions from the standpoint of the evaluator, but in so doing reveal an interesting aspect of control systems. Just as performers attempt to affect evaluations by the level and direction of their effort, so evaluators attempt to use their evaluations to regulate the performers' effort. Fate control—control over sanctions—becomes behavior control when sanctions are made contingent on effort. Here we have an apparent paradox of control systems: participants more in control of their evaluations, in the sense that they can affect evaluations by exerting effort, are more controlled by the evaluation system.

We introduce another factor affecting the importance of evaluations. In addition to importance resulting from influence on sanctions, performers will place more importance on those evaluations that can be affected by their efforts. Evaluations that do not depend on performers' activities are less salient to them. Participants emphasize those aspects of the world that can be affected by their activities. Hence, they attribute more importance to evaluations they can affect.

Definition. Control over performers by evaluations of their performances on a task denotes the extent to which evaluations affect the direction and level of effort by performers on a task.

If effort affects evaluations, greater control can be exercised over performers through evaluations. This relation can be strengthened if evaluations are based on criteria that performers judge to be appropriate. In judging criteria, performers may use standards that conflict with the evaluator's criteria. The performers' standards can be acquired, for example, from previous training or experience or can be derived from persons outside the specified authority system. When performers' standards are congruent with the criteria used by evaluators, however, control is reinforced because performers attach additional importance to evaluations. We will say that performers consider evaluations soundly based to the extent that they believe not only that evaluations are affected by their effort, but also that performances they consider better receive high evaluations. If performers believe evaluations are more soundly based, they attach greater importance to evaluations, are more controlled by evaluations, and are motivated to produce work of higher quality as defined both by their standards and by the criteria used by evaluators.

Definition. A participant considers evaluations soundly based to the extent that he or she believes that (1) the quality of performances or outcomes as judged by the participant is affected by

the performer's effort, and (2) performances or outcomes considered better by the participant receive higher evaluations.

The final set of principles differs from all previous ones in that it deals with the performance of a control task by an organizational evaluator. All earlier principles apply without modification to evaluators who are organizational participants engaged in performing tasks for which they are subject to evaluation by their superiors. We do not propose to restate the foregoing principles by substituting the term evaluator for performer. But we would like to emphasize the special nature of a control task—the task of affecting, by means of evaluations, the direction and level of effort by performers. In order to obtain control over performers through evaluations made of their performances, evaluators need to allow performers to obtain control over the evaluations they receive. This two way process is mutually supporting.

We assert that evaluators will regard the authority system that regulates their exercise of control tasks as more proper if they have more control over performers. This statement is not intended to imply that evaluators, innately power hungry, are satisfied only with systems that provide them with unlimited power. Rather, control over performers is the mechanism by which evaluators pursue their assigned goals. If evaluators are themselves evaluated and sanctioned for their goal attainment, they can be expected to seek and utilize control opportunities provided by the system. The statements in this set assert that an evaluator obtains control over a performer by doing those things that make evaluations more soundly based from the perspective of both performer and evaluator.

Most of these principles would seem to benefit both the controller and the controlled: each has a surer hold on his own fate. Evaluators and performers are locked together in mutual interest. One may question whether all their behavior is mutually advantageous; but it does seem plausible to conclude that in a well-designed and well-functioning evaluation system, the interests of both evaluators and performers may be served by quality performances on the part of the performers. But all evaluation systems in formal organizations are not well designed nor do they function perfectly.

SOURCES OF DATA

In this chapter, we will use data from two collaborative ventures in which the author participated. The first, with Robert R. Hind and W. Richard Scott, interviewed one hundred faculty members at a

major private university, Stanford (Hind, Dornbusch, & Scott, 1974). The sample was randomly selected but stratified so as to have equal members of full professors, associate professors, and assistant professors from the Stanford faculty outside of professional schools. We explained our concept of organizational evaluator:

> For the purposes of this study, I would like to concentrate on some of the activities you may perform as a faculty member, and I would like to group them together into the following categories: (1) classroom teaching; (2) research and scholarship; (3) university service, including committee service, administrative work, advising, and other noninstructional student contacts; (4) external service, including consulting, service to professional organizations, membership on government boards, etc. It is partly on the way in which faculty members carry out some or all of these activities that they are judged by persons who have some influence, either direct or indirect, over university rewards. I have in mind here such tangible rewards as promotion, salary increases, research support, office and clerical support, and the like. Of course, I recognize the importance of intangible rewards for one's efforts, but in this study it is necessary to limit concern to those factors determining tangible rewards.

Thus we have relatively rich interview data from a single institution, but we need to buttress those findings with more representative data drawn from a questionnaire study of a national sample of colleges and universities. The Stanford Project on Academic Governance was led by J. Victor Baldridge. He and another ex-colleague, George Ecker, built questions into their questionnaire to provide an extensive replication of some of our earlier work with the faculty at a single major university. Their project was a major study of academic decisionmaking and governance, published in a series of books and articles. We will note here only the most recent (Baldridge et al., 1977), from which we will draw heavily later in our discussion.

The national sample selected colleges and universities, and faculty and administrators within each college or university, in order to provide representative samples of both institutions and personnel. The sample was drawn from all institutions that had a freshman class, that awarded at least an associate (two year) degree, and that were not service academies. Community colleges were undersampled and then given additional weight in order to produce a representative sample of all institutions and personnel in higher education. When the Baldridge sample of 249 institutions was compared to the total of 2,592 institutions in the nation along five dimensions using the College Entrance Examination Board's data decks, the sample was found to be representative. There were not statistically significant

differences between sample and population on the distribution of such measures as highest degree offered, geographic region, admission selectivity, and sex of the student clientele.

A sampling scheme for selecting faculty respondents was developed in which institutions were stratified by size of faculty. Schools that were smaller had a high proportion of faculty chosen for the study, while in larger institutions, having 350 faculty or more, a maximum of 175 teachers was included. Individual questionnaires were sent to 17,296 individuals randomly selected from lists in their college catalogues. Complete usable questionnaires were returned by 9,237, for a return rate of 53 percent. In the analysis, the stratified samples were weighted in order to estimate the possible results if every faculty member in each institution sampled had been questioned. For this chapter, in which we limit ourselves to schools with some research emphasis, we use unweighted data for each institution and aggregate individual responses.

Within any particular college or university, the sample is not large enough to provide reliable data, particularly when controls by field, rank, age, and sex are introduced. Therefore, we do not say that the findings of this study are applicable to each and every one of the schools in a group of schools nor even imply that. Rather, we will indicate the schools in each group that we create in order to help the reader define the nature of the institutions included within that group.

Almost all faculty data we analyze in this study comes from one section of the questionnaire used in the national sample. It read:

One of the most important functions in any institution is the distribution of faculty rewards—salaries, secretarial help, promotions, research money, course assignments, etc. In order to distribute rewards people are typically evaluated on their work performance. Answer these questions about the evaluation process at your institution.

1. About what percent of your work time do you spend in the following activities? Even though this is very difficult, please just give your best estimate. (Write in percentage)

    _____ % Undergraduate Teaching (including advising)

    _____ % Graduate Teaching (including advising)

    _____ % Research and Scholarship

    _____ % Community Service Outside the Institution

    _____ % Committee Work, Institutional Service, and Administration

    100% Total

Using the same format, with the total equal to 100 percent, each respondent was then asked about the current emphasis of the evaluation system as well as about the preferred evaluation system.

2. In evaluating your performance for salary, promotion and other rewards, how much weight (in percentage terms) is put on each of these activities? (Write in percentage)

3. How much weight would you like to have put on these activities? (Write in percentage)

FINDINGS FROM THE STUDY OF STANFORD FACULTY

Unlike the national sample, the study of Stanford faculty asked numerous questions at each interview. We will report here some of the results that may be potentially applicable to some other educational institutions.

For each of four tasks (classroom teaching, research and scholarship, university service, external service) faculty at Stanford were asked: "How much influence does the evaluation of your (specific task) have in determining your university rewards?" and "How much influence do you think the evaluation of your (specific task) *should* have on your university rewards?" There was a five point scale of influence: Extremely Influential, Very Influential, Moderately Influential, Slightly Influential, and Not At All Influential.

University service and external service were not perceived by Stanford faculty as having much influence on university sanctions. Only 8 percent saw university service as very or extremely influential, and even fewer, 3 percent, saw external service as very or extremely influential. Since the faculty also did not want an appreciable increase in the influence of these two tasks upon university rewards and penalties, we can safely drop these tasks from consideration and focus on classroom teaching and research.

At Stanford, evaluations of research are much more influential than evaluations of teaching. Only 20 percent viewed evaluations of teaching as very or extremely influential, compared to 78 percent for evaluations of research. Most Stanford faculty wanted to reduce somewhat the disparity between the influence of evaluations of the two chief tasks, research and teaching. About half, 51 percent, believed teaching should be very or extremely influential, compared to 67 percent for research. Thus, teachers wanted to reduce the disparity but not to change the existing rank order, in which research was viewed as more influential.

Stanford faculty were asked to report how satisfied they were with the way each task was evaluated and how satisfied they were with the way their total activities as members of the faculty were evaluated. The same five point scale, ranging from Extremely Satisfied to Not At All Satisfied, was used. The relationship between overall satisfaction with the evaluation process and satisfaction with the evaluation of research was higher, with a gamma of 0.90, than the relationship between overall satisfaction and satisfaction with the evaluation of teaching, with a gamma of 0.59. Research was a larger part of the part-whole relationship.

Our theory of evaluation states that authority systems are more incompatible if evaluators do not share a set of criteria (Dornbusch & Scott, 1975: 352). We asked: "How much agreement do you think there is among people in your discipline in their evaluations of (specific task) by their colleagues?" Using a five point scale from Extremely High Agreement to No Agreement At All, we unexpectedly found no difference between research and teaching in the reported amount of agreement among evaluators; 47 percent reported very or extremely high agreement for teaching and 48 percent for research. For both teaching and research, high perceived agreement among evaluators was correlated with overall satisfaction with the evaluation system. Combining both tasks, we found a gamma of 0.59 between perceived agreement among evaluators and overall satisfaction with the evaluation process.

We did find differences among disciplines in perceived agreement among evaluators. We hypothesized that perceived agreement would be more probable among evaluators if they were believed to share a common foundation for criteria, a central body of theory. We asked: "Some academic fields or disciplines are seen as strongly based on a systematic body of theory which serves as the basis for research hypotheses and dominates teaching and scholarship. Other fields are less reliant on a central body of theory. To what extent does your field have a central body of theory to guide research, scholarship and teaching?" As predicted, perceived agreement among evaluators was positively correlated, with a gamma of 0.45, to the perception of a central body of theory in the discipline.

We then predicted that overall satisfaction of a faculty member with the evaluation system would be positively related to the belief that he or she was in a discipline with a central body of theory. Sixty percent of faculty in disciplines reported highly dependent upon a central body of theory were high in overall satisfaction with the evaluation process; 52 percent of those in disciplines with medium dependence upon theory; and 38 percent of faculty in disciplines with

low dependence upon theory. Thus, satisfaction with the evaluation process is positively associated with perceived agreement among evaluators, which in turn is related to perceived dependence of a discipline upon a central body of theory.

We next examined the impact of the evaluation system upon faculty expenditure of effort. We asked: "Here is a schedule showing activities we have been talking about, plus a few others. I would like to get your best estimate of the way in which you divide the time you devote to the activities listed. Would you tell me about what percent of the time you devote to these functions is spent on each one of them? The total, of course, should add to 100 percent." We then asked: "Now would you let me know, if it were simply a matter of your own preference, how you *would like* to divide your time among these same functions?" In connection with the first question, respondents were given a list of the following functions, with spaces for estimating proportion of time spent on each: undergraduate classroom teaching, graduate classroom teaching, other undergraduate teaching, other graduate teaching, research and scholarship, university service, and external service. For the second question, respondents were asked to indicate their preferences beside their responses to the first question. There was no column heading on the response form for these items on preferences so that respondents could not have anticipated the question on preference while responding to the question on actual time spent. This avoided in the Stanford sample a possible bias introduced in the national sample by printing all the columns on the same page.

We have clear findings to show the relation of influential evaluations upon allocation of effort. More faculty wanted to increase the time devoted to research than wanted to reduce their research efforts, and more faculty of every rank and in every disciplinary group indicated they wanted to reduce the time spent on teaching. Faculty wanted to direct their efforts toward those tasks whose evaluations were more influential.

Of course, some faculty find research attractive for intrinsic reasons. Nevertheless, there is a general tendency for professors, like participants in other organizations, to want a balance between the time or effort they spend on a task and the rewards associated with evaluations of that task.

Balance could also be achieved by increasing the influence of teaching on university sanctions. Fifty-three percent of the faculty wanted such a change, compared to only 2 percent who wanted to decrease the influence of evaluations of teaching. (This finding spurred the administration at Stanford to change appointment forms

for faculty to place greater emphasis on evaluations of teaching, so that teaching has become moderately influential. That may not seem like much of a change, but a major shift in evaluations for a faculty, 70 percent of whom have tenure, is really an achievement.)

We can look at the relation of effort to rewards another way. Among professors who saw teaching as relatively high in influence, 65 percent and 77 percent were above the median in time spent on undergraduate and graduate teaching, respectively. Similarly, among those who saw research as relatively more influential, 63 percent were above the median in time spent on research. Faculty who perceive either teaching or research to be more rewarded by the university than is typical of their colleagues are likely to spend more time on that task.

We also inquired about the evaluators of each task and their relative influence:

> Here is a list of people who are potential evaluators of your (specific task). Would you tell me which of them, or others not on the list who might come to mind, make evaluations of your (specific task) which might influence university rewards? (1) students, (2) department head, (3) department colleagues, (4) faculty members in other departments, (5) members of your discipline in other universities, (6) persons having a say in government or foundation grants, (7) other outsiders (please name), (8) dean of the school and his staff, (9) appointment and promotion committee (faculty committee advisory to the dean), (10) other faculty committees, (11) provost and his staff, (12) president, (13) trustees. Among those who evaluate your (specific task) and influence university rewards, I would like to know which ones are the most influential. How influential are (specific evaluators') evaluations of your (specific task)?

Faculty perceived different sets of evaluators as having influence on one task but not on another. More positions evaluated research, a mean of 3.3, than evaluated teaching, a mean of 2.3.

In professional bureaucracies, the professional wants evaluations by colleagues. In this university, that is the pattern. For both teaching and research, the number of collegial evaluators named within Stanford or at another institution was more than three times the number of university administrators named as evaluators. In addition, administrators at Stanford were also seen as lower in influence than were colleagues.

The importance of the visibility of performances can be seen in student evaluations of teaching. Students were equal to departmental colleagues in the influence of their evaluations of teaching. But, in fact, students are viewed as the primary source of information for

department heads and colleagues. Although students are perceived to be the primary source for evaluations of teaching, faculty are split on the soundness of student evaluations.

Visibility plays a role in making university boundaries permeable. For research, 68 percent named colleagues at other institutions as influential evaluators, affecting Stanford's rewards. But teaching was not visible outside the university, and only 15 percent named any outsider as an evaluator of teaching.

Younger faculty, in general and within each rank, were more concerned with the evaluation of research and less concerned with the evaluation of teaching than were older faculty. This follows from the permeability of university boundaries for research. Younger faculty are more mobile and emphasize the research task, whose evaluations often occur outside the home institution. This finding is also reported, without explanation, by Rich and Jolicoeur (1976).

Finally, a brief note on complaints about salary. Contrary to common sense, faculty who volunteered salary complaints to the interviewer were far above average in their current salary level. They were higher, on the average, than their departmental colleagues who did not complain (cf. McKeachie in this volume). It appears that their reference group, their standard of comparison, is internationally known faculty at other institutions. Thus, they feel relatively deprived while receiving higher salaries than their colleagues.

FINDINGS FROM THE NATIONAL SAMPLE

Table 3–1 presents effort, influence, and preferred influence for three broad groups of institutions drawn from the national sample of the Stanford Project on Academic Governance. We examined evaluation processes only in those institutions that considered research as one of the major faculty activities. We did not limit our study to schools that emphasized research more than teaching, but each institution examined in this study paid at least some attention to research and scholarship.

The institutions studied were divided into three broad groups. There are major differences among the schools within each group, but each group differs greatly from the other two groupings with respect to the emphasis on research and teaching in the evaluation system.

The first group of schools consist of universities whose research is nationally and internationally renowned—Duke, Johns Hopkins, Wisconsin, and Yale. Each of these universities not only emphasizes research but produces research whose average quality is considered

Table 3-1. Time Spent, Influence of Evaluations, and Preferred Influence of Evaluations for Five Tasks by Type of School, in Percentages.

	Time Spent				
	Undergraduate Teaching	*Graduate Teaching*	*Research*	*Community Service*	*University Service*
Prestige Universities	22.5	26.3	32.5	4.5	14.0
Research Universities	38.2	21.8	22.8	4.2	12.7
Quality Colleges	64.3	2.7	16.5	2.9	13.3

Table 3-1. continued

	Influence of Evaluations				
	Undergraduate Teaching	*Graduate Teaching*	*Research*	*Community Service*	*University Service*
Prestige Universities	14.3	17.8	51.0	2.8	9.5
Research Universities	27.0	16.5	40.1	3.3	11.8
Quality Colleges	58.4	1.5	22.9	2.5	14.3

Table 3-1. continued

	Preferred Influence of Evaluations				
	Undergraduate Teaching	*Graduate Teaching*	*Research*	*Community Service*	*University Service*
Prestige Universities	22.8	25.3	40.3	4.3	8.3
Research Universities	34.5	22.2	28.3	4.1	10.9
Quality Colleges	61.8	2.4	22.5	2.8	9.8

Source: Data were drawn from the national sample of the Stanford Project on Academic Governance.

extremely high. Of course, this is a matter of judgment and of reputation. The author of this study used no criterion for assignment to this group other than his belief that each of the four schools is a great research center. Accordingly, we call these schools "prestige universities."

The second group of thirteen schools is called "research universities." They vary greatly in the quality of the research by the average faculty member. Perhaps one or more of this group should be considered a prestige university. Yet, on the average, there seems little doubt that the reputation of these schools for research is not as high as that of the group of prestige universities. The research universities in the sample are Arizona State, Auburn, Boston, University of California-Riverside, Connecticut, George Washington, Louisiana State, University of Missouri, Oregon State, Oregon, Pittsburgh, Southern Methodist, and Tulane.

The schools in our third group emphasize undergraduate teaching. The quality of their faculty is such, however, that considerable research is done by some of the professors at each school. Since the primary mission of "quality colleges" is undergraduate teaching, teaching is more important than research in the evaluation of faculty. The quality colleges in the sample are Bennington, Carleton, Earlham, Lawrence, Mills, Mt. Holyoke, Oberlin, Pitzer, Reed, St. Olaf, Scripps, Smith, Swarthmore, Union (NY), and Williams.

Examination of Table 3−1 shows that university service and community service represented minor portions of faculty time and had little influence on the distribution of university rewards. The graduate teaching category was seldom employed among quality colleges, where opportunities for graduate teaching are rare. Thus, in the present analysis we will limit ourselves to two tasks—undergraduate teaching and research—focusing on the time spent on each, the influence of evaluations of each, and the preferred influence of each.

Table 3−1 was encouraging in that the two tasks, undergraduate teaching and research, did indeed differ by type of school in the manner expected. The prestige universities were highest in time, influence of evaluations, and preferred influence for the task of research and lowest on all three measures for undergraduate teaching. Quality colleges, as expected, were highest on undergraduate teaching for all three measures and were lowest for research. It may be appropriate to mention here that these differences represent aggregate data from individual faculty and cannot be used to determine, for example, the time spent on teaching each student. The student-faculty ratio interferes with any such direct assessment.

Table 3−2 presents, for undergraduate teaching and research, by rank and type of school, the correlations between time and the influence of evaluations and between time and the preferred influence of evaluations. There is a tendency for the correlations between time on a task and the preferred influence of evaluations to be higher than the correlations between time on that task and current influence of evaluations of that task. Only for one of nine comparisons, that for associate professors on research, is there a reversal. Faculty in the aggregate prefer the evaluation system to reflect the time expenditure on that task more than is often the case.

The tendency to seek balance between effort on a task and the influence of its evaluations can be shown more directly on an individual basis. Let us compute for each faculty member the discrepancy between time on a task and the influence of evaluations of that task. Let us also calculate the discrepancy between preferred influence of evaluations on a task and current influence of those evaluations. The two discrepancies should be positively correlated with each other. (Time undergraduate teaching minus influence of evaluations undergraduate teaching) should be positively correlated with (preferred influence of evaluations undergraduate teaching minus influence of evaluations undergraduate teaching). The results strongly support this balance prediction for undergraduate teaching. The Pearson product moment correlations are 0.81 for prestige universities, 0.76 for research universities, and 0.73 for quality colleges.

The same pattern is found for the task of research. The discrepancies are positively correlated again: 0.79 for prestige universities, 0.85 for research universities, and 0.78 for quality colleges.

These results provide strong support for the view that faculty members are individually seeking an evaluation system that is more closely attuned to their expenditure of effort (time) on each task.

We can use this pressure toward balance of effort and evaluations in studying the pattern of sexual inequality among faculty. Baldridge et al. (1977) have analyzed data from the national sample in ways that show the power of institutional differences to explain the lower publication rates, salary, and rank of women faculty compared to men. They argue that female faculty appear different from male faculty because they are located at different institutions. Community colleges and nonprestige public institutions are different from other types of colleges and universities. Since women faculty are concentrated in these two types of schools, the distribution of women within the system of higher education explains sex differences in behavior and rewards.

Table 3—2.   Pearson Product Moment Correlations between Time and Influence of Evaluation, and Time and Preferred Influence, for Undergraduate Teaching and Research, by Rank and Type of School.

	Professor		
	Prestige University	*Research University*	*Quality College*
Time Undergraduate Teaching and Influence Undergraduate Teaching	0.64	0.69	0.77
Time Research and Influence Research	0.44	0.69	0.42
Time Undergraduate Teaching and Preferred Influence Undergraduate Teaching	0.70	0.79	0.84
Time Research and Preferred Influence Research	0.58	0.81	0.72
(N)	(123)	(254)	(132)

Source: Data were drawn from the national sample of the Stanford Project on Academic Governance.

In a paper yet to be submitted for publication, Margaret A. Hoag, Gary Natriello, join Baldridge, Ecker, and the author in showing how sex differences within a single institution in its balance of effort and evaluation can produce "Sexism Without Sexists" (1978). Our paper concludes with this application of pressure toward balance:

> What we have found in our study is that women faculty, for unknown reasons that are beyond the scope of this study, were more likely to spend time on undergraduate teaching than were men. This was true particularly for Research Universities. Within Prestige Universities, where the pressure for research is felt throughout the institution, and there are few female faculty, and in Quality Colleges, where there is much less pressure for research anywhere in the institution, the discrepancy between the sexes was not clear. We, therefore, do not feel our findings are sufficiently conclusive to call for remedial action in those institutions. With respect to Research Universities, however, the largest institutions that we studied, there does seem to be sufficient flexibility in assignment and sufficient corners and hideaways in the institutional structure so that women are likely to be spending more time on Undergraduate Teaching. Whether this is based on their own socialization or on institutional pressures we do not know.

Table 3–2. continued

Associate Professor			Assistant Professor		
Prestige University	Research University	Quality College	Prestige University	Research University	Quality College
0.65	0.60	0.51	0.67	0.59	0.36
0.50	0.50	0.30	0.46	0.44	0.24
0.78	0.77	0.70	0.72	0.80	0.66
0.46	0.76	0.64	0.61	0.77	0.63
(58)	(172)	(113)	(38)	(183)	(165)

But the impact of this increased time spent on teaching by women faculty seems to have very clear effects, in accordance with our general theory. Persons who spend more time on an activity wish that activity to be given greater influence in the distribution of organizational rewards and penalties. Similarly, administrators of an organization tend to give more weight to the evaluation of those activities on which more time is spent. Therefore we find that women faculty, once they are teaching more, are evaluated more for their teaching and prefer to be evaluated more for their teaching than do men. The result is a system that perpetuates sex differences in the role of the faculty member, sex differences that produce lower rewards for women under the current market structure.

This finding holds when we control for rank, level of institutional identification, age of the teacher, tenure, and subject matter field. As predicted, the evaluation system in research universities operates in a fashion that permits a circle of discrimination to continue.

CONCLUSION

We have used an abstract theory of evaluation and authority (developed and applied in studies of electronic assemblers, nurses, priests,

doctors, teachers, students, tobacco factory workers, hospital aides, football players, workers on a student newspaper, and members of a physics research group) to study faculty members at American colleges and universities. The abstract ideas have proved useful in understanding and explaining some aspects of faculty behavior.

The full understanding of any concrete institution, certainly one as complex as a university or college, cannot come from any single perspective. Diverse perspectives from different disciplines, plus detailed historical analysis of each case, are needed for the development of insight into a specific faculty's behavior. What this chapter has tried to demonstrate is the power of one set of ideas, abstract and theoretically based, to help us understand some nontrivial aspects of faculty behavior as members of professional bureaucracies: "By their fruits ye shall know them."

Part II

Academic Labor Markets
in Higher Education

Chapter 4 serves as Part Two and presents a conceptual understanding of academic labor markets in higher education. It focuses on the operation of the academic job market and evaluates the potential mode of adjustment to the changes of the 1970s and 1980s. Special attention is given to the economic determinants of the supply of and demand for faculty. Institutional characteristics of academia and an empirical model of the demand for faculty are provided. It is argued that the academic labor market is highly responsive to changing financial conditions.

Chapter 4

The Job Market for College Faculty

Richard B. Freeman

The purpose of this chapter is to examine the operation of the academic job market and to evaluate the potential mode of adjustment to the changes of the 1970s and 1980s.[1] The opening section analyzes several distinctive features of the academic market and considers how they condition the process of adjustment to changes over time. The second section presents an empirical analysis of developments in the faculty market from the 1920s to the 1970s and develops a small econometric model to evaluate the effect of changes in enrollments and in the supply of potential faculty on salaries and employment. The major finding of the chapter is that the faculty job market is highly responsive to changes in the state of higher education, with salaries and employment being greatly influenced by changes in demand and supply conditions, though with some distinctive institutional peculiarities.

CHARACTERISTICS OF FACULTY JOB MARKET

The labor market for college and university faculty has certain distinct characteristics that affect the operation of the market place: the employing institutions are nonprofit enterprises; both employers and faculty are extremely concerned with quality issues; the internal market of colleges and universities limits variation in salaries across fields and is marked by lifetime employment contracts; the future supply of faculty is "produced" within the system; the scale of higher education depends on the demography of the population. This

section analyzes the effect of each of these distinguishing character-
istics of academe on the functioning of the faculty market, particu-
larly on the responses of the system to declines in demand. It shows
that, for various reasons, the faculty market is likely to be highly
sensitive to exogenous "shocks," with much of the burden of adjust-
ment falling on young faculty and potential faculty.

Nonprofit Economic Behavior

It is often asserted that nonprofit institutions, like colleges and
universities, are less responsive to market conditions than comparable
profit-seeking firms. The model of nonprofit behavior developed here
seeks to dispel this preconception. It demonstrates that the nonprofit
budget constraint, which requires that expenditures equal receipts,
actually increases responsiveness to economic incentives, making
employment and wages in existing institutions more responsive to
market ups and downs in the short run than would otherwise be the
case. Overtime entry and exit of new institutions gives academe and
other nonprofit employers similar long-run demand curves to those
of profit-seeking enterprises.

The effect of the nonprofit budget constraint on adjustments to
market conditions can be most readily analyzed with the standard
cost curve apparatus of price theory. In terms of cost curves, there
are two distinguishing features of nonprofit enterprises. First, as Fig-
ure 4−1 shows, if the nonprofit enterprise has no required entre-
preneurial return, its average cost curve will lie below the curve of
the comparable profit-seeking firm ($AC^1 < AC$), leading to greater
output ($Q_2 > Q_0$ at price P_0) and hence employment. Even if the
nonprofit enterprise requires a normal return,[2] output will be greater
in the region where profits are above normal ($P > P_0$), essentially be-
cause the nonprofit constraint requires that potential excesses of
receipts over costs be spent. Second, since profits must be zero, the
nonprofit firm will be governed by average rather than marginal cost
considerations, at least in regions of potential profits, operating along
the AC rather than the MC curve.[3] But, as is obvious in Figure 4−1,
the AC curve is more elastic (less steeply sloped) than the MC curve,
which implies greater responses to changes in prices and costs, in-
cluding faculty salaries, than would be the case under marginal cost
behavior.

Heuristically, when the academic market experiences a boom, col-
leges and universities will increase faculty employment more than
would comparable profit-seeking institutions because they will spend
what would have been profits on additional faculty, while conversely,
in a market decline, they will reduce employment more because of

Figure 4—1. Production Under the Zero Profit Constraint.

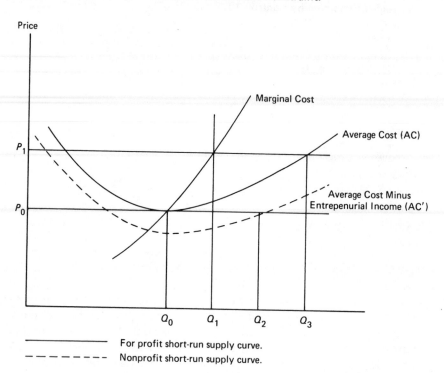

For profit short-run supply curve.
Nonprofit short-run supply curve.

the absence of a "buffer" in the form of profits. The nonprofit status of colleges and universities makes short-run demand for faculty more elastic with respect to wages and to shifts in enrollment than would otherwise be the case. In addition, employment of faculty should be more responsive to shifts in demand and supply than would be the case in a comparable for profit market. Wages should be more responsive to shifts in demand and less responsive to shifts in supply.

While the arguments and model that underly these propositions may ignore too many features of academia to provide a useful guide to actual behavior, they make clear that, contrary to widely held opinion, nonprofit status per se does not imply lack of responsiveness to market incentives.

The Subsidy Market and Budget Constraint. The importance of the nonprofit budget constraint and of subsidies as part of the constraint suggest the value of a more detailed look at those factors in the operation of colleges and universities. To begin with, Table 4—1

Table 4—1. Current Fund Educational and General Revenue of Institutions of Higher Education by Control, 1972—1973.

	All Institutions	*Public Institutions*	*Private Institutions*
Total Educational and General Revenue	100.00	100.00	100.00
Tuition and fees	27.1	16.6	49.9
Federal government	15.4	15.0	16.1
Unrestricted	3.5	4.0	2.2
Research and other sponsored programs	11.9	11.0	13.9
State governments	35.8	51.2	2.4
Local governments	5.2	7.1	.8
Endowment earnings	2.3	.5	6.4
Private gifts and grants	5.8	2.5	13.2
Other	8.4	7.1	11.2

Source: U.S. Office of Education (1976: 222, table 115).

tabulates the receipts of all academic institutions by public and private status, respectively, in 1973. The figures show that overall most of the revenues of colleges and universities come from governmental sources, with just 27 percent received as tuition and fees from students. Decomposed by type of institution, we see that over half of the funds of public colleges and universities (which dominate higher education) comes from state governments, while by contrast, the budget of private institutions is highly dependent on tuition and fees, although nearly 20 percent is obtained from endowment and gifts.

The clear-cut dependence of public institutions on public subsidization and the marked but less striking dependence of private institutions on various private subsidies suggest the value of examining in some detail the mechanism by which those subsidies are awarded to schools. The key analytic distinction is between funds "paid" for particular outputs, which can be viewed as purchase of those outputs at some price, and funds received irrespective of institutional activity.

Subsidies awarded for particular outputs or activities establish a subsidy market where subsidizers and nonprofit schools trade dollars for goods (buildings, minority students, chairs of history, etc.). The supply of subsidies to the market is an upward-sloping curve linking dollars to outputs in accord with subsidizer demands for nonprofit goods. In this market, shadow prices are attached to particular outputs and are important elements in the overall price of the good,

influencing employment and production decisions. The appropriate budget constraint for institutions that receive subsidies for specific output is:

$$G + tE + SE = WF + P_R R \qquad (4\text{--}1)$$

where t = tuition, S = subsidy per student, E = enrollment (assumed for simplicity to be the only output of concern), W = wage of faculty, F = number of faculty, R = other resources, P_R = price of other resources, and G = fixed receipts (endowments, etc.).

If, as Table 4--1 shows, subsidy markets are segmented, with state aid going to public institutions for certain goods (number of students) and private aid to private colleges, subsidy prices will differ by source and institution. This may explain some output and behavior differences among institutions. Differential financing arrangements will, in any case, provide important clues to institutional activities and decisions. In the extreme situation of restricted or tied moneys (donations for buildings, professorial chairs in American studies, etc.) there is a one-to-one correspondence of funds to inputs or outputs. If, as seems to be true, donors prefer tangible capital goods to less tangible purchases of student or faculty quality, the shadow price of such capital will be low, and buildings, stadia, and the like will be excessive in terms of optimal (unrestricted) budget decisionmaking. Physical plant may, accordingly be "underutilized."

What is important about the idea of subsidy markets is that it makes nonprofit receipts dependent on market transactions and not, as might appear to be the case, on exogenous funding. The empirical problem in using subsidy shadow prices to explain phenomena is the absence of explicit price data[4] and the possible confounding of differences in prices and utility functions.[5]

Fixed endowment income or other receipts unrelated to output can be expected to have a distinct effect on the price or tuition policy of institutions. When costs increase, revenues obtained from fixed sources cannot be altered, so that institutions will be forced to raise tuition by larger amounts than if all of the budget had come from variable sources. Formally, if the fixed receipts constitute B percent of the academic budget constraint, then an increase in costs of 1 percent should raise the price of output by $(1/1-B)$ percent. We would therefore expect tuition charges to be highly responsive to faculty salaries and other costs, particularly in the private sector.[6]

Entry and Exit. In the long run, demand for inputs and wage and employment adjustments depend on entry and exit conditions in an

industry. If new enterprises enter whenever existing institutions have receipts above costs at the minimum average cost point, as occurs in competitive markets, firms will operate at the minimum point in the long run and have factor demands appropriate to that equilibrium. If it can be argued that entry and exit of colleges and universities is governed by the possibility of average receipts above the minimum average costs, then demand for faculty in the long run will be the same in academia as in a comparable for profit market.

In higher education, the organizations that subsidize academia, notably state governments, have traditionally performed the entrepreneurial function of forming new enterprises. As long as the states seek to obtain desired output (places for students) at the lowest cost, it can be readily demonstrated that they will tend to create new colleges whenever costs rise above the minimum ($AC > \overline{AC}$), for when this occurs, the subsidizers can obtain ($1/\overline{AC} - 1/AC$) more output per dollar by reducing subsidies to existing institutions and using the funds to form new ones. Maximization of output per subsidy dollar and rational subsidy behavior guarantee an infinitely elastic supply of institutions (barring lumpiness) at the minimum point $\overline{AC}$. While the argument focuses on average cost as the motivating force, the particular way in which excessive costs influence behavior will depend on the institutional structure of the market. If tuition (t) is fixed (as in some state universities), shifts in the demand for education will not alter AC but rather the number of applicants rejected by universities. The resultant "shortage" of places will then motivate entry in the same manner as excessive cost in the preceding discussion. Geographic transportation and residence costs, coalescing in demands for local colleges, offer another specific impetus for new colleges and universities.

Table 4-2 examines the number of institutions in the higher education market in the period under study. It shows a striking increase in the number of colleges and universities from 1960 to 1975, when over 1,000 new educational institutions were formed, primarily by public bodies at the junior and community college level. The rapid influx of institutions suggests that the supply of public colleges and universities is very elastic with respect to the demands of students and their families and to the economic conditions underlying those demands and thus that the long-run demand model is more relevant to changes over time than might initially be expected. While the usual arguments about sunk cost imply that exit will be a more sluggish process, there is some evidence of a marked change in the 1970s. Between 1970 and 1975, forty-four colleges closed and thirty ended

Table 4-2. Numbers of Academic Institutions.

	Four Year	*Two Year*	*Total*
1950	1,322	527	1,847
1960	1,447	593	2,040
1970	1,676	897	2,573
1975	1,914	1,141	3,055
Compound Annual Changes			
1950–1960	0.9	1.2	1.0
1960–1970	1.5	4.2	2.3
1970–1975	2.7	4.9	3.5

Source: American Council on Education (1976: 76, 142; 1977).

independent status by merger.[7] Many states began the task of reducing proliferating graduate programs, and relatively few planned on expansion of higher education. The number of institutions in the market may not fall in the late 1970s and 1980s, but it will surely not rise. Changes in numbers of programs and to a lesser extent in numbers of institutions are likely to play an important role in the demand for faculty in the future, as they did in the expansion of the past.

Quality of Inputs and Outputs

Academic concern with the quality of faculty and of institutions is likely to cause some distinctive patterns of salary and employment behavior in the market. On the demand side, concern with the average quality of faculty means that institutions must choose between numbers used and the quality of those hired, which creates distinct choice sets, along the lines set out by Houthakker's (1952–53) model. The distinctive feature of the quality-quantity interaction is that the cost of increasing the number or quality of a department depends critically on the average quality or size. Assuming concern with average quality, increases in quality are more expensive the greater the size of the department; conversely, the cost of increasing the size of faculty will depend positively on quality. The relative cost of the quality of faculty versus the number hired depends directly on the number and inversely on the quality, with definite consequences for market behavior. On the supply side, individual concern with academic quality leads to division of the market into various subgroups, with Ph.D.s willing to take lower pay in higher rated schools.

The critical role of quality considerations in academia has substantial implications for the market adjustment process. First, it is likely to make changes in the quality of personnel and institutions, as well as in the number of appointees, important in market adjustment. When faculty wages decline due to a weak market, the types of institutions at which new Ph.D.s obtain jobs is likely to drop, while the average quality of institutional appointments rises. It is even possible that the quality adjustment will produce a perverse change in employment, as lower wages and abundant supply lead to improvements in the quality of appointees, which will raise the cost of increasing numbers.[8] While such perverse patterns are not in fact found in the data (see below), evidence on the quality of the academic institutions of first placement shows clearly that the quality of appointments is a major adjustment parameter in the market. In the late 1960s–early 1970s decline in the academic market, the proportion of new doctorates obtaining jobs outside of Cartter's "rated" universities rose from less than one-half in 1967 to over two-thirds in 1971; the proportion in Level I or II universities was halved and, regardless of work activity, new Ph.Ds were increasingly likely to end up in institutions of lower quality than that from which they obtained the degree (Niland, 1973).

Second, the desire of faculty to work in institutions with high average quality drives a wedge between the wages and marginal cost of hiring personnel, which may account, at least in part, for the well-known "rationing" of places in top institutions. This is because a lower quality appointment has two costs: the direct salary paid the individual and the likely increase in the salary demands of other faculty, whose work conditions will be adversely affected by their appointment. As a result, high quality schools will find it very expensive to employ lower quality faculty, while conversely, lower quality schools may have to pay enormous premia to attract the more able, leading to concentration of academic "stars" in a few places and the rationing of appointments in those schools.[9] When student concern for quality makes them willing to pay higher tuition to associate with the more able, a similar pattern in the student market is also likely. Place rationing and concentration of the more qualified in a limited number of institutions will be observed.

Third, quality considerations can be expected to play a major role in salary determination, with those judged of higher quality receiving greater pay. As is shown in Table 4–3, such a pattern is found between even as crude a measure of academic quality as articles published and individual salaries, with virtually all studies of academic salary determination finding that, other factors fixed, number of

Table 4–3. Summary of Studies of the Effect of Number of Publications on Academic Salaries.

Study and Year	Data Set	Controls	Effect of Publications Significant (√)
Tuckman and Leahey (1975)	ACE male full-time economics faculty 1972–1973	1, 3–6, 8, (9)	√
Siegried and White (1973a)	University of Wisconsin Madison, economists 1971	1, 2, 3, (5), (6), (8), (9)	√
Katz (1973)	596 faculty at single university	1, 2, 3, (5), (6), 7, (8), 9	√
Ferber (1974)	132 faculty at single university	1, (5), (6), (8), (9)	√
Freeman (1977c)	ACE sample of 3,500 whites and blacks	1, 2, (4), 6, 7, 8, (9)	√
Astin and Bayer (1972)	ACE sample of 60,000 persons	1, 2, 3, 5, 6, 7, 8, (9)	√

Note to controls

( ) = controlled by focusing on group having single characteristic

1 = years of experience
2 = administrative duties
3 = teaching productivity
4 = race
5 = department quality
6 = region
7 = quality of degree
8 = type of institution
9 = sex

articles significantly raises earnings, constituting one of the major determinants of salary.

Institutional Aspects of Academia

Turning to more specific features of the academic market, three aspects deserve attention: desire for an "equitable" wage structure that rewards faculty roughly equally across specialties; tenure, which guarantees lifetime employment; and recent unionization.

Internal Salary Policies. That most colleges and universities would like to pay faculty of similar rank, experience, and academic ability, but different specialization, the same basic salary is evident from expressed salary goals. A 1973 Dartmouth College compensation committee, for example, stated that "since institutions constitute essential communities of scholars, there is a general feeling of what may be termed academic equity—that differences of compensation among faculty members of equal experience and standing within their own special fields should be as small as is consistent with maintenance of high quality faculty in each department." National Education Association surveys (1972) show that nearly all institutions have explicit faculty salary schedules, providing for minimum-maximum or average pay based on merit, rank, and experience, applying equally across fields.

In essence, in place of market valuations, universities affirm an intellectual value structure that presupposes little or no inherent superiority to knowledge in various fields. According to this nonprofit "price scheme," faculty are judged by their intellectual quality and scholarly output, with differences in the market price of output (which is substantial between, say, economics and hittite archeology) ignored as much as possible in determining wages. Underlying the rejection of market prices is the realization that valuation of knowledge involves considerable uncertainty, nonappropriability, or externalities and time horizons that may be inadequately handled by for profit market prices.

Another factor leading to the equitable wage goal is the tendency for university administrators and members of faculty committees to come from various departments. The Dartmouth compensation committee, for example, included professors of economics, French, mathematics, and sociology, among other fields. Explicit or implicit bargaining on such committees or in administrative decisionmaking, with unclear standards of judgment, diverse evaluations, and similar "bargaining power," is likely to produce symmetric treatment of fields, as some game theory models would predict. When faculties are divided by schools, on the other hand, as among law, business, medi-

cine, and arts and sciences, pressure for wage equity across disciplines will be attenuated.

Whatever the cause, the desire for interfield equity in salaries exacts a cost on the university system when nonacademic opportunity wages differ. This cost must be traded off against other goals and expenditures in the decision process. The use of resources to purchase equity in salaries will produce a narrower interfield dispersion of salaries in academia than in industry, shortages (surpluses) in specialities where opportunity wages are high (low), and reliance on compensatory nonmonetary renumeration schemes to alleviate market problems by widening the real incentive structure, despite the constraint on salaries. Such compensation policies would include differential work conditions (office space, secretarial aid); speeds of promotion; liberal outside time rules; and provision of special professorial chairs, of laboratories, and the like, though equity pressures may also limit these options. As such rewards are possible in the absence of the "constraint" on salaries and substitute imperfectly for flexible salaries, they will only partly alleviate the manpower problems due to the equity goal. Hiring standards are, as a consequence, likely to be an extremely important adjustment tool, with lower quality faculty employed in "shortage" fields and higher quality faculty in "surplus" areas, where job rationing will prevail.

Comparisons of the interfield structure of academic and nonacademic salaries in Table 4–4 suggest an important role for the equity goal in the market. Academic salaries turn out to be much more narrowly dispersed across fields than are industrial salaries, with a range of $3,700 versus $8,200 in the same fields and a coefficients variation across fields of 0.059 in academia versus 0.102 in industry. More importantly in terms of adjustment processes, a similar pattern is found in comparisons of percentage change in salaries. From 1970 to 1975 the standard deviation of the log change of the salaries of academic doctorate scientists was 0.089, while the comparable industrial variation was 0.385.[10] Recruitment also appears to be influenced by the interfield salary structure, as predicted by the analysis. In 1964, when the academic job market was very strong, vacancy rates in universities, defined as the ratio of unfilled budgeted positions to newly filled and unfilled slots, were substantially positively correlated ($r = 0.88$) with the ratio of nonacademic to academic salaries in 1964 (Table 4–5). Vacancies, like high wages, are likely to attract additional specialists due to the increased probability of obtaining desirable jobs and are thus to some extent self-correcting.

Finally, a rigid "equitable salary" policy will alter elasticities of response to supply-demand imbalances in particular fields. Under a

Table 4–4.   Median Annual Salaries and Measures of Dispersion by Field, 1975.

Field	Business/Industry	Four Year Colleges and Universities
Chemists	25,900	20,700
Physicists, Astronomers	25,900	22,200
Mathematicians	26,100	20,400
Statisticians	24,400	22,200
Computer Specialists	23,900	22,700
Earth Scientists	26,400	20,900
Atmospheric Scientists	22,600	23,100
Engineers	26,000	23,600
Biologists	24,900	20,400
Medical Scientists	29,900	24,100
Psychologists	30,500	20,800
Economists	30,800	22,800
Other Social Scientists	22,900	20,500
Agricultural Scientists	23,200	20,800
dispersion statistics		
range	$8,200	$3,700
standard deviation	2,650	1,288
coefficient of variation	0.102	0.059

Sources: National Science Foundation (1977: 63, table B–15).

flexible wage regime, when a 1 percent change in wages clears the market in a specialty accounting for α percent of the faculty budget, average wages change by α percent, while in a world of rigid wages among fields, the same adjustment requires that all salaries change by 1 percent—$1/\alpha$ times as great. Formally, the constraint reduces the elasticity of demand or supply in a field from say η and ϵ to $\alpha\eta$ and $\alpha\epsilon$, necessitating the greater response to attain equilibrium.

Tenure.   Tenure, which guarantees lifetime employment to faculty members except for reasons of institutional financial crisis or incompetency, is a much criticized feature of the academic market, though in some respects it is quite similar to industrial seniority systems, which also protect older workers from the vagaries of the market. Both tenure and seniority result, in part, from worker desires for

Table 4-5. The Impact of the Internal Salary Constraint on the Ratio of Industrial to Academic Salaries and on Unfilled Openings in Universities, 1964.

Field	Incremental Vacancy Rate[a] (1)	Ratio of Industrial to Academic Salaries 1964 (2)	Rank of[b] (1)	(2)
Physics	0.177	1.47	1	3
Economics	0.162	1.72	2	1
Mathematics	0.143	1.65	3	2
Psychology	0.123	1.45	4	4
Chemistry	0.095	1.40	5	5
Biology	0.069	1.33	6	7
Agriculture	0.028	1.08	7	8
Geology	0.017	1.37	8	6

[a]The incremental vacancy rate is the fraction of new budgeted positions unfilled in a given year.

[b]The Spearman coefficient is 0.88; 1 percent level of significance is 0.83.

Sources: National Education Association (1964); National Science Foundation (1964).

job security and their willingness to forego income for seniority, and both place the burden of market adjustments on the young.

What distinguishes tenured faculty from other senior employees is the power to hire additional faculty who do essentially the same work and could replace them on the job. It is this power that makes university departments similar to Yugoslav type collectives, with average quality of departments rather than profits as the maximand and the quality of appointments, not the number, as the policy variable. In the absence of tenure, the operational problems involved in faculty hiring and firing would be immense, with each professor judging possible new colleagues as competitors who could replace him at the workplace and as electors deciding his future. The danger of collusive agreements, bargaining, and coalition formation seriously hampering education and research is substantial. Tenure effectively reduces such "nonproductive" behavior, making "partnership" viable in the nonprofit market where profit and loss sanctions are relatively inoperative, at least in the short run.

The historical development of tenure in the United States lends some support to the hypothesized tenure appointment power link, for "the growing participation of faculty in the recruitment and

selecting of its own members" and "the shrinking of presidential competence" in appointments occurred roughly simultaneously with the beginning of the tenure system. It "was one of the instruments whereby university and college professors gained a nearly exclusive power to determine who was entitled to membership in their ranks."[11] A more formal test of the tenure appointment power link would involve examination of employment in institutions lacking tenure; deans or presidents are predicted to make hiring decisions in such educational enterprises.

Tenure, like other seniority arrangements, makes the age structure of employees and rates of expansion key parameters in market adjustments. When the higher educational system is expanding, the probability of tenure will increase above its steady state level: to attract additional personnel, many lower quality faculty will be promoted, and the income of those of tenure age will be increased relative to that of older faculty. While the number of tenure appointments increases, the proportion may remain constant or even fall, due to rapid expansion. Despite the fixed employment of tenured personnel, there are no difficulties in adjusting the mix of faculty to educational or research demands, as expansion in fields in great demand is an adequate tool (Freeman, 1971). The 1960s were, in general, a period of this type as a result of the extraordinary demand for academic research and educational outputs.

At the opposite end of the spectrum is a period of market contraction in which tenure becomes a serious barrier to the adjustment process. In contracting markets, universities cannot readily keep on young workers of relatively high quality due to tenure commitments and have difficulty in altering the distribution of professors across disciplines to meet changing market demands. While some tools exist for removing less desirable tenured faculty, ranging from closing departments to reducing office space and related prerequisites, failing to award normal salary increases, or cutting salaries, and ultimately to "buying out" a position, such activities are difficult in the university setting. For one thing, the academic job ladder is short, making it difficult to differentiate among permanent employees through promotion or assignment of tasks: the professor rank is the top of the ladder in particular institutions. For another, the collegial pressures needed to push men out of jobs are presumably unpleasant, especially in declining markets, and require decisions of the type that tenure is designed to eliminate—those relating to the status of senior personnel.

Patterns of institutional mobility are also likely to be altered in a contracting market. In steady state or expanding markets, it is

frequent for high quality junior faculty to "invest" several years in top institutions, where they continue their education, and then to move to other colleges and universities. Contraction creates great pressures against such institutional mobility patterns, largely on the part of junior faculty outside the top schools whose promotion is threatened by importing outsiders. The risk that immediate post-degree investments in training will not beat fruit will cause more high quality younger specialists to move outside major universities early rather than late in their careers.

When an expanding market suddenly contracts, adjustment problems are exacerbated, with tenured faculty in younger age categories and relatively small replacement demands for new appointments. Movement to a steady state equilibrium will be extremely difficult, and the entire ethos of the system unpleasant, producing—as Moynihan (1973:11) puts it—"A Balzacian society, where, if you want to be a professor, you wait until the man who is professor dies. Then the 15 of you who want the job compete in various ways. One of you gets it."

Finally, tenure probably reduces the efficiency of academics by removing the possibility of being fired for nonperformance. Those nearing retirement, in particular, may be so affected, since "compensatory firing policies"—failure to grant normal salary increases or salary cuts—are likely to have a small effect due to the short future work life. The danger of loss of pension rights, which exists in industry, is eliminated by the vesting of academic retirement plans.

Unionism. In 1965, effectively no colleges and university faculty were covered by collective bargaining contracts. In 1976 nearly 12 percent of campuses were organized (see Figure 4–2). In the brief span of a decade, organization became an important feature of the academic marketplace. Collective organization can be expected to affect the operation of the faculty job market in several ways. First, it may affect the salary determination process and keep relative wages from falling as rapidly as they might in the 1980s period of declining demand. Second, and perhaps more critically, bargaining may lead to greater stress on internal labor market mobility, with existing faculty obtaining greater job security at the expense of new doctorates. Third, collective organizations can be expected to increase the fringe share of the compensation package, again to the benefit of older more experienced personnel. While faculty unionism is too new for any clear assessment of its impact on adjustment processes, it is important to bear in mind the potential differences in adjustments over time due to unionism. Comparisons of the policies

Figure 4–2. Percentage of Colleges and Universities Organized by Unions.

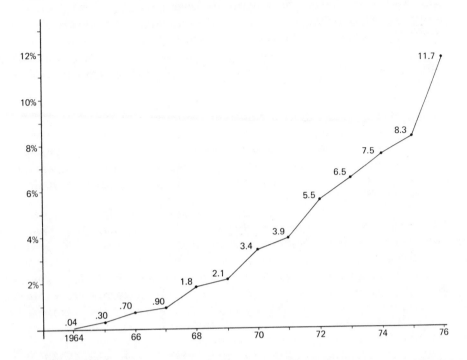

Sources: National Center for the Study of Collective Bargaining in Higher Education (1977); National Center for Education Statistics (1978).

of organized and unorganized institutions in the period of market decline would provide valuable insight into the impact of trade unions on the dynamics of market adjustments.

Capital Goods and Demographic Factors

The dependence of the demand for new faculty on changes in enrollments and the production of new faculty from graduate enrollments suggests application of capital goods accelerator models to the faculty market.[12] These models highlight the dynamic adjustment problems of an industry producing and employing a long-lived capital resource such as faculty and its potential for cyclic fluctuations. Consider first the demand side of the market, which has a capital goods adjustment or accelerator structure with respect to enrollments (E) because demand for faculty depends on enrollments as well as on academic salaries (W). If, as seems reasonable, faculty-student ratios

are fixed save in response to changes in the real cost of faculty, demand (F^d) can be written in linear form as:

$$F^d = aE - bW \qquad (4-2)$$

where a is the parameter for enrollments and b the linear parameter reflecting responses to wages. Then, if δ is the rate at which faculty leave the system for retirement or other reasons, demand for new faculty (NF^d) will be

$$NF^d = F^d - (1-\delta)F_{-1} = aE - bW - (1-\delta)F_{-1} \ . \qquad (4-3)$$

Equation (4−3) is a capital stock adjustment equation in which demand for new faculty depends on output, cost, and size of the existing faculty less "depreciation." If employment of faculty was at the equilibrium level in the last period, so that $F_{-1} = cE_{-1} - bW_{-1}$, equation (4−3) yields the classic accelerator model

$$NF^d = a\triangle E - b\triangle W + \delta F_{-1} \ , \qquad (4-4)$$

which shows that demand for new faculty depends on changes in enrollments, changes in wages, and the rate of outflow. What is important in equation (4−4) is the $\triangle E$ term, which makes demand for new faculty critically dependent on the growth of the educational system: if, as in the early 1970s, $\triangle E$ is small, demand for new faculty will be small; if, as predicted for the 1980s, $\triangle E$ is negative, demand for new faculty may become negative. Moreover, since college and university enrollments consist largely of young persons, dependence of demand on $\triangle E$ makes the faculty market critically dependent on the age structure of the population. While in years past the proportion of a young cohort in college was sufficiently small to provide an important buffer to demographic fluctuations, recent increases in enrollment propensities substantially limit the possible effect of such adjustments to future demographic declines. As a result, instability in higher education due to changes in the age structure of the population is likely to be more important in the future than in the past and deserves serious attention in public policy.

Figure 4−3 graphs log changes in enrollments from 1920 to 1976 and prospective changes (as forecast by Cartter, 1976) from 1976 to 2000. The figure shows considerable fluctuation in the change in enrollments, which implies considerable ups and downs in the market for new faculty and makes clear the potential problem in the 1980s.

Figure 4–3. Log Changes for Enrollment 1920–1976 and Predicted Change 1976–2000.

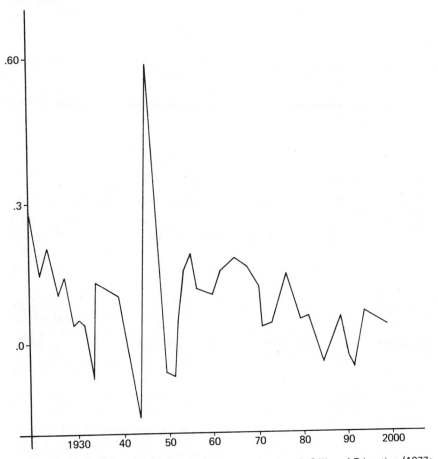

Sources: 1920–1976, U.S. Bureau of Census (Various) and U.S. Office of Education (1977: 177, table 3.03). 1976–2000, Cartter (1976: 58, table 4–9, with *C* series used).

On the supply side, the fact that new faculty are "produced" by the higher educational system from graduate students leads to a more complex market. If, for simplicity, graduate training takes one period and those planning on academic careers (*AG*) base their decision on the basis of conditions a period prior to graduation according to an adaptive expectations process, the supply of new faculty (*NF^S*) can be written as:

$$NF^S = AG_{-1} = \lambda \epsilon W_{-2} + (1 - \lambda) NF^S_{-1} \qquad (4-5)$$

where ϵ is the coefficient of supply response and λ the adjustment coefficient.

With a given parameter relating graduate students to demand (say, for simplicity a) and market clearing ($NF^S = NF^d$), equations (4-3) and (4-5) or (4-4) and (4-5) can be solved to yield a second order difference equation giving the dynamics of market adjustment to shifts in exogenous factors. With reasonable values of the parameters, the equation has complex roots that produce damped cyclic fluctuations.[13] The cycle will be longer than the cobweb cycle in the labor market because demand as well as supply is influenced by enrollment decisions of students. A typical scenario for the cycle would be: On the demand side, high academic salaries → increased graduate enrollments → greater demand for faculty → higher salaries, a response pattern tending to explosive movements; and on the supply side, high academic salaries → increased graduate enrollments → increased supply of new Ph.D.s → increased supply of faculty → decrease in academic salaries, the usual cobweb adjustment process. The demand side cycle is attenuated when graduate students are used as teachers, for the demand-increasing effect of graduate enrollments is reduced and possibly reversed. Investigation of this aspect of the market requires analyses of the substitutability between faculty and graduate teaching assistants and consideration of their relative salaries or costs.

The significance of the endogeneous cyclic mechanism in the faculty market will differ across fields, depending on the relative importance of faculty used to produce faculty. When undergraduate enrollment or graduate enrollments independent of the faculty market account for the bulk of academic demand—as in engineering, for example—fluctuations in the faculty market will be proportionally small. When, on the other hand, graduate students loom large in enrollments and tend primarily to become teachers, as in the more arcane subjects, fluctuations could be substantial until equilibrium is attained.

ECONOMETRIC ANALYSIS OF FACULTY MARKET DEVELOPMENTS

The principal theme of the first part of this chapter is that the academic job market is likely to be, for various reasons, a highly responsive allocative mechanism, though one operating under certain well-defined institutional and structural constraints. It was argued that the nonprofit status of colleges and universities and the capital goods-accelerator structure of the market are likely to produce sizeable adjustments and fluctuations in the face of changing conditions. In

addition, the internal salary structure, tenure system, and concern for quality are likely to create distinct forms of adjustment that should be empirically observable.

This part of the chapter turns to the observed pattern of academic marketplace responsiveness. It examines the major developments in the market in the 1950s, 1960s, and 1970s and then provides estimates of a small econometric model of employment and salary determination that can be used to assess past and to predict likely future responses to changes in market conditions.

Market Developments

The changing economic position of faculty over the long run is examined graphically in Figure 4—4, which records the ratio of faculty salary to industrial earnings and the ratio of faculty to nonagricultural employment.[14] The figure reveals considerable variation in the state of the market over time, presumably in response to changing economic conditions. Relative faculty compensation increased steadily in the 1920s, after declining during World War II; peaked in 1932 due to slow adjustment to depression conditions; and then declined to a minimum of 2.4 : 1 in 1956. From the mid-1950s until the late 1960s academic salaries rose compared to other salaries, as the higher education system entered what has been called a "golden age" of expansion. By contrast, in the late 1960s and the 1970s, the relative gains of the preceding decade were eroded as the market underwent a major turnaround.

The relative employment figures show an upward trend in academic employment, with varying rates over time. There were large increases in the number of faculty per worker in the mid-1950s and the 1960s, following World War II, and at the outset of the 1930s Depression when the number of faculty held steady while total employment dropped sharply. During World War II and the Korean War period, the ratio of faculty to total employment dropped. From 1970 to 1974 the ratio also dropped, presumably as part of the turnaround, but then rose in 1976.

Additional data from the decennial *Census of Population* and annual *Current Population Survey* can be used to examine the growth of faculty relative to other professions requiring considerable education. The ratios of faculty to other professional employment from the census given in Table 4—6 show a pattern similar to that in Figure 4—2, with, however, a more modest trend in post-World War II years due to the professionalization of the work force and a more marked slowdown in the 1970s.

Figure 4–4. Relative Salary and Employment of Faculty.

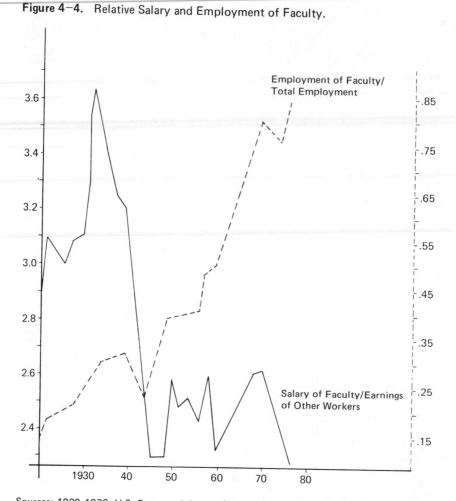

Sources: 1920–1976, U.S. Bureau of Census (Various) and U.S. Office of Education (1977: 177, table 3.03). 1976–2000, Cartter (1976: 58, table 4-9, with C series used).

Turning to enrollments during the boom period of the 1960s, the higher education system enjoyed the benefit of an unprecedented increase in the number of college age (eighteen to twenty-four year old) persons from 1960 to 1970 (U.S. Bureau of the Census, 1972), which together with a high rate of return to college, produced an extraordinary growth of enrollments of 4.8 million students or 126 percent over the decade (U.S. Office of Education, 1977:177). Coincident with this expansion, the receipts of higher educational

Table 4-6.   Relative Number of Faculty.

	1900	1910	1920	1930	1940	1950	1960	1970	1976
College faculty/ all professional	0.006	0.009	0.014	0.019	0.020	0.025	0.024	0.043	0.042
College faculty/ engineers	0.184	0.208	0.246	0.286	0.259	0.234	0.205	0.395	0.451
College faculty/ lawyers	0.065	0.139	0.268	0.385	0.423	0.690	0.840	1.784	1.300
College faculty/ teachers	0.016	0.027	0.044	0.059	0.071	0.111	0.106	0.178	0.173

Sources: U.S. Bureau of the Census, *Historical Statistics of the U.S.* (1977: 1, ser. D-233-682, 140-41) and *Census of Population* (1970: Occupational Characteristics P(2)-7A, 1-2, table 1); U.S. Department of Labor (1975: 186, table A-53).

institutions increased rapidly, tripling from 1960–1961 to 1968–1969 (O'Neill, 1971; U.S. Office of Education, 1972). Total federal aid to academia, including diverse direct student support and facilities and equipment purchases, rose rapidly. The price of education to students, in the form of tuition per full-time equivalent enrollment unadjusted for student aid, declined modestly relative to that of the 1950s, while public tuition and fees increased more slowly than private charges, raising the ratio of private to public tuition from 4.0 in 1960 to 4.7 in 1970.

On the supply side, the major development was the enormous inflow of new Ph.D. and master's degree graduates, which substantially augmented the population of potential faculty (National Academy of Sciences, Annual; U.S. Office of Education, 1972). Between 1960 and 1970, the number of Ph.D. degree recipients tripled; the ratio of new Ph.D.s to enrolled students rose 36 percent, and the total stock of Ph.D.s increased by 80 percent.

Toward the end of the 1960s and in the 1970s, the forces underlying the higher educational boom began to level off or decline. The demographic growth in the number of persons of college age came to an end: in 1970 there were 24.7 million eighteen to twenty-four year olds; in 1975, 27.6 million (U.S. Office of Education, 1977: 146). With the rate of return to college dropping (see Freeman, 1976, 1977a), the proportion enrolled also fell, with a consequent stabilization or reduced rate of increase in college enrollments, depending on the data and group covered. According to the Office of Education (1977), total enrollments increased from 1970 to 1976 at an annual rate of 5.3 percent, compared to an 8.5 percent rate from 1960 to 1970; first year degree credit enrollment grew by 1.5 percent per year from 1970 to 1975, compared to 6.8 percent per year in the previous decade; the rate of increase in graduate enrollments decelerated from the 12.6 percent per year of the 1960s to 4.1 percent in the 1970–1975 period. According to the U.S. Bureau of Census (Various), total college enrollments grew by 5 percent per annum from 1970 to 1976 while freshmen enrollments grew by only 2.9 percent per annum, compared to rates nearly twice as high in the previous decade. In several scientific fields such as physics, first year graduate enrollments fell sharply, despite the increased number of bachelor's graduates from which to draw students (Freeman, 1975b). Federal support for graduate education and research declined in importance, and total income of colleges and universities grew relatively slowly, with the ratio of spending of higher education to GNP barely changing from 1970 to 1976 after having nearly doubled in the decade before.[15] With demand leveling off and with supply growing, the

job market for faculty experienced a sharp slump, which showed up in salaries and employment.

The pattern of change in salaries in the period is examined in Table 4–7, which compares the rate of change in real (1976 dollars) salaries from 1969–1970 to 1975–1976 to the changes from 1960–1961 to 1969–1970. The table tells a clear story about salary adjustments to the changed market. From 1960–1961 to 1969–1970, academic salaries increased in real terms at a more rapid pace than other salaries, so that the ratio of academic compensation to average annual earnings in industry rose from 2.28 to 2.50. From 1969 to 1976 by contrast, academic salaries fell in real terms and relative to other wages and salaries: the ratio of academic compensation to average annual earnings in industry was 2.20 in 1976, below the level at the outset of the 1960s boom.

With respect to employment, the rate of growth of faculty dropped, as can be seen in Figure 4–2 and Table 4–6. From fall 1970 to fall 1976, U.S. Office of Education data (1977:178, table 2.04) show an increase in the number of faculty of 3.1 percent per annum compared to an increase of 7.6 percent per annum from 1960 to 1976, while Bureau of the Census data show a drop in the rate from 10.7 percent per annum in the 1960s to 1.3 percent from 1970 to 1976.[16] The slow growth of faculty had a marked depressant effect on the employment prospects of young academics and greatly altered the age structure of the faculty. Among new Ph.D.s there was a sharp decline in the proportion obtaining academic jobs readily. In 1970, approximately 59 percent of new doctorates had definite prospects in academia upon receipt of their degree; in 1975, just 47 percent were in such a position.[17] As noted earlier, the type of job held by those getting jobs in academia also underwent considerable deterioration in this period, with an increasing number obtaining work in lower quality institutions. The drop in new hires shows up dramatically in the data on the age and rank structure of science faculty in Table 4–8. In 1968, 42 percent of the science faculty had received their Ph.D. within seven years, in 1974, just 29 percent. In 1970, 64 percent of the faculty were full or associate professors, in 1975, 71 percent. After decreasing for about a decade, the median age of faculty rose sharply in the 1970s. Lack of job opportunities for new Ph.D.s became one of the major problems facing higher education. In terms of the theoretic considerations presented earlier in this chapter, the problem reflects both the capital stock–acceleration aspect of demand and the tenure system.

Not surprisingly in view of evidence of the career responses of young persons, the market decline appears to have affected graduate

enrollments substantially. In the areas most severely affected by the turnaround, notably physics, enrollments fell at astounding rates. Between 1965 and 1972, first year graduate enrollments in physics declined by 33 percent; in other physical sciences the decline in enrollments was more moderate but nonetheless striking in view of past trends and the growing number of baccalaureates.[18] Many major universities embarked on policies to reduce graduate classes or at the least to warn entering students of potential market problems (see Figure 4-5). All told, the salary, employment, and supply adjustments of the late 1960s and early 1970s produced a market for faculty that differed drastically from that of the preceding golden age.

Results from an Econometric Modeling

The response of the faculty market to the 1960s boom, the turnaround, and earlier economic conditions can fruitfully be analyzed with small econometric models of employment and salary determination. Estimates of the demand for and supply of faculty from a modeling based on work in part one of this chapter are described in econometric detail in the chapter appendix. Our intent here is to simply provide the general results from this modeling.

The evidence provided in the appendix indicates a long-term elasticity of demand for faculty with respect to salaries of −0.28 to −0.44 and of unity with respect to enrollments. That is, a 10 percent rise in real salaries (salaries corrected for inflation) is associated with a 2.8 to 4.0 percent fall in the demand for faculty; a 10 percent rise in enrollments is associated with a 10 percent rise in demand for faculty. The evidence suggests an adjustment process in which demand for faculty responds to past salaries and current enrollments with a partial adjustment parameter of about one-half.

Estimates of lagged adjustment regressions give a more rapid response of salaries than of employment to market conditions. This may reflect the importance of tenure on employment adjustment and of the key role of quality adjustment in academia. Consistent with the preceding estimate, alternative faculty earning opportunities and enrollments raise salaries of academics, while the number of Ph.D.s in the market reduces salaries, as does the lagged number of faculty.

Unlike most education sector models (Cartter, 1971; Porter, 1965), the above results do not depend on fixed faculty-student ratios. They allow for demand adjustments to changes in academic salaries and the interrelation between employment and salary determination. The computations involved in this education sector model are based on the notion that the academic marketplace responds in

Table 4–7.   Academic Salaries in Periods of Market Boom and Bust.

	Academic and Other Salaries 1960–1976 (in 1976 dollars)			Compound Annual Change in Salaries	
	1960–1961	1969–1970	1975–1976	1960–1969	1969–1975
Professors					
(1) total compensation	20,964	28,089	26,576	3.3	–1.0
(2) salaries	19,554	25,327	23,233	2.9	–1.4
university	22,518	27,114	24,590	1.0	–1.6
public	–	26,455	24,150	–	–1.5
private	–	29,598	26,540	–	–1.8
junior colleges	17,272	23,031	22,136	3.2	–1.6
(3) salaries NEA	19,388	24,448	22,218	2.6	–1.6
Assistant Professors					
(4) total compensation	13,367	17,717	16,487	3.2	–1.2
(5) salaries	12,620	16,057	14,336	2.7	–1.9
university	13,567	16,273	14,670	2.0	–1.7
public	–	16,310	14,690	–	–1.7
private	–	16,289	14,740	–	–1.7
junior colleges	13,533	16,229	15,080	2.0	–1.2

(6) salaries NEA	13,043	15,595	14,069	2.0	-1.7
Other Workers[a]					
(7) annual compensation, industry	9,123	11,243	12,073[b]	2.1	1.1
(8) manufacturing, average hourly wage	4.39	5.20	5.19	1.9	-0.1

[a] Data for other workers relate to the initial year of academic year.
[b] Extrapolated 1974 by rate of change in manufacturing hourly wage from 1974 to 1976.

Sources: Lines 1, 2, 4, 5: American Association of University Professors (1960–1978).
Lines 3, 6: National Education Association (Biennial).
Lines 7, 8: U.S. Department of Commerce (1977); and U.S. Department of Labor (1977).

Figure 4—5.   Graduate School Letter of Acceptance.

STANFORD UNIVERSITY
STANFORD, CALIFORNIA 94305

DEPARTMENT OF ENGLISH

March 11, 1977

I am delighted to inform you that the Graduate Admissions Committee has approved your application for admission to the Department of English next fall.

I enclose a description of our fellowships. I hope you will find it informative. However, it is basically an explanation of departmental policy and does not represent a commitment on the part of the university *per se*. Such commitments are made by the Dean of the Graduate Division, who will contact you by mail on or about March 15 in order to present the university's formal offer.

Before entering this, or any other, Ph.D. program in English, *you should understand that the prospects for permanent employment after you have earned the Ph.D. are generally poor.* As a Department, we work extremely hard at placing our graduates, and they may expect to compete favorably for whatever jobs are available; but *we do not anticipate that there will be many openings in the foreseeable future. Anyone who chooses to pursue a career in college teaching these days is taking a large risk.* Please keep this fact in mind as you weigh your own alternatives.

We think highly of our departmental program, and the fact that we have singled you out of several hundred candidates obviously means that we think highly of you.

You have, as you know, until April 15 to accept the offer. Because we also have a duty to the highly qualified applicants on our waiting list, it would be helpful to us if we could hear from you sooner, however.

Again, congratulations. We look forward to seeing you in September.

Sincerely yours,

David R. Riggs
Director of Graduate Admissions

DRR/da

Enclosure

Table 4-8. Changes in the Experience and Rank Distribution of Doctorate Science Faculty, 1968-1975.

	Percentage of Doctorate Faculty With Seven or Less Years Since Doctorate			Percentage of Doctorate Faculty at Professor or Associate Professor Level		
	1968	*1974*	*Change 1968-1974*	*1970*	*1975*	*Change 1970-1975*
All	42.1	29.4	−12.7	64.4	71.4	7.0
Physics	31.6	18.5	−21.1	60.3	77.1	16.8
Chemistry	34.9	21.4	−13.5	61.5	74.7	13.2
Mathematics	51.9	36.8	−15.1	57.4	67.4	10.0
Economics	42.7	37.4	−5.3	72.1	73.8	1.7
Psychology	43.8	38.7	−5.6	62.2	68.5	6.3

Sources: U.S. National Science Foundation (1968: 10, table 2; 1974: 20, table B-1; 1970: 189-190, table A44; 1975: 110, tables B, B-25).

economically sensible ways to exogenous shocks. The regression results obtained generally support this notion and theoretical modeling of the previous sections of this chapter.

CONCLUSIONS

This chapter has examined the operation of the faculty job market from the perspectives of the theory of derived demand, the institutional characteristics of academia, and a simple econometric model of demand and salary adjustment. The study has emphasized that demand for faculty is responsive to changes in the cost of employment, albeit with peculiarities due to nonprofit motivation and the distinct features of higher education. It has argued that the nonprofit nature of colleges and universities increases responsiveness in the short run while entry and exit conditions of institutions are likely to provide long-run demand behavior similar to that in profit markets.

According to the analysis, concern for quality in academia may produce complex interactions between the number and quality of workers, which are likely to lead to greater quality than quantity adjustments, rationing of places in high level institutions, and a concentration of the most qualified in a limited number of universities. The "equitable" wage goal of universities, to reward comparable faculty similarly regardless of nonacademic opportunities, substantially narrows the interfield wage structure, producing less dispersion than in other sectors of the economy. Equitable wage policies exact a cost

in terms of flexibility of response to market changes and are likely to be loosened in times of financial difficulties.

Tenure also reduces the responsiveness of the higher education system, particularly in periods of market decline when expansion of faculty cannot be used to reallocate resources across disciplines. Issues of academic freedom aside, tenure is critical in a system where senior employees control appointments. Internal production of faculty and the lag structure in producing Ph.D.s create an accelerator type adjustment process with long-dampened cyclic fluctuations. As increasing proportions of cohorts enroll in college, the system becomes especially sensitive to the number of persons of college age.

The empirical analysis in part two has shown that the faculty market has indeed undergone considerable fluctuations, indicative of a highly responsive labor market. The most important change in the market was the termination of the "golden age" of the 1960s toward the end of that decade. With research and related expenditures no longer increasing, enrollments leveling off, and the number of Ph.D.s seeking work increasing as a result of previous market conditions, the academic marketplace underwent a significant turnaround. Real salaries dropped from 1969 to 1976, employment conditions worsened, and new Ph.D.s were forced to take less prestigious jobs. The age structure of the faculty changed dramatically, with the proportion less than thirty years old declining significantly in the period. The econometric estimates lend support to the basic argument of a responsive market, though one subject to lagged adjustments. The elasticity of demand for faculty was estimated to be -0.3 to -0.5, while salaries were found to be substantively influenced by supply and demand forces.

APPENDIX

AN ECONOMETRIC MODEL OF THE DEMAND FOR AND SUPPLY OF ACADEMICS

The response of the faculty market to the 1960s boom, the turn-around, and earlier economic conditions can fruitfully be analyzed with a small econometric model of employment and salary determination. Unlike most education sector models (Cartter, 1971; Porter, 1965), which assume fixed faculty-student ratios, the model allows for demand adjustments to changes in academic salaries and the interrelation between employment and salary determination. Its principal outputs are estimates of long-term elasticities of demand and of the responses of employment to exogenous market developments.

The key equation in the model is the long-run demand for faculty, which will be written in log form as dependent on enrollments and wages:

$$FAC^D = -\eta SAL + ENR + \mu_1 \qquad (4A-1)$$

where the capital letters refer to the natural logs of the variables and where FAC^D = number of faculty demanded, SAL = salary, ENR = enrollment, and μ_1 = random disturbance. The unit coefficient on ENR implies that the faculty-student ratio is fixed except when salaries change.

Actual changes in faculty (FAC) employment can be assumed to move toward the long run according to the standard partial adjustment model

$$\Delta FAC = \lambda (FAC^D - FAC_{-1}) \quad , \qquad (4A-2)$$

which, substituting for FAC^D, yields

$$FAC = -\lambda \eta SAL + \lambda ENR + (1-\lambda) FAC_{-1} + \mu_1 \qquad (4A-3)$$

as the relevant estimating equation. In equation (4A-3), the long-term elasticities are obtained by using the coefficient on FAC_{-1} to obtain λ and dividing into the other coefficients.

On the supply side, the supply of faculty FAC^S will be taken to depend on the number "available" to teach and on salaries in academia and in alternatives ($ASAL$)

$$FAC^S = \epsilon SAL - aASAL + bSTK + \mu_2 = \epsilon SAL - aASAL +$$

$$b_1 FAC_{-1} + b_2 PHD + \mu_2 \qquad\qquad (4A-4)$$

where STK = estimated number of potential faculty, PHD = number of new Ph.D. graduates in the period, and μ_2 = random error. The estimated potential supply (STK) will be calculated as the sum of the number of faculty in the previous period less an estimate of "depreciation" plus the number of Ph.D.s interested in teaching. Changes in the outflow of experienced faculty or in the willingness of new Ph.D.s to teach due to changing market conditions are captured in the responses to SAL and $ASAL$.

If salaries are assumed to clear the market in each period, equation (4A-4) can be combined with equation (4A-1) or equation (4A-3) to yield "reduced form" equations for salaries and employment. Setting FAC^D in equation (4A-1) equal to FAC^S in equation (4A-4) yields

$$FAC = (\epsilon/\epsilon + \eta) ENR + (\eta/\epsilon + \eta)(-aASAL + bSTK) + \mu_2 \ ; $$
$$(4A-5)$$

$$SAL = (1/\epsilon + \eta)(ENR + aASAL - bSTK) + \mu_3 \ .$$
$$(4A-6)$$

With (4A-3) as the demand equation, an additional FAC_{-1} term enters both equations.

If, as seems more reasonable, salaries do not adjust sufficiently rapidly to clear the market in each period, it is necessary to add a salary adjustment equation to the system. One possible adjustment equation postulates that salaries move along a partial adjustment path, toward the market clearing level:

$$\Delta SAL = \psi(SAL^* - SAL_{-1}) \qquad\qquad (4A-7)$$

where SAL^* is the long-term equilibrium as determined by SAL in equation (4A-6). Substituting equation (4A-6) into equation (4A-7) yields the estimating equation:

$$SAL = (\psi/\epsilon + \eta)(ENR + aASAL - bSTK) + (1 - \psi)(SAL_{-1}) + \mu_4 \ .$$
$$(4A-8)$$

An alternative potential salary adjustment model is to make changes depend on the deviation between actual and desired levels of employment:

$$SAL = \phi_1 \, [FAC^D_{-1} - FAC] + \phi_2 \, [FAC - FAC^S_{-1}]$$

(4A–9)

where $FAC^D_{-1} - FAC$ represents the difference between employment demanded at the initial wage and current employment and where $FAC - FAC^S_{-1}$ is the difference between employment and the long-term level of supply at the existing wage. Since salaries will rise when demand exceeds current levels of employment and when employment exceeds long-term supply, ϕ_1 and $\phi_2 > 0$.

Substituting and simplifying, we obtain the following estimating equation:

$$SAL = \phi_1 \, ENR + a\phi_2 \, ASAL + (\phi_2 - \phi_1) \, FAC + (1 - \phi_1 \eta - \phi_2 \epsilon)$$
$$SAL_{-1} + \mu_5 \; . \qquad\qquad (4A–10)$$

Since ϕ_1 is the coefficient that weights the demand influence on salaries and ϕ_2 the coefficient that weights supply influences, if (as seems likely) demand factors are more important in salary determination, $\phi_2 < \phi_1$ and the coefficient on FAC will be negative. If supply factors are more important, the converse will be true. Because economists lack an adequate theory of salary or price adjustments (see Arrow, 1959), there are other possible ways in which to model the salary adjustment process and in which to interpret the resultant coefficients. Since in general the various models have similar basic structures, with lagged salary terms picking up the effect of the past, I will not develop alternatives in this study but instead focus on estimates of equations (4A–8) and (4A–10).

Given partial adjustment equations (4A–3) and (4A–8) or (4A–10) the reduced form of the model can be written in the following matrix form:

$$\begin{pmatrix} FAC \\ SAL \end{pmatrix} = A(X) + B \begin{pmatrix} FAC_{-1} \\ SAL_{-1} \end{pmatrix} \qquad (4A–11)$$

where A and B are matrixes of reduced form coefficients, and X is a column vector of exogenous variables (ALT, $SALA$, and PHD).

This equation highlights the interrelated adjustment of employment and salaries in the market, with lagged values of each affecting

the other. To obtain the long-term impact of the Xs on FAC or SAL, it is necessary to solve the matrix equation

$$\begin{pmatrix} FAC \\ SAL \end{pmatrix} = (I-B)^{-1} A(X) \quad . \tag{4A-12}$$

Because the supply of Ph.D. graduates is taken as exogenous in the model, it does not provide a "full" long-term equilibrium but rather yields employment and salary relations conditional on number of Ph.D.s. The economic factors that influence the supply of Ph.D.s has been examined in detail elsewhere (Freeman, 1971, 1975b, 1977b; Center for Policy Alternatives, 1977) and is not pursued here.

Table 4−9 presents estimates of the demand for faculty equation (4−3) and variants thereof for the period 1920−1976 using the data described in detail in the source note. The calculations in lines 1−4 relate log faculty to the salaries of assistant professors on the hypothesis that demand is more responsive to the pay of younger nontenured than of older faculty, while line 5 uses the salary of full professors as the relevant cost variable. Both variables are deflated by the consumer price index to remove the effect of inflation.[19] Because of sharp abnormal jumps in the period surrounding World War II, the years 1944−1948 are deleted from regressions 1−3 and 5. To make sure that this deletion is not critical to results, line 4 covers the entire period. The calculations are limited to even-numbered numbers (ending academic year) due to data availability.

The main finding in Table 4−9 is that demand for faculty responds to changes in academic salaries with a small but reasonably well-specified elasticity and with some lag. In equation 1, which links faculty employment to the real salary of assistant professors and total enrollments in the current and precedent (two years previous) period, the elasticity with respect to the sum of the two salary variables is −0.28, while the coefficients on enrollment run to the expected unity (1.05). Addition of lagged employment of faculty essentially eliminates the effect of current salaries and lagged enrollments, leading to equation 2, which relates employment to salaries two years earlier, enrollment, and lagged faculty. In this equation, the long-run elasticity of demand is −0.38 (= −0.18/(1−0.53)),[20] somewhat larger than in the first regression. In line 3, the lagged salary variable is replaced by current salaries, instrumented for simultaneity on lagged salaries, number of Ph.D. graduates (in log form), and the other variables in the equation, with similar results. Here the short-run elasticity is −0.20 and the long-run elasticity is −0.38. Addition of the deleted years 1942−1948 in line 4 gives the same short-

Table 4–9. Estimates of Demand for Faculty, 1920–1976.[a]

Regression and Technique	Constant	SAL	SAL (-1)	ENR	ENR (-1)	FAC (-1)	R^2	D.W.
1. OLS	6.4	-0.13 (0.12)	-0.15 (0.10)	0.74 (0.10)	0.31 (0.11)		0.998	0.76
2. OLS	3.3		-0.18 (0.06)	0.52 (0.08)		0.53 (0.08)	0.999	1.30
3. IV	6.3	-0.20 (0.12)		0.58 (0.10)		0.47 (0.10)	0.998	1.37
4. OLS[b]	3.2		-0.20 (0.06)	0.50 (0.05)		0.58 (0.06)	0.998	1.81
5. OLS[c]	3.2		-0.16[c] (0.07)	0.48 (0.08)		0.56 (0.09)	0.999	1.21

[a] Dependent variable is log Faculty (*FAC*); independent variables also in log form; numbers in parentheses are standard errors; D.W. = Durbin Watson statistic; OLS = ordinary least squares; IV = instrumental variables: lagged variables and log Ph.D. as instruments; period covered excludes 1944–1948, except in line 4. Salary variable is salary of assistant professors deflated by C.P.I. except in line 5; observations covered are even-numbered years.

[b] Covers entire period including 1942–1948.

[c] Salary variable is salary of full professors deflated by C.P.I., period 1942–1948 excluded.

Sources: *FAC* = total instructional staff, from U.S. Bureau of the Census (Various: Series H317, 210); U.S. Office of Education (1974–1977: 178, table 3.04 in volume 3); *ENR* = total degree credit enrollment, from same sources (Series H321, 210, table 3.03). *SAL* = salary of assistant (full) professors.

run elasticity and a somewhat higher long-run elasticity (-0.44), indicating that despite the obvious differential developments in those years, the results do not hinge on a particular subset of observations. When the salary of assistant professors is replaced by the salary of full professors in line 5, the results are also comparable, in part because the salaries of the two groups move together. Enrollments obtain a coefficient of about unity in all of the calculations, supporting the notion of a fixed faculty-student ratio, cost incentives held fixed. In short, the evidence indicates a long-term elasticity of demand with respect to salaries of -0.28 and -0.44 and of unity with respect to enrollments and suggests an adjustment process in which demand responds to past salaries and current enrollments with a partial adjustment parameter of about one-half.

A similar set of findings is given in the salary regressions of Table 4–10, which record estimates of equations (4A–8) and (4A–10) with *STK* calculated as described in the table note and with *FAC* entered separately. Alternative salaries are measured by the salary of high

Table 4–10.　Estimates of Alternative Salary Determination Equations for Academic Faculty, 1920–1976.[a]

Constant	ENR	ALT[b]	STK[c]	FAC	SAL (−1)	R^2	D.W.
1. 3.0[d]	0.20 (0.13)	0.66 (0.11)	−0.36 (0.13)		0.36 (0.09)	0.972	1.14
2. 5.2[d]	0.53 (0.20)	0.72 (0.11)		−0.69 (0.21)	0.22 (0.09)	0.975	1.21
3. 3.5[e]	0.14 (0.11)	0.66 (0.10)	−0.26 (0.12)		0.25 (0.09)	0.979	1.09
4. 5.0[e]	0.35 (0.17)	0.71 (0.10)		−0.48 (0.18)	0.16 (0.08)	0.981	1.22

[a] Dependent variable is log salary (*SAL*) of faculty, with salaries of assistant professors used in lines 1 and 2 and salaries of full professors in lines 3 and 4, both deflated by C.P.I. Independent variables in log form. Period covered excludes 1944-1948. Numbers in parentheses are standard errors; D.W. = Durbin-Watson statistic. All estimates by ordinary least squares.

[b] *ALT* = salary of school teachers from U.S. Bureau of Census (Various: Series D728) and from U.S. Office of Education (1972) with 1976 estimated using percent change in average hourly earnings for production workers.

[c] *STK* estimated as log of [0.97 × absolute number of faculty in previous period + 0.70 × number or Ph.D.s graduated in current and precedent year]. This assumes a 3 percent outflow and that 70 percent of new Ph.D.s would on average desire to teach.

[d] Assistant professors salary.

[e] Full professors salary.

Sources: U.S. National Science Foundation (1968: 10, table 2; 1974: 20, table B-1; 1970: 189-190, table A44; 1975: 110, tables B, B-25) with Ph.D.s obtained from U.S. National Academy of Sciences (Annual).

school teachers. While teaching in secondary schools is a significant option for many faculty, especially at the junior and community college levels, the variable was chosen primarily because it is the only professional income series covering the entire 1920–1976 period.[21] Lines 1 and 2 of the table relate the salaries of assistant professors to the estimated stock of faculty enrollment and alternative salaries, while lines 3 and 4 deal with the salaries of full professors. In all of the calculations, the explanatory variables obtain correctly signed and generally significant coefficients of reasonable magnitude. According to line 1, for example, an 11 percent increase in enrollment raises salaries by 0.2 percent in the short run and by 0.3 percent in the long run; increases in alternative earnings have larger positive effects; while the "stock" of available academics reduces salaries with an elasticity of -0.36 in the short run and -0.56 in the long run. The effect of current faculty size in line 2 is even larger, -0.69, providing strong evidence of what may be called a demand tradeoff between employment and earnings. Not surprisingly, perhaps, the effect of the available supply or current employment on the salaries of full professors in lines 3 and 4 is estimated to be much smaller, with long-run effects of -0.35 (line 3) and -0.57 (line 4).

In all of the lagged adjustment regressions of Table 4–10, the estimated adjustment parameter (one minus the coefficient in $SAL\ (-1)$) is larger than in the corresponding employment regression of Table 4–9. This implies a more rapid response of salaries than of employment to market conditions, which may reflect the importance of tenure on employment adjustments and of the key role of quality adjustment in academia.

The way in which faculty employment and salaries are affected by shifts in demand and supply schedules is examined in Table 4–11 by least squares estimation of the reduced form of the model of equation (4A–10). Shifts in demand are measured by enrollments, and alternative salaries by the pay of high school teachers as in previous computations. Because FAC_{-1} enters into the reduced form separately, the STK variable (which consists primarily of $FAC\ (-1)$) is replaced by log Ph.D.s.

The regression results provide general support for the applicability of the model to the faculty market and suggest considerable responsiveness of employment and salaries to exogenous developments. Consistent with preceding estimates, alternative earning opportunities and enrollment raise salaries of academics, while the number of Ph.D.s reduces salaries, as does the lagged number of faculty. The only anomalous coefficient is on the effect of alternatives on faculty employment, which is positive rather than negative, as might be ex-

Table 4–11.   Reduced Form Estimates of the Determinants of Salary and Employment of Faculty, 1920–1976.[a]

	Independent Variable	Coefficients on	
		SAL	*FAC*
1.	ENR	0.12 (0.15)	0.54 (0.09)
2.	ALT	0.74 (0.13)	0.05 (0.08)
3.	Ph.D.	−0.12 (0.11)	0.06 (0.07)
4.	FAC (−1)	−0.17 (0.24)	0.39 (0.14)
5.	SAL (−1)	0.40 (0.10)	−0.21 (0.06)
6. Summary statistics			
	R^2	0.974	0.999
	SEE	0.051	0.030
	D.W.	1.06	1.43
7. Long-run elasticities[b]			
	ALT	1.31	−0.29
	Ph.D.	−0.26	0.17
	ENR	−0.12	0.94

[a] Dependent variables are deflated salary of assistant professors and total number of faculty. Independent variables are in $1n$ form. Numbers in parentheses are standard errors; D.W. = Durbin-Watson statistic; years covered exclude 1942–1948.

[b] Calculated by solving equation $\left(\begin{array}{c} SAL \\ FAC \end{array} \right) = (I-A)^{-1} BX$

where A is the matrix of coefficients on SAL (−1) and FAC (−1).

Sources: U.S. National Science Foundation (1968: 10, table 2; 1974: 20, table B-1; 1970: 189–190, table A44; 1975: 110, tables B, B-25); U.S. Bureau of the Census (Various) and U.S. Office of Education (1974–1977).

pected. Because of the interaction between salaries and employment in both equations, however, this does not necessarily translate into anomalous long-run effects, for the long-run impact of the exogenous factors depends on the interrelation between employment and salaries.

Line 7 presents the results of solving the system to obtain the desired long-term impact coefficients: in the full solution, alternative earnings raise salaries and lower employment, as they should, while the number of Ph.D.s has the opposite effect. Here, however, another anomaly arises: while enrollments have a large positive effect on faculty employment, they are estimated to reduce rather than raise salaries, though by a relatively small amount.

While the computations in Tables 4–9 through 4–11 provide general support for the notion that the academic marketplace responds in economically sensible ways to exogenous shocks, they suffer, it

should be stressed, from several weaknesses. First and most importantly, many of the features of the marketplace discussed in part one of the chapter have been deleted from consideration in order to make use of limited available quantitative data. Second, econometric issues (serial correlation of residuals, simultaneity, possible correlation of residuals across equations lines of causality) have not been seriously examined, in part because previous work (Freeman, 1975a) has found the basic results impervious to these issues. Third, alternative models—for instance, a detailed autoregressive moving average procedure—have not been estimated as a means of testing the robustness of the findings. The basic data are too weak to merit such analysis. What they show is an inverse relation between academic employment and salaries and a link between those variables and the side of the system, which is at least roughly consistent with the notion of a flexible market.

NOTES TO CHAPTER 4

1. This chapter represents a substantive revision and updating of Freeman (1975a).

2. It is unclear whether or not the normal entrepreneurial return is to be included as a cost of the for profit firm, making its operation more expensive than that of the no profit enterprises. If entrepreneurial return is only a reward for risk holding, and risks average out in an industry, we would not want to include it. If, on the other hand, the entrepreneurial return is a reward for "founding" an enterprise requiring future "monitoring," the "free" founding of nonprofit institutions by donors and gratis trusteeship reduce the cost of nonprofits. They face a lower price of entrepreneurship in the market as a result of their nonprofit status.

3. Formally, where ϵ_A = elasticity of average; ϵ_M = elasticity of marginal cost curve; and ϵ_π = elasticity of returns to scale, $\epsilon_A = \epsilon_M + \epsilon_\pi$ so when $\epsilon_\pi < 0$ due to the U shape of the cost curve, $\epsilon_A < \epsilon_M$.

4. In many cases, subsidy prices are explicit—for instance, when a state pays institutions in a per student basis.

5. While confounding could be important in comparing institutions at a given time, time series data on, say, governmental funds can be used to infer changes in "subsidy prices" over time.

6. Since only t changes, balancing the budget requires $\alpha_t \dot{t} = \alpha_f \dot{W}$, which leads to the possibility that increases in academic salaries could raise tuition more than the salary increases.

7. These figures were obtained from American Council on Education (1977).

8. Becker and Lewis (1973) consider this effect in great detail.

9. Since there are relatively many lower quality faculty at poorer schools, it might appear that their change in wages would more than counterbalance the

increased supply price of qualified faculty, leading to dispersion of the more able. The number benefiting from high quality colleagues may, however, be quite limited, and the benefits may be greater for others of similar talent, producing the concentration observed in academia

10. The variances for 1964–1970 were calculated from salary data from National Science Foundation (1970): 84, table A-14. The 1975 figures were obtained from National Science Foundation (1977: 63, table B-15). The analysis covered all fields in Table 4-4 except engineering and other social sciences.

11. The developments are described in Metzger (1973: 142–43).

12. See Porter (1965), Stone (1965), and Tinbergen and Bos (1965) for fixed coefficient models.

13. To see the implications of various parameter values we solve the system. First set equation (4–3) equal to equation (4–5).

(A) $$aE - bW - (1-\delta)F_{-1} = \lambda\epsilon W_{-2} + (1-\lambda)NF^S_{-1} \ .$$

Let $F_{-1} = aE_{-1} - bW_{-1}$ and $NF^S_{-1} = NF^d_{-1} = aE_{-1} - bW_{-1} - (1-\delta)F_{-2}$ and substitute to obtain

(B) $$aE - bW - (1-\delta)(aE_{-1} - bW_{-1}) = \lambda\epsilon W_{-2} + (1-\lambda)[aE_{-1} - bW_{-1} - (1-\delta)aE_{-2} + (1-\delta)bW_{-2}] \ .$$

Focusing on the adjustment of dW, we have the following:

(C) $$-bW = -(1-\delta)bW_{-1} + \lambda\epsilon W_{-2} - (1-\lambda)bW_{-1} + (1-\lambda)(1-\delta)bW_{-2} + X$$

where X represents all non-W terms.

This can be rewritten as

(D) $$W = (2 - \lambda - \delta)W_{-1} - \left[\frac{\lambda\epsilon}{b} + (1-\lambda)(1-\delta)\right]W_{-2} + X \ .$$

A reasonable value for the supply adjustment parameter (λ) is $1/2$; a reasonable value for the outflow of faculty (δ) is $1/20$. Since ϵ refers to the supply response of new Ph.D.s and b to total faculty demand, $\epsilon/b \leq 1$ because the ratio of new Ph.D.s to total faculty is perhaps 1 to 20, so that even if the supply of new Ph.D.s were ten times as elastic as demand, ϵ/b would be at most $1/2$. Taking ϵ/b as $1/2$, we obtain

$$W = 1.45W_{-1} - 0.73W_{-2} + X \ ,$$

which yields imaginary roots with dampened oscillations (since the coefficient on W_{-2} is less than 1) and $(1.45)^2 < 4(0.73)$.

14. The data are obtained from American Council on Education (1976: tables 76.102, 76.108, 76.111, 76.114).

15. The ratio of expenditures to GNP in 1960 was 0.013; in 1970 0.25; in 1976 0.29. Data on GNP from U.S. Department of Labor (1977: 283, table

G—3). Data on expenditures from U.S. Office of Education (1977: 181, table 3.08).

16. The census data are from U.S. Bureau of the Census (Annual: Series P—20).

17. Tabulated from National Academy of Sciences (Annual).

18. See Freeman (1975b) for a detailed analysis of the response of physics to the market turnaround.

19. A more appropriate but unavailable deflator would be the price of output of institutions, including subsidy prices.

20. The long-term equilibria are obtained from the partial adjustment model

$$\Delta X = \lambda [X^* - X(-1)]$$

where ΔX is the change in the variable, X^* is the desired equilibrium level, $X(-1)$ is the previous level, and λ is the partial adjustment parameter.

21. National Educational Association (1965) data reveal that in academic years 1963—1964 and 1964—1965, 17 percent of all new academic hires and one-third of those in two-year institutions come from secondary school teaching.

Part III

Academic Labor Productivity and Its Measurement in Higher Education

The chapters in this section of the book are concerned with some of the conceptual problems and issues in the measurement and understanding of faculty productivity. In Chapter 5, attention is given to the problems inherent in understanding both faculty and institutional outcomes. Problems of "jointness" involving teaching, research, and service as interactive functions and outcomes are of special concern. Chapter 6 identifies and recommends four planning and evaluation criteria (quality of outcomes, centrality to mission, program demand, and cost-effectiveness) for allocating departmental and collegiate resources. Chapter 7 focuses on the use of student evaluations as cues for determining faculty rewards. Review is given to the reliability, validity, generalizability, and "skulduggery" of using student evaluations in faculty personnel decisions.

Chapter 5

Conceptual Problems and Issues in Academic Labor Productivity

Wayne R. Kirschling

INTRODUCTION

The central concern of this book is with academic rewards.
This concern is justified in part by a larger concern with individual and organizational productivity and improved decision-making. In their introductory chapter, the editors said that "Knowledge about what motivates faculty to work hard and to become effective teachers and researchers is of critical importance for rational decisionmaking in higher education." It is the purpose of this chapter to introduce various productivity concepts and issues that have relevance both for the study of faculty productivity and for the study of faculty incentive reward systems.

There are a variety of alternatives that might have an impact on faculty productivity. For example, the composition of the faculty might be altered; faculty might be provided with more assistance in the form of additional support personnel or improved instructional and research aids; programs might be designed and implemented whose purpose is to alter the attitudes, preferences, and/or skills of the faculty; and the reward structure that impinges upon faculty might be altered. It is the latter alternative that is explored in this book. To date, there is no conclusive evidence to suggest that this alternative is either superior or inferior to other possible approaches either in general or in specific settings. Neither is there any compelling evidence that explicit rewards are the most appropriate and powerful incentive for promoting faculty productivity. To date, the reward alternative has received relatively less attention than most

other alternatives. Perhaps because of this, it currently seems to offer a real hope of having a positive impact upon faculty productivity. In part, this book is intended to explore the complexities and the realities of this hope.

This chapter is roughly divided into two major sections. The first describes and examines various productivity concepts, while the second section raises a series of faculty productivity issues. It is suggested that these two approaches—concepts and issues—are complementary to each other. The concepts are intended to provide structure. The issues are intended to demonstrate the subtleness and the humanness of faculty productivity. Concepts without issues tend toward sterility. Issues without concepts tend toward anarchy.

CONCEPTS

At the simplest conceptual level, suggestions on how to increase productivity can be reduced to a series of capsule statements. The nonacademic world tends to use terms such as working smarter not harder, think, cost cutting, getting more bang for the buck, putting one's nose to the grindstone and one's shoulder to the wheel, a fair day's pay for a fair day's labor, and building a better mousetrap. The academic world tends to use terms such as effectiveness, cost-benefit analysis, efficiency, more for less, innovation, and accountability. By themselves, these words and phrases are without specific content. One is reluctant to challenge them because one is never quite sure exactly what they mean. Unfortunately, too much of the dialogue about faculty productivity has been carried on at this level.

Fortunately, some more formal approaches have been suggested that incorporate at least some of the concepts implied by the above statements. Several of these are worth noting. Most of these approaches focus either on input-output distinctions or on behavioral considerations. The former will be discussed first.

Input-Output Approaches

One set of distinctions is that between technical, allocative, and social efficiency (Levin, 1971). Technical efficiency is concerned with whether or not the maximum quantity of outputs is being produced for a given quantity of inputs. Alternatively, this concern can be expressed as whether or not a given quantity of outputs is being produced with the least possible quantity of inputs. Allocative or price efficiency is concerned with whether or not the least costly set of inputs is being used among all the sets of inputs that could be used to produce the same set of outputs. Social or preference efficiency is

concerned with whether the most valuable set of outputs is being produced from the perspective of students, fundors, society, and so forth. To summarize, technical efficiency is concerned with the relationship between inputs and outputs; allocative efficiency is concerned with minimizing the costs of inputs; and social efficiency is concerned with producing the most valuable outputs.

Each of these types of efficiency can be related to higher education productivity. For example, one aspect of social efficiency is the concern with whether or not faculty are providing the goods and services that are expected of them by students, fundors, the institution, and society. A community college professor who produces research reports but no credit hours would fail the test of social efficiency. In general, if higher education is not socially efficient, it will be of little consolation to discover that it is allocatively and technically efficient. Allocative efficiency is the concern with whether or not costs are being kept to an appropriate minimum. For example, are faculty salaries too high; faculty workloads too low; overly expensive research tools and facilities being purchased; or some students being provided with too much financial assistance? Technical efficiency is the concern with whether or not instructional, research, and public service outcomes are being produced with as few inputs (i.e., faculty, facilities, administrators, books, etc.) as possible.

In building reward structures to enhance productivity, it will be necessary to be more specific about what aspect of productivity is to be affected. Reward structures that encourage social efficiency may be substantially different from reward structures that encourage technical or allocative efficiency. For example, if the focus was social efficiency, the reward system might stress activities that were explicitly linked to formalized needs assessment. If the focus was allocative efficiency, then the reward system might stress activities that promote cost consciousness and cost savings. The ideal reward structure would strongly promote all three types of efficiency. Such a reward structure is not yet known to exist.

The above approach does not exhaust all the input-output-related possibilities. For example, another approach would be to focus on the congruence between plans, inputs, and outputs. While this approach is a close relative of the above approach, it suggests some new concerns and permits some additional insights. In this approach, there are three basic relationships: efficiency—are outputs produced with the least input?; effectiveness—do actual outputs match up with plans?; and effort—are resources (inputs) being devoted to the right areas (i.e., those specified in the plan)? These relationships are shown in more detail in Figure 5–1. Figure 5–1 distinguishes ends

Figure 5—1.   An Effort, Efficiency, and Effectiveness Model of Productivity.

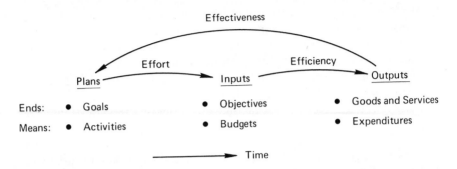

from means. Plans, inputs, and outputs are each disaggregated into more time-specific estimates of means and ends. This finer disaggregation introduces several new considerations.

The first consideration involves the comparison of ends (goals, objectives, and goods and services) and means (planned activities, budgets, and expenditures) across time. If there is to be congruence among ends across time and of means across time, then it is likely that there will need to be considerable control exercised. This concern with congruence across time can be referred to as control productivity. Control productivity is an increasingly important concern in higher education. For some groups, such as state budget officers, productivity, in part, will be judged by the degree to which prior commitments as regards means are carried out—for example, do expenditures match up perfectly with budgets?

A second consideration involves the comparisons of means to ends. For example, would an analysis of plans show that goals are being pursued through the best set of activities? Are specific objectives being pursued with the least cost budget? Are budgets producing adequate (quantitatively and qualitatively) goods and services? This concern with the relationship between means and ends is a concern about transformation productivity—are desired ends being translated into the right means and are means producing adequate ends?

Figure 5—1 suggests some important considerations for the design of faculty reward systems. First, how much emphasis is to be placed on control productivity as compared to transformation productivity? How much emphasis is to be placed on ends as contrasted with means? This latter question is an important one because ends and means are often controlled by different individuals. For example, the academic side of the house controls ends, but the fiscal side of the

house controls means. Often it is only at the presidential level that both of these concerns come together.

Behavioral Approaches

There has been considerable concern expressed about the applicability of input-output approaches to higher education. The basic concern is that these approaches seem to imply the existence of a production line type of environment where individual behavior is determined once management has made their decisions. This environment is not characteristic of most higher education institutions, where both faculty and students are encouraged to exercise a substantial degree of judgment and are given considerable freedom of choice. Kirschling and Staaf (1975: 88) note with regard to their behavioral model of productivity that, "Our focus has been on student and faculty behavior rather than on describing a production-line situation which mechanistically yields degrees, student credit hours, or jobs." Brenneman (1970: 2) notes that:

> None of the [input-output] models introduces behavioral assumptions regarding the objectives of university members. To leave out the human element from analysis of a complex institution like a university is to ignore the potential of the rich body of organizational theory literature that has been developed in the last twenty-five years.

One way of describing behavioral approaches would be to cite a specific example. This is the approach that will be employed here. An early and classic work in this area is Brenneman's (1970) investigation of Ph.D. production at the University of California, Berkeley. In this study, efficiency was defined as "the ratio of [doctoral] degree output to the input of doctoral student time" (p. 5). The purpose of this study was to show how a theory of faculty motivation could be used to explain the rather large differences in Ph.D. efficiency that existed among the various departments at Berkeley. Brenneman summarized his analysis of faculty member and department behavior as follows:

(1) The faculty member is assumed to be rationally attempting to maximize his own prestige, and this behavior on the part of all members of a department is consistent with maximization of departmental prestige.

(2) Departmental prestige is a function of resources and the quality of placement of its Ph.D. students within the prestige system. Individuals who accept industrial or governmental jobs are outside the aca-

demic prestige system, and this type of placement was viewed as neutral, or in some cases, positively prestigious.

(3) Considerations of the quality of placement forces the analysis to include the nature of demand for new Ph.D.'s in each field as a determinant of the prestige maximizing level of doctoral output.

(4) The department was shown to have control over the factors assumed to affect the rate and timing of attrition. These included admissions policy, curriculum design, information, and organization of resources for financial support. (p. 47)

This analysis led Brenneman to develop a theory that Ph.D. attrition rates would be varied by departments in such a way as to maximize the overall prestige of the department. As an example of what a department might do to accomplish this end, Brenneman cited the following examples as applied to "a humanities department desiring a high attrition rate [because of a low demand for new Ph.D.s], but not wanting this to occur within the early years of the student's graduate career [because these students are needed to teach undergraduate courses and generate a need for graduate courses to be taught by faculty]":

(1) Critical hurdles designed to eliminate candidates in the late rather than in the early stages of the program.

(2) A curriculum sufficiently ambiguous and fuzzy to keep students mildly confused about their rate of progress toward the degree.

(3) Conscious minimization of the student's feelings that he is a member of a particular graduate class or cohort. A student should have a minimum of check-points by which to measure his progress.

(4) Feedback from the department designed to keep the student's estimate of success . . . high.

(5) Extremely demanding requirements for the dissertation, this being the final hurdle for the degree.

(6) Use of the same individuals as teaching assistants for several years.

(7) Absence of discussion or information related to the job market for Ph.D.s.

(8) A general lack of information about the historical success rates of graduate students, attrition patterns, and so forth. The best policy for the department would be to minimize information flows to the students.

(9) A tendency for the department not to keep detailed records on the experiences of past graduate students.

(10) Little evidence of major curriculum revisions. (pp. 68, 69)

Quite clearly, Brenneman's behavioral approach has a different cast about it than the typical input-output approach. It attempts to explain not only what is happening, but also why, in motivational terms. In terms of rewards, behavioral approaches such as Brenneman's tend to lead to conclusions such as that individual motivations need to be altered (for example, by getting individuals with different or expended motivations) or that new and strong rewards need to be developed to encourage behavior that is less compatible with existing motivations.

OBSERVATIONS

So what then can be said of formal productivity approaches, whether input-output or behavioral in nature, and their import for the design of reward systems? First, there is not yet widespread agreement on the various components of productivity and the respective importance of each. What is known is that different individuals and groups are apt to focus, often very intensely, on different aspects of productivity. Formal approaches to productivity may be one valuable way of evolving agreement on these components.

Second, there is more than academic interest in the productivity of higher education. There is a desire not only to study and understand it, but also to be able to manipulate it. Different approaches to productivity will suggest and invite different forms of intervention into the current milieu. Simple approaches will tend to encourage simplistic interventions. Complex approaches will tend to encourage cautious interventions; but they may also create the danger of overconfidence because they can easily create a false sense of understanding.

Third, it is unlikely that any one approach will perfectly fit the needs and circumstances of a particular higher education setting. What these more general approaches can do is provide a rough and valuable template to be applied to a specific case. That a revised and individualized template needs to be developed should neither diminish the value of the original template or of such templates in general. As has already been mentioned, without such templates, one's view of productivity is apt to be unfocused and confusing.

Finally, efforts to develop and implement improved reward systems explicitly or implicitly are based upon a specific view of or approach to productivity. Alterations in reward systems are much more likely to succeed if they are based on a well-conceived and explicit approach.

ISSUES

Of course, there is no dearth of issues in the area of faculty productivity. Five issues, or more accurately classes of issues, have been selected for discussion. These issues are neither comprehensive nor independent of each other. These five issues, however, are some of the most interesting and important in the area of faculty productivity. The five issues to be discussed are: (1) faculty responsibility: for what or to whom?; (2) faculty and student productivity: competing or complementary interests?; (3) flexibility and opportunity: precious commodities; (4) productivity: the hidden and not so hidden costs, and (5) jointness: a curse or a blessing?

Faculty Responsibility: For What Or To Whom?

To some observers, higher education is a relatively simple matter. Faculty teach and do research, and students study and learn. Some faculty and students do these things easily and well, and others do them only with great difficulty and often poorly. For these observers there is little mystery in the question of what faculty are responsible for. They are responsible for relatively straightforward matters, such as: (1) preparing adequately for classes, (2) meeting all scheduled classes, (3) being available to students during scheduled office hours, (4) awarding high grades to those students who learn a great deal and failing grades to those who do not learn enough, and (5) publishing articles and presenting papers.

To other observers, higher education is a relatively complex matter. It takes place in over 3,000 institutions whose characteristics, such as mission, governance arrangements, endowment, reputation, and program offerings, vary from being unique to being commonplace. It spans more than 600 recognized disciplines, in which instruction may vary from being remedial to being esoteric. It requires inputs from a larger number of individuals (e.g., students, faculty, trustees, fundors, administrators) with diverse interests. It engages in activities that contribute to academic, social, and economic results that affect both participants and nonparticipants.

Furthermore, it must be admitted that higher education takes place in a region about which little is known, in spite of years of diligent exploration—the human brain. Higher education is a most fragile undertaking. Like a mission to the moon, it can fail when one of the parts or parties fail to perform as expected—for example, a textbook or a professor that does not conform to the learning style of a particular student, a classroom that turns out not to be big

enough to let one or more student(s) enroll in a course that would have sparked a lifelong interest, a student aid grant that cannot be renewed because the definition of "independent student" has been revised by someone in Washington.

For these observers, there is much mystery in the question of what faculty are responsible for. They know that faculty must teach, but they wonder whether they can be responsible for learning. They know that faculty should be sensitive to student concerns about employment prospects, but they wonder what faculty can do about the state of the economy, which, more than anything faculty can do, affects the job market for recent graduates. They know that faculty need to stay abreast of and, if possible, contribute to developments in their field, but they wonder whether it is a good idea to judge every, or even very many, faculty members on how many articles and papers they have contributed to the publishing flood.

For those observers who see higher education in clear relief, it is a relatively easy matter to convert responsibility to productivity. Faculty need to teach more classes and more students, increase their availability by both meeting all scheduled classes and increasing their office hours, preserve the integrity of the grading system by maintaining an appropriate mix of grades, and increase the number of articles and papers that bear their name.

It is more difficult for those observers who see higher education in more complex and subtle relief to establish a relatively clear-cut sense of faculty responsibility. These observers would agree that faculty should act in a responsible manner (e.g., they should fulfill their duties and commitments). To go beyond this requires much more information about the particular people, institution, and discipline involved. For them, responsible action and hence productivity depend upon the situation, and hence few, if any, a priori generalizations are helpful. For them, it would not always be productive to encourage or insist on faculty member's maintaining a given mixture of grades or publish another article.

If there is a reasonable difference of opinion concerning *for what* faculty are responsible, one possible alternative might be to establish *to whom* they are responsible. Then, it would be possible to insist that faculty be responsive to the expectations of these individuals. Productivity could then be reduced to one or more measure(s) of how satisfied these individuals were with what faculty had done for them.

There is no shortage of potential "bosses." Some obvious possibilities are students, administrators, trustees, and legislatures. Some more subtle possibilities are unions, the various fundors of instruc-

tions and research, and the various brokers within the discipline—for example, those in power in professional associations, editorial boards of professional publications, "old boy" networks, tenure review committees, and the like.

In some settings, such as major research universities, it is desirable that in some aggregate sense faculty be responsive to each of these groups. In this instance, to make one group "the boss" would radically change the texture and spirit of these institutions. What distinguishes faculty from these institutions is that they are responsive to multiple constituencies. In other settings, such as community colleges, it is possible to radically reduce the number of potential "bosses." Faculty in these institutions may well be able to be responsible, as well as responsive, to another group without undue conflict among their various roles.

It also needs to be noted that faculty traditionally have not accepted the classical role of an employee. While they might be employed by an institution, they consider themselves to be faculty members and not employees. While the concept of a faculty member includes those concepts associated with being a professional, it goes beyond that. Furniss (1977: 24) points out that:

> A long time ago, the American Association of University Professors defined the college or university teacher as "a citizen, a member of a learned profession, and an officer of an educational institution." . . . The term "officer" designates persons with the authority, the responsibility, and the necessary autonomy to act for the benefit of others in situations requiring special knowledge and training.

Thus, in a very real sense, faculty consider themselves as management and not as employees. Hence, among other things, they would argue that they have an important say in how tradeoffs will be made among the various demands placed upon them and among the opportunities confronting both the institution as a whole and the faculty member as an individual.

So what, if any, general observations can be made about for what and to whom faculty are responsible? First, faculty have a serious responsibility. The creation, transmission, and preservation of knowledge is an important and almost sacred responsibility in most societies. The intellectual development of adults is a wondrous undertaking that has many ramifications for both society and the individual. The extent to which faculty are conscious of and respond to this serious responsibility undoubtedly has a major impact on their productivity.

Second, no comprehensive, standard, unvarying set of responsibilities can be developed that would apply to all faculty, across all situations and institutions. Ultimately, faculty responsibility is more a matter of spirit than of the law.

Third, an effort should be made to establish, in unambiguous terms, the tangible, formal, individualized workload of each faculty member. On an individual faculty member basis, it probably is useful to project the amount of time that will be devoted to each of the various elements of this workload. This should be done in some detail. For example, Mortimer and Lozier (1974: 56) identified twenty-one workload elements in the ninety-two union contracts that they analyzed:

> teaching load . . . office hours . . . length of day, week, or year . . . overload . . . class size . . . number of course preparations . . . calendar . . . advising load . . . required attendance . . . registration duties . . . committee work . . . supervision of student activities . . . professional activities . . . outside employment . . . number of assigned courses . . . organizational work . . . faculty/student ratio . . . research . . . consultative work . . . orientation . . . administrative duty . . .

While the detail of this list may be excessive in some situations, in other situations it could help establish shared expectations and restore confidence in faculty commitment.

Fourth, once formal workloads have been established, faculty should act in a responsible manner by meeting all of their duties and commitments. This is a minimum standard of productivity.

Fifth, faculty should be sensitive and, where possible and appropriate, responsive to the needs and concerns of the various other groups who, along with faculty, make higher education possible. This includes students, fundors, professional groups, administrators, trustees, and if applicable, unions. Thoughtful sensitivity and responsiveness to multiple constituencies is an important step beyond the minimum productivity standard described above.

Sixth, faculty members need to be conscious of the distinct possibility that there may exist incentives that are not coincident with either their formal responsibilities or the formal reward system. For example, a faculty member might realize that promotion, tenure, sabbatical, or compensation decisions are heavily influenced by their performance in only one or two of their responsibilities. In light of this situation, it will take a strong faculty member to be equally conscientious about each element of the workload. Discrepancies among formal workloads, incentive systems, and reward systems, of course, necessarily have a negative impact on a faculty member's productiv-

ity. Such adverse conditions can only be avoided by a careful consideration of the desired relationships among these factors.

In the final analysis, faculty members must be responsible both to their institution and to themselves. Responsibility to the institution can be acquitted by actions such as meeting all the duties and responsibilities contained in or implied by a formal workload; being sensitive and sympathetic to other groups participating in or affected by higher education; and working with other groups to make higher education, individually as well as in the aggregate, more effective and efficient. Responsibility to themselves can be acquitted by actions such as being sensitive to the existence of a trust relationship emanating from students, other faculty, the institution, and society; and, when necessary, placing workload commitments above contrary incentives.

Faculty and Student Productivity: Competing or Complementary Interests?

Faculty productivity cannot be understood without reference to the special relationship that exists between faculty and students. This relationship is special because it is unlike any other in our society where productivity is a major issue. For example, it is not comparable to vertical relationships, such as those that exist between managers and employees or between commanders and soldiers. Nor is it comparable to more horizontal relationships, such as those existing between fellow workers on an assembly line or teammates on a football team.

At first glance, the relationship between faculty and students seems to be straightforward. Their roles are complementary—faculty teach and students learn. This is true as far as it goes. But to understand faculty productivity, it is necessary to go beyond this simple model and to consider some other possibilities.

To use the language of the economist, at the margin, everything is a tradeoff. Said another way, each day faculty members have to decide how much of their efforts will go into activities that will directly interest or benefit them and how much will go into activities that will do the same for students. Thus, for example, a faculty member has to decide between spending the morning going over lecture notes from last year for the next class or working on an article which will eventually be submitted to a journal. The existence of tradeoffs such as these will come as a surprise to no one. But there is more to these tradeoffs than is generally recognized. At least four aspects of these tradeoffs deserve closer scrutiny.

The first aspect to be noted is that student ability and effort can substitute for faculty ability and effort. Kirschling and Staaf (1975: 80) point out that:

> An interdependent relationship underlies a professor's ability to obtain achievement from students. Student achievement not only depends on the professor's ability and effort but also on the ability and behavior of his students. If students exert no effort, there will be no learning. If student abilities are high and we assume a fixed level of student effort, the price of student achievement to the professor is low. Therefore . . . it is quite rational that professors tend to prefer bright . . . and willing . . . students. This . . . also helps to illustrate why many professors may prefer advanced courses to introductory courses. Assuming students in advanced courses have been screened for high aptitudes, whereas introductory courses have no screening, the price of student achievement is lower to the professor in the advanced course.

This interdependent relationship between faculty and student effort and ability suggests some interesting productivity and reward dilemmas. As examples, a professor in a school that admits high ability, high effort students may be able to spend more time promoting his or her own consulting or research interests with no loss in student achievement; a faculty member's time might result in more student learning if it were spent on setting up a very strong reward and penalty system to encourage student effort than if it were spent on teaching; if a faculty member were to increase his or her ability to teach, he or she could devote less time to teaching with no loss in student achievement; a high ability professor may be able to teach three or four classes of high ability, high effort students with the same effort as it would take another, less able teacher to teach one class of low ability or low effort students. Faculty productivity, then, is closely tied to student productivity. If student productivity goes up, then faculty ability and effort can and probably should be directed elsewhere. Hence, what may appear to be radical differences in productivity between two faculty members may be traceable to characteristics of the student body. Whether it is equitable to reward the "more productive" faculty member without taking this into account is, at best, questionable.

A second point can be made about the earlier example of choosing between spending time going over lecture notes or working on a journal article. This point relates to cross-sectional versus longitudinal analysis. At first glance, the tradeoff between lecture notes and the journal article seems to be between instruction and research. This

turns out to be true only if comparisons are made at the time that a decision is made. If longitudinal effects are considered, the tradeoff may well be one of instruction with instruction. As examples, journal articles eventually provide instruction to both graduate students and faculty—hence, the tradeoff may be between undergraduate versus advanced instruction; a journal article may well involve one or more doctoral students—hence, the tradeoff may well be between providing better instruction today or preparing more instructors for the future.

The general point to be made is that the immediate purpose of an activity needs to be distinguished from its long range purpose. How much emphasis a faculty member or an institution places on instruction may well depend as much on their discount rate (their preference for immediate rather than future results) and their degree of catholicity (their preference for widespread rather than local results) as it does on any preference for research versus instruction. An individual or institution with a high, positive discount rate will tend to prefer activities that will result in more and/or better instruction being provided in the future. An individual or institution with a high, positive discount rate will tend to prefer activities that provide direct instruction to students today. An individual or institution with a negative discount rate will tend to prefer activities that will result in more and/or better instruction being provided in the future. An individual or institution with a high degree of catholicity will be more willing to engage in activities that will benefit students in other institutions, while low catholicity would lead to a sharp focus on one's own students.

An interesting aspect of this tradeoff is that the overall system of higher education will work best if all institutions and faculty do not end up making the same decision. It is most desirable that some individuals and institutions focus on the here and now, while others attempt to ensure a better future; it is most desirable that some individuals and institutions have a catholic attitude, while others remain more parochial. In this way, the overall productivity of the system is enhanced. In line with this, it is easy to see why different individuals and institutions can and should have different reward systems even if they are ultimately concerned with the same end.

In some situations, the lecture notes–journal article tradeoff may not be a tradeoff at all. That is, in certain cases, the journal article choice may correspond, even in a "today" sense, to more and better instruction. The issue here is the relationship between student and faculty development. Bailey (1975: 3) captures the dangers inherent

in trading off faculty development for student development. He asks, "How can people who have stopped growing themselves possibly help others grow or help new ideas be born?" Fortunately, faculty are more than teaching machines. They also serve as role models for students. If faculty do not exhibit a lifelong zest for learning, how is this taste to be developed in students? And if it is not developed, how can the benefits of higher education last a lifetime when much of the limited knowledge acquired in college will soon be obsolete or discarded as irrelevant?

It is impossible to understand some important aspects of student-faculty relationships without reference to what Boulding (1973) calls grants. Grants, defined as one way transfers of economic goods, are prevalent in faculty-student relationships. Faculty give students both knowledge and time, which have economic value. Yet because of the incentive system that exists for most faculty, knowledge transfers and time expenditures, beyond some minimum level, are unrewarded. Hence, they become grants. Boulding points out that "The willingness to make grants, indeed, depends on two factors: one, the perception of the efficiency of the grant; and the other, the degree of identification with the welfare of the recipient. That is, the degree of benevolence toward him" (p. 12). Boulding's point is an important one. It suggests many things about faculty effort and hence faculty productivity. As examples, faculty who know, understand, and identify with the needs of students are more likely to make a larger effort to make knowledge and time grants to students; or faculty may identify with students and yet not make a grant to them because they feel that their grant would not have much impact on the student (e.g., the student is not able or is unwilling to make use of the grant).

In summary, then, what can be said of the subtleties of student-faculty relationships and how these subtleties tie into faculty productivity? First, faculty need to allocate their abilities and efforts so that they compensate for, rather than duplicate, student abilities and efforts. To the extent that students take their responsibilities as students seriously, faculty will be free to contribute to higher education in other ways. Second, the instructional impacts of research need to be considered when the tradeoffs between teaching and research are considered. Third, faculty development plays an important, albeit often invisible, role in student development. Because of this lack of visibility, it is all too easy to make a smaller than optimum investment in faculty development, especially for those institutions whose mission emphasizes undergraduate instruction. Fourth, faculty-student relationships cannot be understood without reference to

faculty benevolence towards students, faculty perceptions of their effectiveness in different kinds of activities, and faculty perceptions of how their efforts will be received and used by students.

Flexibility and Opportunity: Precious Commodities

As has already been suggested, productivity depends upon the ability to adjust one's actions to the people and the circumstances involved. If an individual or institution is constrained to few, if any, options, their productivity is likely to steadily decrease over time as the underlying situation changes. Hence, flexibility is a prerequisite for individual and institutional productivity.

Many, if not most, institutions would agree that their flexibility as regards faculty has steadily declined. Some indications of this are: (1) steadily increasing tenure ratios, (2) reduced rates of faculty turnover, (3) increasingly stringent affirmative action requirements, (4) ever more microinterests and specializations on the part of many faculty, (5) escalation of the level at which decisions can be made about changes in the curriculum, (6) movement toward more standardized incentive systems, and (7) where applicable, workload specifications being built into union contracts.

Many of the factors contributing to reduced institutional flexibility also affect individual faculty flexibility—for example, reduced faculty turnover and less control over curriculum. In addition, there are often factors that impinge more directly on faculty opportunities. As examples, the surplus of individuals trained at the doctorate level has tended to reduce both academic and nonacademic opportunities for faculty; and the growth of the community college sector and the decline of the private college sector have affected the kind of institutions to which a junior faculty member might aspire.

These developments in flexibility and opportunity raise serious questions about the potential for improving faculty productivity. In fact, a more realistic concern in many situations may well be whether or not faculty productivity can be maintained at its current levels. It is important to note that there is general agreement across many studies that the average faculty member works very hard. Yuker (1974: 2), in his study of faculty workloads, found that:

> Convergencies in the data from many studies lead to the conclusion that faculty members claim that they work an average of 55 hours per week if a broad definition of workload is used. There are, however, large individual differences as well as differences among disciplines, ranks, and institutions. While these findings of a long work week are sometimes greeted with skepticism . . . convergencies in the data are impressive.

It is important to ask how much of this long work week has been due to the faculty perception that there was ample opportunity for them "to get ahead" if they "worked hard and played their cards right." If faculty opportunities in higher education began to decrease for reasons such as those cited above or because the size of the overall system declines, is it reasonable to expect that the level of faculty effort will remain as high as it is now? If good teaching and publications cannot result in tenure or a position at a "better" institution, is it reasonable to expect that faculty will still work as hard as they have in the past? If the faculty at a given institution undergoes the shock of two or three "cutbacks" in faculty over the next five to ten years, is it reasonable to expect that they will put as much into their work as they did before?

Another concern related to flexibility and opportunity is the level at which efforts to affect productivity will be made in the coming years. Several realistic scenarios can be suggested: an institution decides that it must drop one or more programs for which there is low student demand so that they can expand and improve several other programs for which there is strong student demand; a state level coordinating agency decides that because of declining enrollments, it is better to close one of the institutions completely than to have all of the institutions struggle with cutbacks. In both of these cases, the productivity of individual faculty members will have little to do with whether they are affected or not. Decisions will be made at a much higher level and depend much more on factors out of the control of the faculty—for example, the job market for graduates and politics, both internal and external. As situations such as these begin to take place, where adjustments are made in gulps rather than in nibbles, is it likely that efforts to improve faculty productivity will gain much support or attention from the faculty?

A third concern related to flexibility and opportunity is its impact on how faculty distribute their efforts across activities that promote personal opportunity for them as individuals and those that do not. More than ever, both aggressive and insecure faculty will seek personal accomplishments that are visible and portable to other settings. For example, publications, good teaching awards, positions of responsibility in professional associations, and research awards tend to be much more visible and portable than do activities such as counseling, committee work, student orientation, and supervision of student activities. If faculty have had incentives to sacrifice student and/or collective accomplishment for the sake of personal accomplishment in the past, isn't there a distinct possibility that these incentives will escalate rather than disappear as opportunities become few and far

between? Won't more faculty than ever before have a rational basis for justifying self-centered rather than other-centered activities?

To summarize—the likely impact on productivity of reduced flexibility and opportunity seems dismal at best. If flexibility and opportunity are important ingredients in promoting productivity, then, in a practical rather than a theoretical sense, faculty productivity may have already reached its zenith. If productivity is going to be addressed in a major way in the course of the next decade, it is quite likely to be in macro rather than micro terms. It is likely that the dominant, operative concern will be with the productivity of whole departments and institutions rather than of particular individuals. Finally, there is a distinct possibility that faculty will have increased personal incentives to promote personal opportunity rather than collective productivity over the next decade. Efforts to encourage them to concentrate on activities that contribute to collective productivity, but not to personal opportunity, may well require the creation of much stronger rewards and/or penalties than are generally in use now.

Productivity: Hidden and Not So Hidden Costs

It is intuitively appealing to think that increases in quantitative productivity are always for the good. Upon closer inspection, this turns out in some cases to be a debatable issue.

Suppose, for the sake of illustration, that a decision was being contemplated that would increase both class sizes and faculty teaching loads. One possible rationale for this might be that such an action would allow tuitions to be lower so that enrollments could be maintained or increased. Another possible rationale might be that this increased "productivity" was necessary to "entice" the state legislature to go along with faculty salary increases. Several points need to be made about this so-called "productivity improvement." First, it needs to take into account the other faculty activities that would have to be foregone to make this possible. Some of these activities might be little valued by some individuals—for example, participation in professional associations. But there are often activities that are just as likely to be decreased (e.g., student counseling, involvement in student activities) and that are highly valued by many people. Furthermore, this approach assumes that students will not notice the reduced quality of instructional services (e.g., larger class sizes) but instead will focus only on tuition. While this may work in the short run, the reduction in overall quality of instruction (counseling, classroom contact) may actually cause a drop rather than an increase in enrollments in spite of a decline in tuition. This is a matter of the

relative sensitivity of students to tuition as compared to instructional services. If students are more sensitive to instructional services, enrollments will drop. If it is the other way around and students are more sensitive to tuition, enrollments will increase.

Another factor to be considered is the matter of jobs. Assuming all other factors to be equal—for example, no increases in enrollments or demand for research—real increases in productivity will reduce the number of faculty jobs available. As jobs become an issue, there is every reason to expect that faculty, like other groups, will suggest that real productivity be allowed to decrease so that jobs can be preserved. Accompanying such proposals will be the usual claim that productivity is not being reduced, but that quality is being increased. In fact, the tighter the job market for faculty, the more apparent the tradeoff between productivity and jobs will become. Hard choices have to be made between them. While quality may be expected to increase if jobs are emphasized, it is unlikely that quality increases will be proportional to the number of jobs that are preserved.

Another potential tradeoff related to productivity involves equity. Several important issues can be cited in this general area. First, there is the matter of the advantage created by being productive. Those faculty that have been productive by current standards have also been the faculty who have received the most advantages—namely, higher salaries, lower teaching loads, more travel money, easier access to the "old boy" network, more ready acceptance of their research. But these advantages often have created wide status and monetary differences between faculty within the same department and between departments in the same institution. These differences are not always well received, particularly when the reward structure is perceived as being "too generous" or as rewarding the wrong activities. These perceived inequities are not without their impact on the productivity of the "disadvantaged" faculty.

Another equity issue centers on current efforts to increase the number of women and minority faculty members. On one hand, there is the fear that productivity will be lowered because the best-qualified people will not be hired. On the other hand, there is the hope that productivity will increase because the best-qualified person can be selected from a larger pool of candidates. In either case, there is the additional concern that equity for previously excluded groups may have a higher priority than productivity. In this latter case, unavailable reductions in productivity might well be an acceptable cost to pay for making higher education more equitable.

Finally, there is a not insignificant informational cost to improving productivity. It is difficult to judge or improve productivity without

access to a considerable amount of both descriptive and causal information. In most instances, very little of the necessary information needed to make an accurate judgment or decision is currently available. To assemble this information would cost both time and money. Whether these costs would be offset by the impacts of better judgments or improved productivity remains to be seen. It is only fair to point out, however, that we shall never know with more certainty whether it is or not until a fair number of institutions actually set about collecting and using the needed information.

To summarize—while productivity is concerned with costs, efforts to improve productivity may in some instances actually increase costs. This refers to actual monetary costs, as well as to (1) reduced levels of effectiveness, (2) reductions in jobs, (3) increased alienation because of status and monetary gaps among faculty, (4) lack of progress in providing access to faculty positions for previously excluded groups, and (5) increased data collection and analysis costs.

Jointness: A Curse Or A Blessing?

Bird (1975: 102) concludes that college is "the dumbest investment you can make." Bowen (1977: 447) concludes that, "the sum of the benefits exceeds the total cost by a factor of three or more." Many more such sharply divergent "bottom line" opinions could be cited. To what can these differences be attributed? The single most important factor is the complexity of higher education productivity. It is, to put it mildly, a nightmare for analysts. It is an enterprise whose full individual and social costs have never been measured. It is an enterprise for which new outcomes are constantly being discovered. It is no understatement to say that it is an enterprise that would cost more to measure than to do.

From an analyst's viewpoint, one of the most frustrated aspects of higher education is its jointness. The strict definition of jointness is that as a practical matter, two or more of something cannot be separated. An often-cited example in introductory economic texts is the case of sheep. Raising a sheep produces both mutton and wool. It is impossible, other than on quite arbitrary grounds, to allocate the costs of raising the sheep between the mutton and the wool. A comparable example in higher education is doctoral students. It is possible to roughly estimate the costs of educating a doctoral student, but how are these costs to be allocated among the various outcomes, direct and indirect: undergraduate instruction provided by the graduate student, contributions made to the research of faculty, informal instruction provided to other graduate students, the contribution to the discipline as represented by the dissertation, and so forth.

In theory, there is a need to distinguish between multiple outcomes and joint outcomes. While joint outcomes cannot be disengaged, multiple outcomes can. For example, a large conglomerate produces an array of goods and services, but it is usually possible to analyze the basis of their production on a case-by-case basis. Theoretically, the same should be true for much of higher education. Undergraduate outcomes should be separable from research and public service outcomes. One department's outcomes should be separable from the outcomes of other departments. In practice, such separation is more or less an impossibility. In higher education, most multiple outcome situations are for all practical purposes joint outcome situations. This means that production analysis requires comparing a set of inputs to a set of outputs. The elimination of a particular type of cost will not only affect many outcomes but may also affect other costs. To use the earlier example of a graduate student—if a graduate program were dropped, not only would the above-mentioned instructional and research outcomes be affected, but other costs might increase even more than the savings. For example, the costs of carrying out undergraduate instruction and research might rise sharply as it becomes necessary to substitute faculty for graduate students.

Not only are there multiple inputs and outputs to higher education, there are also multiple and perhaps even joint beneficiaries. For example, how is the impact on the student who is dropped because of failing grades to be separated from the impact on the student's spouse or parents? Is this impact to be counted once for each affected party and then summed, or is only the impact on the student to be counted? The fact that there are multiple outcomes accruing to multiple beneficiaries introduces another difficulty. Each of these beneficiaries is apt to put a different value on each outcome. For example, the student who is helped by a faculty member in getting through one of those many nonacademic crises is apt to put a high value on this faculty member's activity. But what about the student who thereby got "short changed" in terms of the faculty member's attention to the student's difficulty with a recent assignment?

If higher education has a reasonably small number of standard outcomes (the case of inputs or beneficiaries could be used just as easily), the jointness phenomena would not be as staggering as it is. Unfortunately, the outcomes of higher education are controversial, elusive, and legion. Lenning (1977), in a recent review of the literature, compiled a list of over eighty previous attempts to structure educational outcomes and outcome-related concepts. One recent ex-

ample of this is the work by Bowen (1977). He employed the following outcome structure (1977: 55–59).

I. GOALS FOR STUDENTS

A. Cognitive Learning

   (1) Verbal Skills
   (2) Quantitative Skills
   (3) Substantive Knowledge
   (4) Rationality
   (5) Intellectual Tolerance
   (6) Esthetic Sensibility
   (7) Creativeness
   (8) Intellectual Integrity
   (9) Wisdom
 (10) Lifelong Learning

B. Emotional and Moral Development

   (1) Personal Self-Discovery
   (2) Psychological Well-Being
   (3) Human Understanding
   (4) Value and Morals
   (5) Religious Interest

C. Practical Competence

   (1) Traits of Value in Practical Affairs Generally
   (2) Citizenship
   (3) Economic Productivity
   (4) Sound Family Life
   (5) Consumer Efficiency
   (6) Fruitful Leisure
   (7) Health

D. Direct Satisfactions and Enjoyments From College Education

   (1) During the College Years
   (2) In Later Life

E. Avoidance of Negative Outcomes for Individual Students

II. GOALS FOR SOCIETY

A. Advancement of Knowledge

   (1) Preservation and Dissemination of the Cultural Heritage
   (2) Discovery and Dissemination of New Knowledge and Advancement
   (3) Direct Satisfactions and Enjoyment Received by the Population from Living in a World of Advancing Knowledge, Technology, Ideas, and Arts

B. Discovery and Encouragement of Talent

C. Advancement of Social Welfare

   (1) Economic Efficiency and Growth
   (2) Enhancement of National Prestige and Power
   (3) Progress Toward the Identification and Solution of Social Problems
   (4) "Improvement" in the Motives, Values, Aspirations, Attitudes, and Behavior of Members of the General Population

D. Avoidance of Negative Outcomes for Society

Bowen's taxonomy stands as ample testimony to the perceived breadth of outcomes that can be affected by higher education. Because of the complex interrelationships among these outcomes, this

taxonomy cannot be treated like a menu. Higher education productivity is not a case of constructing a meal of one appetizer, one entre, one dessert, and one after dinner drink. In some cases, spinach will be part of the meal no matter what entry is ordered, and it may not be possible to have apple pie as dessert without also having apple cider to drink and applesauce as a side dish.

To summarize—higher education production is characterized as having multiple inputs, outputs, and beneficiaries. In many cases, these multiple relationships are inseparable joint relationships. The study of higher education is thus a fascinating undertaking. The changing of higher education, including its reward structures, is a complex and often perilous undertaking. The intended changes can easily be overwhelmed by unforeseen and unintended changes.

This is not to say that the degree of jointness in higher education is a problem except to those who want to approach it in a hurried fashion and on simple terms. In a very real sense, the multiplicity and jointness of higher education is one of its strengths. For a single investment, a rich array of outcomes that benefit a wide range of people over their lifetimes can be produced. These benefits extend not only to the direct participants but to individuals who are unaware of the origins of the benefits that have come their way.

CLOSING THOUGHTS

Productivity is apt to become a more, rather than a less, frequently discussed issue in higher education. While much of the discussion around this issue to date has centered on how to improve productivity, much of the discussion in the future will center on what to do with individuals, departments, and institutions that have exhibited low levels of productivity. The definition of productivity will be more important than ever. Given the predicted downswing in enrollment, it is quite likely that many of these "low performers" will not survive until the predicted upswing. Thus, sensitive and sensible means of describing and measuring productivity must be employed.

The above discussion hopefully has demonstrated that understanding productivity in higher education is not a simple matter. Furthermore, the shift from steady growth to downswing and upswing means that productivity analysis needs to become more sophisticated than ever. Hence, efforts to improve faculty productivity should proceed with care. At a minimum, a system perspective must be used, because of the crucial linkages that exist between the faculty and the other groups that make up or support higher education.

Finally, it is quite clear that higher education depends as much, if not more, on trust and intrinsic rewards as it does on extrinsic re-

wards. If this trust is lost or if barriers are placed in the way of intrinsic rewards, higher education productivity will likely fall. Whether extrinsic rewards or constraints strong enough to duplicate the effects of trust and intrinsic rewards can be developed is an open question. Unfortunately, there are many indications that this question needs to be answered.

Chapter 6

Planning and Evaluation Criteria for Allocating Departmental and Collegiate Resources in a University Setting [1]

Darrell R. Lewis and
Theodore E. Kellogg

Higher education, as has been well established by experience and in the literature, is increasingly faced with rationalizing its activities and products. Competition for support dollars appears to continue to grow in intensity. Many professional colleges (such as education, dentistry, pharmacy, and public health) face additional problems because of changes in federal support, in student enrollments, and in the types of professional placements available. For all colleges, basic questions are being raised about the numbers and types of college-trained persons that are needed in our society today. In such an environment, special efforts must be made to review the efficiency and effectiveness of existing programs as well as to plan wisely for the future.

While the primary focus in this book is on the individual faculty member and the effects of the various reward structures in higher education on such individuals, it is important to recognize that all of these structures and their effects are clearly conditioned by the collective efficiency and effectiveness of faculty as reflected by the programs with which they are associated. The productivity of individual faculty is a function both of collective departmental and program efficiency and effectiveness and of individual effort. Consequently, any effort to understand and enhance individual faculty productivity must take place in the context of a rational program assessment and resource allocation framework.

This chapter represents an effort to organize various planning and review processes, criteria, and standards into a cohesive framework appropriate for allocating resources within a department or college

in a university setting. The discussion is divided into two major parts: (1) the identification of four basic criteria for planning and evaluation, and (2) a description of the interdependence and interactions among the four criteria, along with a number of policy implications. Quality, centrality, demand, and cost-effectiveness are suggested as the primary criteria to be used in program planning and evaluation. These four criteria, taking into account their relative importance and interrelationships, are presented as the basis for developing program evaluation information and for making resource allocations.

CRITERIA FOR PLANNING AND EVALUATION

Most colleges in major universities have mission statements that identify such obligations as "to extend continuously the frontiers of knowledge and tested skill . . . , to provide education of high quality . . . , and to afford leadership in . . . ." The criteria for evaluating program[2] plans or activities must relate to such goals. However, such goal statements neither state nor imply the criteria that are to be used in making judgments relating to assessment and resource allocation. Operational criteria that can be used in conjunction with these types of goal statements or other statements of priority must be developed. Following such development, rational judgments can then be made (using quantitative measures where these are reasonable) to determine the degree to which these criteria are met.

Based upon a review of existing collegiate statements of mission, planning, context, and priorities as well as other related materials, one can conclude that the major criteria for assessing programs can be summarized as quality of outcomes, centrality to mission, program demand, and cost-effectiveness.[3] The combined evidence based on each of these criteria should provide a useful profile for assessing a program and for rationally allocating resources to and among the many areas of a college or university. However, it is important to recognize that the role of these criteria and the evidence relating to them will likely vary from one area to another according to purposes and functions.[4]

Quality of Outcomes

The quality of program outcomes must be a primary focus of any assessment and allocation effort. Each activity must be viewed in the context of how it contributes to the strength and overall excellence of the programs and departments of the collegiate unit. Evidence of

the quality of departments and programs can come from various sources—for example, rankings by external professional associations, faculty publications, participation of faculty in professional meetings, special awards and other professional recognition, placement of graduate students, number and amounts of grants awarded, peer evaluation, and student evaluation. Distinctions should be made among invited, refereed, and other types of professional contributions; among types of professional contributions; among types of placement; among types of recognition; and among levels of significance of research.

Program evaluations by external bodies such as the American Psychological Association and a graduate school external review committee illustrate important qualitative estimates of a program's vitality over time. For example, does the program periodically assess and address its own perceived strengths and weaknesses in light of such external reviews?

Contributions to professional practice and knowledge are of particular relevance in the qualitative evaluation of the professional programs in a college. The focus of evaluating contributions to practice should be on examining the nature and strength of a program's relationship to the work of agencies and practitioners in the field. For example, has the work of a program faculty or graduate students led to the development of concepts, methods, modes of organizing processes, or other ideas from which new and significant practices or techniques have been derived? The focus of evaluating contributions to knowledge relates to the amount of publication and professional participation, but more complexly to expert judgment as to whether the particular efforts represent a significant contribution to a mission-related knowledge base.

The qualitative assessment of a program should also include the evaluation of teaching at both the graduate and the undergraduate levels. Related evidence includes evaluations by students and peers, as well as followup assessments by graduates. Such assessment also includes whether the program has paid special attention to the task of consolidating, reorganizing, and otherwise revising the structure and content of courses in order to improve instruction and to serve as a model for programs in other institutions. Also included is whether the program has been involved with any new curriculum development or course improvement projects. Evidence of faculty development addressed to meeting new teaching needs should also be reviewed.[5] Similarly, the degree to which each program area has successfully integrated significant dimensions of its disciplined in-

quiry and creative activities within its instructional mission should be evaluated. The unique mission of a school or department in a university setting clearly requires such joint efforts.

Analogous quality concerns apply for noninstructional program and service efforts across a unit. Both external and internal peer and student evaluations are necessary. There must be similar concerns about developing new ideas and procedures; in many such instances there can and should be demonstrated relationships between inquiry and practice.

Centrality to Mission

Centrality refers to the relative germaneness of an activity to the stated programmatic goals and objectives or purposes of an organizational unit. If one considers the programmatic alternatives that contribute to achieving particular goals and purposes, what is the relative necessity of supporting each? The critical question to ask is whether the mission (goals and purposes) of a college would be compromised if the program or activity under review were diminished or not in existence. In what ways would its absence be noted?

A judgment about the centrality of a program or activity is particularly difficult for several reasons. It is a very complex decision and can involve several levels of centrality. It is a decision that necessarily rests more on nonquantitative or subjective determinations than do the other criteria. For these reasons a judgment about the centrality of a program or function may be difficult to rationalize. Agreement on the relative centrality of programs and activities may be difficult to achieve, especially in the absence of fairly specific standards and measures. Nevertheless, the contribution of centrality to resource decisionmaking is programmatic in character and should be considered. To what degree is the substance of an activity pertinent to agreed upon program needs and intentions? In this context, two programs might demonstrate the same degree of quality, demand, and cost-effectiveness but might differ in their centrality to collegiate programmatic intentions.

Because a college is part of a university and a department is part of a college, consideration of centrality suggests concern for at least three levels—centrality to the mission and purposes of the larger university, centrality to the college, and centrality to a specific department. Centrality of activities at the program level might be considered an additional level or perhaps an alternative to considering the departmental level.

While the criteria suggested herein are thought to have application on several organizational levels, the primary focus of this discussion

is on the review of departmental programs at the collegiate level. However, collegiate review must be in the context of the total university—that is, it is always possible that a program or activity might have lesser centrality for a college or a department than it might have for the larger university or institutional framework. When such cases of institutional centrality do exist, it is important that appropriate consultations occur among the various levels, especially as regards decisions affecting resources.

Perhaps the most direct indication of centrality is the degree of correspondence between program activity and stated goals and missions (the more specifically these are stated, the easier it is to establish the degree of correspondence). Another important indicator of centrality is the number of students from other units (or areas) who are enrolled in a program's courses. However, caution should be used when reviewing such data. Such enrollments must be reflective of specific programmatic links with other areas of the college or university. One cannot, for example, have programs in teacher training without learning theory or programs at the graduate level without statistical methodology. Thus, one form of centrality is the degree to which an activity or program provides specific programmatic service to other parts of the college or university.

Yet another view of centrality is the degree to which the program or activity is related to the unique teaching and creative inquiry functions of the college as part of the university. Does it contribute significantly to the interaction of instructional programs with disciplined inquiry, of graduate level programs with undergraduate programs, or of discipline-oriented fields with problem-oriented programs? All such questions must be considered as part of the concern about centrality in relation to mission.

Program Demand

An educational institution is a basic resource and serves societal needs as an important part of its mission. Consequently, based on societal needs and demographic trends, one must try to predict likely future changes in demand and need for presently existing and projected programs.

Three aspects of program demand should be considered: (1) student demand for educational opportunity (i.e., individual student and social choice); (2) demand of the market for personnel (i.e., market and manpower forecasting); and (3) demand for ideas, information, and methods that may be developed through inquiry or testing (i.e., knowledge based social and professional requirements for research and development). These are obviously quite different de-

mands, and each should be viewed on its own merits. Their common element is that each judgment involves a comparison of the present program operation with an estimate of social or student demands or expectations.

Information from departmental and program units regarding their perceived needs for new directions is one way to project student demand changes within and among programs. Such information, along with actual trends in programs and enrollments, should assist in the planning process of a college. For example, considering programs often associated with colleges of education, increasing student and societal interest in early childhood education, recreation, educational technology, adult and community education, and continuing professional education clearly point to some directions for the future.

A review of recent curricular changes concerning the addition or dropping of courses, along with infrequently offered or low enrollment courses, may also suggest student demand changes. Such information, combined with available demographic projections, should provide additional insight as to where an expansion in resources is likely to be needed or where reductions should be considered.

Any argument for program uniqueness in a college is clearly dependent upon social need (demand) for such a program in the region, as well as the limited availability and accessibility of similar programs in other colleges within the state or region. Where such programs or aspects of programs—for example, undergraduate instruction, inservice education, master level studies—are not geographically unique (or central) to a college and when they could be offered or are duplicated in other accessible colleges of the region, serious consideration should be given to the reallocation of such effort and resources. On the other hand, the possibility also exists that entirely new programs are needed (demanded). Periodically, each department and college should review its curriculum and programs and consider whether there are programs offered elsewhere in the nation but not in the region that carry strong social need (demand) and that are clearly within the department's or college's mission. Such programs should be seriously considered for development.

It is important to note that quantitative measures of social demand should not be the only guide for resource allocations in a college. These measures are useful for reviewing areas with either expanding or declining enrollments, but they have limitations. For example, if student enrollments have fallen off in some undergraduate program areas, this may not necessarily justify retrenching large portions of their budgets. The resource base may have been originally inadequate. Or, with programmatic shifts involving new clinical

or laboratory experiences or with an expansion in postbaccalaureate programs, smaller numbers of students may be essential, and additional resources might be required. Perhaps appropriate instructional ratios (e.g., Full Year Equivalent students per academic Full Time Equivalent, degrees per academic Full Time Equivalent, cost per Student Credit Hour, and the like), which would have different interpretations for different areas and program levels, could be used as one type of information in developing guidelines for enrollment-related resource needs. Other ways of operationally defining a "critical mass" of faculty and students (including acceptable floors and ceilings) might also be developed for the different areas and programs across a college.

With respect to the market (manpower) demand for personnel, one should review very carefully the history of placements for the program graduates wherein both the quality and proportion of such placements are examined. However, the most common form of projecting market demand for personnel in educational planning has been the use of manpower-forecasting techniques. In its simpliest form, manpower-forecasting attempts to signal future labor market surpluses or shortages. When such models have been carefully developed with field-specific observations, they can provide useful guidelines as to the direction and intensity of expected changes. On the other hand, it is important to note that manpower forecasting has generally proved to be a most elusive guide to social and economic policy in both macro- and microeducation planning. The very real limits of such forecasting techniques have been frequently documented in the policy and planning literature.

Cost-Effectiveness

The extent of cost-effectiveness in any given program or activity is usually measured by comparing the costs or resources used with the outcomes or benefits achieved. It is a technique of selecting from alternative activities the one that will attain a given outcome at the lowest cost or the greatest benefits at given costs. The greater the benefits with given costs, or the lower the costs with given benefits, the greater the cost-effectiveness. It is particularly useful where benefits cannot be measured in money terms. Such comparisons for determining cost-effectiveness are often expressed as ratios, sometimes employing other terms and techniques such as input-output or cost-benefit analysis. However, the underlying concept in all such comparisons is that the use of resources involves a cost and that the outcomes should be compared with that cost. Thinking in "real" terms, the real cost of producing anything is the alternatives that are

foregone. For example, the real cost of any given program or activity in a college would be the outcomes of the best alternative program or activity given up that might otherwise have been produced with the same resources. Thus, for any resource allocation decision within a college, the extent of cost-effectiveness must be assessed by comparing the outcomes (at the margin) with the outcomes that might have been achieved if the same resources had been used in an alternative activity. To decide whether a department or a program should be maintained, expanded, or contracted, one must assess whether more desirable outcomes could be realized by reallocating resources into an area or out of it.

In discussions dealing with cost-effectiveness, three fallacies are frequently stated: (1) lower costs are better, (2) quality should not be related to cost, and (3) reduced costs mean reduced quality. Lowest or lower cost is not necessarily better. The key question is, What outcomes of what quality for what cost? Too often administrators fail to view the substantive differences in training methods and modes such as between professional and general education, between graduate and undergraduate education, and between a college with a relatively simple mission and a college in a multipurpose university. Significant differences in quality of output are also frequently ignored. A second error is to judge cost-effectiveness only in relation to outcomes by assuming that certain improved outcomes are desirable and should be sought irrespective of cost. The third error is the assumption that the quality of outcomes will necessarily fall if the costs for a given outcome are reduced. Comparisons of similar data among peer programs in other institutions often show this not to be the case. In higher education (as in any production process), there are a number of alternative ways in which contributing resources (primarily faculty and students) can function in order to produce outcomes. Some of these alternatives are obviously more cost-effective than others. The important idea is to recognize that cost-effectiveness involves a relationship between costs and outcomes. For example, to add to costs in a program area would not be cost-effective if the outcomes gained were less valuable than the outcomes that the added resources would have yielded in another area. On the other hand, to cut costs would not be cost-effective if the outcomes given up were more valuable than the outcomes of the saved resources used in another area.

A major problem in all such assessments is how best to conceptualize and measure (or describe) the inputs and outputs in order that they may be compared and evaluated. In higher education, inputs have often been thought of as dollar costs, although they might also be thought of as activity levels of students, faculty, and staff or

numbers of Full Time Equivalent faculty and staff, or student and faculty characteristics, or possibly some measure of educational process.[6] Outcomes tend to be more complex and often more difficult to measure. Simplest measures of output variables are weighted (by level) student credit hours, student counts (Full Time Equivalent or headcounts), numbers of graduates, or numbers of placements. Examples of more complex outcome variables include cognitive changes in students, affective changes in students, research and development contributions, economic benefits to the student or society, and other social benefits. The choice of which inputs and which outcomes will be used and how they will be defined, weighted, and related are crucial determinations and should involve the most informed judgments of faculty and administrators. In a large university, useful comparisons can be made among similar types of departments and programs within a college as well as with other "peer" programs in the parent institution and in other colleges and universities.

It is important to note that departments and programs that operate at a low rate of expenditure per student are not necessarily cost-effective because of their limited resources. They may be cost-effective because of the way in which they manage their inputs (i.e., the consolidation of courses or sections with low enrollments) or because they do not require specialized training methods (i.e., large lecture classes versus individualized laboratory sessions). Significantly, departments and programs that are cost-effective are not necessarily the lowest quality or lowest cost. In fact, examples of almost all combinations can be found across most institutions. Again, the critical question underlying advice on cost-effectiveness is, How are program effectiveness and cost related? For example, how can program outcomes be maintained (or enhanced) while reducing (or holding constant) costs? Or, what will be the tradeoffs in outcomes if resources are transferred between programs?

Rather than seeking to establish an acceptable and comprehensive definition of program output for all units within a college (which is probably not possible), it seems best to make use of the concept of cost-effectiveness by determining selected indexes of effectiveness and by considering these indexes in relation to measures of cost.

POLICY IMPLICATIONS AND INTERACTIONS OF THE CRITERIA

The criteria described in this chapter suggest four dimensions of programmatic evaluation that are fundamental to making resource allocation decisions. However, programs across a college vary greatly in

centrality, demand, cost-effectiveness, and quality; and the cost (or savings) of significantly expanding or improving (or reducing) them will be different for each area. Thus, any consideration of these criteria in specific situations makes it clear that their use involves many complexities.

These complexities are the result of several factors:

1. Usually the criteria cannot be used separately because they are interrelated and interactive. In each instance the four basic criteria need to be considered jointly.

2. The criteria cannot be assigned equal importance because their significance is relative. The fact that one activity or program has one sort of emphasis may be the very reason a different sort of emphasis is possible elsewhere.

3. While the extent to which a criterion is met can be based on a variety of indicators, the most appropriate indicator(s) to use will always be conditioned by the type of program and its purposes.

4. The types of information provided by the various indicators will vary from quantitative measures to judgmental narratives; in some instances the desired information may not be available.

5. As a consequence of the factors cited above, significant portions of appropriate information cannot be processed by formula. The extent to which the criteria are met cannot be completely described by a set of numbers, averages, or scales.

Thus, while certain processes or outcomes may be summarized quantitatively, all final resource allocations decisions need to be subjective and judgmental. Many different kinds of evidence are part of the process, and the relative importance of a particular criterion, the importance of the relationships among programs, and the idiosyncratic circumstances of a particular program all must be considered. Nevertheless, the overall program profile that emerges from considering all elements and their relationships will make a useful contribution to the complicated and judgmental resource allocation process.

Such judgments can be assisted by considering some of the variations that might occur among the four basic criteria. Examples of situations where conclusions may be reasonably clear are the easiest to illustrate and to make judgments about. It is obvious that an optimal program and resource situation exists when high quality, high centrality, and high demand are all coupled with a high level of cost-effectiveness. Similarly, programs with high quality and high centrality need to be preserved and nourished when necessary. In these

latter circumstances, attention must also be paid to questions of program demand and cost-effectiveness, but these are of lesser priority and must not dominate decisions concerning the program's long-term welfare. On the other hand, those few programs that are found to be low in centrality, demand, and quality (independent of costs) will need to be phased out or significantly reshaped with appropriate faculty renewal efforts.

Unfortunately, decisions about resource support are less clear for most other variations of the criteria. For example, situational factors will always play a significant role in any related resource decision. These factors include the likelihood that change can be facilitated with reasonable expenditure of effort, personnel, and tenure considerations; the total amount of resources available for (re)allocation; the general institutional; community, and political climate; the relative importance of the various dimensions of mission; and the time scale over which change might be expected. In light of these situational factors, the criteria become all the more important as guidelines for making judgments.

Programs for which there is high demand but that tend to be marginal with respect to the other criteria are especially bothersome. Such programs must be reviewed very carefully so as not to detract from other more central programs and from the primary mission of a college. Support decisions are also difficult when highly central programs are of generally low quality combined with limited demand and high cost. Special extra effort should be directed to improving the quality and cost-effectiveness of such programs. Similar problems arise when a program exhibits generally high quality but is viewed as being low with respect to the other criteria. A judgment about a program's role in the total scheme of a college, especially relative to its cost-effectiveness under conditions of reallocation, will be essential in all of these cases.

The fact that resource allocation decisions are very complicated implies that difficult problems are to be expected. There will be uncertainties, reasonable disagreements about conclusions, and in some cases, decisions that are difficult to explain to the satisfaction of all parties. These sorts of difficulties should be anticipated. Their resolution or alleviation can be facilitated by the prior development of appropriate institutional policies concerning the process of decision-making.

A number of such policy implications follow from the above discussion. For example, the criteria and the processes by which decisions will be made should be arrived at by broad and open consultation throughout a college. This should lead to some consensus

about basic principles and should assist everyone in attempting to change or improve where necessary. Such criteria and processes should be described in written form. Additionally, the nature of all major resource (re)allocation decisions should be openly discussed, so it is clear to all concerned what directions and guidance are emerging from the process. Also, policies are needed that more clearly take into account the importance of the individual human contribution—that is, faculty development policies and adaptive change strategies and policies are needed at both individual and organizational levels. Existing faculty in a college represent the most available and important resource for meeting new challenges. As a matter of policy, the types of information that will be regularly collected and used to assist in making decisions should be made explicit. The information used should be available to program units and should be as widely shared as appropriate. There is also a need for an explicit planning strategy (including both process and desired outcomes) for both the short- and long-term future. The purpose of such planning should be to consciously look to the future of the organizational unit in setting directions and to provide appropriate tests of whether outcomes are consistent with intentions.

CONCLUSION

In summary, the four basic planning and evaluation criteria identified in this chapter (quality of outcomes, centrality to mission, program demand, and cost-effectiveness) provide a conceptual framework that can be useful in collegiate decisionmaking for resource (re)allocation. Additional discussion has illustrated the great variety of indicators that may aid in determining the degree to which the criteria are satisfied. Such variation is due partly to the complexity of the four criteria, but it is also due to the inherent differences among programs. In the final stages of any (re)allocation process, one will be faced with informational profiles for a set of programs that are competitive in nature. Patterns of relative strength in satisfying the criteria will vary within and between programs. In addition, some information will be qualitative while some will be quantitative; some will be ambiguous and some will be clear and precise; some may prove to be unavailable; some will not be comparable among programs. This chapter suggests that the resolution of these differences in kind and character and the processing of this diverse information will necessarily be based on subjective judgmental decisions rather than upon any predetermined formula.

Finally, it has been suggested that the resource allocation process clearly has implications for college and departmental policy. Information needs should be clearly stated, decision processes should be described, open discussion and consultation that are essential to good communication and improvement are needed, adaptive change strategies should be developed, and full recognition should be given to the critical role of existing faculty. These are all illustrative of areas in which collegiate policy needs to be refined or developed as the situation dictates.

NOTES TO CHAPTER 6

1. This chapter has been adapted from a similar statement developed by the authors as a working draft for the College of Education at the University of Minnesota during the fall of 1977. The authors believe that the principles and criteria developed for their college are generalizable to other collegiate settings in higher education. Special acknowledgement must be given to the contributions of the Administrative Council and Educational Policies Committee of the College of Education and to earlier related works by Mary Corcoran and an unpublished paper that proposes a similar structure by May Brodbeck, G.C. Christensen, and J.G. Martin (1976).

2. For purposes of this discussion, a program is thought of as an organized set of collegiate activities, the exact nature of which may vary from a department or center to a curricular major or emphasis.

3. The unpublished report to the Iowa Board of Regents by M. Brodbeck, G.C. Christensen, and J.G. Martin (1976) was especially useful in the identification of these criteria.

4. Note also should be taken of the special difficulties that relate to developing and proposing a new program. While the same criteria apply, it is apparent that one may be dealing with projections or expectations rather than experience.

5. In the near future, the planning assumption most likely for higher education is for a "steady state" condition. Under such an assumption, faculty development and renewal is likely to be one of the least costly and most practical ways for insuring program flexibility and instructional quality.

6. The advantage of defining input in dollar terms is to establish a readily available measure of input that is comparable across programs. In no sense should this conceptualization of inputs be assumed to mean that finances are the only important inputs to higher education. In some instances dollars may be a poor surrogate or indirect measure of the true resources that contribute to outcomes.

Chapter 7

Use of Student Evaluations in Faculty Personnel Decisions

Kenneth O. Doyle, Jr.

There is no perfect way to evaluate teaching. There may not even be a really excellent way. There are, however, good and responsible ways to evaluate teaching that are within the reach of any college or university.

This chapter will explore some practical aspects of one important component in a good and responsible evaluation system—student evaluation of instruction. People who study this chapter should come away with a fundamental grasp of the more important parts of the enormous literature on student evaluations as well as beginning answers to some of the trying questions that face people who need to make decisions that involve those data. More importantly perhaps, people should find in this chapter a set of facts, opinions, ideas, and conclusions to which they can react while trying to build a better instructional evaluation system.

It is essential to keep perspective. Student evaluations are not intended to evaluate all of instruction. Instruction involves scholarship, or the instructor's knowledge of the subject; it involves dissemination or presentation or communication of this knowledge to students; and it involves the students' learning of that knowledge. Student evaluations focus on the presentation of knowledge and sometimes—through students' self-reports of achievement—on student learning. But student evaluations are seldom intended to evaluate scholarship. Nor are they intended to supplant tests as measures of student learning.

Neither are student evaluations intended to be the sole evaluation of classroom presentation. Other kinds of appraisal are desirable sup-

plements to student evaluations—peer visitations, for example, or peer review of videotapes. Self-evaluation also plays an important role, even in evaluation for promotion and salary purposes.

No one of these forms of evaluation—self-appraisal, peer review, student learning, student evaluations—is a sufficient basis in itself for important personnel decisions. Each has its own strengths and weaknesses. A good and responsible evaluation program is one that capitalizes on the strengths of each kind of data and protects against its peculiar weaknesses. Toward that end, the rest of this chapter will focus on the strengths and weaknesses of student evaluations. The first section will examine some of the more important research on student evaluations. The second section will deal with some practical questions.

STUDENT EVALUATION RESEARCH

Researchers worry about four qualities of any data, including student evaluations: reliability, validity, generalizability—and skulduggery.

Reliability

Reliability describes the extent to which evaluations are unencumbered by errors of observation, perception, or communication. An example of an obvious error of observation is failure to see important events because one was absent or distracted. Thus students (or, for that matter, colleagues) who do not come to class often enough, or who are too distracted from what is going on, cannot give reliable evaluations of what occurred. It is difficult to say how often one needs to come to a class to evaluate it reliably. Centra (1974a) found that colleagues who visited a class two times each gave fairly reliable ratings, but their ratings were considerably less reliable than those of students who (presumably) had attended many more classes. Bejar and Doyle (1976) found that student ratings were reliable as early as the end of the first class period. Frequency of attendance, then, is not likely to be a problem for most student ratings. If frequency of attendance does seem to be a problem in a particular situation, it would be a simple matter to include on the evaluation form a question asking about the rater's attendance; ratings from students who said they attended relatively infrequently could then be analyzed separately from the ratings of the rest of the students.

It is even more difficult to say how distracted is too distracted, but it seems unlikely that so many of the students in a class will be so often so distracted that their ratings will be much affected. The technical data on reliability of student ratings supports this conclusion (Costin, Greenough, & Menges, 1971; Doyle, 1975: ch. 3).

Usually more important than errors of observation are errors of perception. One kind of perceptual error, the "halo effect," occurs when people's overall impressions of an instructor blind them to that instructor's specific strengths and weaknesses. Thus students of a very charismatic instructor might fail to see, or see less clearly, the deficiencies in that instructor's presentation, or students of a very dull instructor might fail to appreciate the excellent way that the course is organized. Halo will probably never be completely eliminated from ratings, but by the same token, it rarely seems to cripple them. It is probably more of a problem in course improvement ratings, in which identification of particular strengths and weaknesses is important, than in promotion and salary ratings, where overall judgments are the goal. It can be countered to some extent by warning raters about this tendency and advising them of the importance of distinguishing among instructor characteristics.

A second kind of perceptual error has to do with expectations. If people are led to believe that an experience will be especially good or bad, they may in fact see it as better or worse than they would have, had their expectations been neutral (Asch, 1946). Moreover, if the experience turns out to be at extreme variance with people's expectations, their evaluations may be considerably more favorable (relief?) or unfavorable (disappointment?) than they would otherwise have been (Helson, 1959). Expectations seem most likely to have an effect on student evaluations in situations in which there is an active, trusted student "grapevine," when evaluations are published for students to use in selecting courses, and when the instructor at hand is seen as an exceptionally good or poor teacher. The best protection against the effects of expectations is probably time—that is, they seem less likely to be a problem in actual courses, in which students observe an instructor several times a week for several months, than in the single, experimental sessions in which they are usually studied (e.g., Perry, Niemi, & Jones, 1974). Other perceptual errors are discussed in social psychology texts such as Schneider (1976) and in measurement books like Guilford (1954).

At least as important as perceptual errors are errors of communication. One kind of communication error would be mismarking the answer sheet, circling a 2, say, when one had intended to circle a 6. This kind of occasional error is quite likely to be absorbed into the whole set of ratings, especially in larger courses, and thus to become insignificant; it is best controlled by clearly laid out and labeled questionnaires. A more serious communications error involves deliberately giving higher or lower ratings than the rater believes would be accurate. Most often this kind of error will be leniency, rising from social prescriptions to "take it easy on the guy." (The opposite of

leniency, harshness, will be dealt with in a later section.) Leniency is likely to be especially pronounced when raters believe that the data will be used in promotion and salary decisions (Sharon, 1970). The danger here is that one instructor may suggest to the students that the ratings are for personnel purposes while an equally good instructor indicates that they are strictly for course improvement purposes. The former instructor is likely to receive the higher rating. A simple device to guard against this kind of inequity would be to print on all questionnaires a statement that the data may be used in personnel decisions.

It is important to remember that errors of observation, perception, and communication can also occur when faculty and administrators interpret student ratings. The most reliable student evaluations are useless for promotion and salary purposes unless the review committees (1) look at them, (2) alert themselves to their own propensities toward halo, (3) separate their interpretation of the data from their expectations about the instructor, and (4) attend to their own tendencies to be inconsistently lenient or harsh. Since the best protection against these kinds of errors of interpretation may be simply to keep people aware of them, a sheet of "cautions and suggestions for review committees" might be a good addition to a personnel system.

Validity

Validity describes the meaningfulness or importance of a rating item: How important is the instructor or course characteristic a particular evaluation item measures?

The usual ways of establishing or documenting the validity of rating items can be arranged on a continuum from more subjective to more objective. All of these ways, subjective as well as objective, have something to contribute. Each way has its own strengths and its own weaknesses.

A typical subjective way might involve interviewing or surveying faculty, students, instructional specialists, and so forth for their opinions regarding the importance of particular ratings items. One might simply ask them to rate the importance of each of a collection of items (e.g., Wherry, 1952). Or one might ask them to judge the extent to which the instructor or course characteristic described by each item bears on student learning. Or one might ask them to describe good and bad teachers and take as important those characteristics that distinguish the good from the bad (e.g., Doyle, 1972; Hildebrand, Wilson, & Dienst, 1971). Finally, one could also study the research literature on learning and teaching to see which instruc-

tor and course characteristics are likely to facilitate student learning in different kinds of courses (e.g., Gagné, 1977). The element common to each of these methods is that they all depend on human judgment.

A typical objective way to validate a rating item might involve correlating student and peer ratings on that item with some measure of student outcome (e.g., Elliott, 1950; Doyle & Whitely, 1974; Frey, 1973). Like the subjective ways, this approach asks the extent to which the characteristic bears on student learning.

The essential difference between objective and subjective ways is that the one uses judgment to estimate a characteristic's relationship to learning, while the other uses test scores. Which route one prefers will depend on how much he or she trusts judgment and how much he or she trusts tests. Ideally, of course, both routes would provide the same answers, but unfortunately, this is not often the case. The inconsistency in results between subjective and objective approaches to validation has been the source of a great deal of controversy about student evaluations. It is also a primary reason why it is important to look closely at both kinds of validation.

Both kinds of validation—through judgment and with tests—have their own strengths and weaknesses. Judgment, for example, may be able to provide more subtle, penetrating, and complex information than current test technology can supply. On the other hand, judgment may be capricious, uninformed, or just plain wrong. Tests may be able to measure student learning without bias and with minimal error. But tests may fail to measure the breadth and depth of learning or may be so encumbered by statistical complexity (e.g., gain score computations [Glass, 1974]) that their results may be deceiving.

Most studies of the validity of rating items have been based on judgment. Indeed, most of the better known student evaluation forms have been developed in the light of surveys of student and/or faculty opinion about item importance—for example, at the University of California (Hildebrand, Wilson, & Dienst, 1971); at Educational Testing Service (Centra, 1972); and at the University of Minnesota (Doyle, 1972, 1977). Table 7—1 presents categories of items that appear quite consistently in these studies, along with illustrative items.

Objective studies of the validity of items like these typically involve correlating student gain (tested progress in the course) with ratings on these items. Seldom are such correlations extremely large; rarely are they negative. Although many objective studies lack the rigor necessary to answer validity questions, a few well-designed

Table 7-1.   Common Categories of Evaluation Items.

Expositional Skills
  The instructor presents the subject matter clearly.
  The instructor identifies what he or she considers important.

Interpersonal Skills
  The instructor is approachable.
  The instructor has a genuine interest in students.

Motivational Skills
  The instructor raises challenging questions.
  The instructor is enthusiastic about the subject.

"Feedback" to Students
  The instructor provides adequate information about student progress.
  The instructor tells students when they have done a particularly good job.

Workload
  The instructor expects a lot from students.
  The instructor maintains definite standards of student performance.

studies of specific items have recently furnished quite consistent results (e.g., Frey, 1973; Sullivan & Skanes, 1974; Doyle & Whitely, 1974). In these studies, expositional skills, motivational skills, and workload usually showed positive correlations with learning gain, while interpersonal skills showed near zero correlations. (Feedback items were unfortunately not included in these studies.) Correlational studies carried out in the framework of instructional evaluation thus provide some objective evidence for the validity of commonly used items.

Often neglected, however, are many other studies that bear on the validity of these items. Gagné's (1977) excellent discussion of external events that influence learning cites empirical studies that support items relating to expositional skills, motivational skills, and feedback. Similarly, Skinner (1968), along with other literature on instructional technology, empirically reinforces the importance of feedback about student performance. In counseling psychology, such interpersonal phenomena as empathy, unconditional positive regard, and warmth have often been shown to be necessary conditions of effective therapy, which in many ways is similar to teaching (e.g., Truax & Mitchell, 1971; Goldstein, 1971; Strong, 1968). And in social psychology, personal likability has been documented as an important influence on affective or attitudinal learning, sometimes on cognitive learning (Uranowitz & Doyle, 1978). Thus, there actually is a fair amount of consistency between what the objective and the subjective approaches to item validation provide as support for the validity of commonly used evaluation items.

However, it would be dangerous to infer from this that these five categories of items are absolute requirements of good teaching. For

example, few people would argue with the proposition that different teachers can be equally effective in their own very different ways. One instructor might capitalize on expositional skills, another on interpersonal skills, another on motivational skills, yet they may all be equally effective teachers. And the importance of these different characteristics might vary as the mode of instruction changes. In large lectures, for example, expositional skills may be more important than interpersonal skills, while in small discussion groups the opposite may be the case. Moreover, for some characteristics (e.g., clarity, approachability) it may not be necessary to be more than sufficient, while for other characteristics (e.g., some motivational skills) the more of the characteristic the instructor exhibits, the better a teacher he or she may be. It is not difficult to conceive of an instructor who in some kinds of courses is too clear (and boring) or too approachable (and distracting) or too demanding (and unfair), but it is harder to envision an instructor who is too stimulating. Finally, different kinds of students may need different things from their instructors. Students who are required to take a course the content of which they find unpalatable may need an especially stimulating instructor, but students who are already excited about the material may only need someone to guide them. Students who are haphazard in their approach may need a particularly firm and organized instructor, while students who are controlled and rigid may need someone to challenge their positions and broaden their perspectives. In short, there are a multitude of situational considerations that bear on the validity of specific rating items and on the weight that should be assigned to each of them. Clearly it would be impossible to quantify all of these considerations. But a good approximation may be for review committees to think a while about the instructor, course, and students, perhaps to talk with the instructor, and only then to begin to examine and interpret the evaluations.

There is a somewhat different kind of item that may be simpler for review committees to use and yet still provide valid ratings—the general, summary item. One version of this summarizes evaluations of the teaching process:

How would you rate this instructor's overall teaching?

Very poor   Poor   Fair   Good   Very Good   Excellent

Another version summarizes student outcome:

How much have you learned as a result of this course?

| Very Little | Little | Some | Much | Very Much | A Tremendous Amount |

Together these two items summarize most if not all of what students can say about a course and an instructor.

There are a number of advantages to items like these in promotion and salary decisions. They are applicable to all kinds of courses. They do not require the ad hoc weighting that more specific items do. And they are easy for students to answer and for review committees to interpret. Moreover, they correlate significantly (albeit modestly) and quite consistently with tested student learning (Sullivan & Skanes, 1974; Doyle & Whitely, 1974; Centra, 1976). These items can be faulted for being too general and therefore ambiguous, but when they are studied ("regression") along with more specific items, the patterns of results ("beta weights") indicate that the general items do a good job of summarizing what seem to be the more important specific items (clarity, motivational skills [Doyle & Whitely, 1974]). There is even some indication that the students' interpretations of these items change to reflect the important features of different kinds of courses (Wilson & Doyle, 1975). In short, there are some very good reasons to include these general, summary items on student evaluation forms that are intended for use in personnel decisions.

The best practice may be to construct a questionnaire that contains both the commonly used specific items and the general, summary items. Review committees could emphasize the summary items, but they would still have the specific items to supplement the general ratings. In fact, the patterns of ratings on the specific items could help explain what the students meant by their ratings of overall teaching quality.

Generalizability

In this context, generalizability describes the special features of students and teaching situations that deserve attention in interpreting student evaluations. The research literature provides quite a consistent statement that student evaluations are essentially unrelated to such demographic variables as student sex and ability (Doyle, 1975: ch. 5). Even when correlations of these sorts are relatively large, they still explain very little of the total (multivariate) variability in ratings. Usually, then, it is not especially important to know about these kinds of student characteristics.

On the other hand, there is some evidence that evaluations are meaningfully related to student year in school, to degree and kind of motivation, and perhaps, to cognitive style or way of thinking. Similarly, student ratings seem related to type or size of course (e.g., large lecture, small seminar) and to curriculum (humanities, sciences). So

it is important, at least for a thorough interpretation of a set of student evaluations, to know about student year, motivation, and way of thinking and about course type, size, and content. Knowledge about the course characteristics permits separating too different courses from one another so that unfair comparisons are not made — a senior humanities seminar versus an introductory science lecture, for example. Knowledge about the student characteristics permits looking separately at the evaluations of different subgroups of students within a class so that average ratings do not mask important differences of opinion from different kinds of students.

Most of these characteristics can be easily measured, either by adding questions to the student questionnaire or by asking the instructor to describe the course. The characteristics that are likely to be the most difficult to measure are student motivation and cognitive style. One way to measure motivation might be to add to the questionnaire a short checklist of reasons for taking the course, along with self-ratings of how interested the students were in the subject, how badly they wanted to take the course, or how much effort they put into it. Another way might be to construct a brief version of an academic motivations inventory (Moen & Doyle, 1977; Doyle & Moen, 1978). Measuring cognitive style may be even more difficult, but one could conceivably use a question like, Did you feel you were on the same wavelength with the instructor? More rigorously, a short form of an inventory of learning processes (Schmeck, Ribich, & Ramanaiah, 1977) might serve. The problem, of course, will be to devise measures of motivation and cognitive style that are at once effective and short.

Although, as already mentioned, student characteristics like sex and ability are usually not related to ratings, there are times when these variables—or any other student factors—may take on considerable importance. If an instructor "teaches to" the brightest students in the class and neglects the weakest students, there probably will be a correlation between evaluations and student ability. If an instructor teaches course content in such a way that it offends or frightens various subsets of students (e.g., modern sex roles from an extremely feminist or antifeminist point of view; statistical procedure to a mixed group of humanities and mathematics premajors), there may well be a relationship between evaluations and student characteristics. In these cases, information about student characteristics may be very important to a full interpretation of the evaluation. Because there are so many possible relationships of these sorts, it would be impossible to anticipate all of them. One solution might be to leave a few blank items on the evaluation form and to invite

instructors to add a question or two designed to identify groups of students who might have very different reactions to the course. These questions can then be used to sort the evaluations into different sets, and the instructor—and the review committee—can judge the extent to which the course is serving the students for whom it was principally designed.

Skulduggery

Some people cheat. Student evaluations—like peer and self evaluations—are instances of human perception, and it is clear that human perception can be manipulated. So one kind of cheating involves attempts to manipulate student perception in such a way that students will give undeservedly favorable evaluations. As already discussed, an instructor might suggest to his or her students that their evaluations will be a pivotal factor in an upcoming promotion review. Because students—like other people—seem inclined to be generous when they believe their opinions will affect important personnel decisions (Sharon, 1970), this instructor might very well receive higher ratings than an instructor whose students believed their evaluations would be used only for personal feedback. A straightforward way to deal with this possibility might be to print on all evaluation forms a statement to the effect that the data may be used in important personnel decisions. In this way, although every instructor's ratings might be a bit inflated, no instructor should be able to take special advantage of student generosity.

An instructor might also indicate to students that there is a relationship between evaluations and grades. A blatant attempt to set up such a quid pro quo would be very risky—if it outraged a single student, it could create a very difficult situation for the instructor. A subtle suggestion, however, might work on at least enough students to affect the average rating. For this reason, evaluations ought to be anonymous. Perhaps, too, the evaluation reports should not be given to instructors until after course grades have been assigned, but this step might discourage the good practice of collecting course improvement evaluations earlier in the term. Review committees could examine grade reports along with evaluations to see if an unusual percentage of high or low grades paralleled an unusual percentage of high or low evaluations. But the results of that extra effort would still be equivocal; it would be very difficult to tell if the grades were a response to the evaluations or if the evaluations were a response to (anticipated) grades or if both sets of data were as they should be. Probably the easiest and best—but still not wholly satisfactory—solution to this problem is a system of checks and balances, with review committees looking for themes and patterns in evaluations from

course to course and from year to year and supplementing student evaluations with whatever other evaluations might be available.

Some students might try to use very harsh ratings to penalize an instructor for, say, his or her political or social views, for what they consider too demanding a course, to be "cute," or simply because they are angry or frustrated or frightened about something that may not have much to do with the instructor. If a large proportion of the students in a course give very negative ratings, those ratings should certainly receive close attention. They might indicate a genuine problem with the instructor; but they might also describe some other kind of problem that is interfering with the students' education, or they might indicate pure malice. Students do not give extremely low ratings without reason; the important thing is to identify the reason and respond to it.

If only some of the students give very unfavorable evaluations, the meaning could be the same, different only in that fewer students are involved. To some unknown extent, these ratings will probably be balanced out by unduly high ratings from other students, but it may still be important to pursue the reasons for the ratings. Review committees could discuss the matter with the instructor, or the instructor (or a representative) could talk with some students, who might know more about the reasons for students' reactions than any member of the faculty. In any case of very low ratings, the system of checks and balances becomes doubly important, not as a means for explaining away low ratings but as a way to test the dependability of the various kinds of data.

In another form of cheating, an instructor who has been, say, hostile and uncooperative during the term might try to "win points" just before an evaluation by being exceptionally helpful and cordial. This kind of manipulation does not seem likely to be very effective. First, it seems improbable that a sudden change in behavior will override the effects of typical behavior. Second, there is no reason to expect that students are any less able to identify brownnosing faculty than faculty are to identify brownnosing students. Moreover, such practices are very risky; there is a substantial literature in social psychology that indicates that "ingratiators" are likely to receive more negative evaluations than they would have otherwise received. Some institutions have set up systems in which instructors absent themselves from the classroom during the evaluation so that their behavior does not bias the evaluations. These systems probably help, but they cannot control behavior in the class preceding the evaluation or in the class before that. Probably the best defense against this kind of manipulation is the perceptiveness of the students.

A final form of cheating is less subtle than any of the preceding. Some instructors who administer their own evaluations read through the questionnaires before sending them out for processing and remove or even change the most unfavorable evaluations. An obvious way to deal with this problem is to have a student, teaching assistant, or secretary collect the evaluations from the students and deliver the forms to the processing center. A decision to institute this sort of system should be a thoughtful one however, and the system itself should be graceful; otherwise the cost in institutional morale may be too steep a price to pay.

There can never be a fail-safe evaluation system. Institutions or departments can take steps to reduce if not eliminate the more obvious forms of cheating, but no administration can prevail against the collective genius of a faculty or student body that is determined to subvert an evaluation system. Infinitely more desirable than a system heavy with distrust is a program that is developed or negotiated by representatives of the faculty, administration, and students to the point that it is accepted by a least most people in the various constituencies. If the system is widely accepted, then there will be a general monitoring, and attempts to beat the system should become quite evident. This kind of climate, coupled with worldwise perceptiveness on the part of review committees and administrators, may turn out to be the best deterrent to skulduggery.

PRACTICAL QUESTIONS

This final section will deal with some practical questions about student evaluations of instruction. The most frequently raised questions seem to be of three sorts: What data should we collect from whom, and when? How should those data be tabulated, reported, and interpreted? What features of an evaluation system can ward off complaints and dissatisfactions?

Deciding what data to collect means deciding which questions to ask and in what form to ask them. Decisions about which questions to ask are essentially matters of validity: What most likely constitutes good teaching?, or better, What most likely constitutes good teaching in this particular course? The objective and subjective routes to validity, as already described, along with the judgments of people who are familiar with the subject, the students, and the instructor, probably provide the best available answers to this question. No certain answer can be given yet. And certainly no absolute answer.

Questions may be in the form of conversation or dialogue, prose essays, or ratings. Dialogues are probably of little use in personnel

evaluation because they are hard to record, tabulate, and norm. (But they may be the most useful kind of evaluation for instructional improvement.) Prose essays may or may not be useful, depending on whether the question is structured enough to elicit answers that are "on target" and whether review committees are willing to go through the considerable effort of reading and systematically studying them. Although essays will probably never be as technically reliable as ratings, there may be times when essays are preferable to ratings, even for personnel decisions. For example, if the personal tastes of faculty and students in a given discipline are such that these people will cooperate with prose evaluations but not with ratings, then essays are distinctly preferable. In general, though, the rule of thumb for essay evaluations in personnel decisions is the same as the rule for essay examinations: use them only if more objective measures cannot do the job. Thus ratings, which are probably the least desirable form for course improvement evaluations, are probably the best form for personnel evaluations. A good personnel package might include ratings on general, summary items (discussed above), supplemented by ratings on situationally important specific items, supplemented by short, pointed essays.

Distinguishing a good evaluation questionnaire from a bad one is a tricky business, because a thorough appraisal of a questionnaire requires a good bit of empirical study. With or without empirical study, however, the people who are going to use the questionnaire should study the content of the questions to be sure that the collection of items covers the important aspects of teaching in the situations in which the questionnaire will be used, and they should examine the form of the questions to be sure that the rating task will be clear to the people who will fill out the form and interpret the results. It is very unlikely that empirical study will say that a questionnaire is good unless the questions on that form are important and clear.

From whom to collect ratings raises two questions: First, from what proportion of the students in a class? Second, from which classes that the instructor teaches? The goal in both cases is representativeness—that is, the students who fill out the questionnaire should represent the students who actually took the course, and the courses evaluated should represent the full complement of the instructor's courses. If fewer than all students in a class complete the questionnaire, representativeness becomes a question. The smaller the proportion of respondents, the greater the problem. There is unfortunately no satisfactory way to determine what percent of students will assure a representative sample; even the sophisticated for-

mulas for sample selection assume random selection, and it seems unlikely that nonrespondents are an entirely random sample of students in the course. The best one can do if the percent of respondents becomes lower than one is comfortable with is to check the tabulation of demographics on the questionnaire to see if there is gross disproportionality between those data and the actual student group, estimate how much influence the nonrespondents could have had on the mean had they given mostly favorable or mostly unfavorable ratings, make a judgment about whether the data from the group at hand "make sense," and rely on other data for checks and balances. While some data are usually better than no data, there is likely to be a point—somewhere—when a subset of evaluations become so unrepresentative as to be misleading.

Designing a representative sample of courses is easier. One needs only to decide which types of courses an instructor teaches and choose courses of each type, keeping in mind that patterns of evaluations from year to year (for the same type of course) may be more meaningful than a set of evaluations for a single year. Whether all courses or a sample should be evaluated should probably be governed by the need for data and the tolerance of the students and instructors. Faculty facing promotion decisions may do well to collect as much evidence of their teaching quality as possible, but it is probably not good practice to require student evaluation of every course each time the course is offered. Too much evaluation will tire everyone and may work to the long-run detriment of the system.

Student evaluations are often collected immediately before or after the final examination. This is probably the worst possible time, since anxiety or relief could bias the ratings and because it provides no opportunity to summarize the evaluations to the students, to ask for clarification from them, or to describe one's plans to respond to the evaluation or one's reasons for disagreeing with it. Evaluations early in the term are excellent for course improvement purposes but may not provide a good description of the course as a whole. Take home or mailed evaluations seldom seem to work. One never knows the conditions—at a party?—under which the forms were filled out, or by whom; and response rates are often very low. Perhaps the best solution is to administer personnel evaluations toward the end of the term, late enough so that the students have been exposed to most of the course, but early enough so that the students are not too focused on the exam. A two or three item evaluation of the exam itself could also be attached to the test, along with a repeat of the general, summary item.

How should student evaluations be tabulated, reported, and interpreted? Essay evaluations, if they are used for personnel purposes, should be treated like a well-graded essay test (cf. Gronlund, 1976: ch. 10)—that is, they should be read and tallied question by question and, within questions, theme by theme. Ratings should be tabulated for basic descriptive statistics—frequency distribution, central tendency (mean or median), and variability (standard deviation or, conceivably, interquartile range). The frequency distribution stays closest to the data. It simply counts how many people chose each alternative on each item. It is probably the best summary statistic for conveying the range and spread of evaluations. There is some controversy about means versus medians. The median is less affected by extremely favorable or unfavorable responses, which is either good or bad depending on how much one wants to attend to extreme scores; the median is also less influenced by some technical properties of scales (i.e., "equal intervals"). However, given that the goal is to sort instructors into three or four broad categories (e.g., unsatisfactory, satisfactory, outstanding), either the median or the mean should work (Baker, Hardyck, & Petronovick, 1966). One should not, of course, compare medians to means. The standard deviation, an index of difference of opinion among students, completes the basic set of descriptive statistics. This statistic might best be considered a "warning flag"; if the standard deviation exceeds, say, 1.0 on a five or seven point scale, people should be sure to look at the frequency distribution because the mean may be masking important differences of opinion.

In addition to these basic statistics, a good tabulation system should provide the capability of analyzing subsets of the data—descriptive statistics for majors versus nonmajors, for example, or those who wanted to take the course versus those who did not (see the discussion on generalizability, above). Instructors could have the option of separate tabulation to supplement the overall tabulation.

Student ratings are usually reported as tables of descriptive statistics. But many people may find graphical presentations more interpretable, either bar graphs or "boxes and whiskers" in which the boxes (or xs) show, say, the middle 25 percent of ratings and the adjacent whiskers (or dashes) show another 25 percent in each direction:

$$- - - - \text{xxxx (median) xxxx} - - - -$$

Two things are especially important in interpreting ratings. The first, already discussed, is the choice of which questions to empha-

size. The second is the statistics themselves. With regard to the statistics, a frequent temptation is to overinterpret small differences. Although more rigorous tests of how small a difference is too small are available, a good rule of thumb is to disregard differences that are not at least half to three-quarters the size of the standard deviation. This will sometimes result in no differences among instructors, but to interpret smaller differences could be to create differences where there are none.

Also useful in the interpretation of evaluations is a "faculty handbook." A simple handbook could include some comments about the various descriptive statistics and some suggestions for getting more out of the evaluation (e.g., rate yourself first, then compare your ratings to the student ratings; go over the ratings with some students to learn more about their rationales; try to summarize the students' ratings in your own words). A handbook could also list books and services available for instructional development (e.g., McKeachie, 1969; Bergquist & Phillips, 1975; Bormann & Bormann, 1972; Verderber, 1973).

A final topic on interpretation of student ratings is norms. The purpose of norms is to show what rating the "average" or "typical" instructor got, so that one knows how high or low one's own ratings are by comparison. There are dangers to norms, however. First, they are sometimes tricky to interpret. For example, if most of the faculty are in reality very good teachers, one could be "below average" on the norms and still be good; conversely, if most of the faculty are very poor teachers, a poor teacher will still be "above average." Second, norms can cause some morale problems, because half the faculty will have to be below average. And third, unless they are very carefully developed, norms can be more misleading than helpful. Probably the most frequent error in developing norms is to compute the average rating in all courses. The problem is that courses are different, some harder to teach than others. An overall average might end up comparing a senior seminar on a "fun" topic with an unpopular required lecture. A better practice would be to group courses according to the task facing the instructor—that is, according to course objectives, format, content, and type of students—and then to compute the average of the mean ratings for each group of courses. Even then, however, one really ought to look at the words on the rating scale associated with the average rating, so that an instructor who is below average but "good" is seen differently from one who is below average and "poor." In short, a good interpretation is both norm-referenced and absolute, or criterion-referenced.

Finally, there are a number of things an institution can do to ward off complaints—and, simultaneously, to develop a better evaluation system. The first is to develop the details of the system jointly with all the people who will be affected by it—faculty, students, administrators, and maybe even trustees. Otherwise the chances are good that it will be seen as an imposition to be resented or a game to be outwitted. The second thing is to make provision for the instructor's own view of the course: how well it went, what was especially difficult about it, what new teaching technique was tried but failed, and so forth. This kind of information should be as much a part of the system as the student ratings. And it should be routine—perhaps on a standard questionnaire—so that the instructor who has a legitimate reason for disagreeing with the students or who has valid mitigating information to provide is not forced to be seen as defensive or unable to take criticism. A third thing an institution can do to build a better system is to review that system regularly. Are the questions on the questionnaire still important and clear or could they be improved? Are there any kinds of courses for which the system is just not working, that need some different evaluation system to meet their special needs (e.g., studio courses, team-taught courses, tutorial courses)? Is there any skulduggery going on that should be checked? Is the procedure for tabulating, reporting, and interpreting evaluations still satisfactory? And lastly, are there any other valid complaints that can suggest ways the system might be improved?

To complement a thoughtful evaluation system, institutions should make sure that instructors have some good resources to help them improve teaching. At the very least, the institution should have a small, accessible, well-publicized library of good books on instruction (e.g., McKeachie, 1969; Bergquist & Phillips, 1975; Bormann & Bormann, 1972; Verderber, 1973). Better would be some instructional consultants, either professional educational development specialists or just plain good teachers (with freed time) who are willing and able to help their colleagues. And best, an institution (or a consortium of institutions) might establish policies to reward faculty for efforts and success at improving teaching and set up an office to provide whatever instructional development services the faculty need.

All of these practices together should make for a good and responsible evaluation program.

Part IV

Reward Structures in Higher Education

The chapters in Part Four focus on the empirical aspects of current reward structures in American higher education.

Although all forms of faculty reward structures are reviewed, primary attention is given to salaries. Chapter 8 introduces this part by reviewing the various types of rewards commonly available to faculty members and the various incentives these rewards create. Chapter 9 reviews the historical and current economic status of salaries in higher education. Sex differences in academic rewards are examined in Chapters 10 and 11. Chapter 12 is concerned with the likely relationships between faculty reward systems and the recent emergence of unionization in higher education. Wherever possible, from the data and analysis, policy alternatives are presented.

Chapter 8

The Academic Reward Structure in American Higher Education

Howard P. Tuckman

Over the years a variety of laws, customs, and practices have been established that provide an incentive for faculty to engage in some activities and to ignore others. At the same time, the academic labor markets have assigned a premium to certain types of skills while placing no value on others. Virtually all departments bestow rewards on their faculty. These take the form of salary increments, assignments to prestigious committees, trips to conventions, and the like. Departments also dispense what at least some faculty will regard as penalties. These take the form of higher teaching loads, assignments to less desirable courses, more student advising, and so forth.

To the extent that engaging in one particular type of activity gives rise to rewards while engaging in another gives rise to penalties, faculty members have an incentive to alter their behavior.[1] The decision is a voluntary one; no one compels a faculty member to respond to an incentive. Nevertheless, failure to respond to the reward structure can lead to a reduced rate of salary growth (usually as measured in real terms), a less desirable teaching schedule, an inability to move to another position, and so forth. It seems reasonable to hypothesize that the academic reward structure plays a role in determining how at least some faculty allocate their time among competing uses. For this reason, it is important for us to understand both the nature of that structure and the incentives it creates.

The purpose of this chapter is to explore the academic reward structure, its possible consequences, and its future. We begin by de-

fining four types of rewards available to faculty members. Data are then presented both from a twenty-two field sample and for two individual disciplines to provide quantitative evidence of how the activities faculty undertake affect their salaries and their chances for promotion.[2] The importance of the time span of an activity is then analyzed, and data on the time allocation of different age cohorts are presented. The chapter concludes with a discussion of recent changes in academe and their likely effects on the academic reward structure.

FOUR MAJOR CATEGORIES OF REWARDS

I have argued elsewhere that at least four forms of rewards are available to faculty.[3] The most direct is the salary increment or merit raise provided faculty by their department or by higher administrative levels. In good times this increment is likely to be over and above the amount received to cover cost of living changes; in bad times, it comes at the expense of a decline in the real salaries of nonproductive faculty. The size of this increment will depend on the finances of the employing department and institution, the productivity of the other members of the department, whether an outside job offer has been received, and the faculty member's base salary.

The lifetime value of a direct salary increment is significantly greater than one would suppose if it is viewed only in the year of receipt. A merit increase of $150 given to a young assistant professor may be reflected throughout that person's career. To calculate its true value, a researcher may find it useful to employ an investment framework and to discount the salary increment over the person's working lifetime. We shall return to this point later in the chapter.

Direct nonmonetary satisfactions provide a second form of remuneration. These include acclaim from students and peers and feelings of self-satisfaction and self-worth. The importance of these factors as incentives for faculty should not be minimized. No doubt some faculty trade prestige for monetary rewards in deciding which activities to undertake (Marsh & Stafford, 1967). Unfortunately, the empirical evidence on this point is limited.

Promotion to a higher rank represents a third form of reward. In some departments the probability of promotion to a higher rank increases with publication; in a few, teaching and departmental service are also important. Promotion represents an indirect form of reward. The person undertakes an activity valued by his department. As a result he may be promoted. Promotion brings prestige, self-esteem, and a higher salary. But the rewards are obtained only if the promotion is obtained.

The career options, both internal and external, that result from engaging in an activity provide a fourth form of reward. Internal options usually involve positions in the administrative hierarchy of the university; external options include access to research grants, outside consulting, opportunities to move into and out of government jobs, and so forth.[4] To the extent that the exercise of these options involves behavior consistent with the internal structure of academe, this is likely to be sanctioned by the reward structure. Some of the external options may require behavior that conflicts with academic norms and thus may give rise to negative sanctions. For example, a young assistant professor may increase his income by writing many short reports on business conditions for local industry. If, as a result, he fails to publish, he may never achieve a higher rank.

These four categories are not exhaustive. Excluded, for example, are rewards in the form of reduced teaching loads or more favorable hours. This is because of the difficulty involved in obtaining a reasonable monetary equivalent for such items. Also excluded are the rewards faculty receive in the form of increased resources such as more graduate students. An accurate reckoning of these involves a balancing of both the benefits and the costs to the faculty member. Ideally, all of these elements should be included in the reward structure; the evidence presented in this chapter represents a humble first step toward providing quantitative estimates of the incentives provided by this structure.

THE DIRECT REWARDS TO FACULTY

The first step in our analysis is to examine the rewards to those engaged in four areas—teaching, research, public service, and administration. These activities are chosen as the ones most directly linked to the academic labor markets for faculty. A more complete discussion of how these markets operate, particularly in regard to determining a reward for the successful exercise of a skill may be found elsewhere (Tuckman, 1976; ch. 3). Used to capture the effects of these activities are data from the 1972–1973 American Council on Education's national survey of faculty. From this data source of 53,034 faculty in over seventy-two fields, we have selected 16,421 faculty in twenty-two fields.[5] The results reported below are based solely on the responses of full-time faculty employed at public and private universities.

To obtain estimates of the direct effects on salaries of engaging in each activity, a regression equation is run, with institutional salary as the dependent variable. The independent variables, chosen on the

basis of earlier work by researchers in this area, include years of experience, length of time required to complete the highest degree, whether the faculty member has a Ph.D., several interaction variables between time required to obtain the degree and the Ph.D. and experience variables, and race.[6] Also included are dummy variables for the faculty member's region and field. For present purposes, our sole interest is in the activity variables. The regression coefficients for these are shown in Table 8–1.

A dummy variable that assumes a value of 1 if the number of articles published by a faculty member falls into the corresponding category is used to capture the effect of publication on salary. A similar procedure is used to capture the effect of the books published by a faculty member. This formulation is necessitated by the survey instrument and has the advantage of enabling us to capture nonlinearities in the data. The teaching variable assumes a 1 if the faculty

Table 8–1. Average Dollar Increments Received by Faculty Engaged in the Four Major Activities, Holding Other Salary-determining Elements Constant.

Variable Name	Male		Female	
	Regression Coefficient	*Percent of The Sample in This Category*	*Regression Coefficient*	*Percent of The Sample in This Category*
Articles				
1–2	$714*	11	$181	20
3–4	882*	11	1,342*	16
5–10	1,467*	20	1,860*	17
11–20	2,325*	19	3,142*	13
21–50	3,766*	19	5,054*	9
50 +	6,505*	11	6,232*	3
Books				
1–2	106	32	−434	32
3–4	397	14	−390	10
5–10	915*	9	402	6
10 +	321	3	−1,126	1
Teaching	174	16	−43	18
Public Service	535*	49	209	56
Administration				
Current	3,044*	15	2,345*	14
Previous	1,260*	32	860**	24

*Coefficient for this variable significant at 1 percent confidence level.
**Coefficient significant at a 5 percent level.
Source: Based on Tuckman (1976: 57).

member has received a teaching award from his or her home institution. Likewise, the public service variable assumes a 1 if the faculty member has engaged in unpaid public service. Administrative skills are captured by two variables. The first equals 1 if the person is currently primarily engaged in administration, while the second equals 1 if the person was previously a department head or dean. In comparison to the publications variables, the latter three variables measure whether a person participated in an activity, not the intensity of participation.[7]

These results suggest several interesting insights into the direct salary rewards obtained by faculty. Note that both males and females receive sizable salary increments from publication (except in the first category). In fact, the rewards to those with a large number of articles swamp those to faculty engaged in virtually any other activity. For example, a male faculty member with over fifty articles averages more than two times as much as a male administrator. What is not immediately obvious from the table, however, is that the returns to each additional article diminish. When a curve is fit to smooth out the data and the value of each incremental article is calculated, the data indicate that a male faculty member averages a $472 salary increment for his first article and a female $250; the fifth article yields each $156 and $175, respectively, and the twenty-fifth, $79 and $138. We have analyzed the differential rewards to the two sexes by field elsewhere (Tuckman, Gapinski, & Hagemann, 1977). It is sufficient to note here that the incentive structure is different for the two sexes and that it favors publication by females to a greater extent than publication by males.

While these figures do not take into account the effects of publication on income received outside the academic institution, they are nonetheless suggestive. Unless the costs of producing an article fall more rapidly than the benefits (a prospect that is not likely for most faculty members), the incentive to publish will diminish for the faculty member as the number of articles he or she produces increases.

Equally interesting is the fact that for the 16 percent of the men and the 18 percent of the women who received an award for outstanding teaching, no monetary reward was observed. Of course, some persons may have received a financial award, but on average, no statistically significant salary increment was observed for either sex. Males engaged in unpaid public service fared slightly better, although the monetary reward revealed by the regression is appreciably smaller than that to the prolific publisher or the current or past administrator. In fact, the results indicate that the highest rewards go to those who can both publish extensively and pursue a career in administration.[8]

DIRECT REWARDS IN
THE DIFFERENT FIELDS

Researchers have long argued that the labor market for academics is balkanized into separate submarkets by field.[9] This is partially due to the low degree of skill substitution and to the difference in the demand for various faculty skills across fields. It also reflects different tastes and preferences regarding the lifestyle implied by entry into a particular field. If the market forces differ among fields, it is likely that the rewards also differ.

To test this hypothesis, we divided the faculty in our sample into five groups and ran a regression identical to the one presented above for each.[10] Only males were included, since too few females were available in the sample to permit the estimation of separate equations. The same variables are used to estimate the rewards to the four skills in each field, even though other variables might have been added to improve the specification. For example, the salary of an artist is affected by the number of performances (exhibitions) he gives and, in some schools, by the number of students he teaches. Because our primary goal is to examine whether and how the returns to the four activities differ by field, we accept the possibility of misspecification of the equations. It is important to note, however, that different dollar estimates of the rewards to the activities might be obtained if the estimation equations were tailored to include the salary determinants unique to the individual fields.

Social Science. In all of the social sciences except anthropology, those with articles earn more than those with no articles, but in some fields, salary does not rise systematically as the number of articles produced increases. In economics, geography, and sociology, salaries increase monotonically with the number of articles produced. In history, those with over fifty articles receive $3,217 more than those with no articles, but the salary increments below this level show no clear pattern. Political scientists with eleven to twenty or twenty-one to fifty articles receive statistically significant returns ($1,301 and $3,010, respectively), but above and below this range the link between articles and salary is tenuous. In psychology, the statistically significant categories are twenty-one to fifty and fifty plus.

Book publication is rewarded, albeit less than article publication, in economics, psychology, history, political science, and sociology. In the latter three fields, the pattern is uneven. In geography it is barely significant, and in anthropology it is not rewarded. Teaching is rewarded only in geography ($1,060), while public service brings a

reward of $541 in economics, $1,110 in history, $789 in political science, and $922 in sociology. The reward for public service is higher than that reported in the last section in three of these fields and roughly equal in one (economics). Both current and previous administration receive large and statistically significant salary increments in all of the fields. Current administration increases average salaries by $3,987 in economics, $3,063 in geography, $5,314 in history, $3,927 in political science, $2,497 in psychology, and $2,045 in sociology.

Engineering and Math. Article publication is associated with a rising salary in all of the three fields included in this category. With a few exceptions the relationship is monotonic, and in all cases the effect on salaries is statistically significant. Book publication has no effect on salaries in civil engineering; in electrical engineering and mathematics, it augments salaries only within the three to ten book range. Outstanding teaching is not rewarded in any of the three fields, while public service is not significant in electrical engineering, but raises salaries an average of $1,215 in civil engineering and $576 in mathematics. Current and past administration are rewarded by large and statistically significant salary increments; the former raises salaries by $2,563 in civil engineering, $2,945 in electrical engineering, and $2,440 in mathematics.

Physical Sciences. The physical sciences are characterized by large salary increments to those who have published over fifty articles—$4,955 in chemistry, $4,855 in earth science, and $7,764 in physics. Below the twenty-one to fifty category the pattern is uneven, and it is unclear that article publication has a direct effect on salary. This may be related to the fact that virtually all of the faculty in these fields publish articles.[11]

Book publication brings a significant reward in chemistry; the pattern is less clear in the earth sciences and physics. Once again, teaching is not rewarded in any of the fields—and may even be penalized in earth science—while public service apparently yields a monetary reward of $486 in chemistry and $1,070 in physics. Current and past administration again produce large and significant rewards. For the former, the reward is $2,557 in chemistry, $5,179 in earth science, and $3,326 in physics.

Liberal Arts. In both English and music, article publication is associated with a significant increase in salary. The relationship in the former field is a monotonic one; in the latter, the pattern is uneven,

and significant increments are observed only in the eleven to twenty and twenty-one to fifty articles categories. Book publication brings a positive and significant increment in salary in English; it is significant only for those with more than ten books in music. Outstanding teaching brings a reward in neither field, and public service is rewarded by a statistically significant increment ($645) only in music. Both current and past administration bring higher salaries. For the former, the salary increment is $2,216 in English and $4,074 in music.

The Professions. In law and education, salary increases as the number of articles published increases. In medicine and pharmacy the returns to article publication are negative and not significant, perhaps reflecting the fact that researchers earn less than practitioners in these fields. Book publication is rewarded only in the field of education. Outstanding teaching is not rewarded in any of the four fields, and public service brings a statistically significant reward of $648 only in education. Current administration is rewarded in education ($2,670), law ($3,944), and medicine ($4,278). Past administration is rewarded only in education and medicine.

Biological Sciences. As in the case of the physical sciences, article publication carries a monetary reward only for the most prolific publishers, perhaps reflecting the fact that virtually all of the faculty in these fields publish. Those who write books do not receive a systematic monetary reward in any of the fields, and public service is also not rewarded. Outstanding teaching appears to be rewarded in botany but not in the other two fields, while current administration carries an average salary increment of $4,598 in biochemistry, $4,497 in botany, and $2,673 in zoology. Previous administration is rewarded in biochemistry and zoology.

Summary

Together, these findings suggest that while it may be useful to talk about a single reward structure for some purposes, the direct monetary rewards differ, in some cases dramatically, by academic field. Thus, faculty are subject to a different relative set of incentives depending on which discipline they are in. There are, however, several commonalities in the data that merit further exploration. In all fields, for example, participation in current administration, with rare exceptions, brings a large and statistically significant salary increment. The estimates presented here may understate this increment

since they ignore the increased access that administrators have to eleven or twelve month appointments.[12] However, they also ignore the opportunities for outside employment that administrators may forego as a result of their administrative duties. On the basis of these figures, it seems likely that a faculty member wishing to increase his institutional income, and either unwilling or unable to publish large quantities of articles, has a strong incentive to attempt a career in academic administration.

Article publication brings a salary increment in almost all of the fields studied. In the sciences the direct rewards appear to accrue only to those who publish in excess of the median number of articles in their fields; for many other disciplines, an incremental article creates an incremental salary increase. In contrast, those who choose to publish books can expect to receive smaller rewards from their institutions or to receive no rewards at all. For most fields, the first few articles carry substantially higher rewards than the first few books. However, because of the presence of diminishing returns, a point exists where it becomes more profitable to publish a book than to publish one more article. Where this point occurs depends on the particular field, on the relative costs of producing the book rather than the article, on the indirect rewards to each form of publication, and on the non-university-provided revenues that an author can expect to receive from each type of publication. On the basis of the evidence presented in this chapter, the incentives in most fields favor an initial investment of time in article publication.

Outstanding teaching is rewarded in two of the twenty-two fields in our study and may be penalized in one. While this finding may be due to the particular measure used to capture quality teaching, it fits with both intuition and with what can be observed at most universities. Whether a similar finding would hold for other types of academic institutions remains an open question.

Finally, the evidence with respect to the rewards to public service is mixed. In 45 percent of the fields, public service is rewarded; in the remainder it is not. Generally, public service appears to be more highly valued in the social sciences and less valued in the professions. No clear pattern emerges in the sciences and professions, perhaps reflecting the broad and basically amorphous nature of this activity.

On balance, these results suggest that, in terms of direct salary increments, monetary incentives exist for faculty to choose some activities over others. The second step is examine the extent to which these incentives exist at the promotion level.

THE FOUR ACTIVITIES AND THEIR
EFFECT ON PROMOTION

While a fairly large body of literature exists on the determinants of salaries in academe, surprisingly little information is available on the determinants of promotion. Data of this type are difficult to obtain, since promotion and tenure committees rarely announce their criteria for promotion with specificity, the weights given to the individual criteria change from one year to the next, and the folders of both those considered and those rejected are usually not open to public scrutiny. Nonetheless, the activities examined above, with the exception of administration, are the ones normally cited as having a substantial effect on a person's chances for promotion. Thus, it is useful to explore the actual extent to which they increase the probability of promotion to a higher rank.

A multivariate technique is used to estimate the probability of promotion to the associate and full professor ranks with the faculty member's publications, teaching experience, public service, degree level, and experience as the independent variables.[13] For each rank, an equation is fit for a subsample of faculty that includes both those promoted in the year of and in the year preceding the ACE study and those not promoted. Separate equations are run for males and females. Table 8−2 shows the unsmoothed probabilities obtained from these equations.

The findings reported in Table 8−2 once again suggest a strong incentive for faculty to publish, especially at the assistant professor level. Note the rising probability of promotion (with one partial exception) associated with article publication at the associate level. In contrast, the link becomes more tenuous for males at the full professor level, with the probability increasing significantly only in the over twenty articles categories; for females only, the eleven to twenty and twenty-one to fifty categories are significant. For both sexes, publication has a greater effect on the probability of promotion to associate than to full professor, perhaps reflecting the existence of other productivity criteria at the latter rank.

The effect of publishing a book is uneven both by rank and by sex. While it seems likely that those who have published a book have a greater chance for promotion in three out of the four cases (the exception being females at the associate level), the relationship is not well defined, as can be seen by the drop in the ten plus category.[14]

The results also clearly suggest that an outstanding teaching award increases the probability of promotion by an amount roughly equal to about 2.5 articles for males; for females the relationship is not

Table 8–2. Probability of Promotion to a Higher Rank by Type of Activity, Rank, and Sex.

Activity	Males		Females	
	Promotion to the Rank of		Promotion to the Rank of	
	Associate	Full	Associate	Full
Articles				
1–2	0.022	0.002	0.003	0.016
3–4	0.074*	0.026	0.122*	0.052
5–10	0.152*	0.014	0.184*	0.017
11–20	0.231*	0.076*	0.185*	0.117*
21–50	0.373*	0.149*	0.270*	0.156*
50 +	0.512*	0.311*	0.850*	+
Books				
1–2	0.096**	0.063*	0.063	0.026
3–4	0.183*	0.110*	0.018	0.146*
5–10	0.165	0.163*	−0.085	0.311*
10 +	0.190*	0.155*	−0.051	0.052
Teaching	0.064	0.003	0.065	0.072
Public Service	0.018	0.023*	0.032	−0.009

*Denotes coefficient significant at 1 percent level.
**Significant at 5 percent level.
+Insufficient observations in this cell.
Source: Based on the procedure described in the text and on American Council on Education data.

statistically significant. The outstanding male teacher with none of the other activities to his credit would have less than a 7 percent chance of promotion, holding years of experience constant. For promotion to the full professor level, outstanding teaching appears to have no statistically significant effect on the probability of promotion for either sex.

Those who engage in public service also do not substantially increase their chances for promotion. At the associate professor level, neither coefficient is statistically significant, and both are small. At the full professor level, public service has a statistically significant effect on male promotions, but the 2 percent increase implied by the coefficient is hardly cause for optimism for those solely engaged in this activity.

It is difficult to avoid the conclusion that article publication has the greatest impact on a faculty member's chances for promotion in academe, at least when viewed in terms of the average person in

our twenty-two field sample. This impression is further borne out when the data are examined for the individual fields. Table 8−3 shows the smoothed probabilities of promotion for the males in the fields of economics and education, the two fields to which we have applied the model.[15]

Note that once again article publication contributes significantly to the probability of promotion. As in the regression for all fields, the contribution is stronger at the associate professor than at the full professor level. Likewise, in both fields publication of articles gives rise to a higher probability of promotion than publication of books, especially when consideration is given to the fact that several articles can be written in the time required to write one book.[16] The probabilities for the other activities (not shown) approximate those shown in Table 8−3; neither teaching nor public service activities compare to publication activities in their contribution to promotion. The academic rewards clearly accrue to those who publish.

FACULTY ACTIVITIES AND THEIR EFFECT ON CAREER OPTIONS

It seems reasonable to hypothesize that the activities faculty perform within academe give rise to career options that they may later choose

Table 8−3.   **Effects of Publication on the Probability of Promotion to a Higher Rank for Males in the Fields of Economics and Education.**

| | Economics | | Education | |
| | Promotion to the Rank of | | Promotion to the Rank of | |
Activity	Associate	Full	Associate	Full
Articles				
1	0.074	0.138	0.083	0.000
5	0.221	0.199	0.136	0.002
10	0.320	0.273	0.206	0.022
15	0.481	0.342	0.279	0.041
20	0.552	0.468	0.350	0.059
Books				
1	0.001	0.000	0.061	0.000
3	0.052	0.021	0.076	0.017
5	0.103	0.021	0.094	0.037
7	0.147	0.040	0.114	0.050
10	0.196	0.103	0.151	0.060

Source: See Tuckman & Hagemann (1976: 456-61). Note that these represent smoothed probabilities. Thus, the significance levels of the individual coefficients are not reported.

to exercise. These may be of an internal type, such as promotion to dean, provost, or another administrative position. They may also take the form of external opportunities to consult for business and industry, to serve in government positions for short periods, and so forth.

Experiments with several predictive equations failed to reveal a systematic relationship between the four activities discussed in this chapter and the various internal and external career options. In part, this is due to the limited data available to analyze external career options; a far more extensive data source is necessary to deal with this issue than that provided by the ACE.[17] It may also be related to the fact that many faculty who exercise an external option are self-selected out of our sample. However, our experiments do suggest that internal options are related to faculty rank and age. Likewise, external options are related to both of these variables and to the faculty member's field of specialization.

The finding that both external and internal career options are related to rank suggests an indirect relationship between the four activities and career options that has provocative implications. While engaging in an activity such as publication may not have a direct effect on one's career options, it nonetheless increases access through its effects on the probability of promotion. Thus, the faculty member is provided an incentive to participate in these activities that is greater than it would be if career options were purely exogeneous. However, if the link is indeed solely an indirect one, then once the faculty member is promoted to the full professor rank, the incentives provided by the desire to generate external and internal career options may diminish.[18] To the extent that this is the case, a shift in the allocation of time among activities would be observed after faculty reach the full professor rank.

Field of specialization proves to be an important explanatory variable in explaining external career options.[19] The largest number of external options are available to faculty in the professions, particularly those in business, education, and the medical schools. Those in the sciences, math, and engineering also appear to have a large number of options, although these vary substantially among the fields. The social sciences as a group have the next largest number of options, but once again there is a substantial variance among fields. Music and liberal arts faculty have the fewest options available.

To test the robustness of these findings, the faculty in our sample were separated by ten year cohorts starting with age twenty-five, and the equations were rerun. With few exceptions, the ranking of the dscipline groups held constant, although the position of several of

the fields within the discipline groups reversed. The results appear to refute the hypothesis that the activities a person performs directly affect his career options.[20]

INCENTIVES AND FACULTY AGE

Studies of the determinants of faculty salaries focus either on age or experience as an important independent variable. In fact, age can be decomposed into two separate components: (1) Start: year of highest degree minus year of birth. This variable measures length of time required to obtain the highest degree. (2) Experience: year of the study minus year of highest degree. This is not a true experience variable since the faculty member may not have spent all of his time since receiving his last degree in academe. For current purposes, it is useful to distinguish a third variable, "left," which equals age of retirement minus current age. As age increases, "left" diminishes.

Most studies of faculty and their environment focus on either age or experience, although a recent study of faculty salaries included a measure of when faculty started their career.[21] In terms of the incentives that confront faculty, left is probably the key variable. The importance of left can be illustrated by a simple example. Suppose a new assistant professor hired at age thirty has thirty-five years of work left. Suppose too that during his second year, he publishes an article and receives a $500 increment over the amount received by his colleague. The value of that increment will grow through time as his salary grows. Column 1 of Table 8–4 shows the value of that increment in his tenth, twentieth, and thirtieth year of experience.

The figures in this table are based on the assumption that increments are given as a percentage of the base salary and that salaries rise by 5 percent a year. Under this assumption, a $500 salary increment grows by almost four times its initial value in thirty years.

Suppose, however, that instead of publishing in his second year the person published in his fifth year and received the same $500.

Table 8–4. Growth in Salary Increment by Time at Which Increment is Received.

Value at End of His	Increment at End of:				
	2nd	*5th*	*9th*	*15th*	*25th*
10th year	$739	$638	$525	—	—
20th year	1,203	1,039	855	638	—
30th year	1,960	1,693	1,392	1,039	638

The comparable values at each level of experience are shown in the column marked "5th." As can be seen, at the end of the thirtieth year, the salary increment is only about 3.4 times greater than the initial increment. Comparable figures are also shown for faculty in their ninth, fifteenth, and twenty-fifth year, and fairly hefty reductions in the value of the increment can be observed.

Table 8-4 is open to several criticisms, but the basic point it makes is a sound one. Because a salary increment enters the base, it becomes a permanent part of a faculty member's salary. To the extent that raises are made as a percentage of the base, the value of the increment increases through time. But the later in life the increment is received, the less its value. Thus, faculty with a large "left" value have the greatest incentive to respond to differential rewards.

There are two other effects that relate to these variables. The longer the time left to the faculty member, the larger the present value of his salary increment. This is because the increment is not received in only one year, but rather represents a flow of payments throughout the faculty member's career.[22] As in the case just described, faculty with a larger left value have the greatest incentive to strive for a salary increment. Second, because of the indirect incentives discussed earlier, faculty at the lower ranks (usually those with the largest left variables) have a greater incentive to respond to incentives than those at upper ranks. For the assistant professor, the incentive is the strongest because his activities contribute to promotion to both the associate and full professor rank and to the opening of future career options.

Taken in total, these results suggest the rather substantial incentives to those with a long work life remaining and the more restricted incentives to those with a short work life.

CHANGES IN THE ACTIVITIES FACULTY PERFORM THROUGH TIME

To what extent are the changes in the allocation of faculty time across activities in accord with the incentives discussed above? If faculty respond to the set of rewards outlined in this chapter, we would expect to see several behavioral changes through time: (1) Since teaching is not rewarded as an activity, at least some faculty might be expected to seek out other types of primary activities while remaining in academe; hours spent in teaching preparation might also be expected to decline. (2) Since research (at least if translated into publications) is rewarded, the proportion of faculty engaged in research might be expected to increase through time.[23] However, as

faculty age, the time remaining to receive the rewards of research diminishes. Which of the two forces is stronger remains to be seen; the data favor the latter, however. (3) For faculty close to retirement, there is little, if any, reward to further productivity, and thus, the hours spent in all forms of academic activity for this group are likely to be low.

Table 8—5 breaks the faculty in our sample into seven experience cohorts. The faculty in each cohort are subdivided in terms of the primary work activity they reported on the ACE questionnaire. Finally, males and females are separated to permit a contrasting of the two groups.

Table 8—5 suggests somewhat different changes through time in the primary work activities of males and females. For males, a shift toward administration and away from teaching occurs. In the first cohort, nearly 7 percent are in administration; in the fifth, over 21 percent. Recall that our analysis of the incentive structure suggests no significant direct rewards to teaching and indirect rewards only at the early stages of a male faculty member's career. In contrast, there are large direct rewards to administration. Thus, the patterns observed in this table are consistent with our hypothesized behavior. No appreciable differences in the long-run percentage of males engaged in research is observed. The rise in the first three cohorts is consistent with the hypothesis that the returns to research (and its handmaiden, publication) are greatest in the early stages of a faculty member's career; the later shifts away from research and into administration also accord well with the observed rewards to each activity.

The pattern for females is difficult to interpret in terms of our proposed hypotheses. Recall that in Table 8—1, in all article categories except the first and last, females earn more per article than males. Moreover, the average salary increment that females receive for being administrators ($2,345) is less than that for males ($3,044). These facts suggest that a larger proportion of females should prefer research to administration than should males. Yet, an analysis of the data suggests a smaller proportion of females in research. The movement toward research in later years might suggest that structural impediments prevent females from achieving their research goals until later in their careers. In this case the data would be consistent with our hypotheses.

Alternatively, the observed patterns may be due to the effects of affirmative action, which could affect the data in two ways. First, to obtain more female administrators, the universities may be offering administrative positions to females of younger ages. This would

Table 8–5. Primary Work Activity of Faculty by Experience Level.

Experience Cohort	Males				Females			
	Administration	Teaching	Research	Other	Administration	Teaching	Research	Other
0–5	6.7	81.1	10.6	1.6	13.6	78.0	3.7	4.7
6–10	10.8	74.4	13.1	1.7	13.6	77.0	5.8	3.6
11–15	17.3	65.8	14.4	2.6	15.1	74.7	7.2	3.0
16–20	18.7	67.0	11.8	2.6	11.6	76.1	9.7	2.6
21–25	21.5	67.6	9.1	1.8	16.1	66.4	11.7	5.8
26–30	22.0	63.4	11.6	2.9	9.7	79.0	4.8	6.5
31–35	20.5	66.9	10.6	2.0	9.4	77.4	9.4	3.8

Source: Tuckman (1976: 98).

raise the percentage in the initial cohorts relative to that in the later ones. Second, affirmative action may have opened research positions not previously available to females. Females not previously able to obtain research positions and wanting them would be more likely to be in the more experienced cohorts.

In the absence of longitudinal data that follow the same persons through time, it is difficult to discriminate among these alternative explanations. Thus, the materials presented here and those below might best be regarded as inconclusive.[24] They do appear to support the hypothesis that females are treated differently than males, however.

As a second basis for evaluating the above hypotheses, it is useful to look at the distribution of faculty hours among alternative activities and how it changes through time. The two measures used here are time spent in preparing for teaching each week and time spent in research each week. Unfortunately, the hours are reported in terms of intervals rather than actual values. The interval data are not as sensitive to changes in faculty behavior, since small changes in hours could leave the faculty member in the same interval. To avoid this problem, and to permit comparisons across fields with widely divergent time requirements, we constructed a new measure: the proportion of faculty spending less than or the same number of hours as the median for their field. An increase in this measure suggests a decline in the percentage of time spent in the activity. Table 8-6 shows the relevant percentages for males in three discipline groups—the biological sciences, the liberal arts, and the social sciences. The median hours for each field are shown in the bottom row of the table.

The percentage of male faculty spending the median number of hours or less in preparation for teaching rises in all three fields.[25] About twenty percentage points more of the faculty are below the median in the cohort thirty-one to thirty-five than in the cohort zero to five in the biological sciences, and a roughly similar percentage point increase is observed for the liberal arts; for the social sciences, the percentage point increase is substantially less, although there is a 16 percent increase in the midrange experience cohorts. The dropoff in research hours is less pronounced in two of the fields and fails to occur in the liberal arts. The data at least suggest the possibility that the dropoff is more severe the greater the median hours spent in research.

Similar patterns are observed for the females in our sample (not shown). In all three fields, the percentage of faculty spending the median amount of time or less on teaching diminishes—in the first

Table 8–6. Percentage of Male Faculty Spending the Median Number of Hours or Less in Preparation for Teaching and Research, Select Fields.

Experience Cohort	Biological Sciences		Liberal Arts		Social Sciences	
	Teaching	Research	Teaching	Research	Teaching	Research
0–5	42.3	57.3	52.2	53.9	54.5	46.4
6–10	51.5	57.6	57.7	49.3	65.7	46.6
11–15	50.5	63.5	79.8	56.0	68.7	55.0
16–20	54.4	64.9	71.1	61.6	70.3	57.0
21–25	50.9	74.3	65.1	61.8	70.6	57.0
26–30	55.7	72.0	73.2	50.0	61.8	56.5
31–35	61.5	74.7	72.1	50.7	61.9	57.7
Median Hours	5–8	17–20	13–16	5–8	9–12	9–12

Source: Tuckman (1976: 101, 102).

two, by twenty percentage points, and in the third, by over twenty-five percentage points. Likewise, the proportion spending the median amount of time or less on research diminishes by twenty percentage points in the first two fields, but decreases seventeen percentage points in the social sciences. The unevenness of the pattern for research makes generalizations hazardous. Nonetheless, in at least two out of the three disciplines for both males and females, hours spent in teaching and research declined relative to the median as faculty aged.

Several caveats are needed in analyzing these data. First, they ignore many of the other factors that affect the options available to faculty as they age, including their previous accomplishments, work history, field of specialty, and so forth. Moreover, the reward structure may change through time. Our crude analysis compares existing incentives to existing work behavior. To the extent that behavior operates with a lag and incentives change rapidly, the comparisons made here may be misleading. Third, biological, environmental, and psychological forces come into play that are excluded from the present analysis (Merton, 1968; Cole, 1973; Allison & Steward, 1974). Fourth, the patterns reported above are consistent with other hypotheses regarding changes in faculty productivity as a result of aging. The crude comparisons made here do not discriminate among the several explanations.

Despite these limitations, it seems reasonable to suggest that the observed behavior patterns reported above are not inconsistent with the hypothesis that the reward structure affects faculty behavior. A more rigorous test of this hypothesis must await better data.

RECENT CHANGES IN THE REWARD STRUCTURE

The recent belt-tightening in academe has the potential to change the reward structure in the following ways:

1. As the money available for salary increments becomes scarcer, it becomes more difficult for departments to provide large salary increases for merit relative to cost of living.

2. A compression may be occurring due to the slow growth of academic salaries relative to those outside of academe. This is because salaries of assistant professors are often more closely linked to outside markets than are those of associate and full professors. The result is a reduction in the relative rewards of productive faculty.

3. As the number of positions in academe diminish, the probability of promotion to a higher rank also diminishes. At the same time, the use of merit criteria may increase. The question is which of the two effects predominates.

4. Internal career options for faculty diminish as the number of positions in academe decreases. It is difficult to forecast the effects of these changes on the external options of faculty.

Evidence on the first point is difficult to obtain. However, recent issues of the *AAUP Bulletin* have shown academic salaries either barely keeping pace with cost of living increases or falling behind. Under these circumstances, merit money is likely to be obtained, if at all, by reducing cost of living increases to nonproductive faculty. Merit money provided by this means increases the relative income position of productive faculty relative to their nonproductive colleagues. Unfortunately, it probably leaves them relatively worse off compared to persons outside academe, and there are limits on how much merit money can be extracted from this source.[26]

Compression occurs when the salaries of those in the lower levels of the income distribution for a given industry or firm grow relative to those persons at the upper end of the distribution. A consequence is that the differentials attributable to merit are reduced in value relative to the rising salaries of faculty in the lower ranks. To explore whether compression is occurring in academe, two types of measures are formulated. The first is a ratio with the average compensation for a full professor in the ninth decile of the AAUP survey as the numerator and the average compensation for an assistant professor in the first as the denominator.[27] This ratio is 2.27 in 1972–1973, the first year for which data are available. In the following years the ratio falls slightly and then rises to 2.37 in 1976–1977. A similar comparison of full professors to instructors results in a ratio of 2.7 in 1972–1973 and of 2.8 in 1976–1977. These ratios suggest that within the five year period for which data are available, no compression occurred. In the 1976–1977 year, the evidence suggests a widening between ranks rather than a compression.[28]

A second form of compression can occur if the salary differentials of faculty within a rank narrow. Where this occurs, it is possible that the differentials between productive and nonproductive faculty also diminish. However, evidence of within rank compression does not necessarily suggest that the rewards to productivity are decreasing— for example, this result would also be observed if faculty became equally productive. The ratio of the average compensation of full professors in the ninth decile of the AAUP survey to the average

compensation of those in the first is computed for the period 1972–1973 to 1976–1977. Again, no evidence of a compression is found, and in 1976–1977, the ratio suggests a widening.[29]

Taken together, these two pieces of evidence suggest that the distribution of academic compensation has not narrowed in the last five years. But they leave unanswered the question of whether the rewards to different types of activities have changed. It is possible, for example, that the existing differential was preserved by flat, across the board increases to faculty; that some rewards were given to various types of behavior but at a lesser rate than in the past; or even that the reward structure reported earlier was altered somewhat from its previous form. The evidence reported above at least leaves open the possibility that direct monetary rewards were given to faculty for meritorious activities during this period.

The much heralded aging of the faculty has resulted in a slight decline in the proportion of assistant professors and instructors in academe, from 48 percent for the two ranks in 1972–1973 to 44 percent in 1976–1977.[30] Some growth has also occurred in the number of faculty at the associate professor rank, suggesting at least the early beginnings of a reduction in access to full professors positions; the trends are not strong enough to attach much weight to them, however.

It seems likely that if the number of academic positions begins to shrink in response to the enrollment decreases now forecast for the 1980s, the probability that a faculty member will be promoted will also shrink. At the same time, the weight given to merit in the promotion process may very well increase. The net effect of these offsetting influences on faculty incentives will depend on whether the increased rewards to merit offset the shrinking number of high level positions. At the moment this seems unlikely, and a net decrease in indirect incentives seems a more reasonable possibility.

Faculty access to internal career options will almost surely diminish in the next few years. A reduction in the number of academic institutions is almost certain to occur as an increasing number of institutions face pressure from declining enrollments and reduced federal funding. At the same time, the projected decrease in the demand for faculty is likely to reduce the number of administrators demanded, while forcing at least some faculty out of career administrative positions. Partially as a result of these events, an increasing number of academics are likely to seek out and exercise outside career options. In the short run this will probably reduce the number of external options available to those remaining in academe; it is also likely to result in an upgrading of the degree requirements for jobs involving research skills.

WHITHER THE ACADEMIC
REWARD STRUCTURE?

Several insights seem to emerge from our exploration of the academic reward structure. First, the rewards tend to be greatest for those at the lowest ranks. While the relative size of these rewards could diminish if the amount of money available for salary increments shrinks, we have found no evidence of this occurring in the last five years. What is not clear, however, is whether the advent of unionism and the increased emphasis on teaching by some state legislatures has altered the process by which salary raises are conferred. Our inquiry suggests that the funds are available to reward faculty according to merit; whether they are distributed this way at present and whether they will be in the future remains an open question.

Several speculations seem in order, however. The possibility exists that as the number of faculty shrinks in the late 1970s and early 1980s, those remaining will become more alike in their characteristics. If, for example, publication is made a prerequisite for promotion and retention, more faculty will find it necessary to publish than have in the past. To the extent that this occurs, we may find a pattern developing similar to that in the sciences; only those with publications in excess of the median may achieve direct salary rewards. But this does not seem to be a likely possibility given the relatively low publication levels of existing faculty. More likely is the prospect that publications will continue to distinguish among faculty, partially because they provide a quantitative, albeit imperfect, measure of productivity and partially because some older faculty are likely to stop publishing. While the relative reward to publication is likely to diminish, it seems unlikely that publication will go unrewarded.

The same cannot be said for teaching, committee work, advising, and the host of other activities that confront a faculty member. Success in these activities is hard to quantify and unlikely to bring professional recognition. Its rewards are most likely to be immediate ones, primarily in the form of increases in prestige and self-esteem. While legislatures, regents, trustees, and other governing boards may mandate standards for faculty to perform against, it is unlikely that these will have a major effect on faculty behavior in the absence of a more explicit and direct set of rewards for these activities.

Perhaps the most distressing aspect of our inquiry is the observation that the reward structure primarily favors performance when faculty have a large number of years left to work. In the absence of a change in the existing reward structure, it seems likely that as faculty members age, their incentive to remain productive will diminish. Given the expected aging of our nation's faculty members, this im-

plies a reduction in the overall productivity at American universities. It is difficult to interpret what this will mean for the intellectual development of our nation; it is almost certain to have an impact on the lives of individual faculty.

What is needed is a reward structure that recognizes the need for incentives at the associate and full professor levels. This might involve an increase in the number of ranks that faculty can hold and a concomitant increase in salary. It might also involve a system of rewards to senior faculty who excell in teaching and related activities. In the absence of such incentives, it seems likely that some senior faculty will lose interest in their work. The effects that this will have on the quality of their teaching, and on their students, are difficult to measure.

The academic reward structure is an amalgam of rules, precedents, rewards, and reactions to changes in academic labor markets. It has evolved piecemeal, and it has responded to changing markets most rapidly at the assistant professor and instructor levels. As the market for faculty contracts, and the academic community shrinks along with it, the need to pay greater attention to the signals sent out by the reward structure is virtually certain to grow. A well-designed set of incentives is likely to be one of the main means by which we can preserve the development and transfer of knowledge in the lean years that threaten to come upon us.

NOTES TO CHAPTER 8

1. Some authors argue that deans, department chairmen, and other decisionmakers are highly secretive about the types of behavior they reward. If this were widely the case, faculty would have little incentive to engage in an activity, since the effects of their behavior would be unknown. What is more likely is that faculty know that some behavior will be rewarded (i.e., publication); the dollar amount of the reward is not known, however.

2. It is useful to distinguish between an activity and a skill. An activity is something that a faculty member does. In the process of engaging in an activity or through study or inheritance, a faculty member acquires a skill. Faculty are probably rewarded for their skills rather than for engaging in an activity. In this chapter we use the two terms interchangeably, however.

3. The discussion in this chapter is drawn largely from the materials presented in Tuckman (1976).

4. It should be noted, however, that these options are often field-specific. In some fields there are many options; in others, there are few.

5. Included are the following fields grouped according to the HEGIS taxonomy: *Social Science*—anthropology, geography, economics, history, political science, psychology, and sociology; *Liberal Arts*—English, music; *Math-Engineering*—civil and electrical engineering, mathematics; *Biological Sciences*—biochem-

istry, botony, zoology; *Physical Sciences*—chemistry, earth sciences, physics; *Professions*—education, law, medicine, pharmacy.

6. For a more extensive discussion of this work, see Tuckman (1976: ch. 2).

7. A critique of these variables may be found in Tuckman and Hagemann (1976).

8. No allowance is made here for the differential in the amount of hours spent in each activity by faculty, however. The possibility exists that the wage rates of faculty are the same while the amount of time spent in the activities differs. But adjusting for hours alone would not be sufficient to meet this objection, since an hour spent in one activity may be more demanding than an hour spent in another.

9. See, for example, Brown (1967: 62–63, 66).

10. See note 5 for listing of these fields.

11. The median number of articles in all fields exceeds eleven and in one case exceeds twenty-one. This is substantially larger than the median for the other fields described above.

12. A separate variable is included in the equation to control for this.

13. For a more extensive discussion of the technique used here, see Tuckman (1976: ch. 6). Note that the coefficients obtained from the equation are interpreted as conditional probabilities. See Goldberge (1964: 248–55).

14. Entering and removing the book coefficients as a group, however, reveals that in all three regressions, they are statistically significant.

15. The data presented in this table are analyzed in greater detail in Tuckman and Hagemann (1976: 456–61).

16. Unfortunately, our data do not allow us to distinguish between scholarly books with long lead times and readers or monographs that take comparatively little effort. Had we been able to make this distinction, it is possible that scholarly works would have higher values than those reported here.

17. The ACE questionnaire contains data on days of paid and unpaid consulting, number of grants held, and jobs held outside of academe. Unfortunately, dates are not given for the latter variable, so that it is difficult to determine whether these jobs were held prior to or subsequent to the person's data of academic employment.

18. The term "diminish" is used here because activities like publication do provide a measure of national visibility, albeit often to a different group of persons than those the faculty member may wish to reach.

19. The results reported here represent a synthesis of several explanatory equations using different proxies for the dependent variable and broken down both by the HEGIS categories and for the individual fields.

20. At least two caveats apply to this conclusion. First, a career in academic administration (i.e., as a department head) often increases one's chances of reaching a higher office. But the results suggest that access to any administrative office is related to academic rank. Thus, there is a conceptual problem in deciding whether the administrative activity is the dependent or the independent variable. Second, this conclusion is based on a structural equation where field is controlled by a dummy variable that shifts the intercept term but does not allow for changes in slope. The possibility exists that within individual fields, the four activities may not be equally important.

21. For a list of these see the footnotes in Tuckman (1976: chs. 2 and 6).

22. For quantitative evidence on this point see Tuckman and Leahey (1975).

23. This statement assumes that the supply of research positions is not a factor impeding faculty choice of a primary work activity. At least at the university level this may not be a bad assumption, since faculty create research positions by the grant money they bring in. Of course, this leaves open the possibility that the grant agencies favor faculty at a certain age. For evidence on this point, see Tuckman (1976: 105—107).

24. For a discussion of the limitations of cross-section data for this purpose, see Tuckman (1976: 45).

25. The objection may be raised that this dropoff occurs because as faculty become more experienced, they require less time to prepare. One cannot help but wonder about the lack of obsolescence and senescence effects in later years, however.

26. This is especially true where a department chairman is elected by majority vote. In this case, 51 percent of the department must consistently receive at least some cost of living money, placing a limit on the amount available for raises. A 6 percent cost of living raise, for example, would yield an additional 5.8 percent merit raise to the 51 percent of the faculty if 49 percent were required to forego their cost of living increase. The same raise would be given to 25 percent of the faculty if the 49 percent received half of their cost of living increase. Whether a few highly productive faculty receive a modest increase or all productive faculty receive a small increase, the rewards to productive faculty are limited.

27. The figures used in this comparison are based on various issues of the *AAUP Bulletin* from 1972—1973 to 1976—1977. Average compensation is used in the comparison to allow for differences among ranks in fringe benefits received.

28. This conclusion is supported by analysis of the yearly salary increases for continuing faculty in each rank. No evidence appears of substantial differences in the salary increases received by each rank.

29. Within the full professor rank, the ratio of average compensation in the ninth decile to that in the first rose from 1.66 in 1975—1976 to 1.8 in 1976—1977. For associates, the comparable ratios are 1.53 and 1.61.

30. Once again, these data are taken from various *AAUP Bulletins*. In 1974—1975 and thereafter, separate data are published for males and females. These suggest a declining percentage of female faculty in the upper ranks, from 33 percent for associate and full professors in 1974—1975 to 28 percent in 1976—1977.

Chapter 9

Academic Compensation in Higher Education[1]

Howard R. Bowen

American higher education employs more than 1.5 million persons in 1.3 million full-time equivalent positions (National Center for Education Statistics, 1976b: 7, 12–13). The total payroll costs of colleges and universities, including fringe benefits, make up at least two-thirds of all current expenditures (Halstead, 1977: 5–6). How well paid are the faculty members, administrators, and general service workers who are employed in higher education? What levels of compensation should be paid to these people to get the work of higher education done acceptably? These are the questions addressed in this report. They are important questions for those concerned with the costs and financing of higher education; they are also important for those who depend upon academic salaries and wages for their livelihood.

The question of academic remuneration may be viewed from various standpoints. For those who must put up the money—taxpayers, donors, students, and parents of students—faculty and staff pay is the major cost of operating colleges and universities. Their interest seemingly lies in the direction of holding down salary and wage rates. For faculty and staff, their pay is a major source of income and also of personal reward and recognition. Their interest usually lies in the direction of higher levels of compensation. For governing boards, administrators, and others who are responsible for particular institutions, salaries and wages are viewed as the chief means of attracting and holding qualified faculty and staff. They tend to favor high compensation levels as a means of raising the quality and distinction of their institutions—though they must balance personnel costs against

other needs. For legislative bodies, state coordinating commissions, federal bureaus concerned with education, other broadly representative groups, and also disinterested observers, salary and wage rates are presumably considered in relation to the broad public interest. Needs and demands of higher education are weighed against those of other parts of the economy, and a balance is sought between compensation in higher education and in other industries and occupations. In this chapter, the intended point of view is that of the public interest.

In the past, most studies of academic compensation have dealt mainly or exclusively with faculty. This special concern has grown out of the conviction that faculty, through their engagement in teaching and research, are the front line personnel of the academic enterprise and that the success of higher education depends primarily on them. As a result, considerable data have been collected on trends and levels of faculty compensation, and many analyses have been made. However, instructional faculty members make up only 38 percent of the higher educational labor force. On the average, to place one faculty member on the front line of teaching and research, about 1.6 other employees are needed to provide logistical support and complementary services. The amount of money spent in the aggregate to meet the nonfaculty payroll is probably as large as that paid the faculty. Moreover, though nonfaculty people serve in backup positions, their work is clearly indispensable. Their level of compensation is an important factor in the success of higher education and also a major ingredient of higher educational costs. Thus, a serious study of academic compensation must include not only faculty but also other workers. Unfortunately, available data on nonfaculty workers are scarce. Though information is beginning to accumulate on the compensation of administrators, little is known systematically about the compensation of secretarial, clerical, and blue collar workers who make up a substantial part of the payroll of every college or university. The original report from which this chapter is adapted (Bowen, 1978) assembles a great deal of data about academic remuneration.[2] This chapter presents an overview of the whole report, including a summary of findings, conclusions, and recommendations.

The report as a whole leads toward a consideration of present and future compensation policy in a period when academic faculty and other staff are experiencing a weak market position owing to the large number of qualified people in the market, a possible decline in enrollments, and the precarious finances of many institutions.

LONG-TERM TRENDS IN THE PAY
OF ACADEMIC PEOPLE

The first task in this study was to assemble information about historic trends in the remuneration of academic people.[3] The purpose was to learn about the effects of changing economic and social conditions upon the pay of faculty and staff—with special emphasis on the effects of inflation, which is a dominant factor today. Annual data were gathered on average faculty salaries and fringe benefits for the period from 1903–1904 to the present. Since trends in faculty compensation were found to be quite similar for the several faculty ranks and for administrators as well, no special study of each subgroup was necessary. Unfortunately, however, there were no usable historical data on general service workers such as secretaries, clerks, and physical plant employees.

The period since 1903–1904 may be divided into twelve distinct episodes, each defined by prevailing economic conditions at the time. Table 9–1 describes these episodes and shows what happened to faculty compensation during each one. Table 9–1 and the related discussion refer exclusively to average faculty compensation expressed in dollars of constant (1967) purchasing power. Table 9–1 shows that World War II was a major watershed in the evolution of faculty compensation. Consider first the eight episodes in the period prior to World War II (1903–1904 to 1942–1943):

1. In the three periods of orderly economic growth and stable prices (1903–1904 to 1913–1914, 1922–1923 to 1929–1930, and 1934–1935 to 1939–1940), faculty compensation increased steadily but slowly at 1 to 1.5 percent a year.

2. In the two periods of rapid inflation (1913–1914 to 1919–1920 and 1939–1940 to 1942–1943), faculty compensation declined sharply at the rate of about 5 percent a year. Pay raises failed to keep pace with inflation.

3. In the three deflationary periods (1919–1920 to 1922–1923, 1929–1930 to 1931–1932, and 1931–1932 to 1934–1935), the response of faculty compensation was mixed. In the first two, it increased sharply at the rate of 9 to 11 percent a year because current dollar compensation held fairly steady while the price level plummeted. But when the Great Depression took hold in 1931–1932 to 1934–1935, compensation fell even faster than the price level, and the net decline was at the rate of nearly 3 percent a year.

Table 9-1.   Twelve Episodes in the History of Faculty Compensation, 1903-1904 to 1976-1977.

Periods	Conditions in National Economy		Trend of Constant Dollar Faculty Compensation Average Annual Percentage Change[a]	
	Description and Average Annual Percentage Change in Consumer Price Index[a]			
1903-1904 to 1913-1914	Steady economic growth; stable prices	+ 1.03	Steady slow advance	+ 1.09
1913-1914 to 1919-1920	War; rapid economic growth; rapid inflation	+11.0	Sharp decline	- 5.29
1919-1920 to 1922-1923	Depression and deflation	- 3.2	Rapid advance	+10.75
1922-1923 to 1929-1930	Steady economic growth; stable prices	0	Steady slow advance	+ 1.42
1929-1930 to 1931-1932	Crisis; early stages of Great Depression; deflation	- 7.59	Rapid advance	+ 8.92
1931-1932 to 1934-1935	Deep Depression; continued deflation	- 2.12	Moderate decline	- 2.87
1934-1935 to 1939-1940	Slow recovery; stable prices	+ 0.58	Steady slow advance	+ 1.45
1939-1940 to 1942-1943	Rapid recovery; rapid inflation	+ 6.36	Sharp decline	- 4.93
1942-1943 to 1945-1946	World War II; rapid economic growth; substantial inflation	+ 3.77	Substantial advance	+ 2.95
1945-1946 to 1951-1952	Korean War; erratic economic growth; rapid inflation	+ 5.77	Slow decline	- 0.91
1951-1952 to 1969-1970	Steady economic growth; slow but accelerating inflation	+ 2.04	Steady rapid advance	+ 3.61
1969-1970 to 1976-1977	Slow and erratic economic growth; rapid inflation	+ 6.51	Stable with slight downward trend	- 0.33

[a]Compound growth rates.
Source: Bowen, (1978: Appendix A, Table A).

This pattern seemed to change around the beginning of World War II.

1. In the one period of orderly economic growth and reasonably stable prices (1951–1952 to 1969–1970), compensation increased by about 3.6 percent a year—as compared with 1 to 1.5 percent in comparable prewar periods.

2. In the three periods of rapid inflation (1942–1943 to 1945–1946, 1945–1946 to 1951–1952, and 1969–1970 to 1976–1977), faculty compensation did not decline drastically in the prewar manner. During World War II (1942–1943 to 1945–1946), when inflation was substantial even though held in check by price controls, compensation increased by nearly 3 percent a year. And during the two later periods of acute inflation (1945–1946 to 1951–1952 and 1969–1970 to 1976–1977), compensation declined only slightly—in the most recent episode at the rate of one-third of one percent a year.

3. There were no episodes of deflation in the period after 1942–1943.

Clearly, something changed around the beginning of World War II. Since then, during periods of economic stability and growth, the rate of increase in compensation has been greater than formerly; and since then, inflation has not triggered serious setbacks in faculty compensation. Indeed, during the entire period 1942–1943 to 1976–1977, the average rate of increase in faculty compensation was about 2 percent a year; whereas in the period 1903–1904 to 1942–1943 it had been a mere 0.5 percent a year. How does one explain the difference?

The explanation undoubtedly lies in a marked change in public attitudes toward higher education (Bowen, 1968). Around the time of World War II, college attendance began to be seen not merely as a privilege for a small minority but as opportunity for the masses of youth. Moreover, from the events of the Great Depression and World War II, the nation was gaining a new appreciation of higher education as a source of economic productivity and national power. These attitudes led to the adoption of the G.I. Bill, and in turn, they were greatly reinforced by the striking success of that law. Later, the launching of Sputnik and the reports that began to filter in about educational achievements in the USSR also strengthened public concern for higher education. Corporations and government gained increasing appreciation of the returns from research and development and of the need for educated people in managerial and technical

work. Moreover, in the early 1950s, it became generally clear that the college age population would expand greatly in the 1960s and 1970s and that higher education would have to operate at dramatically higher levels. In this atmosphere, it was widely recognized that faculty had suffered from neglect and that compensation needed to be raised if the academic profession were to attract and hold adequate talent. In the climate of the time, the financing necessary to improving faculty compensation became available. Parents were becoming more interested in higher education and more willing to pay tuitions. Private donors and foundations were becoming increasingly generous in support of higher education, state legislators were expanding appropriations, and the federal government entered the field with increasing determination and more money, as manifested by the Higher Education Facilities Act of 1963 and the Higher Education Act of 1965. Meanwhile the leadership of the colleges and universities themselves had become increasingly sensitive to the need for higher compensation to retain capable faculty members and to recruit new people into academic positions.

Though support of higher education had been gathering steam since 1942, the effect of new attitudes and initiatives became apparent around 1951–1952. Beginning in that year, faculty compensation (in constant dollars) increased at an average rate of 3.61 percent a year and continued at that rate until around 1969–1970, when rapid inflation set in (Table 9–1). But even after 1969–1970, the efforts of the colleges and universities, backed up by public concern for the academic enterprise, were sufficient to maintain constant dollar compensation at nearly the 1969–1970 level and to prevent inflation from seriously eroding the gains of previous years. Indeed, much of the financial stress among institutions of higher education since 1969–1970 has been due to the determined effort of colleges and universities to keep faculty compensation at least in pace with inflation and to avoid the kind of slippage that had occurred in prewar inflationary periods. Maintaining faculty compensation slowed institutional progress in other respects.

The basic trend in faculty salaries has been more closely linked to public attitudes about the value of higher education than to market demand as indicated by enrollments or to market supply as indicated by numbers of new Ph.D.s and other indicators. The turning point in the rate of growth of faculty compensation occurred around 1942–1943, precisely when enrollments were declining at the onset of World War II. The acceleration of this growth around 1951–1952 coincided exactly with an enrollment trough following the departure of the GIs and preceding the arrival of the postwar baby generation.

Moreover, there has been no drastic decline in faculty compensation since 1969–1970, despite a slowing of the growth in enrollment and a rapidly increasing supply of persons qualified for college teaching.

COMPARATIVE TRENDS IN COMPENSATION

The next step in the analysis was to compare progress in the compensation of faculty and staff in higher education with that of other elements of the national labor force. For this purpose, a mass of data on earnings of various groups was assembled and analyzed. These data were all expressed in current dollars. There was no need to adjust them for price level changes, since all groups were faced with similar costs of living. Among the groups with which faculty were compared were:

- All civilian full-time employees;
- Full-time employees in manufacturing;
- Domestic airline employees;
- Telephone and telegraph employees;
- Unionized workers in building trades, printing trades, and trucking;
- Workers paid the legal minimum wage;
- Executive and supervisory employees of large companies;
- Employees of the federal government;
- State and local government employees; and
- Nonsalaried professional practitioners.

The findings are briefly summarized in the following paragraphs.[5]

1904–1930. The rate of growth of academic pay was substantially lower than that for almost all other occupational groups for that data were available. One exception was federal civilian employees, who fared even less well. Whereas faculty pay increased during this period at the rate of 3.19 percent a year, the pay of most other groups increased by annual percentages averaging from 3.5 to 6.21 percent. The percentage for all civilian full-time employees in all occupations was 4.17.

1930–1952. The relative progress of academic pay was even less in this period than in the years 1904–1930—slightly over 2 percent a year. Most other groups were enjoying average annual increases of 2.5 to 4.5 percent—though federal professional and administrative employees were gaining less rapidly than academic workers. The rate of increase in compensation for all civilian employees was 4.42 per-

cent. In view of these disparities, it is little wonder that academic people were discouraged in the early 1950s and that the inadequacy of academic salaries was widely acknowledged at that time.

1952–1961.   The situation changed abruptly in this period. It was the time of Sputnik, a new appreciation of science and learning as major ingredients of national economic growth and power, and the dramatic Ford Foundation faculty salary grants. It was also the time when it was widely recognized that higher education should be extended to a larger percentage of the revelant age groups and expected that the postwar baby boom would soon materialize in a horde of eighteen year olds ready for college. Improvement of academic salaries became a major national objective. Under these conditions, faculty salaries rose by 5.21 percent a year and faculty compensation by 5.41 percent a year (indicating the growing importance of fringe supplements). The rates of increase for other groups ranged mostly from 2.75 percent to 5.25 percent, the figure for all civilian employees being 4.46 percent. Only a few groups received raises larger than those in higher education, among them state and local government employees, lawyers, physicians, engineers, and members of Congress. Clearly, academic people were near the head of the pack in the annual rate of pay raises.

1961–1970.   The situation was mixed, but the gains in higher education were ahead of those for workers in most other occupations and industries. In this period, the compensation of academic faculty and staff increased by 6.03 percent, as compared with 5.23 percent for compensation of all civilian full-time employees. The comparative growth of compensation in higher education was somewhat slower than in the preceding period, but it could not be said that higher education was falling behind.

1970–1975.   The situation changed drastically. The rate of increase in academic compensation was substantially below that of most other groups. The average annual increase in compensation was 6.01 percent, as compared with 8.07 percent for all civilian full-time employees—leaving a gap of more than two percentage points. However, the gap was somewhat less for faculty compensation compared with particular occupational groups that are weighted toward white collar work. For example, the average annual increase in compensation for executives in large corporations was 7.1 to 7.67 percent, for civilian employees of the federal government, 6.51 percent; for city employees, 7.38 percent; and for public school teachers, 6.35 percent. On the basis of these and similar figures, one might conclude that between 1970 and 1975, the average annual increase in faculty compensation of 6.01 percent, compared with average annual in-

creases of roughly 7 to 8 percent for other groups, leaving a gap of from 1 to 2 percentage points.

Since 1975. As is well known, no improvement in the relative position of higher education has occurred in the past several years. Such data as are available suggest that while faculty compensation has been increasing at the rate of around 6.4 percent a year, the compensation of other groups has continued to grow at the rate of 7 to 8 percent a year. A significant gap remains.

Conclusions. When all the periods are combined and comparisons made for the entire period 1904 to 1975, it becomes clear that the periods of relative academic prosperity during 1952–1961 and 1961–1970 were not sufficient to offset the loss of ground in the less prosperous periods of 1904–1930, 1930–1952, and 1970–1975. Over the nearly three-quarters of a century from 1904, faculty compensation increased on the average at the rate of 3.71 percent a year, whereas compensation of all civilian full-time employees increased at the average rate of 4.69 percent, a difference of about one percentage point a year. The comparability of the data over such a long period may be in question, and conclusions about relative progress in rates of pay must be accepted with caution. However, in the most recent period since 1970, which is of the greatest interest, compensation in higher education, though it has nearly kept up with the cost of living, has clearly failed to keep pace with compensation in the rest of the economy. These conclusions are generally applicable to the compensation of academic administrators as well as of faculty. As indicated earlier, the trend of administrative compensation tends to run parallel to that of faculty compensation.

COMPARATIVE COMPENSATION
IN 1976–1977

In comparing the compensation of academic people with that of other groups of workers, the actual contemporary situation is perhaps more significant than past trends. How are faculty, administrators, and general service workers paid today relative to persons in other industries and occupations? There is a wealth of data pertinent to this question. Among the sources are statistics gathered by the Bureau of the Census, the Bureau of Labor Statistics, the National Science Foundation, and the American Management Association. In some cases, these statistics must be adjusted to make them comparable or to bring them up to date, but there is no dearth of reliable information. However, their interpretation does raise problems because of the difficulty of comparing jobs in higher education with

those in other industries. Nevertheless, when considered in their entirety, the data lead to firm conclusions.

As compared with the rank and file of American workers, faculty and administrators in higher education are relatively highly paid. Their average annual compensation is in the range of $20,000 to $30,000, depending on the nature of their work and the length of their annual contracts. In contrast, the average compensation of all civilian workers is $13,300; of public elementary and secondary teachers, $12,800; and of all federal civilian workers on the Civil Service General Schedule, $16,700.[6] However, 1969 census data on salaries of male workers present a somewhat less favorable comparison. When women are excluded from the salary data, academic administrators are still near the top among professional occupations, faculty on calendar year contracts are in a relatively good position, but faculty on academic year contracts are considerably below the average for all "professional, technical, and kindred workers."[7]

Data compiled by the National Science Foundation (1977: 62–63) on salaries of engineers and scientists show that the federal government and private business pay on the average a quarter more than four year institutions and a third more than two year colleges—even when academic year salaries are adjusted to a calendar year basis. The NSF data indicate that the salaries of scientists and engineers in higher education are roughly comparable to those in state government and in hospitals. Comparisons of administrative salaries tend to confirm that hospital pay scales are roughly similar to those in higher education.[8]

Salary comparisons of professional people employed in business and of academic faculty on eleven to twelve month appointments show that on the whole business pays more, the difference being especially marked in the lower ranks.[9] Similar comparisons for professional people employed in the federal government and for academic faculty on eleven to twelve month appointments show that the overall differences are not great, but that the federal government pays somewhat more in the lower and upper ranks and a bit less in the middle ranks.[10] It is noteworthy that academic salaries in the upper professional ranks for persons on eleven to twelve month appointments begin to overlap with those of important business executives in substantial companies. Faculty members on nine to ten month appointments earn 20 to 30 percent less than their counterparts in business who are employed the year around, and 10 to 20 percent less than their opposite numbers in the federal government.[11]

Administrators' salaries in higher education are from half to two-thirds of the salaries of those occupying comparable jobs in busi-

nesses of similar scale.[12] Physical plant workers in higher education are paid wages that are at least 10 percent lower than the wages paid to comparable workers in business.[13]

The conclusion from these findings is that faculty salaries for eleven to twelve month appointees, though on the whole considerably lower than those in business and perhaps a bit lower than those in the federal government, are relatively good. The disparities are not shockingly great. The position of the majority of faculty, who are on nine to ten month appointments, however, is not so favorable. If they are regarded as year round workers who happen to be paid on an archaic nine to ten month basis, they are clearly underpaid as compared to persons doing comparable work in the federal government and in business. On the other hand, if they are regarded as part-time employees, then their rate of pay may be construed to be about as good as that of colleagues who are on eleven to twelve month appointments. The salaries of administrators in higher education are drastically lower than those in business even for comparable jobs in organizations of similar size, and the wages of physical plant workers in higher education are about 10 percent lower than those for comparable employees in business.

NONMONETARY BENEFITS
AND OUTSIDE EARNINGS

Before reaching conclusions about relative earnings in higher education and those in other industries, nonmonetary benefits and outside earnings must be taken into account. These are modest for most academic administrators and general service employees, significant for faculty on eleven to twelve months contract, and substantial for faculty on nine to ten months contracts.

Among the nonmonetary benefits are the following (those marked with an asterisk are often available to administrators and general service workers as well as to faculty):

- *Tuition remission for faculty members and their families;
- *Access to sports facilities such as golf courses, tennis courts, gymnasiums;
- *Subsidized housing;
- Tenure;
- Substantial freedom and flexibility in the use of time;
- Long vacations;
- Subsidized sabbatical leaves; and
- Membership in a collegial academic community and in the "company of scholars."

Many other minor benefits could be mentioned. These benefits are widely but by no means universally available. Moreover, they are valued differently by different people. But almost certainly they are of sufficient value to most academic people to offset some part of any gap between their pay and the pay of persons in other occupations. In addition to these nonmonetary benefits, faculty members usually have the opportunity for outside earnings, not only after hours or during vacations, but even in regular working time (though for administrators and general service workers this opportunity is much more restricted). The main sources of these outside earnings are summer or part-time teaching, consulting, research, private practice fees, royalties from inventions, royalties from writing, sale of works of art, lecture fees, and miscellaneous "moonlighting." According to one study (Dunham, Wright, & Chandler, 1966: 145–49), outside income is earned by 74 percent of faculty members on academic year appointments and by 51 percent of those on calendar year appointments.[14] In the aggregate, outside earnings amount to 19 percent of base salaries for those on nine to ten month appointments and 11 percent for those on eleven to twelve month appointments. A recent study (Ladd, 1978: 17), in which no distinction was made between academic year and calendar year appointees, reported that 83 percent of faculty receive some outside earnings and that the amount averaged 15 percent of base salary. Outside earnings are not distributed equitably among all the ranks or among all the disciplines, but in total they are substantial and go a long way to offset disparities between academic people and their counterparts in other vineyards.

The augmentation of compensation by substantial nonmonetary benefits or outside income places faculty in a strong position relative to comparable workers in other industries. Faculty on eleven to twelve month appointments may be better off than their counterparts in business and government when nonmonetary benefits and outside earnings averaging 11 percent of base salary are taken into account. Similarly, the overall position of faculty on nine to ten month appointments may be comparatively good when the nonmonetary advantages and outside earnings averaging 19 percent of base salary are considered. Another indication that faculty remuneration may be not too far out of line is the notable absence of any rush to leave the profession or any shortage of young people who are willing to enter when jobs can be found. But it must be remembered that the position of administrators and general service workers is not significantly improved by the inclusion of nonmonetary benefits and outside income.

FUTURE POLICY: FACULTY COMPENSATION

History has shown that the level of faculty compensation has not been determined solely by the spontaneous forces of the market, but has been heavily influenced by conscious public attitudes and conscious policy toward higher education. This was demonstrated by the deliberate effort to raise faculty compensation in the early 1950s. At that time, there was a wave of public recognition that higher education is a critical ingredient of societal welfare and progress and widespread realization that compensation was too low to attract to the profession people of appropriate talents. The result was a determined effort by those supplying the funds to higher education and by the leaders of the institutions to make faculty compensation competitive with that of talented people in other industries and occupations. This effort succeeded, and by the late 1960s, the position of faculty (including salaries, fringe benefits, nonmonetary benefits, and outside income) was almost certainly equal or superior to that of persons in comparable jobs elsewhere; not surprisingly, an abundant supply of capable people came seeking entry to the academic profession. At about that time, however, public attitudes toward higher education changed. Student unrest, rising costs, congestion in the job market for graduates, the shift of public attention toward competing priorities, and the need to control inflation all contributed to this disenchantment. Under these conditions, the institutions faced a gradual but persistent financial squeeze, and faculty compensation began slowly to lose ground as compared with the pay of workers in other industries and occupations. Nevertheless, colleges and universities almost uniformly continued to place high priority on faculty compensation, often at the sacrifice of plant maintenance, student services, new programs, financial reserves, and general institutional advancement. As a result, faculty compensation on the whole nearly kept pace with inflation, even if it did not stay abreast of the wages and salaries of other groups, who received productivity increases in addition to cost of living increases. This record is in sharp contrast to that before World War II, when episodes of inflation were uniformly accompanied by sharp declines in the "real" earnings of faculty after allowance for increases in the price level. In spite of great efforts, however, faculty have been slowly losing ground in recent years relative to other groups—though the relative economic position of faculty today is still relatively good.

The critical policy question is, What should be done in the years ahead about faculty compensation? Or, to phrase it differently, What

trend of compensation will be in the broad public interest? This question is posed at a time when the market for faculty is decidedly weak. On the supply side, the number of persons qualified for the academic profession is large relative to the market, and great numbers of newly minted Ph.D.s are being turned out each year. On the demand side, the enrollment outlook at least through the 1980s is uncertain, and public attitudes toward higher education, though not antagonistic, are less than enthusiastic.

There are three plausible policy options:

1. To continue the present trend. Faculty compensation would nearly keep pace with the cost of living but would increase at a slower rate than average compensation in the rest of the economy.

2. To increase the rate of growth of faculty compensation to keep pace with earnings in the rest of the economy. This would call for average annual increases of perhaps 7 to 8 percent a year, as compared with recent increases averaging just above 6 percent a year.

3. To lower the priority now attached to faculty compensation in favor of other priorities (either inside or outside higher education). The rate of growth of faculty compensation could then be slowed up to take advantage of the undoubted market weakness of the academic profession. In this scenario, faculty compensation (in constant dollars) would almost certainly fall absolutely as well as relatively.

Clearly, the temptation for institutions to adopt the third option is very great and could become greater if the financial squeeze should worsen. From the point of view of those who supply the finances, the temptation is also great to force salaries down by withholding the money to pay the salaries. Indeed, it would be possible, in the short run at least, to "solve" the financial problems of higher education simply by slowing up the rate of growth of faculty compensation—for example, by placing a freeze on faculty salaries or even by imposing cuts. Under the circumstances, it is remarkable that this temptation has been resisted. One must ask not why has faculty compensation failed to keep pace with pay in other industries and occupations, but why has faculty compensation fared so well in view of its past history and in view of the present weak market situation?

There are many reasons for the surprisingly strong performance of faculty compensation. One is that the public disenchantment with

higher education has been less profound than often alleged. Many studies show that both students and alumni overwhelmingly indicate satisfaction with their college experience and that a vast majority of parents want their sons and daughters to attend college (Bowen, 1977: 226–35). Other reasons for the strength of faculty compensation are a general wish to be fair with a profession that has happened to run into a weak bargaining position, the desire to avoid undermining faculty morale, and the hope of forestalling collective bargaining. The pressure to raise the pay of minorities and women also has had a part in keeping average compensation up.

But more important than these factors has been the belief both on and off the campus that the improvement in relative compensation during the 1950s and 1960s had resulted overall in the attraction and retention of thousands of capable and well-trained people, that these hard won gains had been in the broad public interest, and that these gains should not be sacrificed to short-run financial expediency. It has been strongly suspected that with the recent deterioration in the relative economic position of faculty, many of the most able people would eventually slip away to other callings; that the academic profession would attract substantially fewer capable young people; and that the quality of the profession and of the institutions it serves would gradually decline.

It is often argued that higher education does not need to be concerned about keeping compensation up to levels of comparable positions in other industries because higher education is entering the "steady state" when it will not need to hire many faculty members—especially since the present faculty lack easy mobility. This argument is far from conclusive. In the first place, it is not necessarily true that higher education is entering the steady state. As I often point out, enrollments could rise in the next couple of decades. The size of future enrollments will depend, as they have in the past, on the kinds of higher education offered and on the terms on which it is made available, not merely on demographic trends. Also, it is not true that faculty members lack mobility. Virtually all of them in professional fields can readily move to other industries, and many in the natural sciences, economics, psychology, and other social sciences are capable of changing careers and often do. Moreover, even those in the humanities can shift careers, and it would be a good thing for the country if more of them found their way into business, journalism, and government, where they could represent a new and much-needed outlook.

But even if one assumes that the steady state is likely and that faculty are not very mobile, the academic community will still need to

recruit many new people in the next several decades. Nearly 30 percent of all faculty are over fifty years of age (Bayer, 1973: 27; Dunham, Wright, & Chandler, 1966: 59). Allowing for mortality, some early retirement, and some shifting to other occupations, at least a third of all faculty will have to be replaced within the next fifteen to twenty years—even assuming that the normal retirement age is raised. Nearly 60 percent of the present faculty are over forty. Again allowing for mortality, early retirement, and mobility, at least two-thirds of the faculty will have to be replaced in the next twenty-five to thirty years. Should faculty compensation fall significantly, then the number of faculty retiring early and shifting to other occupations would be greater, and the problem of securing competent people would be compounded. If there is enrollment growth, as is possible in the 1980s and likely in the 1990s, the recruitment problem will be still further complicated. No one doubts that all available faculty positions could be filled at lower relative compensation than now obtains, but they probably could not be filled with people at the level of competence of those recently recruited. In my judgment, the third option, that of drastically lowering the compensation of faculty relative to that in other industries and occupations, is almost surely not in the public interest.

The first option—namely, to allow the present trend to continue—is one of slow deterioration rather than sharp cuts. Faculty compensation has been increasing at the rate of about 6 percent a year, whereas the compensation of various other occupational groups has been growing at the rate of about 7 to 8 percent a year. The difference, which represents the rate of deterioration for faculty, is about one to two percentage points a year. Over a decade the effect would be substantial, and over two decades it would be catastrophic. It would eventually put faculty back in the weak position they experienced just before World War II. Slow deterioration would of course be preferable to drastic cutting, but it is not a recommended solution for the long run.

This leaves only the second option, which is to raise the annual rate of faculty compensation so that it approaches or matches the average rate for workers in other industries and occupations. To achieve this objective, higher education would either need more money or it would have to achieve cost-cutting improvements in efficiency.

There are undoubtedly opportunities for improvements in efficiency—that is, for cost cutting without unduly impairing outcomes—but these opportunities are not as great as is often alleged by critics of higher education. The higher educational community has already

achieved considerable budgetary tightening under the pressure of the financial squeeze of the past eight or nine years. Among the results of this tightening have been undermaintenance of plant and some reduction in quality of services. But economies such as these can be instituted only once. For example, if the standard of building maintenance, the quality of the food service, the rate of library acquisitions, or the ratio of faculty to students are cut in 1978, these savings may be continued from year to year, but additional savings will require new cuts in 1979, again in 1980, and so forth. As the cutting goes on, to find new objects of economy becomes harder and harder. Meanwhile, the need to economize would reduce the ability to undertake innovation and institutional development in response to changing conditions. Thus, while one may freely concede that substantial economies are possible, it is doubtful that they could be sufficient to add increases to faculty compensation of the order of 1–2 percent a year, year after year.

If the rate of increase in faculty compensation continues to lag behind pay raises in other occupations, the position of higher education will deteriorate. As has been shown, the current relative position of faculty even after several years of failing to keep pace with other occupations is not bad. But if the disparity of one to two percentage points in annual rate of increase continues (6 percent for faculty versus 7–8 percent for other occupations), in ten years faculty compensation would be 9–18 percent below that of other occupations and in twenty years, 18–33 percent below. At some point fairly soon the present disparity should be corrected. To do so would require an increased flow of funds into higher education. Potential improvements in efficiency are unlikely to bridge the gap without socially unacceptable impairment of quality. The correct policy for the nation, in my judgment, is to deal with the compensation problem over a period of years. For example, the gap in average annual increases might be halved in three years and eliminated in five years. This timetable would eventually bring about parity in rates of growth, but relative levels of compensation would be considerably less favorable for faculty than at present.

Perhaps a word is in order about nonmonetary income and outside earnings of faculty. If growth in faculty compensation could be kept closer to parity with the rest of the labor force, many of the privileges and prerequisites might be curtailed. Many of them were instituted at a time when faculty were grossly underpaid. But as we are now again moving away from parity, the justification for these various items of nonmonetary income increases apace. The same holds for outside earnings. But the case for outside earnings on a fairly

generous basis is even stronger. The opportunity to earn outside income encourages faculty members to take part in the affairs of the world, to gain practical experience in their professional fields, and to become proficient in their disciplines. This opportunity also offers a special incentive to ambitious persons because it provides the chance within the academic profession to earn substantial amounts and even in some cases to get rich. In other words, it removes the ceiling on earnings that are possible within the academic world and thus strengthens incentives for adventurous and imaginative people to enter the profession. Moreover, outside work is an antidote to the boredom that afflicts many faculty people in midcareer. There are, of course, disadvantages in the opportunity for outside earnings. Some faculty neglect their academic duties, some lose their loyalty to their institution, some misuse their status as academic people when operating in the public arena. But on the whole, the opportunity for outside earnings is socially advantageous. It tends to narrow the gap between academic compensation and earnings in other occupations in a way that is mainly constructive.

COMPENSATION OF ADMINISTRATORS AND GENERAL SERVICE WORKERS

The earnings of academic administrators are reasonably comparable with those of administrators in hospitals and government but far below those of business executives in comparable jobs within organizations of similar size.[15] For instance, the earnings of presidents or chancellors of colleges and universities are less than half those of chief executive officers in private business; the salaries of admissions and development officers—the sales executives of higher education—are far below those of sales managers in industry; and so on down the whole roster of administrative officers. I see no reason to believe that the administration of a college or university is any less difficult or entails any less responsibility than the management of a company of similar size. Under these circumstances, the questions must be posed, Would colleges and universities be more successful over a period of time if they paid higher salaries to their administrators? Would they attract and hold more capable and better prepared people? Would these people perform with greater energy and dedication? Would the higher costs be returned in greater efficiency and in greater income? One may of course argue that higher education attracts many very capable and dedicated administrators at existing salary levels. One may suspect also that higher salaries for administrators might merely attract people who are interested in money and lacking in dedication.

However, my opinion is that on balance, a gradual upgrading of administrative salaries, on a highly selective basis, would be sound policy for higher education.

On the basis of limited data, I found that the wages and salaries of general service workers probably average around 10 percent below those for comparable jobs in private business.[16] Some or all of this differential may be justified by relatively pleasant working conditions and steady employment in colleges and universities.[17]

CONCLUSION

The dominant item of cost in institutions of higher education is the compensation of faculty and staff. Faculty compensation (including nonmonetary income and outside earnings) relative to earnings in other occupations and industries is reasonably good as of 1976–1977. Administrative compensation is probably comparable to that in government or hospitals but far less than that in business. The compensation of general service workers is probably on the whole lower in higher education than in other parts of the economy. Faculty and administrative compensation is slipping relative to trends in other industries and occupations. The slow relative attrition of compensation in higher education threatens to impair its future soundness. Policies are needed to bring about reasonable parity between the rates of growth in compensation in higher education and in other occupations and industries.

Currently, the salary goals of most institutions are (1) to keep up with other academic institutions and (2) to keep pace with the cost of living. These goals are not adequate for the future soundness of American higher education. Instead, the goal should be to keep pace with the growth of compensation in the economy generally. Institutions and those who control their financial support should endeavor to relate their salary increases to those prevailing in the economy at large, not merely to those of other colleges or universities or to the cost of living.

NOTES TO CHAPTER 9

1. This chapter is adapted from Bowen (1978: chs. I and II). Reprinted with permission from TIAA/CREF.

2. The reader is encouraged to read the entire report (Bowen, 1978), which is divided into three parts. Chapter II presents an overview of the report and is adapted for this chapter. Chapters III, IV, and V are the body of the report. Appendixes provide detailed data and serve as backup for the chapters.

3. The basic data used in this section are presented and discussed in Bowen (1978: ch. III and App. A).

4. See the final section of Chapter III and Appendix B in Bowen (1978).

5. For detailed data, see Tables 7 to 11, Chapter III in Bowen (1978).

6. For detailed data, see Table 12 in Bowen (1978).

7. For detailed data, see Table 13 in Bowen (1978).

8. For detailed data, see Table 16 in Bowen (1978).

9. For detailed data, see Tables 17 and 18 in Bowen (1978).

10. For detailed data, see Table 17 in Bowen (1978).

11. For detailed data, see Tables 17 and 18 in Bowen (1978).

12. For detailed data, see Table 19 in Bowen (1978).

13. For detailed data, see Table 20 in Bowen (1978).

14. Refers to four year institutions only.

15. For detailed data, see Tables 16 and 19 in Bowen (1978).

16. For detailed data, see Table 20 in Bowen (1978).

17. In some cases, however, colleges and universities are forced to pay union scales despite their offering more steady employment than is available elsewhere.

Chapter 10

Pervasive Sex Differences in the Academic Reward System: Scholarship, Marriage, and What Else?

Helen S. Astin and
Alan E. Bayer

Rank and salary represent two important aspects of the reward system in academe. However, these rewards vary substantially from one institution to another and often from one department to another within the same institution. Faculty activities, such as teaching, research, service, or administration, are valued differently in different types of institutions within the system of higher education. For example, research may be rewarded more highly in elite colleges and universities, whereas teaching skills have greater value in community and junior colleges. Similarly, publication productivity may be rewarded more highly in the natural sciences than in education. Teaching ability may be valued more in the humanities and less in the hard sciences. To the extent that academic men and women vary in their backgrounds, professional activities, and institutional settings, it is important to consider these factors in any analysis of differences between the sexes in academic rewards.

In a study of sex differences in academic rewards, certain variables are critical. One must keep in mind how the rewards, such as salary and rank, are distributed in the academic sector. First, these rewards depend on a faculty member's productivity in research and scholarship, in teaching, and in service activities. Second, the rewards are a function of the faculty member's level of education and years of experience. Third, such rewards vary with the supply and demand conditions of various fields. That is, persons in fields in which the supply is short and the demand is great are much more likely to receive higher remuneration than those in fields with high supply and relatively low demand.

STUDIES OF SEX DIFFERENCES

In 1965, a Commission on Human Resources and Higher Education was established to examine the development and utilization of human resources in the United States (Folger, Astin, & Bayer, 1970). This commission was interested in assessing the development and utilization of both highly trained men and women. As part of its work, the commission undertook a national study of women doctorates, with the primary goal to assess the extent to which these women were members of the labor force, to examine their career patterns over time, and to look at their status in the professions (Astin, 1969). The women in the study, in describing their current status, indicated that they had experienced discrimination in salaries and in promotions. About the same time, Jessie Bernard's book, *Academic Women* (1964), reported on the lower status of academic women with respect to salaries and ranks. The research division of the National Education Association examined salaries of faculty in higher education and also reported differentials between men and women (NEA, 1965). In reviewing these findings, it became apparent that there was a need for a better assessment of the extent to which differentials in salaries and rank could be attributed to sex discrimination or to other factors, such as differences in characteristics critical to achieving status in academe. There was a need to identify the critical variables that should be controlled to assess the status of academic women more accurately, since one could not attribute the salary differentials to sex discrimination without considering a person's labor market experience, work performance, specialization, employer, or the type of work.

The first study on sex differences in academic rewards utilized a sample of scientists in the National Register of Scientific Personnel of the National Science Foundation (Bayer & Astin, 1968). It included scientists with doctorates who were employed in academic institutions. The study sample comprised faculty in beginning teaching positions (two years after the doctorate) and scientists who had been teaching five to six years. The primary interest was to examine whether salary and rank differentials exist at the beginning of the academic career and the extent to which they persist or increase over time. The subjects were classified into two major categories—natural sciences and social sciences. Persons were grouped into high ranks (associate and full professors) and low ranks (assistant professor and lower). Type of institution was also controlled.

The analyses yielded the following observations: Within each major field, academic setting, and career length category, no significant

sex differences in academic rank emerged. At a later point, after five to six years in the labor force, major field differences appeared. In the natural sciences, women who persisted in academic teaching tended toward an aggregate higher rank than did their male colleagues. However, men in social sciences obtained higher ranks over time than did women. With respect to salary, across all work settings, fields, and ranks, women experienced a significant lower average academic income than men at the beginning of their careers, as well as over time. The salaries of women social scientists were not generally as discrepant from those of men as were the salaries of the women natural scientists.

The second study on sex differentials in academe utilized data from a national survey of college and university teaching faculty (Astin & Bayer, 1972). The survey was undertaken in spring 1969 by the Carnegie Commission on Higher Education (now the Carnegie Council on Policy Studies in Higher Education) and the American Council on Education. The study examined sex differentials in rank, tenure, and salary, controlling for relevant variables. After applying the men's derived weights to predict the women's rank and salary, it was observed that the average compensatory increase in rank would be from slightly below to somewhat above the assistant professor level, an average of one-fifth step. To award women the same salary as men of similar rank, background, achievements, and work settings would require a compensatory average raise of more than $1,000. This is the amount of actual salary discrimination identified as not attributable to discrimination in rank. The amount of actual salary discrimination attributable to discrimination in advancement would substantially increase this figure.

Subsequent to the 1968 and 1972 articles on the topic, interest in this area has increased among social science researchers. Among the social scientists, economists have been the group primarily interested in these issues. The research reported in economics journals has included a number of articles on the topic. There have been reports by Johnson and Stafford (1974, 1977), Emily Hoffman (1976), Stephen Farber (1977), and Barbara Kehrer (1976). The findings from these studies can be summarized as follows: Johnson and Stafford viewed the sex differentials in rewards as resulting primarily from a market reaction to voluntary choices made by women about lifetime labor force participation and on the job training. That is, they attributed the differences in salaries primarily to the differences between the sexes in their work patterns. Hoffman argued that rank itself determines salary and that women receive lower salaries because of discrimination in promotions. Kehrer, in a study of income

differences between women and men physicians, concluded that women physicians, even though they possess professional character- istics less favorable in terms of earning potential, tend to realize greater marginal returns to specific characteristics than do men phy- sicians. She attributed this to a natural selection phenomenon for women. For example, the short supply of women in fields and in practices that are the most highly paid, such as surgery, implies greater competence due to survival factors. Farber (1977), using longitudinal data to compare life cycle salary increases and rank pro- motions for men and women academic scientists, concluded that sal- ary differences between men and women vary with age cohorts. For example, he found a significant increase in salary differences for the younger cohorts but not for the older ones, contrary to Johnson and Stafford. With respect to rank, he observed that women in the younger cohort had a significantly lower chance of being promoted than men. Furthermore, he concluded that women had farther to climb on the promotion scale than men. From these brief results, it appears that the various investigators attributed the differences to different factors; some focused more on "person" explanations and others on "system" attributions.

The late 1960s and early 1970s witnessed the emergence of legis- lation to bring about equity in the treatment of the sexes in employ- ment. This new legislation and interest in issues of equity prompted another study (Bayer & Astin, 1975) designed to assess the extent to which equality may have been approached since the antibias regu- lations have been in effect.

Sample and Research Design

In the academic year 1972–1973, the American Council on Edu- cation (Bayer, 1973) undertook a general purpose survey of more than 100,000 college and university faculty members in a nationally representative sample of 301 institutions—80 universities, 179 four year colleges, and 42 two year colleges. Some 53,034 college and uni- versity faculty members responded, of whom 42,345 were currently active teaching faculty—that is, each was teaching at least one course that year at one of the 301 institutions.

The study focused on two outcome variables of academic status and achievement—rank and salary. Four sets of predictor variables were used—demographic characteristics (age, race, parents' educa- tion); educational characteristics (degree, field); professional or work variables (department, years employed); and characteristics of the employing institution (type, region).

Differences in Academic Men and Women

Academic men and women differ in the educational backgrounds, professional activities, work settings, and related characteristics that affect rewards in academe: 40 percent of the men but only 20 percent of the women hold a doctorate; larger proportions of women than of men specialize in education (23 versus 13 percent), humanities (21 versus 17 percent), and health sciences (10 versus 3 percent); larger proportions of the men than of the women are in the physical sciences or engineering (21 versus 5 percent) or in the social sciences (13 versus 9 percent); of the women, 39 percent spend more than twelve hours a week in scheduled classroom teaching; of the men, less than one-third devote that amount of time to teaching. Less than one-fifth of the women but one-third of the men spend more than eight hours in an average week in research and scholarly writing. These differences are also reflected in publication productivity: of the men, over one-third had published at least five articles and 12 percent at least one book; in contrast, one in ten women had published at least five articles and 7 percent at least one book.

Academic Rank

In the 1972–1973 survey, 30 percent of the men but only 11 percent of the women faculty members were full professors; 24 percent of the women and 10 percent of the men were instructors. In part this variation reflects the difference in degree attainment, traditionally an important criterion in achieving high academic rank. Differences in rank (and salary) have been explained to some extent by specialization, research performance, and other differences in background and work activities. The analysis examined sex differentials in rank, controlling for virtually all major demographic, educational, work experience, and institutional variables that might affect rank attainment.

Of the sixty potential predictors, nineteen were statistically significant. The five most important were productivity as measured by published articles, age, degree level, years of continuous service at the present institution, and time in administration. After all nineteen variables were controlled, the partial correlation (-0.13) between being a woman and holding a high rank was significant ($F = 85.92$). That is, even after a sizable number of other variables were considered, much of the differential in rank was still attributable to sex per se.

Academic Salary

In the 1972–1973 survey, the average salary of the men exceeded that of the women by more than $3,000. Much of this differential

is attributable to differences in rank, years of employment, specialization, research productivity, work setting, and related background and work activities. In the examination of salary differentials, controlling for these relevant variables, the three most important factors were rank, productivity, and number of years in professional life. After controlling for rank and an additional nine statistically significant predictors of salary (such as years since highest degree, articles published, department), the partial correlation (-0.04) between sex (female) and salary was again statistically significant ($F = 9.29$).

These results suggest that the sex differential in salary is due in part to differences in rates of promotion. Analysis of salary differentials within rank supports this inference. In the junior ranks (instructor or lecturer, assistant professor), women are paid at about the same rate as men; senior women (full professor, associate professor) have lower salaries than their male counterparts. For full professors ($F = 20.03$), the residual effect (partial r) of sex (female) on salary was much greater (-0.12).

If the same predictors of rank with the same weights that were applied to men in 1972–1973 are used to predict rank for women, the average expected rank is about one-tenth of a step above the observed rank, rising from somewhat below to slightly above midway between the assistant and associate professor levels. The parallel analysis in the 1968–1969 data indicated a differential of one-fifth step. Thus, some gains in the academic rank of women compared with that of men have been made over the past half decade, though substantial differences persist.

The case for salary is somewhat more complicated. In 1968–1969, an average raise for women of more than \$1,000 across all ranks would have been required for equity in accordance with the predictors of men's salaries. The comparable figure in 1972–1973 was \$600. Both these figures are conservative, since they are based on accepting all preceding differentials, including rank, as unrelated to sex. If rank is excluded as a predictor of salary, application of the men's regression equation to the women's data yields an average gross salary differential in 1972–1973 of more than \$1,000 between the actual and the predicted salaries of academic women.

This is an average differential for all ranks. However, although equity in salary between men and women has been virtually achieved in the junior ranks, the differentials persist in the senior ranks, particularly at the level of full professor. Calculating the differences between actual salaries of women full professors and salaries for men full professors predicted by the regression equation, the difference, \$1,680, is the amount of underpayment in 1972–1973 to women in

high rank with characteristics in educational attainment, speciali-
zation, productivity, and so forth statistically identical to those of
men.

In summary, even after controlling for differences between aca-
demic men and women for degrees, fields, productivity, continuous
employment, and so forth—all primary criteria for rewards in the
present system—sex differences in rank and salary are still obtained.
It is possible that there are some additional variables not considered.
Lester (1974: 55), for example, indicated that some of the additional
variance attributed to sex per se may actually be a function of "ca-
reer motivation, ability to perform demanding teaching assignments,
standing in the discipline and the profession," and other factors that
he labeled "unmeasurable quality aspects." However, several vari-
ables included in the present analyses are proxies for some of these
"unmeasurables"; some have not been shown to be distinctively
possessed by men more than by women, and others may merely re-
flect the cumulative effects of sex discrimination before a woman
enters academe as a trained professional. Indeed, if there is cumula-
tive discrimination, one would expect the women entering academe
and surviving there to be particularly well qualified. The differences
between expected and actual rewards revealed when the weights de-
rived from the men's analysis were applied to the women's data dem-
onstrate powerfully the presence of sex bias, especially since the
variables used can be measured and are widely accepted as the basic
factors in promotion decisions.

FACTORS IN SCHOLARLY PRODUCTIVITY

From the findings above, it is evident that scholarly productivity
is an important index of performance in academe (for more on this
topic, see Astin, 1978). The rewards—rank and salary—are based
largely on productivity. Scholarship demonstrated in published
works does indeed increase one's status.

Often a woman's lower status in academe has been attributed to
her lower productivity. However, studies have demonstrated the im-
portance of a number of institutional factors that affect productiv-
ity. These factors emerge in studies independent of sample or time.
Invariably, a person's graduate institution is a significant factor in
later productivity. For example, among women doctorates, produc-
tivity as measured by published articles is greatly determined by the
quality of the graduate institution (Astin, 1969).

Explaining the relationship of institutional quality to later pro-
ductivity is a complicated task. The positive relationship may result

primarily from a person's characteristics rather than from the institution. For example, it is likely that the more achievement-oriented and creative persons select and are being selected by high quality institutions. By the same token, it is possible that the atmosphere in a highly selective institution increases motivation and achievement orientation and, thus, that a graduate of a selective institution becomes a productive scholar.

A study of the determinants of scientific productivity (Folger, Astin, & Bayer, 1970) observed that the training institution is important in later scientific accomplishment, as indicated by the citation index, which measures scholarly visibility by the number of times articles, books, or other published works are cited by researchers. No relationship obtains between academic performance and citations. However, those who attended selective graduate institutions have a higher index rating. These findings suggest that persons who attend highly selective institutions are further socialized to achieve by engaging in research and scholarship.

Another important variable in productivity is the type of institution at which a faculty member is employed. Fulton and Trow (1974), in a study of faculty productivity, found that persons employed at universities are more productive than those employed at four year colleges. The importance of teaching at a university compared with a college is further illustrated by the fact that faculty at low quality universities are likely to be more productive than faculty at high quality four year colleges. Crane (1965) substantiated this relationship; she reported that, after controlling for the quality of the training institution, a faculty member's affiliation with a major university is an important correlate of scholarly productivity.

One can offer a number of interpretations for relationships between institution of affiliation and productivity: A person interested in research and publications is probably more likely to be attracted by a university than one who receives great satisfaction from teaching and interacting with students. Productive people are also more likely to be hired by universities. Universities more often than four year colleges expect their faculty to engage in research. Often, four year colleges focus on teaching and interaction with students, while universities strive to be centers of new knowledge in science and technology. Because of their size and resources, universities have greater facilities for research. Furthermore, granting agencies may be more willing to fund research at larger institutions with their large faculties, laboratories, libraries, and other facilities. Thus, the environment at a university is designed to facilitate research and scientific and scholarly productivity.

Discipline or specialization may also play an important role in scholarly productivity. If productivity is measured by published articles and books, persons in the biological and physical sciences are more productive than persons in social sciences, humanities, education, or arts (Astin, 1969; Fulton & Trow, 1974; Startup & Gruneberg, 1976). There are some field differences, however, depending on the type of published work. For example, if productivity is measured solely by published articles, biological and physical scientists have the highest productivity rates; if productivity is measured by published books, those in the humanities are more likely to have the highest productivity rates (Astin, 1969). Nevertheless, people who are productive in general tend to publish books, as well as articles, and to present papers, write reports, and review books (Astin, 1969; Startup & Gruneberg, 1976).

Faculty rank has also been identified as a correlate of productivity. Fulton and Trow (1974), in examining productivity rate, reported that full professors are more productive than associate and assistant professors. However, Bayer and Dutton (1977) have shown that this relationship is confounded by the selection process in promotion and rank and by the effects of age on scholarly productivity. The relationship of rank and productivity could be interpreted in a variety of additional ways. Full professors, because of their past record of productivity and visibility, may have been productive during a given period because they were asked to present major addresses, contribute chapters to edited books, or edit volumes of their own.

In summary, the findings reviewed so far indicate that the important correlates of scholarly productivity for both men and women faculty members are equality of graduate training institution, specialization, type of institution of current employment, and rank.

Sex Differences in Productivity

Some studies on productivity have focused on sex differences in publication rates (Astin, 1969; Bernard, 1964; Simon, Clark, & Galway, 1967; Ladd & Lipset, 1976). In general, they have reported that women are less productive than men. Part of this lower productivity is due to lower degree attainment, since fewer women have attained the doctorate. Some is due to the type of institution with which women are affiliated—quite likely two and four year colleges. Part is also due to women's greater interest in teaching and to the fact that they carry heavier teaching loads.

In fields with the highest productivity, such as the natural sciences, women constitute a small minority—only 4 percent of the women

are in physical sciences, compared with 14 percent of the men. Women are much more heavily concentrated in education and humanities, both fields with low productivity as measured by published articles. Thus, the sex differences in productivity result in part from differences in specialization, current institutional affiliation, and teaching load.

Predictors of Productivity

Because productivity is a critical factor in achieving academic status, a study was designed to clarify some important issues about women's scholarly productivity.

It has been argued (Lester, 1974; Sowell, 1975) that attributing sex differentials in rank and salary to sex discrimination can be misleading and incorrect if the analysis combines single and married women. This argument assumes that single women's career paths and achievements parallel those of men, whereas married women's lower achievement results from family constraints and not from discrimination. The study reported here deals with these assumptions by examining scholarly productivity, work status, and career paths of single and married women separately.

Sample and Procedures

This examination of scholarly productivity of faculty women and men utilized a subsample from the faculty surveyed in 1972–1973. All 1,800 women who held doctorates were selected for analysis. A similar sample, selected by choosing every tenth man who held a doctorate, yielded 2,041 men.

The analyses examined productivity, as measured by published articles and books, among single women, married women, and men in five major disciplines—biological sciences, physical sciences, education, social sciences, and humanities. The faculty members were classified by their publication of one or two articles, three or more, or none. The same classification was used for books.

Differences in Productivity

An examination of the overall productivity of women and men indicated that, while there is a difference in favor of men, there is no difference in the productivity of single and married women when all fields are combined. Regarding published books, the differences between men and women are not as marked.

An examination of the productivity of faculty within each of the five major disciplines indicated that, independent of sex, the most productive persons for articles are those in the biological sciences, with those in the physical sciences next, whereas those in the hu-

manities are the least productive. For books, the least productive persons are in physical and biological sciences and the most productive are in social sciences and education. An examination of the productivity of single compared with married women within each major field showed that a higher proportion of married women in education, biological sciences, physical sciences, and social sciences publish three or more articles. Also, more married women in education, physical sciences, and humanities publish three or more books, whereas single women in social sciences are more productive than married women. Although single and married women publish about the same number of articles and books across all fields, in most specific fields, married women publish somewhat more than single women. These differences between married and single women on overall productivity versus productivity within fields result from differences in the proportions of married compared with single women who choose various fields and to differences in publication rates for persons in the different fields.

While the findings indicated that rank relates to number of publications over time, the effect of rank per se on the rate of publication is also of interest. Men assistant professors are less productive than either associate or full professors. Men associate and full professors are similar in overall productivity. The productivity of married women is greater with each higher rank in the major fields—assistant professors are the least productive, associate professors are next, and full professors are the most productive. The patterns for single women are more erratic: assistant and associate professors tend to be somewhat more productive than full professors. The earlier interpretation that reaching the rank of full professor is in itself beneficial because it provides greater visibility and productivity is not valid for single women.

Overall, within each rank, married women are more productive than single women. Furthermore, married women full professors are more productive than men full professors in education, physical sciences, and social sciences. That assistant professors among married women are the least productive may result in part from their younger age and accompanying familial status—that is, married assistant professors are more likely to have young children, a barrier of sorts to scholarly productivity. The fact that, among single women, full professors tend to be less productive could result from greater administrative responsibility: a higher proportion of single than of married women have administrative responsibilities.

If rank and period of time are not controlled, men are more productive than women. However, married women are more productive

than single women and men in some fields when rank is controlled. Differences in overall productivity among the three groups could result from differences in educational and work characteristics. Examining the distribution of the three groups with respect to type of research revealed that, in some ways, married women more closely resemble men. An examination of stipends during training indicated that a higher proportion of married than of single women have been teaching or research assistants or have held fellowships or scholarships at some point. However, more men than women have had stipend support of some sort during graduate training.

An examination of the percentages of women and men who have attended high quality undergraduate and graduate institutions revealed that married women are more similar to men than to single women in the quality of their training institutions and their institutions of current employment. The differences between married and single women in stipend support and experiences, research activities, and quality of training institution may be, in part, the factors that can explain the higher productivity of married women.

Married women also differ from single women in specialization. For example, a higher proportion of married women are in social sciences and humanities. However, a higher proportion of single women are in education—18 percent, compared with 9 percent of married women. Institutional affiliation is also a factor in productivity. Men are more likely to be employed at universities, while women are found in higher proportions in two and four year institutions, colleges of low selectivity, and predominantly black institutions. Quality of institution is also a variable in scholarly productivity. A somewhat higher proportion of married (16 percent) than of single women (13 percent) are affiliated with highly selective universities.

Do married and single women follow different career paths that could account for their differences in productivity? Higher proportions of single women in colleges and universities have come from teaching and administrative posts at the elementary and secondary level. However, more married women have been postdoctoral fellows or researchers in nonacademic settings. These differences in previous employment could account somewhat for the differences in productivity between married and single women.

Determinants of Productivity
In addition to the cross-tabulations used to examine productivity for single and married women and men by specialization, multiple regression analyses were performed separately for the three groups. These analyses indicated that the one variable that appears to make a

difference in the type of productivity is specialization: the biological and physical sciences are important predictors of published articles, whereas humanities and education are important predictors of published books. The type of institution is an important variable in productivity in general: being at a university or at a high quality institution are both important predictors or are at least variables associated with high productivity. For married women, a former nonteaching research position predicts productivity. In the past, married women were less likely to receive academic appointments in institutions where their husbands were employed because of anti-nepotism regulations. Thus, these women were often affiliated with research institutes and centers where their primary activity was research, leading to higher productivity rates.

The stipend support during training affects later productivity: a research assistantship appears to affect men and married women positively, while a teaching assistantship affects married women negatively. However, having a fellowship or scholarship affects all three groups in positive ways.

These analyses of factors of scholarly productivity highlight some differences in career paths not only between men and women but also between married and single women. Contrary to current thought, which maintains that the academic careers of single women resemble those of men more closely than do the careers of married women, the present study demonstrates that the careers of men and married women are actually more similar with respect to educational preparation, field of study, and publications. The only two similarities in the careers of single women and men concern their activities in administration. Also, if age, which in part accounts for this observation, is not controlled, a higher proportion of single than of married women are at the professor rank. Statements by Lester (1974) and Sowell (1975), who tended to attribute academic women's lower status to the constraints of marriage and family life, need to be reexamined in view of the finding in the present study that the scholarly productivity of married women is higher than that of single women.

PREDICTING RANK AND SALARY

The issues left unsettled by Lester (1974), Sowell (1975), as well as by Johnson and Stafford (1974), prompted an examination of rank and salary differentials separately for married and single women. They believe that differences in the rewards result from constraints on women imposed by marriage rather than by sex discrimination. This "shortcoming" was described by Sowell (1975) and repeated

by Lester (1977). Our analysis was designed to deal with some of these concerns:

> Even the comprehensive studies by Helen S. Astin and Alan E. Bayer make the fatal mistake of holding marital status constant in comparing male-female career differences. But marriage has opposite effects on the careers of male and female academics, advancing the man professionally and re-tarding the woman's progress. Not only do men and women themselves say so, but the Astin-Bayer data (and other data) also show it. Therefore to treat as "discrimination" all residual differences for men and women of the same characteristics—including marriage—is completely invalid and misleading. (Sowell, 1975: 55)

Using the variables described earlier in this chapter, the stepwise regression analysis for single and married women separately was run using rank first and then salary as a dependent variable. The salaries of assistant, associate, and full professors were also examined. The actual and predicted rank and salaries were compared, applying the weights of men to single women and then to married women. For these estimates, all significant predictor variables were used first; the estimates were recomputed by excluding rank, which has been differentially awarded to men and women.

The sample for these analyses comprised a random subsample ($N = 6,219$) of all respondents who held regular full-time appointments, with or without tenure, and who indicated their sex, salary, and rank on the survey questionnaire. This subsample included 2,071 single women, 1,694 married women, and 2,454 men.

Rank

In predicting rank, an R of 0.756 for married women and 0.771 for single women was obtained. In achieving rank, there are certain characteristics and behaviors that are critical for men, as well as for single or married women (Table 10–1). Having a doctorate, publishing, being continuously employed with an institution, and spending time in administrative activities are all significant variables. Career interruptions affect single and married women negatively in achieving rank. However, having had a scholarship or fellowship as a stipend in graduate school affects both positively. Children as a predictor entered the equation for single women (not presently married) and men, but not for married women. However, the relationship was positive for men but negative for women.

The fact that "children" as a variable entered the analysis for single but not for married women has some interesting implications:

Table 10—1. Predictors of Rank for Academic Men and Women.

Variable	Men (R = .787)			Single Women (R = .771)			Married Women (R = .756)		
	Step at Entry	Beta	F-ratio	Step at Entry	Beta	F-ratio	Step at Entry	Beta	F-ratio
Age	1	0.303	212.59	1	0.271	165.17	2	0.201	85.24
Articles	2	0.235	190.28	3	0.170	84.96	1	0.210	92.07
Highest degree: doctorate	3	0.174	68.57	2	0.274	72.60	3	0.312	89.19
Years of continuous service	4	0.142	76.96	4	0.130	52.45	4	0.160	70.84
Time spent in administration	5	0.092	51.40	5	0.106	47.73	5	0.106	41.51
Years since degree	6	0.203	81.28	6	0.157	52.11	6	0.125	32.85
Children	7	0.095	54.02	7	-0.067	20.16			
Field: biology	8	-0.068	26.88	11	-0.072	22.72	11	-0.061	12.64
Four-year institution	9	0.064	22.93	8	0.098	44.42			
Paid consulting	10	0.055	17.02						
Department: art	11	0.043	10.44						
Two-year institution	12	-0.045	11.33						
Books	13	0.054	14.29	13	0.055	11.97	7	0.084	20.95
Department: education	14	-0.047	10.06						
Race: white	15	0.033	6.76						
Department: humanities	16	-0.036	7.29	10	-0.083	29.97			
Department: health	17	-0.043	10.03						
Degree: masters	18	-0.055	7.02	14	-0.089	7.93	13	-0.113	12.42
Degree: bachelors				9	-0.098	32.08	12	-0.099	23.28
Field: physical sciences				12	-0.058	15.51			
Career interruption				15	-0.044	8.19	14	-0.050	8.63
Received stipend				16	0.033	4.81	16	0.039	4.88
Time spent in teaching				17	0.033	4.31			
Institution: university							8	-0.089	27.88
Was teaching assistant							9	-0.056	10.85
Field: humanities							10	-0.074	18.83
Department: engineering							15	0.036	5.09

apparently, the effect of children has many more negative conse-
quences for women who are single parents than for women with a
spouse. The career progress for these single parents is slower, because
of the greater demands on their time from raising children alone.
This finding has implications for public policy on child care facilities
at universities and at other public and private institutions.

In addition to common predictors, some other variables were
unique in explaining the variance in rank for each subpopulation.
Being white and doing outside paid consulting benefited men in ad-
vancing in rank. Spending more time in teaching activities benefited
single women. Married women who were teaching assistants as gradu-
ate students were less likely to achieve high ranks.

One might speculate that a person who engages in outside consult-
ing is more assertive, entrepreneurial, and thus able to negotiate a
better rank and salary at the parent institution. However, paid con-
sulting might reflect some "quality" characteristics that are impor-
tant in making persons visible and in demand nationally and in their
achieving higher status at their parent institution.

Teaching time as a predictor of higher rank for single women is
harder to explain, especially since field and institutional affiliation
were controlled. The finding suggests that a woman must be a super-
woman to advance in academe. That is, after she has published and
participated in administration, engaging in a great deal of teaching
ensures that she will overcome barriers that might result from "sin-
gle" status. That being a teaching assistant is not much more of an
advantage for a woman than being a research assistant is easily ex-
plained: having any sponsor or mentor can have long-term benefits
for one's career development.

Applying the weights derived in predicting rank for men to the
single women yielded a predicted rank score of 2.582 (a little over
midpoint between associate and assistant), compared with the actual
rank of 2.567. For married women, the differential was somewhat
greater—the predicted score was 2.520, the actual, 2.253. This sug-
gests that it may be somewhat harder for married than for single
women to be promoted.

The results of the analysis for salary are presented in Table 10−2.
The *R*s are 0.744 for single women, 0.766 for married women, and
0.700 for men. The most important predictors for either sex or mari-
tal status were publications, having a professional degree (i.e., M.D.
or J.D.), engaging in administrative activities, doing less teaching,
being at an institution in the Northeast or at a two year college, and
number of years since obtaining the degree. A conservative political
orientation enters with a negative sign for men and single women.

Table 10-2. Predictors of Salary for Academic Men and Women.

Variable	Men (R = .700)			Single Women (R = .744)			Married Women (R = .766)		
	Step at Entry	Beta	F-ratio	Step at Entry	Beta	F-ratio	Step at Entry	Beta	F-ratio
Salary base	1	0.195	154.01	1	0.179	130.28	1	0.165	96.37
Rank	2	0.275	146.17	2	0.349	243.66	2	0.379	269.43
Years since degree	3	0.208	63.50	16	0.103	21.39	20	0.043	4.16
Articles	4	0.158	65.77	3	0.159	68.35	3	0.191	80.55
Time spent in administration	5	0.099	40.91	9	0.068	16.97	12	0.048	7.92
Department: health	6	0.095	31.91	19	0.041	6.39			
Two-year institution	7	0.095	38.57	8	0.107	47.26	7	0.115	46.34
Time spent in teaching	8	-0.064	15.85	7	-0.058	11.43	8	-0.063	12.31
Field: biology	9	-0.054	12.26						
Degree: masters	10	-0.049	7.62						
Institutional region: Northeast	11	0.065	18.15	5	0.129	68.97	5	0.153	82.68
Institutional control: public	12	-0.064	17.42	4	-0.121	47.87	6	-0.109	36.72
Top 12 institutions	13	0.049	10.32						
Degree: professional	14	0.051	9.21	6	0.124	65.62	4	0.161	90.44
Department: engineering	15	0.044	8.53						
Years of continuous service	16	-0.061	10.26						
Conservative (politically)	17	-0.048	9.59	11	-0.073	22.20			
Age	18	0.072	8.40	10	0.032	2.02	14	0.062	8.58
Department: humanities	19	-0.041	7.39	12	-0.058	12.65			
Time spent in research				13	0.135	40.64	19	-0.036	4.44
Degree: doctorate				14	0.066	14.23	15	0.092	16.48
Institution: coeducational				15	-0.061	13.56	17	0.041	5.66
Field: humanities				17	-0.047	9.28			
Field: art				18	0.040	6.56			
Paid consulting				20	-0.037	5.74	11	0.048	8.14
Mother's education				21	0.040	5.78			
Books				22	-0.035	5.16	10	0.059	10.77
Degree: bachelors				23	-0.029	3.83			
Race: oriental									
Field: health							9	0.088	25.76
Department: art							13	-0.041	6.41
Career interruption							16	-0.043	6.75
Field: social sciences							18	0.037	5.03

All but the political orientation variable are easy to understand and explain; these variables have been recognized as important factors in advancing in academe. In understanding why political ideology might relate to achieved status, it is important to identify other characteristics and behaviors that might describe academics with a conservative political ideology. Some 43 percent of the men and 46 percent of the women said they are politically conservative. Some of the variables that correlate with political conservatism are time spent teaching, having a master's rather than a doctoral degree, being in education, and not having taken a graduate program at one of the top twelve institutions. Furthermore, those with a conservative ideology are less likely to have been in social sciences or to have had a fellowship while in graduate study. Apparently, conservative faculty possess professional characteristics that are valued less among academics in general. Thus, their lower status in the profession could explain, in part, their lower salaries.

Among predictors that entered the equation for both single and married women but not for men were publishing books, spending less time in research, doing outside paid consulting, and being at a coeducational institution. For men, having done graduate work at a prestigious institution predicted a higher salary. Also, continuous service at an institution entered the men's equation with a negative weight. Mother's education was a negative predictor for single women, whereas career interruptions affected married women negatively.

A look at the variables that differentiate women from men, independent of marital status, indicated that, for women, there is more pressure to prove themselves by publishing not only articles, but also books. The effect of the sex composition of the institution on salary differences reinforces some other observations: there is a higher proportion of women in women's colleges than in coeducational institutions, and at those institutions, the average salaries are lower (Astin, Harway, & McNamara, 1976).

Mobility has had positive consequences for men in increasing their job prospects, but not for women. In the past, women were likely to move if their husbands accepted a new job in a different location. Before affirmative action, the academic tradition and ethos ignored and often looked down on persons who approached an institution on their own rather than being recruited and courted. Unfortunately, this bias persists today at some institutions.

As in estimating differences between predicted and actual rank, the weights derived from the analysis of salary with the men's sample were applied to the two groups of women. First, predicted and

actual salaries were computed for the total samples of single women and of married women. Then the discrepancies were examined separately for assistant, associate, and full professors. The predicted and actual salaries, excluding rank as a predictor, were also computed (Table 10-3).

The differential between predicted and actual salaries was greater for single women. Across all ranks, single women are underpaid by about $1,895, compared with married women, for whom the difference is $1,622. The greatest difference, however, lies with full professors: for single women, the amount is $2,424; for married women, $1,639. That the predicted salary is higher for single than for married women could result from differences in age and in administrative experience. Excluding rank, the differential between "married" and "single" in the discrepancy between "predicted" and "actual" diminishes. This finding further supports the interpretation that promotions might be easier for single than for married women.

Apparently, the difference between "predicted" and "actual" is greater for single than for married women, which suggests that some subtle discrimination may operate more substantially against single women because single status for women is looked down on in society. But the pervasiveness of continuing sex differentials in the academic reward system, independent of traditional and nontraditional criteria for these rewards, cannot be denied.

Table 10-3. Predicted and Actual Salaries for Single and Married Women.

Status and Rank	Predicted	Actual	Difference
Single Women	$15,898	$14,002	$1,896
Married Women	14,901	13,279	1,622
Single Women Excluding Rank	16,152	14,002	2,150
Married Women Excluding Rank	15,436	13,279	2,157
Full Professor			
Single	20,769	18,345	2,424
Married	21,219	19,580	1,639
Associate Professor			
Single	16,137	14,737	1,400
Married	16,152	14,836	1,316
Assistant Professor			
Single	13,105	12,106	999
Married	12,850	12,113	737

Chapter 11

Pecuniary Rewards to Men and Women Faculty

George E. Johnson and
Frank P. Stafford

The purpose of this chapter is to examine the extent to which the salaries of men and women academics differ and to ask why these differences exist. The first section reviews a variety of available evidence from a descriptive point of view, and the second section offers various interpretations of this evidence. One hypothesis is that women earn less in academia because they are on average less productive because their work histories are typically somewhat different from men's. An alternative hypothesis is that the lower earnings of women result from discrimination.

THE EARNINGS STRUCTURE OF WOMEN AND MEN ACADEMICS

The starting point of any analysis of the earnings of academics is a description of the basic facts. What is the pattern of earnings differences between men and women in academia? The data presently available to answer this question are from periods prior to the affirmative action thrust of the mid-1970s. We are thus looking at the situation before policies were encacted to correct a perceived problem.[1] In a sense, however, this is more interesting from both an analytical and a policy point of view, for it permits us to explore the reasons for the gap between the salaries of men and women.

Table 11-1 shows the relationship in 1970 by sex for six separate academic disciplines between the average nine month salary of academics with a Ph.D. and the number of years of experience since receipt of the doctorate. The nine month salary figure is for most

Table 11–1.   Average Nine Month Salaries of Men and Women Academics,[a] Annual Salaries at HEW,[b] and Hourly Wage Rates in the General Labor Force,[c] by Years of Experience.

Category		Years of Experience			
		0	10	20	30
Academics					
Economics	Men	11,610	16,260	19,550	20,170
	Women	11,000	14,250	16,580	17,330
Sociology	Men	10,560	15,020	17,840	17,720
	Women	10,130	13,340	15,270	15,190
Anthropology	Men	10,400	15,230	19,310	21,180
	Women	9,520	12,710	14,870	15,250
Mathematics	Men	10,510	15,980	20,010	20,600
	Women	9,860	12,980	14,790	14,610
Physics	Men	9,440	15,320	19,810	20,400
	Women	8,590	12,000	14,740	15,910
Biology	Men	9,680	14,090	17,360	18,130
	Women	8,590	11,850	13,990	14,150
HEW	Men	10,940	18,210	25,850	30,330
	Women	11,970	16,840	19,540	20,320
General Labor Force	Men	2.22	2.71	3.00	3.15
	Women	1.60	1.86	2.01	2.02

Sources:

[a]From Johnson and Stafford (1974). Estimates refer to persons with Ph.D.s from a university not in the top ten of his or her field at the time of receipt of degree and with four years of pre-Ph.D. experience (which is not included in "years of experience"). Time period is 1970.

[b]From Borjas (1978). Estimates refer to whites with sixteen years of schooling, employed in Washington, D.C. Time period is 1977.

[c]From Oaxaca (1974). Estimates refer to men and women who are white, married with spouse present and one child, high school graduates, and residents of the Northeast. Time period is 1967.

academics equivalent to a "wage rate" received by most workers in the economy, and accordingly, estimates of the hourly wage rate by sex of all workers in the economy in 1967 are shown in the last row of the table.[2] A recent study of the sex differential in the earnings of employees at the Department of Health, Education, and Welfare offers another set of estimates. What is especially interesting is the percentage wage disadvantage of women, and this is shown by years of experience for the six academic disciplines and for the general labor force. To provide a further explanation, Table 11–2 says, for example, that, holding "quality" of Ph.D. and years of pre-Ph.D. experience, women academic economists earned 18.8 percent less than their male counterparts in 1970, men earned $100/(100-18.8) = 24.4$ percent more than their female counterparts.

Table 11–2. Percentage Salary Disadvantage of Women Relative to Men by Academic Discipline and for the General Labor Force.

Category	Years of Experience			
Academics	0	10	20	30
Economics	5.3	18.8	15.2	14.1
Sociology	4.1	18.9	14.4	14.3
Anthropology	8.5	16.5	23.0	28.0
Mathematics	6.2	18.8	26.4	29.1
Physics	9.0	21.7	25.6	22.0
Biology	11.3	15.9	19.4	22.0
HEW	−9.4	7.5	24.4	33.0
General Labor Force	27.9	31.4	38.0	35.9

Sources: Johnson and Stafford (1974); Borjas (1978) and Oaxaca (1974).

Three facts stand out from an examination of Table 11–2. First, the relative wage disadvantage of academic women is considerably less than in the case of the more or less typical worker in the general labor force. However, because academic salaries are so much higher than the average salary in the economy, the absolute dollar disadvantage is still about the same for academic women as for women in the middle of the skill distribution.[3] Further, because women professors may serve as a role model for women undergraduates, the possibility that they may be subject to labor market discrimination takes on greater importance than simply the inequity per se.

Second, for all groups of academic women, the size of the relative salary disadvantage is small for entry level positions and rises fairly dramatically over the next ten to twenty years. In three fields, the disadvantage falls toward the latter half of women's careers, but in the other three fields it increases. The wage disadvantage of women in the general labor force also rises with time for the general labor force, but the rise is less pronounced than in academia. This tendency does not appear to be due to "cohort effects" (i.e., women trained in 1970—experience equals zero—are substantively different relative to their male cohort because they received better training relative to men or were more assertive or whatever than, say, those trained in 1940—experience equals thirty), for a very similar pattern of wage differentials by discipline existed in 1964.

Third, among the six disciplines for which the analysis of salaries was made, there are substantial differences in the relative wage disadvantage of women. These differences do not appear to follow any discernible pattern (for example, from least to most technical). The

same pattern of variation in salaries is apparent in an analysis of more disaggregated data. Table 11–3 shows the percentage salary disadvantage and the percent of the discipline who are women for a dozen disciplines within the biological sciences. The salary disadvantage ranges from 6 percent for nutritionists to 24 percent for biochemists, but these differences are not related to the proportion of the discipline who are women.

ALTERNATIVE EXPLANATIONS OF THE STRUCTURE OF ACADEMIC EARNINGS

The most interesting—and, alas, the most controversial—question about the salaries of academic women is why they are less than those of men. Although there are several variants of each, there are basically two explanations of the academic salary structure by sex.

1. Women academics have an average lower productivity than their male counterparts and consequently lower salaries. Because of the lifetime pattern of their work attachment, the fall in the productivity of the average woman academic relative to men is especially acute during the first ten years of experience.

Table 11–3. Percent of Academics Who Are Women and Average Percentage Salary Disadvantage of Women for Twelve Specialities Within the Biological Sciences, 1970.

Discipline	Percent Women	Percentage Salary Disadvantage
Anatomy	10.2	13
Biochemistry	9.5	24
Biophysics	5.5	16
Botany	9.4	10
Ecology	3.8	8
Entomology	2.1	19
Genetics	9.6	18
Microbiology	13.6	14
Nutrition	16.3	6
Pharmacology	9.0	14
Physiology	9.4	15
Zoology	8.4	16

Source: Johnson and Stafford (1974).

2. Women are, given equivalent training and experience, just as productive as men but receive lower salaries because of labor market discrimination against them—that is, they are paid lower salaries given their productivity than males are.

In principle, the percentage salary disadvantage of women (in any particular discipline-experience category), which we shall call S, is equal to the percentage productivity difference, P, plus the percentage "tax" put on women by discrimination, D. Hypothesis A implies that $D = 0$ and hypothesis B that $P = 0$. The observed salary differences in Table 11–2 could, of course, arise due to any combination of the two hypotheses. Since the two hypotheses have very different implications concerning both the effect and desirability of affirmative action and reward policies in academia, it is thus useful to examine each in detail.

Productivity Differences

The productivity explanation of the observed differential between the wage and salaries of men and women rests on the relation between earnings potential and skill accumulated through experience. Consider three groups of workers: (1) men (A), who will most likely be in the labor force without significant interruption from the point of completion of formal schooling until retirement; (2) those women (B) whose lifetime labor market attachment resembles that of the "typical" man; and (3) those women (C) who anticipate a significant interruption of their labor market attachment to bear and raise children. For occupations in which there is a significant "learning by doing" component and a necessity to learn of new developments on a continuous basis, we would obviously expect that the third category—those women who interrupt their careers to raise families—would incur a significant deterioration of their earnings potential during any period of career interruption. Academic occupations are, of course, excellent examples of high technical change professions.

The qualitative effect of a career interruption on the skill (productivity, potential earnings) of a person in an academic discipline is shown in Figure 11–1. From the point at which the Ph.D. is completed (time 0) until time T_1, a C worker accumulates skill at the same rate as A and B workers. At time T_1, however, the C worker drops out of the labor force to raise a family, until T_2, when she[4] returns. During the period from T_1 to T_2, the C worker forgets much of what she once knew about her field and is ignorant of new developments, so her skill falls absolutely as well as relatively. After she reenters the labor market at T_2, she begins to accumulate skills again, but she never catches up with the A and B workers.

Figure 11-1. Qualitative Effect of Career Disruption.

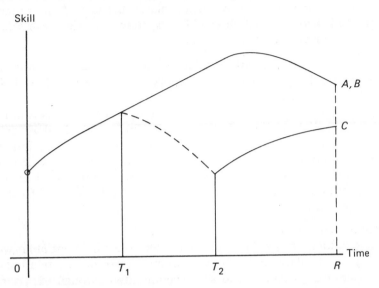

This hypothetical model is too extreme to account for the differences in earnings between men and women academics, for it is not necessary for women academics to drop out of the labor force altogether if they wish to spend time raising children. Instead, they can go on part-time status (or on a full-time payroll but with less time allocated to research and keeping up study). In fact, the NSF data show that for biologists between the ages of thirty and thirty-four, 11.8 percent of women versus 1.1 percent of men worked part-time in 1970; for ages thirty-five to forty-four, the figures were 7.2 and 0.5. Second, in 1960, 26 percent of women who had experience within the preceding ten years as college professors were out of the labor force, but the corresponding figure for men was only 6 percent (U.S. Bureau of the Census, 1963). Third, in 1960, 34.5 percent of women college professors worked fifty to fifty-two weeks per year, compared with 58.3 percent of men.

Despite the overall differences in labor market participation between men and women, there are two important characteristics that mitigate against obsolescence and limited professional development through lack of labor market participation, reduced hours, or on the job training. First, marriage rates for women doctorates are significantly lower than for other women of similar age. Only 55 percent of the women doctorates in a 1965 survey were or had been married. "In a comparable age group (40-44 years) in the general population, . . . 86 percent were married" (Astin, 1969: 26).[5] Second, "among

women of comparable ages in the general population only 45 percent worked as compared with 91 percent of the women in this sample" (Astin, 1969: 58). Among the women Ph.D.s, however, reduced labor market activity was most strongly influenced by present marital status (as well as by husband's income level) and the presence of preschool age children (Astin, 1969: 63). Further, Astin (1969: 73) found that women doctorates were less likely to be engaged in research and administration, and these are activities that receive substantial financial compensation in the academic labor market. In light of the evidence on differential participation in the labor market by men and women Ph.D.s, the question is then, What is the effect of this participation on salary? Further support for the productivity explanation of salary differentials between academic men and women comes from a recent study by Stephen Farber (1977). Between the years 1960 and 1966, Farber was able to infer how many years of additional experience each of a large sample of academics actually accumulated. The results suggest that the impact of additional experience on salaries was essentially the same for men and women. This means that the dropoff in the female-male relative salary observed during the first half of the career—see Table 11–1—is consistent with the hypothesized effect of differential experience accumulation during the interval.

If reduced labor market effort leads to less professional achievements, then this should be indicated by fewer publications and by less administrative and public service. One of the limitations on most previous research (including our own) on the subject of male-female salary is that "true" productivity or achievement must be proxied by variables such as years since the Ph.D. or crude work history measures. Some new data sets, however, do permit direct estimates of productivity—even though these are admittedly imperfect. A recent paper by Howard Tuckman and others (1977) was based on variables that included the quantity of publications (books and articles separately), whether or not the person has received a teaching award, whether or not the person is currently engaged in public service, and whether or not he or she is currently or was previously holding an administrative position. The effects of these activities on the eleven month salaries of male and female academics are shown in Table 11–4.

These results suggest that men and women academics receive approximately equal rewards for teaching excellence, public service, past administration, and (up to ten) the publication of books. Where women lose relative to men is in the current holding of an administrative position and in the salary increment due to publishing arti-

Table 11–4.   **Estimated Effects of Additional Publications, Superior Teaching, Public Service, and Administrative Responsibilities on the Earnings of Men and Women Academics in the Social Sciences, 1972–1973.**

Publications	*Men*	*Women*
Number of Articles		
1–2	285	141
3–4	161	208
5–10	135	117
11–20	113	75
21–50	74	69
> 50	65	3
Number of Books		
1–2	284	237
3–4	407	378
5–10	335	273
> 10	166	−11
Teaching Award	276	418
Public Service	643	722
Administration		
Current	3403	1530
Previous	1448	1956

Source: Tuckman, Gapinski & Hageman (1977).

cles. For the latter, the effect on salary due to having published ten articles is $1,567 for men and $1,283 for women—that is, men would receive 22 percent more (women 18 percent less). What is not clear is the extent to which such a differential reflects quality differences in the articles—just as it is not clear to what extent the male-female differential in the reward for current administration may reflect time requirements and responsibilities between the jobs the sample of men and women happened to take.

It is thus very difficult to tell from data that include measures of individual productivity whether or not women academics' salaries are equal to what they are worth from a market point of view. What is necessary to answer this question are productivity measures that reflect the quality of each person's performance. Variables like the number of articles and books and whether or not the faculty member engages in administrative functions are not sufficiently discerning to answer this question.[6] Another difficulty is that if women are less able to receive research funding because of discrimination rather than because of their own voluntary choices, then productivity measures

will not by themselves permit inferences about the role of discrimination. Nonetheless the results of the studies based on productivity variables suggest that women with achievements similar to their male colleagues receive similar compensation. Whether or not there are discriminatory barriers in access to research funding, release time for writing, or departmental administration is an issue that needs additional research. To our knowledge there have not been studies of discrimination in funding and release time for women faculty nor have there been studies of the process of assigning faculty to administrative posts.

Discrimination

The alternative to the productivity explanation of differences in academic salaries by sex is that women are subject to systematic labor market discrimination. There are several variants of this hypothesis, and it is interesting to examine each of them.

First, women academics may be subject to some form of direct discrimination such that they are paid less per unit of productivity than their male counterparts. One way that this could happen is that (predominantly male) deans and department chairpersons could have a preference for having male colleagues. With a given salary budget, they will then be willing to pay more to hire a male of a given productivity than to hire a woman. Put differently, they are willing to sacrifice college and/or departmental quality in order to have men rather than women on the faculty. If students, alumni, legislators, or other supporters will offer smaller payment because of reduced quality, this could mean that the discriminating male decisionmakers would achieve discrimination against women at the cost of lower financial rewards. Most colleges and universities, however, probably do not have their revenues tied that directly to the educational services provided. Hence, it is indeed possible for direct labor market discrimination against women academics to occur and to continue indefinitely without major sacrifices in personal income to the discriminators.

Another approach to the description of the way women faculty could receive less than men for each unit of productivity centers on collusive behavior among the majority group (males). By this view, the men in charge of the college or department define a set of rules by which the "excess" funds available for salaries (i.e., in excess of the amount necessary to meet costs of services) are distributed among the faculty so as to maximize their own incomes. Some of the obvious characteristics for reward under such a situation would be the extent of association with the group in power rather than with "out-

siders." A leading candidate as an index of association with the group in power would be years of continuous experience at the college (and since receipt of the doctorate), for this would be highly correlated with various empirical measures of work history and experience used in empirical studies. Women, as was argued above, would be less likely to have a record of continuous service (because of family responsibilities, movement because of husband's career, etc.) and would thus lose by the use of experience as the major determinant of salary.

A second general form of discrimination is "statistical" discrimination (Aigner and Cain, 1977). In this case, women would be perceived to be less productive on average than men (because of some of the arguments in the preceding section) as well as having less easily predictable future productivity based on indicators available to employers at completion of the degree and would thus be less likely to be hired by the best colleges and departments. Yet, because so much of the productivity of academics is acquired on the job after receipt of the Ph.D., this perception would be to some extent self-fulfilling; women's skills would not grow as fast as those of the average male academic because their typical work environment would be inferior to those of men.

Similarly, if the persons who select new Ph.D.s to fill the available vacancies for the best jobs assume that women will not perform as well as men because of the "dropping out" phenomenon discussed previously, women will take jobs that are associated with lower skill growth and lower eventual remuneration. This will then mean that they will be more likely to drop out of regular work attachment because the alternatives are poorer—again, a self-fulfilling assumption.[7]

A third set of possibilities is that potential women academics may be subject to indirect or societal discrimination. Women have traditionally been expected to perform roles as wives and mothers and thus subordinate their own career aspirations to the needs of their husbands and children. Such expectations would make it more difficult for women to receive the requisite training for entry into academic professions. For example, some academic departments may have systematically given smaller fellowships to women than to men graduate students on the grounds that women "need" less support. Attitudes of this sort would discourage women from entering (and completing) graduate programs and thus would restrict their numbers in academic employment. Further, discriminatory practices during graduate programs might have influenced the relative initial skill levels of women as they began their academic careers.

It is very difficult to sort out the likely effects of these three types of discrimination, for they are obviously interrelated. Moreover, many of the variants of the discrimination hypothesis predict essentially what the productivity explanation predicts—that the earnings differential between men and women will rise during the years after receipt of the doctorate. Perhaps the best test of the two explanations rests on the evidence of what happens to the relative salaries of men and women in the 1980s and 1990s. With the changes in the roles of expected roles of married men and women that are associated with women's liberation, women should have a more regular attachment to the labor market. By the productivity explanation, this would mean that the differential would tend to disappear. By the hypothesis of direct labor market discrimination, on the other hand, women will continue to earn less than men. The only complication with this test, however, is that HEW pressure may eliminate (indeed, may have already eliminated) the differential for new cohorts, so one could not tell whether the narrowing in salaries is due to changes in productivity or to changes in the exercise of discrimination.

CONCLUSION

A variety of empirical studies based on cross-sectional and panel data, notably the National Science Foundation Register data by academic discipline, have shown that women and men Ph.D.s start with salaries that are only slightly different upon completion of graduate studies. As time passes, the earnings differential between the sexes grows, and this can be attributed to cumulative effects of discrimination or to the market's reaction to voluntary choices for reduced hours of work and on the job training by women. One implication of the latter interpretation is that never married women Ph.D.s or those who accumulate on the job experience consistently from one year to the next should do better relative to their male colleagues than do married women or those whose work history includes reduced hours or years out of the labor force or less research. A variety of evidence supports this prediction. A market discrimination hypothesis would require that there be greater discrimination against married women or women whose work history has periods of labor market withdrawal. Moreover, women faculty have been less likely to alter their labor market effort because of family situations than have all women. As a consequence, the earnings differential would be predicted to be smaller for women faculty than for all women. Empirical evidence supports this prediction.

Another kind of analysis attempts to augment the earnings analysis by measures of academic productivity—books and articles written, thesis supervision, administration, and other forms of academic output. This analysis is an alternative way of looking at differential on the job training by men and women, since many of the output measures are simply indexes of past investments in skills that are rewarded in the academic labor market. The results of such studies have offered at least a tentative explanation for some of the potential postdegree growth in the earnings differentials between men and women faculty. One limitation of this type of analysis is that various forms of discrimination may reduce the access that young women faculty have had to research funds or appointments at research-oriented graduate departments. Evidence on this form of discrimination is virtually nonexistent, though one study by Lewis Solmon (1973) has suggested that graduate schools did not engage in widespread discrimination in offering fellowship support to women, even before federal antidiscrimination efforts.

A broader question is whether various forms of premarket discrimination have discouraged women from pursuing certain fields, such as engineering. This is beyond the scope of our inquiry, since if this is the source of scarcity of women faculty in certain fields, it is unlikely that the federal policy for employment in higher education will remove much of this. (However, removing discriminatory earnings differentials would increase the net return to market activity and would probably influence long-run career choices by school age females.)

While we believe that the voluntary-choice-acquired skill hypothesis is important in explaining much of the disadvantage pecuniary rewards to women faculty, it is also true that much of the evidence could also be consistent with various models of discrimination. As a result, informed persons could have reasonable bases for different positions on the role of discrimination vis-à-vis acquired skill differences. Our hope is that those involved in the dialogue on salary differentials between men and women faculty would understand the different interpretations of the evidence. The importance of the different interpretations in part lies in the policy implications.

If discrimination is the major source of the earnings differentials, then federal policies may be effective, since they would provide greater incentives for women to function in the academic labor market and would attract new cohorts of women to university teaching. On the other hand, if there is merit to the voluntary choice–labor market participation interpretation, then marital and fertility decisions and intrafamily assignment of responsibility for housework and childcare will have a major impact on future earnings differentials

in the academic labor market. It is possible that there have been major changes on this score already and that future evaluation of the impact of federal antidiscrimination policy should be designed to protect against attributing effects to the policy that actually arise from changes in family decisionmaking. Moreover, federal policy on deductibility of childcare expenses and treatment of married women under the Social Security laws may have a broader and more significant effect than direct antidiscrimination policy.

NOTES TO CHAPTER 11

1. Salary data are, of course, available from specific academic institutions. One recent analysis (of Illinois State University) concluded that affirmative action policies changed the situation from one of salary discrimination against women to against men (see J. Koch and J. Chizmar, 1976b). This conclusion is debatable and, needless to say, not necessarily generalizable to the average academic institution. There is, however, little doubt that the average salaries of incumbent women faculty have risen much faster during the past few years than those of men and than they would have risen in the absence of HEW pressure.

2. From 1970 to 1978, average wages in the United States have grown by about 76 percent (112 percent from 1967 to 1978), so a rough translation of these figures to 1978 terms could be performed by multiplying 1.76 times the appropriate academic salary (2.12 times the general wage level). This might exaggerate somewhat the average salaries of male academics—because of the slackening in the demand for academic labor during the 1970s—and underestimate the salaries of female academics—because of the likely impact of affirmative action programs—but it does provide an order of magnitude adjustment.

3. For example, converting the estimated 1970 salaries of academic sociologists into 1978 dollars, we obtain values of $26,440 and $23,480 for men and women, respectively. Converting the Oaxaca wage rates into 1978 annual earnings by multiplying the adjusted wage rates by 2,000 hours, we get $11,490 for men and $7,890 for women, with ten years of experience. In this case, women sociologists earn $2,960 less than men; women in the general labor force, $3,600 less than men.

4. This word would be "he" if, for example, we were talking about a male physicist who took a ten year leave of absence to travel around the world to collect pottery—or about a male physicist who stayed home with the children while his M.D. wife worked.

5. It can be noted that never married women fare better than married women in reaching the rank of full professor. See Johnson and Stafford (1974: 896–97).

6. On this point see R.A. Lester (1977).

7. An argument along these lines has been presented by Marianne Ferber and Betty Kordick (1978). Specifically, they argue that if women earn less than men because of labor market discrimination, it is efficient for the former to specialize in home production rather than market activity, thus compounding salary differences due to discrimination.

Chapter 12

Faculty Bargaining and
Faculty Reward

James P. Begin

INTRODUCTION

In order to attract and retain employees and to keep them performing at acceptable levels, organizations offer a set of rewards to their employees. Over time, the employees develop a range of expectations about the particular reward system that has evolved in their work organization. Schein (1965) describes this relationship between employee expectations and reward systems a "psychological contract." Kuhn (1974: 225) defines an explicit or implicit agreement that a particular relationship will be continued as a "major bargain." As indicated by Hammer and Bacharach (1977: 1), "These expectations cover not only the amount of work that should be performed for given amounts of pay, but also the rights, privileges, and obligations each party has with respect to the other."

In higher education, a complex and diverse system of rewards has evolved as faculties have attempted to achieve control of those resources necessary for their adaptation to increasingly bureaucratic organizations. Many observers have noted that institutions of higher education traditionally provided a reasonable balance between professional faculty needs and bureaucratic, organizational goals. Vollmer (1966: 276–82), for example, pointed out that research entrepreneurship was one mechanism that developed in higher education to accommodate professional and organizational needs. Clark (1966: 283–91) argued that the growth of institutions of higher education and the development of disciplines produced a federated system of organization that has permitted a maximum degree of professional

participation. Governance mechanisms providing for faculty input to policy development, administration, and tenure systems providing for the protection of academic freedom represent other forms of adaptation.

However, the reward systems in higher education have not evolved identical patterns at all types of institutions. For example, a task force report issued by the American Association of Higher Education (1967: 10) reported that: "the case studies indicate that the greatest discontent and most visible tendencies toward unionization are found at the junior college level . . . there was considerable faculty dissatisfaction over the complete control by the administration of curricula and promotions and the rigid application of rules governing the conduct of professional duties . . . similar developments have taken place in the new or emerging four-year colleges and universities." In contrast, Barbash (1970: 27) stated that in prestigious universities, "professional autonomy and control are embedded in the structure of government."

Are these disparaties in faculty reward systems the basis for the current faculty union movement? What major bargains or psychological contracts in respect to faculty reward systems have been violated by higher education organizations such that faculties now perceive the need to adapt to their work organizations through the process of unionization? It is the purpose of this chapter to review the empirical literature for the purpose of setting out those factors that are important to understanding both the evolution of faculty reward systems that created the faculty bargaining movement and the further evolution of these systems under collective bargaining.

THE ORIGINS AND GROWTH
OF FACULTY BARGAINING

A few years ago, Garbarino (1974: 309) used the term "creeping unionism" to describe the expansion of faculty collective bargaining. As Table 12–1 indicates, the annual growth of faculty bargaining has continued to creep. At the end of 1977, over one-sixth of all institutions were unionized. In total, just over one-quarter of the faculty have been unionized. Additionally, about a quarter of the two year institutions, 12 percent of the four year institutions, and less than 5 percent of the private institutions have been unionized. While these results indicate a definite unionization trend, faculty unionism has proceeded at a much slower rate than teachers. In a nine year period (1965–1973), it was estimated that at least 70 percent of the elementary and secondary school teachers were organized (*Government Employee Relations Report*, 1974: D–2).

Table 12-1. Faculty Union Activity: 1966-1977.

Year	New Institutions Each Year	Total Institutions
1966	1	23
1967	14	37
1968	33	70
1969	68	138
1970	39	177
1971	68	245
1972	40	285
1973	25	310
1974	27	337
1975	61	398
1976	53	450[a]
1977	30	480

[a]One bargaining unit was decertified in 1976.
Sources: Garbarino (1975b: 110-11); Garbarino and Lawler (1977: 105-106; 1978).

Over the thirteen year history of the faculty bargaining movement, an extensive literature, mostly case studies, has emerged assessing the determinants of faculty bargaining. This discussion is a summary of a more detailed integration of this literature reported elsewhere (Begin, Settle, & Alexander, 1975). In sorting out and clarifying the factors important to the movement of faculty in establishing collective bargaining relationships, an effort will be made to distinguish the environmental, organizational, and individual variables affecting acceptance of unionization.

An analysis of the national pattern of unionization illustrates the dynamic nature of faculty unionization. Faculty bargaining started at a core of institutions (the pioneers) and then spread outward along several paths. The pioneer institutions can be described as those for which most of the following factors are relevant:

1. *Located in states where earliest bargaining legislation developed.* The location of the organized institutions in geographical areas traditionally supportive of unions reflects the importance of legislation in providing access to collective bargaining. Clearly, institutions of higher education were caught up in the public sector union movement of the 1960s after lobbying for labor legislation had been accomplished by other occupational groups. It is no coincidence that most of the public institutions in which faculty bargaining has occurred are located in states with labor legislation covering public em-

ployees (Begin, 1974a: 78). As Garbarino (1975a: 63) points out, about 90 percent of the organized institutions are located in states with the strongest legislation. Moreover, the recent slowdown of the growth of faculty bargaining is a reflection of the fact that most of the public institutions in states with legislation are organized (Begin, 1974a: 79).

In states without legislation, there have been few higher education administrators willing to permit elections for a faculty bargaining agent without a statutory requirement. The most notable examples of this position are institutions in Wisconsin, California, and Washington. Administrators in Ohio and Illinois have been less reluctant to proceed to bargaining without statutory authority.

The legislative variable, however, does have limitations. It does not explain the low penetration of collective bargaining into higher quality institutions or into private institutions. Furthermore, while nearly 40 percent of the elections in private institutions to mid-1975 ended in "no union" votes, only three four year public institutions had voted "no union" (Garbarino, 1975: 57–58, 67). Clearly other forces must therefore be at work in private institutions.

The experience in New Jersey, for example, illustrates that faculty adaptation to perceived internal and external authority problems had preceded the passage of legislation. For several years, the state colleges, Rutgers University, and other institutions had bargained informally with institutional administrations and state authorities and had lobbied the legislature. The various faculty organizations sometimes formed coalitions for these activities. The reorganization of higher education in 1966, just two years before the passage of the bargaining law, was another step strengthening state authority which threatened faculty influence (Begin, Settle, & Alexander, 1975: 20–21). Clearly, as described below, other forces in addition to legislation are at the base of faculty unionism.

2. *Experienced greatest faculty-administration strife due to organizational change and/or leadership style.* While faculty-administration strife is not unique to current times, accelerated change in enrollments, missions, and structures in the context of perceived autocratic leadership styles led to the adoption of bargaining as a means of coping with the changes (Garbarino, 1975: ch. 1). Studies of the causes of faculty bargaining at particular institutions or systems of higher education indicate that faculty dissatisfaction with a wide range of working conditions does distinguish among faculty who support collective bargaining (Lussier, 1974; Edgar, 1974; Feuille & Blandin, 1974: 682; Seidman, Kelley, & Edge, 1974;

Lozier & Mortimer, 1974: 67; Mortimer & Ross, 1975: 22; Mortimer, Johnson, & Weiss, 1975: 41; Shoup, 1969; Haehn, 1970; Sawicki, 1975: 11–12; Moore, 1971: 39). However, the specific issues about which faculty who support collective bargaining are dissatisfied vary from institution to institution. This finding from the literature, coupled with statistics on the extent and pattern of faculty unionization, lend support to a conclusion that it is not absolute differences in working conditions among institutions that primarily explain variations in the pattern of unionization. These differences between types of institutions have always existed (for example, salaries have usually been higher and governance usually more extensive at four year colleges). Rather, it appears that changes in higher education that have differentially affected various types of institutions play an important part in explaining the pattern of faculty unionization.

Changes in structure and function were more important at an early point in the bargaining movement; external economic pressures in terms of declining enrollment and funding problems have exerted a stronger effect in recent times. Predominant among the first four year institutions to organize were those experiencing changes in structure and function—the former teacher's colleges. As a body, the private institutions were spared the massive growth and reorganization of public institutions and this very likely accounts in an important way for the low rate of unionization. But the New Jersey experience indicates that those private institutions which have unionized have been likely to experience substantial tension from changes (Begin, Settle, & Alexander, 1975: 21). The rapid growth in size and structure of the two year colleges in the context of authoritarian leadership styles created substantial faculty-administration strife in many institutions, which provided an impetus to faculty bargaining.

3. *Had a history of informal faculty bargaining that rereflected faculty concern with decisionmaking authority that predated bargaining movement.* This factor is related to the previous one in that the political, economic, and social forces that started to reshape and restructure higher education in the 1960s had already initiated a different form of faculty participation in some institutions. So when bargaining laws were passed, established organizations headed by senior faculty and acceptable to the larger faculty body were in place to ease the transition into unionism. Faculty bargaining was not a revolutionary changing of the guard; it was an evolutionary recognition by established faculty leadership that collective bargaining appeared to be a viable alternative for achieving or protecting faculty

rights and benefits under conditions of change. At the City University of New York it was the Legislative Conference, an organization in existence for many years, which provided the link to unionization. At Rutgers University it was the AAUP, and at the New Jersey State Colleges, an NEA affiliate which had been very active in serving faculty interests prior to the passage of bargaining legislation.

4. *Existence of faculty acceptance of unions deriving from prior relationships.* The missions of the teacher's colleges brought them into close contact with the public school establishment, and the missions of the two year colleges led them to hire many former public school teachers. Thus, the faculty in the earliest institutions to unionize not only had been subject to a greater degree of organizational change as noted previously, but they also had prior relationships to the more extensively unionized public education sector (Lozier & Mortimer, 1974; Haehn, 1970; Moore, 1971; Edgar, 1974; Angell, 1971: 34; Carr & Van Eyck, 1973: 62). On the other hand, the presence of the nonmilitant AAUP at most private institutions, where the missions of the institutions did not provide easy contact with the AFT or NEA, not only has led to the dominance of the AAUP in private institutions but very likely has contributed to the lower rate of unionization of private schools. Important as well was the previously noted fact that private institutions generally had been spared the same degree of organizational change in public institutions.

From the pioneer institutions bargaining flows out along some or all of the following paths:

1. *Passage of further legislation.*

2. *Organizational relationships dictated by structure.* These relationships will tend to override differences between institutions in individual faculty characteristics. For example, Rutgers University and the New Jersey Institute of Technology (NJIT) were defensively organized as a consequence of membership in a statewide system, even though the bargaining unit was not systemwide. The New York state universities (Buffalo, Stonybrook, Albany, and Binghamton) were organized as part of a statewide bargaining unit, as were the four year elements of the University of Hawaii. Obviously, private institutions are not subject to these forces. As a consequence, the quality variable is more operable in explaining variations in collective bargaining in the private sector. Gold (1974: 326) and later Chandler, Julius, and Mannix (1977) found that high prestige institutions in the public sector are experiencing a higher proportion of unionization. But these authors have ignored the system linkages described above,

which tend to override varying faculty values in different types of institutions.

3. *Changing social values in respect to unions as favorable faculty perceptions of bargaining experiences at other institutions break down attitudinal barriers to unionism.* Growing faculty acceptance of unionism reduces the need for informal prebargaining relationships such as the AAUP at Rutgers and the Legislative Conference at CUNY, since the adoption of bargaining at other institutions makes unionization a less unprofessional alternative. Changing values toward collective bargaining may also eventually force the national AAUP into greater support for bargaining.

4. *Sites of significant faculty-administration stress created by organizational change and/or leadership style.* Changes deriving from economic pressures are now generally more important than when the bargaining movement was initiated in the 1960s and early 1970s.

5. *Situations where union competition produces a bargaining agent where the other forces for bargaining are not strong.* Union competition often serves to override differences in faculty support for collective bargaining caused by varying demographical and value orientations. For example, faculty members may have strong reactions against one or more of the competitors and will thus decide not to vote "no union" but to vote defensively for the union they feel most nearly reflects their values or interests. This factor may account for the finding of Seidman, Kelley, and Edge (1974) that some of the factors which explained faculty attitudes toward bargaining in a preelection attitude survey were not as useful to explain actual voting behavior. In three separate studies, Mortimer and his colleagues have identified the presence of this defensive force (Lozier & Mortimer, 1974: 67; Mortimer & Ross, 1975: 22; Mortimer, Johnson, & Weiss, 1975: 41).

The New Jersey experience suggests that union competition will more likely produce a bargaining agent where none would otherwise have developed (a) when the other forces for unionization are not strong (e.g., antiadministration sentiment is not strong), and/or (b) when system relationships produce defensive unionism (NJIT and Rutgers) (Begin, Settle, & Alexander, 1975: 15). The two-tiered voting system adopted or recommended for adoption by some states (first vote yes or no for bargaining, then for specific union if yes) may prevent unionization from developing in the first instance, but such a system is unlikely to prevent unionism where the other forces creating faculty dissatisfaction and support for bargaining are very

strong. To the extent that the pioneer institutions in collective bargaining represent the ones in which the other forces for bargaining are most strong, then the two-tiered system would be expected to be more applicable to later attempts to unionize faculty where the "bandwagon" effect generated out of perceptions of bargaining experiences at other institutions might be stronger, the other basic causes perhaps weaker.

Generally speaking, while the competition between the AAUP, AFT, and NEA has been identified as creating bargaining relationships at some colleges and universities where none might otherwise have developed, the faculty bargaining movement, when compared to the school teacher bargaining movement, has not been marked with substantial competition. To date, the AAUP has not responded strongly at the national level to the AFT or NEA competition, and this less aggressive stance by the national organization most acceptable to large numbers of faculty might account in part for the slower rate of unionization of faculty, particularly in private institutions where the educational missions have not brought the faculty into frequent contact with the AFT or NEA.

6. *Instances in which systematic management or faculty opposition does not emerge.*   Bain (1969: 246) indicates that the degree to which employers are willing to recognize unions is an important explanatory factor in producing white collar unionism. The fuzzy boundary between management and professional employees is felt to make professionals particularly sensitive to management attitudes in respect to collective bargaining. A study by Mortimer, Johnson, and Weiss (1975) of thirty-two situations in which the faculty rejected collective bargaining in an election indicated that organized administrative opposition was a common element in most instances.

While the above evidence tends to indicate that systematic administrative opposition can be effective in heading off unionism, it is doubtful that an administrative effort to defeat a union would be effective in a context where there are strong antiadministration feelings. Such efforts in fact might serve to further polarize faculty-administration relationships as they did at Delaware (Sawicki, 1975).

The success of administrative opposition seems to be related in a major way to the ability of an administration to foster active opposition among senior faculty—that is, to the extent to which a subtle or not so subtle administration–senior faculty coalition develops. Thus, the role of senior faculty in a recognition campaign emerges as a crucial one. Where, as noted previously, the senior faculty leadership supports bargaining, administrative campaigns are likely doomed.

Summary: Origins and Growth

The above explanation of the origins of faculty bargaining focuses on organizational change and its effects on faculty expectations. This is not the first historical period in which change has produced an altered authority structure in higher education. In the earlier part of this century, faculty at many institutions adapted to the growing size of academic institutions, the development of the disciplines, and the emergence of full-time administrators by developing internal governance mechanisms. The eventual emergence of academic tenure was essentially another adaptive mechanism facilitating the interaction between academic professionals and the bureaucratic organizations in which they worked.

As academic organizations continued to grow, as administrative structures became increasingly complex and bureaucratic, as administrators began to reflect more of the professional bureaucrat's frame of mind, and as the economic climate worsened, the faculty needed a stronger means of relating to the bureaucratic organizations in order to protect and/or achieve professional status. With the failure of traditional mechanisms to cope with the changes, the process to which many faculty have turned is the one traditionally used in this country to ameliorate employee-employer tension—collective bargaining. As Light (1974: 21) indicated, "Just as tenure once signaled the power of the new academic professions over a small, elite network of institutions, now faculty unions signal the power of teaching cadres over a massive, universal system of higher education."

THE CONSEQUENCES OF FACULTY BARGAINING

We now turn to a discussion of the impact of faculty bargaining on the reward systems the faculty are seeking to protect or improve through unionization.

The available empirical literature will be reviewed with respect to the changes in faculty reward systems that have been created by collective bargaining. Other institutional effects are likely to occur, but will not be dealt with in depth. The bulk of the literature consists of unrelated case studies that rarely carefully delineate pre- and post-bargaining states of faculty reward systems, of surveys of contract provisions unrelated to the context of bargaining relationships or the prebargaining status of benefits, or of subjective attitude surveys of union effects (for example, Kemerer & Baldridge, 1975). Additionally, the independent effects of other forces for change in higher

education—for example, market factors and affirmative action—are not frequently considered. Another caveat is related to the fact that the types of institutions unionized to date may represent a skewed distribution of higher education institutions generally. Since they may represent the institutions with the greatest problems, the changes under collective bargaining would be expected to be skewed in that direction as well. So any conclusions stated below about the effects of bargaining must be measured against these limitations of the data.

The effects of collective bargaining on faculty reward systems are conceptualized as the outputs of the bargaining exchange process (Begin, 1973: 35). Basically, employees, through their bargaining agent, seek to share in making the decisions that govern their employment relationships for the sake of improving their wages and other conditions of employment.

As pointed out by Gustad (1969), the concerns of faculty for participation in policy development and administration, for the protection of academic freedom and job security, for collegial relationships with other members of the organization, and for adequate compensation comprise important components of faculty reward systems.

As indicated in Figure 12-1, it is expected that bargaining will affect faculty reward systems through:

1. A rationalization of institutional policies and practices, particularly those related to personnel issues;

2. A rationalization of grievance procedures, with a corresponding improvement in due process;

3. A redistribution of authority among faculty, administrators, and students;

4. Changes in the quality of relationships brought about by the adversary nature of the collective bargaining process; and,

5. Changes in the level of compensation, with possible resulting effects on resource allocation.

Rationalization of Institutional Policies and Practices

It is expected that faculty unions will promote rationalized institutional policies by negotiating and enforcing through the grievance procedure (1) more systematic promotion, tenure, reappointment, dismissal, and appeals procedures for protecting individual rights and

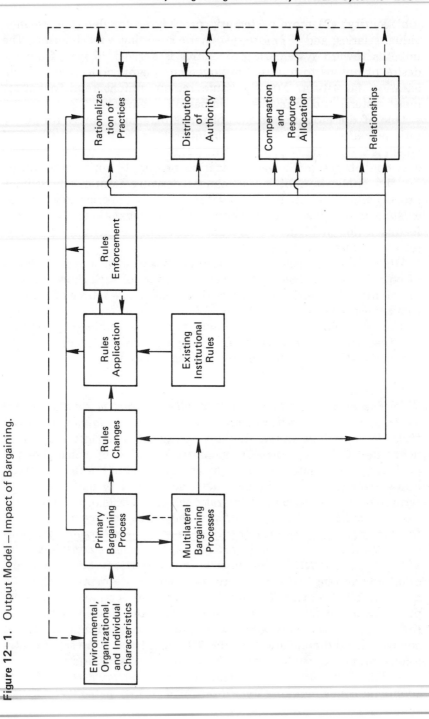

Figure 12–1. Output Model – Impact of Bargaining.

job security; (2) more systematic procedures for determining individual salaries; and (3) more systematic governance mechanisms. The impetus toward systematic procedures is derived, in part, from the desire of unions to mollify employee complaints concerning administration favoritism. For the same reason, unions tend to oppose merit systems and to favor criteria based on seniority.

One of the most important collective bargaining forces for policy rationalization is the contract administration process, at the base of which is the grievance procedure negotiated in the contract. This process contributes to the rationalization process by uniformly enforcing the application of rules changes deriving from the bargaining process and, where permitted by the scope of the grievance process, existing noncontractual university rules and regulations. The dotted feedback line in Figure 12—1 from Rules Enforcement to Rules Application illustrates this effect.

While the regularization of procedures has positive aspects in terms of equity, the expected negative consequences of such procedures on the ability of an institution to reward quality is a source of concern to many observers.

The rationalizing effects of unions will be determined by examining, first, the policies deriving from negotiations and, second, the enforcement of policies through the grievance process.

Negotiations
1. *The evidence indicates that faculty contract negotiations have led to a substantial rationalization of institutional policies and practices.* It should be noted that the source of most information on negotiated policies derives from contract studies in which pre- and postbargaining changes must be inferred, at least in the first contract. Subsequent changes in the contracts, however, very likely can be interpreted as an indication of the rationalizing effects of unions.

a. *A longitudinal analysis of the change in contracts as support for the growing rationalization of policies under bargaining is provided by a study by Andes (1974) that compares contracts from 1971, 1972, and 1973.* Increases in the proportion of contracts covering a wide range of issues were indicated. Since many of the contracts in 1972 and 1973 were first year contracts, his results were probably understated; a comparison across the three years of only the 1971 contracts very likely would have produced more extensive changes. He did conclude that the 1973 contracts were significantly longer, no matter what year the first contract was negotiated.

b. *Bargaining has had its greatest impact on policies relating to economic issues, working conditions, and faculty personnel policies.*

To date, educational policies have received little treatment in contracts and bargaining statutes do not require mandatory negotiations over these issues. (For detailed discussion of court and administrative decisions see the section on Authority Distribution, below.)

c. *There is a trend toward writing faculty governance procedures into the contracts, even though most bargaining statutes do not require mandatory negotiations over governance procedures.* For example, Andes (1974) reported that the 1973 contracts contained far more governance items than previous years. Also, Mortimer (1973) reported that one-quarter of the contracts he reviewed had some provision for the formation of joint administration-faculty committees to handle a range of issues.

Sixty-four percent of 417 respondents from six two year colleges in New York indicated that they felt that bargaining had been helpful in establishing a more formalized governance structure (Falcone, 1975). (For a detailed discussion of governance under bargaining, see the Authority Distribution section.)

d. *Faculty contracts also deal extensively with merit and other compensation procedures, although the extent of rationalization through bargaining is unclear due to the absence of prebargaining comparisons.* (For a discussion of the data and their limitations, see the section on Compensation and Resource Allocation, below)

e. *Union security provisions, except for dues checkoff, are not widely reported in faculty contracts, although they have presented major negotiating problems for the unions.* (For a detailed discussion, see Authority Distribution.)

f. *The inclusion of tenure provisions in two-thirds of the contracts at two and four year institutions underlines the objective of unions and faculty in protecting faculty job security through the preservation of traditional tenure procedures, particularly at four year institutions, where 71 percent of the contracts studied had tenure provisions* (Andes, 1974). Sixty-one percent of the respondents to an opinion survey conducted in six New York two year colleges (Falcone, 1975) reported that they felt that formal academic freedom policies existed after the initiation of bargaining. Thirty-four percent felt that such policies had existed prior to bargaining. In respect to formal tenure and promotion procedures, 88 percent felt that these procedures existed after bargaining, and 66 percent indicated that the formal procedures also existed prior to bargaining.

Tenure provisions have been one of the most sensitive negotiating areas, and it has been the purpose of the unions to protect and refine the traditional system rather than be parties to major overhauls. In fact, unions attempting to implement major changes have run into

problems. At the University of Hawaii, faculty dissatisfaction with changes in the tenure system negotiated by the AFT were an important factor leading to a turnover in the bargaining agent to a merged NEA–AAUP representative. A five year contract mechanism had been agreed to as an alternative to the traditional tenure system.

In a two year college studied by Mortimer and Richardson (1977: 84), many of the faculty were dissatisfied with the negotiation of multiyear contracts for tenure, even though the contracts required statements of cause and due process before dismissals could take place: "tenure is an emotional issue with the faculty and this issue has been used by the college administration to support their claims that the faculty were sold down the river by the NEA in order to end negotiations."

At Bloomfield College (New Jersey) abolition of the tenure system and substitution of multiyear contracts for those faculty remaining after a layoff required by a financial exigency led first to the unionization of the faculty (AAUP) and then to very difficult negotiations and a court case. The college was subsequently required to re-hire all the faculty when the court found no basis for the declaration of financial exigency, in part because the college still owned some very expensive real estate on which a golf course was situated (Begin, Settle, & Alexander, 1975: 165–91).

The negotiation of grievance mechanisms as a means of providing due process in the promotion and tenure process are discussed below.

2. *Variation in the extent of rationalization has occurred along some dimensions.*

a. The evidence on the effect of the *type of bargaining agent* on the contract language is mixed. A multivariate analysis of the factors associated with variations in contract content at fifty-nine four year institutions found that most clauses were not systematically related to the type of bargaining agent (Bognanno, Estenson, & Suntrup, 1977). Another study of only nineteen institutions, which did not employ multivariate techniques, concluded that the variations in the contracts did reflect a bargaining agent effect (Butcher & Schenker, 1976).

b. Where *bargaining units* are mixed occupationally and institutionally, there is some evidence that nonteaching professionals, administrators, part-time faculty, and two year college faculty have used the contract to "catch up." (For a detailed discussion, see the section on Compensation and Resource Allocation, below.)

c. The *type of control* of institutions (public, private) was not found to be systematically related to the extent and type of contract content in one study (Bognanno, Estenson, & Suntrup, 1977).

d. Variations were found across different *types of institutions.* A New Jersey study found that the most extensive contracts were in three private institutions, followed by the two year colleges and the state colleges, and far behind were the graduate and research institutions (Begin, Settle, & Berke-Weiss, 1977).

In another study, two year college contracts were more extensive than four year contracts and appeared to be rapidly approaching the public school teacher model in many instances (Andes, 1974).

Contract Enforcement

1. *While the literature on prebargaining complaint procedures within institutions of higher education is sparse, the onset of negotiations has clearly produced more systematic grievance procedures.* Falcone (1975), for example, in an opinion survey of six New York two year colleges, found that the 92 percent of the respondents felt that formal grievance procedures existed after bargaining. Half of the respondents felt that formal grievance procedures had existed prior to bargaining.

2. *While few, if any, institutions had external arbitration available in the prebargaining period, faculty unions and administrators have broadly accepted the concept of arbitration.* Even at an early stage of the faculty bargaining movement, 75 percent of the four year contracts and 83 percent of the two year contracts contained binding or advisory arbitration provisions (Benewitz, 1973: 145; Mannix, 1974: 24).

3. *An examination of the issues that can be grieved indicates that the parties in higher education have shaped the scope provisions to reflect prebargaining practices.* Usually omitted from the definition of a grievance in faculty contracts are substantive matters of academic judgment: only procedural violations, such as improper compliance with evaluation procedures, may be grieved or arbitrated through the negotiated procedures (Benewitz, 1973: 146). Two year institutions do not follow this pattern as closely as four year institutions.

The limitation of personnel grievances to procedural questions, after the historical pattern of the national AAUP, developed primarily because the parties did not feel that the usual just cause model was as relevant in a context in which (i) the union members were participants in personnel decisions on the basis of their professional knowledge of individual qualifications, or (ii) decisions not to reappoint an individual were made on the basis of one's failure to achieve a minimum level of excellence and not on an individual's ability to meet minimum job requirements.

Only one study reviewed the important question of whether limitations on the scope of the grievance procedure have sacrificed individual due process for the protection of academic judgments. At Rutgers University it was found that due process was achieved under such procedures even in the absence of external review; the president was the final step (Begin, 1978a). However, there is a growing evidence that the parties at a number of institutions are, through experience, evolving procedures that either substitute internal due process for external review of academic judgment (for example, Temple University, the University of Hawaii, Rutgers University, and CUNY provide internal committees) or open up arbitration to some or all academic judgment issues, often by developing special arbitration procedures (for example, Oakland University provides a form of tripartite arbitration and the University of Rhode Island provides for arbitration of all issues).

4. *The literature indicates that faculty grievance and arbitration rates generally have not been high.* A 1974 survey of seventeen four year units reported minimal usage of the final step. Even though the City University of New York (CUNY) and the State University of New York (SUNY) have had many cases in absolute terms, if the cases are ratioed to faculty size, the ratios at these institutions are lower than many other institutions (Begin & Weinberg, 1976: 98). In addition, at SUNY, a fifth of the grievances were filed by nonteaching professionals (Satryb, 1974: 135). The arbitration rate at Temple University was also reported to be low (Lee, 1977: 178−98), as were rates in many two year colleges (Begin, Settle, & Berke-Weiss, 1977: 130; Gershenfeld & Mortimer, 1976: 160).

5. *The low grievance and arbitration rates and the variation in the rates between institutions seem, based on a limited literature, to be related to faculty values, the extent of the contract (including the scope of the grievance procedure), and the nature of the bargaining relationship.* In terms of faculty values, the low number of cases raises the question as to whether all aggrieved faculty are taking the opportunity to use the procedures. At Rutgers University, the AAUP counselors and officers perceived that some faculty with tenure and/or promotion grievances that the AAUP felt were legitimate either quietly left the university or decided to wait for reevaluation the next year in instances where the probationary period had not expired or where the grievant already had tenure. The additional finding that only five grievances were filed by faculty who faced future peer reviews indicates that the fear of biasing future peer judgments is powerful and tends to delay the filing of grievances, if filed at all, until termination is imminent (Begin, 1978a). As economic condi-

tions worsen and/or faculty perceptions about bargaining change, perhaps faculty will be less reluctant to grieve.

The extent of the contract and the nature of the bargaining relationship were also factors in the grievance and arbitration rates (Begin & Storholm, 1978; Begin, Settle, & Berke-Weiss, 1977: 136–37; Newton, 1973: 64; Satryb, 1974: 74; Weisberger, 1976: 30).

6. *To date, the policies most subject to rationalization through the grievance process have been those involving personnel actions such as reappointment, promotion, and tenure.* At most four year institutions, even those with broader contracts, faculty personnel actions have produced the bulk of the grievances (Begin & Weinberg, 1976: 98; Begin, 1978a; Gershenfeld & Mortimer, 1976: 40, 146–56, 185; Weisberger, 1976: 13, 24). In two year institutions, other grievance issues appear frequently and sometimes dominate, in large measure because the contracts are much thicker (Begin, Settle, & Berke-Weiss, 1977: 131; Levy, 1975a: 2).

Most of the studies described above discuss postbargaining grievance or arbitration rates and decisions; thus, an impact on prebargaining policies can only be inferred from the types of issues grieved. If the experience at Rutgers University is any indication, however, the rationalizing effects are substantial. Decisions in the grievance process either produced a number of faculty personnel policy changes, particularly in respect to hiring practices and evaluation procedures, or have led to a more uniform application of existing policies (Begin, 1978a). In the New Jersey State Colleges similar results have obtained, as the bargaining agent (AFT) has grieved just about every possible provision in the contract; subsequent policy changes also derived from the grievances (Begin & Storholm, 1978).

7. *The question of whether the more systematic negotiated grievance procedures have produced improvement in due process is again one that must be answered through inference since few studies were found that dealt specifically with this issue.* At Rutgers University, even though the grievants won exactly what they wanted in only a quarter of the cases, it was concluded that due process had been achieved, even in the absence of external review (Begin, 1978a). In the New Jersey State Colleges, where the arbitrators had upheld the union in about a third of the first forty cases, it was also concluded that due process had increased substantially (Begin & Storholm, 1978). In both New Jersey examples, it was concluded, as well, that the more systematic procedures provided a higher quality of due process. At Rutgers University, for example, the complaint process had been cleansed of many potential conflicts of interest, and the right of both parties to be present and to cross-examine witnesses was more

firmly established. It probably would not be stretching it too much to infer that the same outcomes were experienced at other institutions.

In terms of outcomes, the New Jersey experience was generally comparable with other situations. At SUNY, the union lost all nine arbitration cases. Of the 135 cases going to the chancellor's level, the union won a remand or a partial or full victory in about one-fifth of the cases (Satryb, 1974: 71). At CUNY, the union reportedly was upheld in about 40 percent of the first 105 arbitration awards (Mintz & Golden, 1974: 35). In the sixteen New Jersey two year colleges, the unions were upheld in less than a third of the arbitration awards (Begin, Settle, & Berke-Weiss, 1977: 134).

8. *While it has been commonly believed that the rationalizing effects of the grievance process will have a negative impact on institutional quality (for example, see Oberer, 1969: 143), there is not sufficient empirical literature on this question to provide firm conclusions.* At Rutgers University an examination of the number of faculty returned to departments because of favorable grievance decisions where the departmental faculty had previously rejected them indicated that it was extremely difficult to overcome negative peer reviews in the grievance process. Thus, there was little diminution of the existing quality of Rutgers faculty due to the grievance process (Begin, 1978a). No study was found that examined pre- and post-bargaining promotion and tenure rejection rates, controlled for the effects of affirmative action and the market, so that the hypothesis concerning the tendency of faculty to automatically recommend promotions to colleagues under pressures of external review of the grievance process could be tested. Brown and Stone (1977) did find, however, that there were no differences in the promotion rates between the thirty-seven unionized four year institutions they studied and national rates.

Kemerer and Baldridge (1975: 128) offered the opinion that "The major negative consequence of faculty unionism may be a protectionist, job-security orientation that could thwart personnel policies so that incompetency is protected and seniority, not merit, becomes the main decision-making criterion." But would not reactions to severe economic conditions produce the same types of employee adaptations, union or not? The relative contributions to due process by negotiated grievance procedures, market forces, and affirmative action were considered in a study of Rutgers University. While it was found that most of the grievances were generated by nonbargaining forces and may have occurred with or without bargaining, the negotiated grievance process provided a more efficient internal accommo-

dation to affirmative action complaints and grievances arising from institutional responses to market forces. Policy responses to problems were also quicker (Begin, 1978a). A review of the experiences at SUNY, CUNY, and the Pennsylvania State Colleges also concluded that many of the grievances at those institutions would have occurred without collective bargaining (Weisberger, 1976: 42).

Compensation and Resource Allocation

One of the common expectations concerning the effects of unions is that they will interfere with the free operation of the labor market by reallocating resources in less than optimal ways. Unions accomplish this in part by negotiating higher wages for their constituents than nonunionized faculty receive, even though relative productivity is equivalent. Additionally, unions tend to negotiate structured salary systems that emphasize seniority over merit and insulate some groups more than others from the market. To the extent that union wage and benefit increases are funded by allocating resources from nonsalary accounts—for example, library books or classroom facilities— a possible misallocation of the factors of production occurs that diminishes the quality of the product. The findings generated by the literature on these factors are as follows:

1. *The growing literature on the effect of faculty unions on relative wages produces mixed results as to union impact, but most estimates fall within a range of 0 to 10 percent.* Some of the articles (Birnbaum, 1974, 1976; Morgan & Kearney, 1977) identified a union wage impact. Birnbaum (1976) in a study of fifty matched pairs of union and nonunion four year institutions found a positive union differential of $1,500 (8.1 percent). Morgan and Kearney (1977) in a study of forty-six pairs of matched four year institutions found an average union effect of $625. In a regression analysis using salary change from 1969–1970 to 1974–1975 as the dependent variable, the union-nonunion variable was the largest predictor (Morgan & Kearney, 1977: 37). Some of the recent studies reported a lessening (Birnbaum, 1977) or insignificant effect (Brown & Stone, 1977).

The relatively low union effect measured by the studies and the varying results of the studies would not be surprising to labor economists. Most studies of private sector relative wage rates have concluded that the union impact ranges from 0–20 percent, with considerable variation across time and across occupations (Rees, 1962: 75–80, 90–94; also see Lewis, 1963). Private sector studies show that relative wage impacts are the greatest in earlier years of a bargaining relationship (Rees, 1962: 87–94). A review of the literature of public employer union impacts concluded that "the 'average'

wage effect of unionism in government is roughly on the order of five percent, a much smaller impact than is popularly supposed and smaller than the average union wage impact in private industry" (Lewin, 1977: 374).

2. *As can be expected at this stage, the researchers are still sorting out the methodology to be used to compare union and nonunion faculty salaries, the proper variables, and data limitations.* The Birnbaum and the Morgan and Kearney studies used a matching technique in which a union and a nonunion institution were matched in accordance with several criteria. But as pointed out by Brown and Stone (1977), since the matches required researcher judgment to balance the criteria to get the best match, the results obtained can be very unreliable. Brown and Stone properly pointed out that uncontrolled variables in the Birnbaum and the Morgan and Kearney studies could reduce the union wage impact to nothing. In the first place, Birnbaum and Morgan and Kearney matched across geographical regions with different labor markets and different average wages. This was necessary since the public institutions in some states or regions were almost entirely unionized. But regional salary differences appeared to account for some of the union wage effect, since the unionized institutions came from regions with higher average salaries (Brown & Stone, 1977: 310–11). Second, Birnbaum and Morgan and Kearney had not controlled for changes in institutional quality, and Brown and Stone (p. 312) indicated that there was evidence that unionized institutions, using the average number of professional accreditations as a criteria for quality, had increased in quality faster than the nonunion institutions over the period of the studies. Lastly, Brown and Stone argued that the authors had not identified precisely within their study periods when the institutions had negotiated the initial contract. Thus, the union effect was not precisely identified and was very likely overstated.

Brown and Stone compared salaries of unionized institutions to national salary trends utilizing AAUP salary data and found no union salary effects. However, they did not identify the possible response biases in the AAUP data, which might have affected their results. Are institutions unionized by non-AAUP organizations still cooperating with the AAUP survey? Furthermore, the response rates of two year institutions from certain states, particularly the heavily unionized states, are so low as to render the data almost useless for any type of generalizations concerning two year colleges.

Another limitation of the studies to date is that they do not control for possible relationships of faculty salaries, particularly those in public institutions, to salaries of other public employees. For exam-

ple, Bain (1976) pointed out that salary increases at CUNY, at least in the early stages of bargaining, were determined by a system of parity with public school administrators and teachers. In New Jersey, the eleven public four year institutions have always received essentially the same wage increases as other state employees. Sometimes the package has been carved up differentially—for example, Rutgers University on three occasions has negotiated merit increases with the AAUP—but the total packages across state bargaining units almost always have been identical. The union effect here may be not that faculty unions have got more than other state employees, but that they preserved parity in across the board increases where the pattern was set by nonfaculty and non-higher-education state employee units. Garbarino (1975a: 171) also reported a parity relationship between SUNY and other state employees for the first contract. In fact, he concluded that public college and university salaries have "moved upwards more or less in line with the salaries of other state employees." His conclusion was confirmed by another study in which it was found that faculty economic increases are tied to those of other state employees in New Jersey, New York, Pennsylvania, Massachusetts, and Hawaii (Weinberg, 1976: 106). It should be noted that this parity in most instances also existed prior to bargaining. Clearly these relationships must be controlled in wage studies that attempt to separate out the impact of faculty unions.

The empirical analyses of union effects would also be more useful if other types of economic and noneconomic faculty union impacts were included in the analysis—for example, governance, grievance procedures, and fringes. Until these broader studies of union-nonunion effects are completed, the overall effects of unions will be unclear. One study, for example, indicated that tradeoffs among economic issues and between economic and noneconomic issues do occur (Begin, Settle, & Berke-Weiss, 1977: 71).

3. *While longitudinal and cross-sectional economic comparisons of union and nonunion institutions will continue to be of interest as long as there are sufficient nonunion institutions to make such comparisons useful, an essentially untapped area of analysis is the variation in effects found in unionized institutions.* An understanding of the forces causing variable accommodations of collective bargaining to institutions of higher education would seem to be a useful area of inquiry if optimal adaptations are to occur. What are the different tradeoffs that occur in negotiations and what are the environmental, organizational, and individual factors that condition the tradeoffs? One study of two year colleges, for example, found inverse relationships between economic and noneconomic contract content and

between contract content and the effectiveness of noncontractual faculty governance (Begin, Settle, & Berke-Weiss, 1977: 6, 15). In the same study, the salary variation among unionized two year institutions was found to be 28 percent (p. 68). This large variation among unionized institutions at this point in the history of faculty bargaining may account in part for the small union-nonunion effects found in other studies.

4. *Studies of faculty contracts have reported that "virtually" all contracts provide for the use of salary schedules* (Goeres, 1977a, 1977b). While faculty unions likely have contributed to the rationalization of faculty salary policies, the contract studies do not provide an indication of pre- and postbargaining changes. Most of the unionized institutions are two year colleges or former teachers colleges with a high incidence of prebargaining salary schedules. Many of the public four year institutions also had schedules prior to the onset of bargaining—for example, all eleven public four year institutions in New Jersey, SUNY, and CUNY. If the institutions already had such procedures prior to bargaining, it can hardly be argued that collective bargaining has eliminated the free market differentials between disciplines, ranks, and faculty quality.

5. *A review of a limited literature produced mixed results concerning the effects of faculty unions on rank and occupational differentials. The more extensive literature on differentials between types of institutions indicated a strong union effect on the reduction of such differentials.*

a. *Rank*: Bain (1976: 212) reported a leveling downward under the first CUNY contract, with the lower ranks receiving the largest increases. In the recent Rutgers University contract, a smaller increase was given to the senior faculty so that a merit pot could be established. However, at both CUNY and Rutgers, full professors are among the best paid in the country while junior faculty are paid much closer to national averages. Usually at the New Jersey four year institutions, across the board increases have tended to broaden inter-rank differences. Brown and Stone (1977) in their large study of unionized campuses also reported that the salaries of junior faculty had not increased relative to senior faculty. Garbarino (1975a: 171–72) reported that while some unions negotiated increases that tended to favor lower ranks—for example, absolute dollar increases—the AAUP data showed little change in rank relationships.

b. *Occupation*: Garbarino (1975a: 174) reported that at SUNY there was pressure for parity between the four year colleges, the university centers, and the nonteaching professionals and faculty, but

not from the two year agricultural and vocational schools that are a part of the unit. Garbarino (1974) concluded that the nonteaching professionals in the SUNY unit had made major gains in noneconomic issues, particularly in respect to personnel and governance procedures, while the faculty gains in these areas, with the exception of the grievance procedure, were negligible (p. 330). The nonteaching professionals did get a slightly larger salary increase for one year, 5.5 percent versus 5 for the faculty (p. 328). Some professional occupations, such as doctors, dentists, and lawyers, have protected themselves against potential leveling by successfully seeking out separate bargaining units. Chandler and Julius (n.d.) in a preliminary report indicated that only three of thirteen law school units have ever negotiated contracts, further illustrating the defensive nature of their unionization. At Rutgers University, the law school faculty stayed in the faculty unit without negative economic consequences since they retained their special salary ranges in an already highly structured salary system.

c. *Type of Institution*: Garbarino (1974: 327) reported that the community college faculty in the combined two and four year unit at CUNY received parity with four year colleges under collective bargaining, yielding a 42.5 percent increase for the top of the two year college full professor range compared to 20.5 percent at the same level in the senior colleges. In a more recent study, Begin, Settle, and Berke-Weiss (1977: 74–79) reported the following findings in respect to relationships between two and four year salaries:

i. In a four year period from 1973 to 1976, two year college salaries in New Jersey had increased relative to Rutgers University, the New Jersey Institute of Technology, the private institutions, and the eight state colleges. The shift was caused by (*a*) the greater two year salary increases; they exceeded the state college increases at every rank by a total of 4 to 6 percent over the four year period, and (*b*) the greater shift of faculty upward to higher ranks in the two year colleges as their relatively low seniority faculty moved up (p. 75). Two year college salaries now overlap state college salaries at the instructor and assistant professor ranks, and the differences between the other ranks have decreased substantially (p. 74).

ii. A review by the authors of available printed information and a telephone survey of community college administrators at the state level in other states indicated that two year college salaries are, or soon will be, overlapping four year college salaries in

many states (p. 76). With the exception of New Jersey, however, no relationship between collective bargaining and this decline in relative salary differentials was established in the literature.

iii. Differences in two year and four year salary differentials tended to be maintained to a greater degree where there was full state control and funding (Connecticut, Minnesota, Massachusetts); shared control (state and local) with substantial state funding (Florida, Montana); active state involvement in negotiations (Hawaii); or some combination of these factors. Only one state with shared state and local control over two year colleges reported that differentials were being maintained (Pennsylvania). Where two and four year institutions are combined in a single unit, salary schedules and/or increases were identical in three of the four units. In several states, it was reported that increasing teacher salaries pushed two year college faculty salaries into the four year territory (p. 77).

6. *Merit does live in faculty contracts to reward the "stars" despite expectations to the contrary.* It would probably not be too extreme to conclude that the incidence of merit has not changed substantially under collective bargaining to date, given that most of the institutions that have been unionized have not traditionally had merit provisions. An analysis of merit provisions in forty-one four year contracts produced a surprising number of merit provisions; eighteen contracts provided for merit increases, while one prohibited such increases. Ten of eighty-three two year college contracts contained merit provisions. So 46 percent of the four year contracts compared to 10 percent of the two year contracts made reference to merit (The National Center for the Study of Collective Bargaining in Higher Education, 1975b: 1–7). Unfortunately, no information on prebargaining merit systems was available to determine whether the incidence of such mechanisms was affected by unionization. AAUP contracts in the four year institutions were more likely to have merit increases, but this was probably more a function of the type of institution that the AAUP has organized. Another study of sixty-one four year agreements found that just less than half contained merit provisions (Bognanno, Estenson, & Suntrup, 1977: 13–14).

As the experience at Rutgers University indicates, merit is a difficult negotiating issue. The administration always places a high priority on negotiating such provisions. But the faculty who provide input to the AAUP through surveys before the negotiating package is developed and at AAUP meetings where votes are taken on the issue clearly do not support the use of merit. Most of them do not disagree

with the concept, but indicate that it is the implementation that causes problems. The AAUP's bargaining position has always reflected this particular faculty orientation. Currently, the issue of merit is one of the most difficult issues in a very difficult set of negotiations. Substantial dissatisfaction with the manner in which the last contractual merit increase was implemented has tended to undermine support for such a system. Hedgepeth (1974: 698) reported similar experiences at the State University College at Cortland, New York, a part of the SUNY bargaining unit. Whether over the long run merit systems can survive the political nature of collective bargaining, which requires the leadership to respond to majority views, is still open to question.

7. *While many administrations claim that reallocations have occurred to faculty salary accounts from nonsalary accounts, the absence of systematic, empirical inquiry into this area prevents any meaningful generalizations.* However, if increased funds are not available externally to fund faculty economic increases, a faculty at some point may have to consider whether it needs a better pension system or more library books and secretarial help. The problem with any inquiring into this area is that nonunion institutions may also be reallocating resources in this manner to provide faculty with salary increases in times of continuation budgets. Additionally, measuring the impact of these reallocations on the quality of education is subject to the usual caveats about studies in this area.

Authority Distribution

Power is one of the most important resources to professional employees. Society has long recognized the validity of the claims of certain occupations—professors, doctors, lawyers—to exercise significant control over recruitment, training, certification, and standards of practice due to the possession by these occupations of an esoteric body of knowledge. As noted earlier, the development of traditional collegial mechanisms in higher education were the evolutionary product of the interaction between faculty as professionals and increasingly bureaucratic educational organizations. In this stage of our history, some faculties have reached out for stronger leverage. To what extent are faculties enhancing their power, or simply changing the structure through which they express it, by supplanting traditional collegial mechanisms with collective bargaining? To what extent is the adoption of an alternative form of governance causing a shift of influence within the faculty? Faculty influence under bargaining in relation to that of administrators, students, and faculty subgroups will be discussed.

Faculty versus Administration

1. *Most unionized institutions did not have strong traditions of faculty participation in governance prior to bargaining.* Even though Garbarino (1975a: 70), using 1969 AAUP survey data, found that unionized institutions on average had higher levels of faculty participation, the response bias of the AAUP survey data discussed elsewhere, when coupled with the small differences in the level of governance between union and nonunion institutions indicated by the AAUP data, makes his conclusion subject to question. Furthermore, if the 1969 AAUP survey is an accurate depiction of reality (and one author thinks the results are an overstatement of the level of faculty participation due to the overrepresentation of prestigious institutions [Walker, 1976]), then the general level of faculty participation in this country has been low. Even in the area of personnel decisions, Garbarino (1975a: 37) interpreted the AAUP data as indicating that "faculty dominance in personnel decisions does not apply to large absolute numbers of institutions."

Other evidence supports a conclusion that the prebargaining state of governance in unionized institutions was not extensive. Gershenfeld and Mortimer (1976) found that prebargaining governance at the state colleges and two year colleges in Pennsylvania was only recently established and rarely influential. A similar pattern exists for the same types of institutions in New Jersey. Mortimer and Richardson's (1977) study of six institutions, some in Massachusetts, produced similar findings. Kemerer and Baldridge's (1974: 140) survey of unionized institutions produced the finding that about 65 percent of the senates had been established in the last decade.

2. *Generally, faculty influence has tended to be enhanced at institutional and, for public institutions, at state levels at the cost of senate influence over some issues. But the senates' influence over remaining issues has likely been strengthened as the bargaining agent performs a "watchdog" role. The greatest power losers have been presidents, particularly in public systems, and deans. In the Pennsylvania State Colleges, for example, Johnson and Mortimer (1977: 81–82) concluded that the faculty had been the benefactors of bargaining at the cost of institutional autonomy.* The below discussion will examine this generalization in respect to faculty influence under bargaining in more detail.

3. *The nature of faculty bargaining and traditional governance is evolving and unstable. There is a wide variation in experience in respect to developing bargaining-governance relationships.* Indeed, one author concluded that the diversity of relationships was the most

prevalent characteristic of collective bargaining (White, 1976: 22). Another author has indicated, "there is probably evidence or an incident to illustrate whatever case one wants to make about the relationships between senates and/or faculty governing structures and collective bargaining" (Mortimer, 1977: 9).

The instability of evolving governing patterns under collective bargaining is indicated by the New Jersey findings discussed in more detail below. In only four of the sixteen two year colleges has the mode of faculty participation outside of collective bargaining not changed in important ways. In at least three institutions, traditional governance mechanisms have gone out of existence, in all cases because of perceived jurisdictional conflicts with the collective bargaining process. However, in two of these institutions representative bodies have been reinstated and continue to operate, and in the third institution recent difficult negotiations produced an agreement to reinstitute a governance body (Begin, Settle, & Berke-Weiss, 1977: 121).

The uncertainty over the respective jurisdictions of the two modes of faculty participation that created the above instability is now diminishing. Over time the boundaries between the two mechanisms have been evolving as the parties have gained experience and as decisions on the scope of negotiations delineating mandatory, permissive, and illegal subjects of bargaining have been handed down by administrative agencies and the courts.

4. *Despite the instability noted above, the expectation that traditional governance and bargaining would be inherently competitive at the cost of traditional mechanisms has not been fulfilled. What is most often found, instead, at least to date, is a new governance form that integrates both collective bargaining and traditional governance and that seems to enhance faculty power.*

In earlier work, both Garbarino (1975a) and Begin (1974b) reported that the dominant pattern of union-senate relationships was one of cooperation rather than competition or cooptation. In *cooperative* bargaining agent–senate relationships, a dual system of faculty participation operates in which the cooperative linkages between the separate bargaining and traditional governance mechanisms are informal. Union leadership or participation in both fora sometimes forms the linkage. In the *competitive* model, the mechanisms are still separate but are competing to be the instrument of faculty power. In the *cooptive* model, the union serves the faculty interest on all issues, either through direct negotiations or consultation, or it agrees to delegate its consultation activities (and perhaps some negotiable

issues) to other forms of faculty participation. In the latter instance, the other forms are usually protected by a contract that establishes the procedures for faculty participation on the delegated issues.

This author would suggest a revision in Garbarino's models as defined above that separates the nature of union–senate relationships from the effect of those relationships on governance structure as indicated below:

Nature of Union-Senate Relations → *Structural Effects*

Competitive	Dual/informal governance model
Cooperative	Dual/formal governance model
	Union model

The three effects in this conceptualization form a continuum from situations in which the two governance systems exist separately with only loose connections (dual/informal), to separate but formalized relationships in which broader faculty participation is protected procedurally in a contract (dual/formal), to, finally, situations in which all faculty input to decisionmaking is channeled through union leadership (union model). It would be expected that the more cooperative the relationship between the senate and the union, the more likely a governance structure on the dual/informal end of the continuum would result. Of course, other factors affect the nature of the governance structure in a particular institution, and these will be discussed at a later point.

a. *Using the above definitions, there are few examples of the union model to date (some two year contracts come closest to the mark) primarily because union–traditional governance relationships have been mostly cooperative.* While competition between governance fora on particular issues arises in many unionized institutions, generalized competition occurs infrequently. Additionally, as will be discussed in more detail below, faculty union leaders and administrators alike have preferred broader faculty participation than union leadership on certain issues.

b. *There is no survey that permits an accurate distribution of bargaining relationships between the other two models. But on the bargaining relationships for which data are available, the trend is in the direction of greater contractual delineation of faculty authority (dual/formal model).* The evidence supporting these tentative conclusions is as follows:

i. Only in one state has widespread dismantling of senates been reported; otherwise such occurrences have been isolated. In Penn-

sylvania, Gershenfeld and Mortimer (1976: 48−51, 160) reported that in the fourteen state colleges, two senates had been dissolved and four appeared to fulfill only social or clerical purposes. The remaining eight senates dealt primarily with curriculum and student affairs. It should also be noted that the state college contract (all colleges are in the same bargaining unit) is one of the most comprehensive faculty contracts and that the state college senates were not developed until the latter 1960s. The two year colleges had a worse experience: five of nine prebargaining senates were dissolved, two were found to be inactive, and the remaining two weakened. Elaborate contractual and extra contractual systems of faculty-administration committees had appeared as alternatives at most of the campuses. Less severe effects were reported for Lincoln, Temple, and the Temple Law School.

ii. In another study of governance, Mortimer and Richardson (1977: 178−79) reported that prebargaining governance mechanisms at six Massachusetts and Pennsylvania institutions had been supplanted by contractual governance mechanisms (dual/formal model). In other words, the collegial procedures by which the faculty participated in policy recommendations were incorporated into the contracts. As noted elsewhere, however, had the administrations followed precedent in other jurisdictions, they would not have had to negotiate governance issues.

iii. The results in New Jersey vary to some extent from the above-reported results. In the sixteen two year colleges, for example, nine have developed representative forms of faculty participation outside of bargaining, and four have committee structures (three were the product of negotiations). An additional college is developing a governance mechanism after having dismantled it at an earlier point in the bargaining relationship. These bodies deal primarily with educational policy; the contracts do not delve into these areas. This pattern of governance developed despite the fact that there was no governance tradition at these institutions, since the beginning of the two year colleges coincided very closely with the passage of collective bargaining legislation (Begin, Settle, & Berke-Weiss, 1977: 120).

At the eight state colleges, stable governance relationships under bargaining have not yet evolved, although there are major differences in this respect across the colleges. The adaptation process has been complicated by the competition for faculty loyalty between two bargaining agents. When an NEA affiliate won the initial elections at the campuses, there was not a great dislocation of faculty authority because the association had long been active

in serving faculty interests in the state colleges. In addition, the local NEA leaderships were active in the campus government mechanisms, the first of which had been established in the late 1960s. As an AFT affiliate sought to become the exclusive representative, they sought to take over governance leaderships on some campuses, complicating the operation of those organizations. When the AFT became the bargaining agent, conflicts between local NEA leaders, many of whom still occupied local governance positions, continued. Additional efforts by the NEA affiliate to resume power have created further instability. Despite this competition, no state college has dismantled its nonbargaining governance mechanisms, but there is common agreement that the AFT locals have made substantial contractual inroads into local institutional governance. The union competition and the militancy of the AFT in the face of a state negotiating strategy that the AFT perceived as overly conservative, including a strike in 1974, very likely speeded up the development of the dual/formal model, with elements of the union model, as the union needed to show concrete progress.

At the other public institutions—Rutgers University, New Jersey Institute of Technology (NJIT), and the College of Medicine and Dentistry of New Jersey (CMDNJ)—the dual/informal model is more descriptive of events, although the jurisdiction of the governance bodies has diminished to some extent as bargaining has moved into economic and personnel areas previously considered by these bodies. At Rutgers University there was never a strong central governance mechanism; faculty power was in the colleges, and they had wanted to keep it there. A restructured centralized senate began functioning at the same time that bargaining began, and it has evolved in the context of bargaining. Its existence is partly a function of the centralization of decisionmaking in recent years above the college level. The development of this body represents a response to a shift in faculty authority, not necessarily an increase. In fact, the perceived absence of authority in this new body led the AAUP in one set of negotiations to challenge administrative authority by filing scope of negotiations petitions and unfair labor practices with the New Jersey Public Employment Relations Commission. The AAUP did not perceive its actions so much as being directly competitive with the senate; it felt it was protecting faculty authority vis-à-vis the administration. But if the AAUP had won, the result would have been the same. Most of the disputed issues were found to be only permissibly negotiable (New Jersey Public Employment Relations Com-

mission, 1976), but on some of the issues, the administration subsequently turned to the senate for recommendations. Additionally, the senate has increasingly become the battleground over issues under negotiation as the faculty senators attempt to influence the progress of difficult negotiations, usually by supporting AAUP bargaining issues.

At NJIT, the independent bargaining agent and the faculty council have cooperated to maintain a dual/informal structure: the independent bargaining agent, in fact, had been the product of the faculty council. At CMDNJ, separate mechanisms also continue. The AAUP initially supported the development of faculty personnel procedures and a governance system external to the bargaining agreement. The AAUP did not participate as a unit in the development of the personnel and governance procedures though individual members were active in the study committee. The AAUP did create leverage by negotiating a provision that required the changes to be approved by a certain date or the AAUP would have the option of opening negotiations on the issues; the changes were approved on time!

Two unionized private institutions in New Jersey—Rider College and Fairleigh Dickinson University—have adopted the dual/formal model more fully than other New Jersey institutions by incorporating many faculty personnel procedures and the governance mechanisms into the labor contracts. Difficult governance problems at both institutions produced this result.

iv. Mortimer and Lozier (1973) reported that one-quarter of the contracts they reviewed had some provision for the formation of joint administration-faculty committees to handle various issues.

v. Falcone (1975: 3–4), in an opinion survey of faculty and administrators in six community colleges in upstate New York, found that "64 percent of the respondents felt that collective bargaining had served as an important catalyst in the establishment of a more formalized, written governance structure at their institutions." The respondents also felt that faculty power had increased under bargaining; a third felt faculty and administration shared power equally in a variety of areas prior to bargaining, while 63 percent felt that was so only after bargaining.

5. *To date, the authority of traditional governance mechanisms has diminished primarily in the areas of faculty economic benefits and personnel policies. Negotiations have not dealt in a major way with educational policy. The creeping expansion of negotiations into*

permissive areas of managerial authority (often delegated to faculty for recommendations through traditional governance) may undermine traditional governance over the long haul. Both attitudinal and objective data support this pattern.

a. Kemerer and Baldridge's (1975: 149) survey of the attitudes of institutional and union leadership in unionized institutions indicated that unions dominated economic issues, senates prevailed in respect to academic issues, and they shared influence in gray areas such as faculty working conditions and long-range planning. Andes' (1974) analysis of contract provisions and a New Jersey contract study (Begin, Settle, & Berke-Weiss, 1977) found that the contracts dealt primarily with economic issues and working conditions.

b. The authority and structure of traditional governance mechanisms have not been generally threatened by the decisions of courts or administrative agencies, but on specific issues, the decisions complicate union–senate accommodations by bifurcating faculty authority. By entering into collective bargaining relationships, faculty have introduced environmental influences heretofore not present into the decisionmaking processes of higher education. In almost all instances, faculty bargaining units emerged after either the passage of legislation (public sector) or the expansion of legislative jurisdiction (private sector) permitting collective bargaining. The various public or private bargaining statutes have the potential to alter traditional governance mechanisms through the interpretation of the statutory scope of negotiations obligations either by agencies set up to administer the laws (for example, the National Labor Relations Board) or by the courts.[1]

Traditional governance mechanisms could be affected by the interpretation of bargaining statutes by courts or administrative agencies in two ways: (i) by the alteration of the structure of the governance mechanisms or, (ii) by findings on a case-by-case basis that individual issues previously dealt with through traditional governance procedures were subject to mandatory negotiations.[2] In the first instance, the external bodies might determine that the traditional procedures were subject to alteration through mandatory negotiations or that the traditional procedures should cease to exist because they were employer-dominated and thus represented an unlawful interference with the bargaining process. A study of eighteen major higher education decisions of the courts and administrative agencies in respect to negotiable terms and conditions of employment produces the following conclusions:[3]

i. *The courts and the administrative agencies do not consider traditional governance procedures to be employer-dominated bodies.*

Only one case has been decided that deals directly with this issue. A decision by the Michigan Employment Relations Commission indicated that Michigan State University, by establishing departmental advisory committees, was not interfering with statutory employee bargaining rights. Another case was initiated at Pennsylvania State University by a National Education Association affiliate, but the charge was dropped before the case was decided. Both cases emanated from recognition campaigns, apparently as part of the campaign strategy of the faculty unions filing the charges.

Two rulings by the NLRB that the senates at Northeastern University and the Argonne National Laboratory were not labor organizations apparently would lead to a conclusion that they were also not employer-dominated company unions unless they attempted to interfere with the mandatory bargaining responsibilities of a union.

The risk of alienating faculty supportive of traditional governance procedures most likely accounts, in part, for the few direct challenges by unions of the jurisdictions of senates. As an example, a decertification campaign at Central Michigan University was believed to be partly based on the union's competitive relationship with the senate on some issues.

While there are few cases dealing directly with the treatment of governance procedures as employer unions, it probably can be implied from the cases that deal directly with the negotiability of governance procedures that the boards or commissions do not perceive that the existence of traditional governance mechanisms, per se, represents an attempt by the employer to undermine the collective bargaining process. Comments by the New Jersey Public Employment Relations Commission in a case between the American Association of University Professors and Rutgers University are typical of other cases dealing with this issue. The commission did not argue for the complete elimination of traditional governance by any means:

As viewed by the Commission, . . . there is no reason why the systems of collegiality and collective negotiations may not function harmoniously. Neither system need impose upon the other, with one exception: terms and conditions of employment including grievances. The University is free to continue to delegate to collegial entities whatever managerial functions it chooses, subject, of course, to applicable law. The Act is among the laws applicable to the University as a public employer, and therefore collective negotiations under the Act would only mandate a change in the collegial system if that system were to operate so as to alter

the University's obligation to deal exclusively with the AAUP with regard to the grievances and terms and conditions of employment of unit employees. Beyond that, both systems are free to operate without necessarily interfering with one another. (New Jersey Public Employment Relations Commission, 1976)

ii. *Most governance structures are not subject to mandatory negotiaations.* Public and private administrative agencies alike have agreed that procedures providing for faculty participation in policy development and policy application activities are not mandatorily negotiable except to the extent that the procedures have an impact on terms and conditions of employment. The rationale put forth for this outcome is that the employer has the right to determine how it wants to organize itself for making or applying policy. University administrations have delegated and can continue to delegate managerial functions to faculty through a variety of mechanisms, but it remains the prerogative of the administrations to permit or not permit this type of delegation. Thus, the administrative agencies have found the following issues to be permissive and not mandatory areas for negotiations: governance procedures in general; 1966 AAUP statement on governance of colleges and universities; union, faculty, or student participation in tenure and promotion committees; faculty participation in administration search committees or administrator evaluation; union appearances at governing board meetings or faculty participation on boards.

iii. *An analysis of the available cases in respect to specific, substantive issues indicates that once again the agencies are restricting the mandatory scope of negotiations to clear terms and conditions of employment.* Curriculum issues, budget matters, physical facilities, course offerings, teaching materials, qualifications and responsibilities of administrators, tenure quotas, tenure criteria, academic calendar, studies on faculty evaluation, professional development programs, work location, methods of teaching and testing, and student advising programs have been found to be permissive issues, although the impact of policy changes in these areas on terms and conditions of employment issues were found to be mandatory subjects of negotiations.

At this time, the agencies and courts have dealt with some complex issues only in general terms, and it will take a number of decisions before the line of demarcation between mandatory and permissive issues is more clearly drawn. For example, union, faculty, or student participation in promotion and tenure commit-

tees and the criteria to be used by the committees generally have been found to be permissive areas. But the application of the "impact" test may find many aspects of the procedures to be mandatorily negotiable. As an example, the New Jersey Public Employment Relations Commission in the Rutgers decision found the scope of tenure (e.g., by campus or universitywide) to be a negotiable issue.

The same observation could be made about the issue of the academic calendar. Issues such as the time that classes start in September and the time they stop in the spring or whether a semester or trimester system should be used have been found to be permissive subjects of negotiations. But the impact of the calendar on such things as workload, vacations, holidays, and compensation are likely to be mandatory issues unless restricted by statute.

A major implication of the division of issues into mandatory and permissive categories is that faculty jurisdiction on given issues becomes scattered. If the administration wants to seek faculty input, for example, on a major overhaul of the faculty evaluation system, it would have to balance between the senate on one hand for the permissive areas and the bargaining agent on the other mandatory issues of negotiations. Over time, the administration may find it easier to deal totally with the bargaining agent. The interesting aspect is that the preservation of traditional modes of governance is essentially in the hands of the administration, unless faculty support to protect traditional governance emerges in given situations. The campaign at Central Michigan University to decertify the union indicates that such opposition may arise in some instances.

c. Further erosion in the jurisdiction of traditional governance mechanisms is occurring as administrations agree to include permissive areas within the scope of the contract. At this time, there is little evidence to indicate that faculty unions have negotiated contract provisions dealing with curriculum, teaching methods, or similar types of issues. But both public and private sector agreements give some evidence of a trend to incorporate permissive issues in the governance area into the collective bargaining agreement. The Rider College and Fairleigh Dickinson University agreements in the private sector and, in the public sector, some of the agreements from Massachusetts state colleges incorporate complete senate type structures into the contract.

Many agreements also incorporate faculty evaluation systems and promotion and tenure procedures in the contract, as well as committees to deal with various issues. The evidence to date suggests that

the expansion of negotiations into these areas is more likely to occur where prebargaining governance procedures were ineffective or non-existent, as was the case in the institutions noted above. Thus, the incorporation of governance procedures into the contract in these instances represents an attempt to improve prebargaining procedures, and it provides the unions with some security that the administration cannot unilaterally change the procedures. As a consequence, the union may be less likely to demand negotiations on permissive issues with which the senate would otherwise deal.

In the long run, the creeping expansion of collective bargaining into areas previously dealt with by senates may undermine faculty interest in the senates. In some New Jersey institutions, for example, faculty and union interest in the senates appears to have waned as the bargaining process has become the focal point for issues holding the greatest interest to faculty (Begin, Settle, & Berke-Weiss, 1977: 122). To date, this occurrence has evolved primarily at institutions where the prebargaining governance procedures were not well established.

One way to limit union intrusion into traditional governance would be to place statutory boundaries on the scope of negotiations. A Montana bargaining statute passed in 1974 did just that by prohibiting interference with faculty senates or committees. But statutory limitations otherwise have been slow to develop. Since widespread statutory limitations on the scope of negotiations are not likely to develop due to union opposition, the authority of traditional governance mechanisms will be diminished (i) by case-by-case administrative decisions that will fractionate faculty authority between collective bargaining and other governance mechanisms on certain issues, and (ii) by the gradual expansion of negotiations into permissive areas as dictated by the conditions of particular bargaining relationships.

6. *Limited evidence indicates that the type of union–senate accommodations that develop is a product of a number of factors, including the extent of governance before bargaining; the responsiveness of traditional mechanisms to problems; the attitudes of the administration, faculty, and union concerning the function of the senate; the nature of the bargaining relationship; the existence of union competition; the type of bargaining agent; and the bargaining structure.*

a. The importance of the prebargaining state of governance is illustrated by the finding of Mortimer and Richardson (1977:166) that the fastest institutional accommodation to collective bargaining occurred at the institutions that "had the most positive experience

with faculty involvement in governance prior to organization." In New Jersey and other places, such as Temple University, institutions with a tradition of established prebargaining governance have not as yet suffered major alterations in prebargaining patterns.

b. A study of bargaining in New Jersey two year institutions found that where the noncontractual governance system was perceived to be operating most effectively, the overall scope of the contract tended to be below that of institutions with nonexistent or more ineffective systems of governance (Begin, Settle, & Berke-Weiss, 1977:123).

c. The prevailing attitude of administrators and faculty union leaders in most unionized institutions, after acquiring some experience with negotiations, is to recognize a need for noncollective-bargaining modes of faculty participation. Scattered union leaders and administrators have called for the demise or major alteration of senates in collective bargaining situations. But over the long run, there seems to be a need that is recognized by both sides to maintain faculty input other than through union leadership (see Mortimer & Richardson, 1977; Begin, Settle, & Berke-Weiss, 1977). The New Jersey experience indicates that a number of accommodations between bargaining and governance have evolved out of active administration and bargaining agent efforts to preserve an alternate forum to union consultation machinery for faculty participation on issues not dealt with in negotiations. In one two year college, for example, the administration and the faculty union engaged in a lengthy retreat to develop a new governance mechanism to replace one previously voted out of existence by the faculty.

The Kemerer and Baldridge attitudinal data would seem to indicate that presidents would not be inclined to work out compromises since they feel bargaining will ultimately undermine senates (Kemerer & Baldridge, 1975: 150), but the objective evidence indicates that when confronted with the reality of negotiations, administrations have striven to preserve aspects of traditional governance for some issues.

Mortimer and Richardson (1977) reported that in one university the parties reconstituted a senate when after five or six years of bargaining, the parties agreed that there were matters best handled by a senate and informally negotiated a new organization. Begin (1974b: 590) reported a number of institutions where the administrations had taken positive initiatives to balance governance and bargaining.

d. An adversary bargaining relationship that is generalized to overall faculty-administration relationships complicates, in the short run, accommodations between bargaining and traditional governance. A

problem-solving approach was found in New Jersey to have enabled faculty and administrators in two year colleges to work cooperatively rather than competitively to reach accommodations in respect to governance issues (Begin, Settle, & Berke-Weiss, 1977: 122–23). Another study of six institutions across two states also concluded that accommodation to bargaining was more efficient where the bargaining relationship was more open (Mortimer & Richardson, 1977: 163). The authors of that study also concluded that the nature of the relationship was highly related to the style of the administrative leadership. Where the style was most authoritarian, the union leadership was the most militant and least amenable to cooperative activities (p. 173).

At Rutgers University, for the first time difficult negotiations have spilled over into senate discussions, as the AAUP has sought to exert maximum pressure. One consequence of senate discussions of bargaining issues is that it awakened student interest in negotiations.

e. Dual union participation in both bargaining and governance fora generally has contributed to the stability of traditional senates where the bargaining relationship is otherwise good (Begin, Settle, & Berke-Weiss, 1977: 123). Apparently, dual union participation provides the union some assurance that the bargaining relationship will not be undermined. And as long as the unions do not assume militant stances in the governance mechanisms, the administrations are willing to continue consulting the membership of the governance mechanisms. As reported by Julius (1977), Mannix indicated that in the early phases of faculty collective bargaining, employers were concerned that the senates would attempt to "unbargain" or rebargain issues agreed to or discussed in negotiations. But as the separate jurisdictions have been clarified, the fear over the "two bites of the apple" alternative has diminished.

f. Union competition can inhibit the interaction of bargaining and traditional governance. As Mortimer and Richardson (1977:174) pointed out, "there does seem to be a higher degree of accommodation in those institutions where the union is well-established and a majority of the faculty belong." As indicated by the experience in the New Jersey State Colleges, a union would be less likely to delegate negotiating or consulting authority to a senate if a rival organization has influence in those bodies.

g. No study shows a systematic relationship between the type of bargaining agent and the type of governance model that evolves; but each bargaining agent has produced examples of every type of bargaining-governance model. It appears that the model that evolves at a particular institution is less related to the type of agent than it is

a product of local environmental, organizational, and individual characteristics. Because of similarities in contract output, in fact, Andes (1974) no longer controls for the type of agent in their reports on contract content.

h. The occupational and organizational composition of a bargaining unit can influence governance patterns. Systemwide units, for example, tend to centralize authority beyond individual institutions if the "before" locus of authority is at the institutional level. However, in New Jersey and probably in other states as well, local informal and formal agreements between local administrations and union leaders to solve local problems tend to offset centralizing tendencies on some issues (Begin, 1976: 30—31).

But where administrative authority is clearly beyond the campus level and the senate is clearly a local organization, the stability of the dual model is more questionable, as noted by the Kemerer and Baldridge analysis of the CUNY situation (1975: 161—64). In New Jersey, the absence of a statewide senate in the state colleges almost guaranteed that the faculty union would take on all statewide faculty representation functions. Indeed, when the senates of the individual institutions attempted to form a statewide coalition, the union effectively discouraged the efforts.

The accommodation is complicated also where the occupational composition of the bargaining unit and senate differ. Students in the senate, for example, may make the union hesitant to work cooperatively with that body because of the uncertainty of outcomes. Nonteaching professionals in the bargaining unit may also complicate the bargaining-governance accommodation process, particularly if they tend to dominate the union leadership as they have in the past at SUNY.

7. *By providing for the systematic review of faculty complaints, faculty grievance procedures clearly make faculty peer recommendations subject to greater review, but it is not clear that this, per se, diminishes faculty authority.*

a. The literature review indicates that large numbers of cases are resolved at higher administrative levels or at arbitration. At CUNY, 600 cases reached the highest internal level (the chancellor) and 105 went on to arbitration (Mintz & Golden, 1974: 35). At SUNY, about half of the cases were estimated to have reached the chancellor's level (Satryb, 1974: 74—76). About three-quarters of the cases at Rutgers University reached the highest level, the president. However, as previously noted, it has been very difficult for a grievant at Rutgers to overturn a negative peer review and thus undermine faculty peer authority (Begin, 1978a). The bulk of the other studies have

focused on the question of whether academic judgments have been undermined by the grievance process, particularly by the external review of arbitrators. Most researchers agree with the conclusions of one author that "the effect of grievance arbitration awards on college and university governance to date has been neither uniform nor substantial" (Levy, 1975: 2; also see Finkin, 1976). Other authors, in fact, concluded that the more equitable decisions deriving from the rationalized personnel process have probably reinforced faculty authority (Weisberger, 1977: 16–17; Begin, 1978a).

b. As noted above, negotiated grievance mechanisms have developed as an internal alternative to courts, state and federal affirmative action appeals procedures, the AAUP, and other national organizations. At Rutgers University, all administrators interviewed felt that the negotiated grievance procedures had played a useful role in speeding up the needed policy changes and in providing a quicker internal procedure for responding to affirmative action complaints (Begin, 1978a). A female chief negotiator for the AAUP, who later became president, also preferred the internal processing of affirmative action complaints (Smith, 1973: 405). Of course, if nonunionized institutions developed systematic grievance procedures, similar results might be obtained. It has been reported that Northeastern University and the California State Colleges have adopted advisory or binding arbitration in the absence of unionization (Weisberger, 1977: 1).

The development of internal procedures ending in arbitration has reduced reliance on the national offices of the AAUP for external review of complaints at unionized institutions. Local AAUP chapters at many union institutions where they are the bargaining agent no longer call on the national AAUP for help to any great degree, and the administrations of many campuses unionized by AFT or NEA affiliates have refused to deal with AAUP, primarily because it would complicate relations with the established agent. Accordingly, faculty at unionized institutions have lost the resources previously provided by the national AAUP for protecting academic freedom. In return they have gained more extensive local protections. In essence, the policing of faculty rights has been decentralized under bargaining to the institutional level.

8. *Faculty influence at the state level has been increased, particularly under conditions of statewide or systemwide bargaining.*

a. In New Jersey, for example, the centralizing effects of the Department of Higher Education, in addition to having created pressure for unionization, have forced the unions into court on a number of occasions in an attempt to protect faculty authority. The AAUP at Rutgers University challenged the Department of Higher Education

in court for alledgedly violating the autonomy of Rutgers in adopting a student-faculty funding ratio and a new sixteen week budget calendar (Begin, 1976: 28–29). While the AAUP lost the case, the incident illustrates the "watchdog" role that the union plays in representing faculty authority at the state level, even if the issues are not subject to mandatory bargaining.

b. Johnson and Mortimer (1977: 82) pointed out that state level officials in Pennsylvania clearly tried to use bargaining as a means of centralizing authority in the state colleges, but would have attempted to reach the same end even if bargaining had not occurred.

c. In an analysis of the governance system of Hunter College, a part of CUNY, it was concluded that systemwide contracts reinforce the already decreasing authority of local campuses (Kemerer & Baldridge, 1975: 163).

d. Collective bargaining in higher education is clearly a part of a larger trend toward centralized decisionmaking and rationalization of policies and procedures, particularly in public institutions. Faculty bargaining has tended to take faculty influence to the increasingly centralized sources of authority in higher education, in the process reinforcing the centralizing process. The relationship of bargaining centralizing effects to state bureaucracy was identified by the findings of a study of eight states:

1. The more highly placed within the state bureaucracy the office of employee relations, the more power within the office, and the more pressure for centralization and state control. Those states with no central state apparatus for state employee bargaining have the most decentralized relationship with higher education administration: Michigan, Ohio, Delaware. In situations where the state is defined to be the employer, institutional governing boards and administrators tend to lose a degree of their previous authority. In cases where systemwide boards or administrators are the employer, campus officials are relegated to advisory and/or consultative administrative roles on those issues within the scope of the contract (e.g., New York and the Pennsylvania and New Jersey state colleges). Whatever control campus officials retain over these items is based on influence rather than authority relationships.

. . . .

4. The degree of centralization under collective bargaining is strongly influenced by the prebargaining structure and degree of centralization. Bargaining appears to have little impact on the structure of higher education. Those states with strong state government involvement or systemwide governing boards tend to centralize bargaining responsibility in those boards. Those states with strong traditions of decentralized authority and/or high degrees of autonomy tend to reflect these traditions in their bargaining relations. (Weinberg, 1976: 106)

Faculty versus Students

While students have participated in negotiations in a variety of ways at some institutions (in some states, a student role is mandated by statute), there is little evidence that this participation has reduced faculty influence. The continuing opposition of many union leaders and administrators to student participation would seem, in part, to be a reflection of concerns with authority.

Mortimer and Richardson (1977: 177) indicate that students placed little priority on using new procedures providing for their participation. Students influenced decisions in areas of greatest concern to them—for example, the allocation of student funds—and were satisfied to operate in these areas. In New Jersey, students were able to influence events to some degree in extreme situations such as strikes, but otherwise their influence on collective bargaining activities has been minimal.

Faculty versus Faculty

1. *There is little evidence available to support or reject the common expectation that a stronger voice may be acquired by faculty traditionally excluded from traditional participation in decisionmaking, particulary young nontenured faculty, women and minority faculty, lower quality faculty, and nonfaculty groups where the latter are included in the bargaining units.*

a. The faculty bargaining movement is predominantly the product of senior faculty—in almost every reported instance it has been senior faculty in positions of union leadership that brought bargaining to an institution.

b. There is no objective evidence indicating that lower quality faculty were in union leadership positions or have "taken over" the union leadership or that lower quality faculty have benefited disproportionately from bargaining outcomes. The little evidence available on the latter point is to the contrary; under a previous discussion of grievance procedures, it was related that promotions at unionized institutions do not occur any faster and that faculty rejected by peers for promotion and tenure have not found the grievance procedure to be a useful forum for upsetting negative peer recommendations. There are plenty of opinions offered by administrators that the quality of union leadership has declined; the administrations of many New Jersey institutions, for example, believed this. But in the absence of objective evidence in the form of changes in the individual qualifications of union leaders over time and a comparison of these qualifications with those of faculty who are leaders in other governance fora, it is difficult to generalize on this issue.

c. As a subgroup, it appears that females have gained benefits from collective bargaining in instances in which they have chosen to become active in bargaining activities. Inequity payments, maternity leaves, sabbatical leaves, affirmative action statements, and quicker internal resolution of grievances represent some of the gains (Reuben and Hoffman, 1975).

d. As discussed in the section on Compensation and Resource Allocation, there is some evidence that nonfaculty groups, junior faculty, and two year college faculty have achieved the greatest gains through bargaining. Based on the evidence available, it is difficult to assess the equity of these results.

2. *One rule change that might conflict with existing faculty rights is the negotiation of union security provisions by the bargaining agent.* The question as to whether clauses requiring union membership or payment of dues will constitute a requirement for the retention of tenure is unanswered at this point, although some courts have supported such a relationship in the instance of public school teachers.

Despite expectations that faculty would not support union security because of its likely effect on academic freedom protections, a 1974 contract study by the Baruch National Center indicated that 10 percent (12 of 105 two year contracts and 6 of 37 four-year contracts) contained some form of union security, usually an agency shop (The National Center for the Study of Collective Bargaining in Higher Education, 1975: 1, 2). However, little experience with these provisions has been reported. At Ferris State College in Michigan, four faculty members apparently were threatened with dismissal for failure to pay an agency fee. Three eventually paid and one resigned (Kemerer & Baldridge, 1975).

But faculty at some institutions have not been happy with the development of union security requirements. Faculty at Minnesota's two year colleges challenged the statutory fair share requirement. At Central Michigan University, opposition to an agency shop provision was one of the reasons the faculty unsuccessfully attempted to decertify the faculty union. The union had permitted only union members to ratify the contract containing the provision.

The contracts at Central Michigan, Rider College (New Jersey), and the New York Institute of Technology do not require the dismissal of faculty refusing to pay the fee. At Central Michigan, the union has to file a civil suit against those refusing to pay. At the other institutions, faculty may apply for a conscientious objector status and be exempted from paying a fee.

Collective Bargaining and
Institutional Relationships

Another common expectation concerning the consequences of faculty bargaining is that the nature of the faculty-administration relationships will become adversarial and polarized as a result of the organizational stresses and strains that accompany the rationalization of policies and authority redistribution under collective bargaining. The private sector experience does not necessarily bear this prediction out; there are thousands of bargaining relationships in which generalized employee-employer relations are not continually adversary. But then again, most private sector bargaining units do not cover professional employees. A review of the literature produces the following conclusions:

1. *Much of the data available for analysis on relationships consists of interviews with parties directly involved in negotiations whose feelings are likely biased in an adversary direction due to their direct participation in the process.* Conclusions in respect to generalized faculty-administration relations are difficult to draw from this type of data.

2. *The weight of the available evidence is that the collective bargaining process is a reactive process that reflects and reinforces basic institutional relationships. In some instances, bargaining has led to improved faculty-administration relationships by providing a channel through which faculty have vented and resolved tension. Most faculty bargaining relationships are at an early stage of development, but in many instances, as the parties have adopted to the new process, adversary relationships have tended to be focused on formal negotiations, not personal relationships of the negotiators or generalized faculty-administration relationships. Administrative style and/or organizational change have been key factors in setting the tone of bargaining relationships.*

a. Falcone's (1975: 4) opinion survey of 407 faculty, nonteaching faculty, and administrators at six New York two year colleges indicated that about two-thirds of the respondents felt that faculty-administration relationships had become more adversary. Other studies, however, were not willing to attribute such a strong independent contribution of bargaining to generalized faculty-administration relationships.

b. A study by Hedgepeth (1974: 698) of early experience under bargaining at the State University College at Cortland, New York, found that the majority of the twenty-nine faculty and administrators interviewed "felt that, though there might have been a basis for

adversary relations in pre-existing conditions, collective bargaining has extended and intensified those conditions.''

c. In a study of unionized institutions in Pennsylvania (fourteen state colleges, ten two year colleges, three state-related institutions, and three private colleges), Gershenfeld and Mortimer (1976) found a variety of faculty-administration relationships and concluded that adversary relationships were as much a product of prebargaining relationships as they were of the collective bargaining process. They felt that the militancy exhibited by union leaders during the early stages of negotiations diminished and that adversarial relationships were then primarily restricted to formal collective bargaining activities, not personal relationships.

d. Research on twenty-six unionized institutions in New Jersey also produced a mixed range of findings in terms of relationships. Generally, the relations between negotiators were somewhat adversary, though not always unfriendly or uncooperative, even at institutions like Rutgers University (AAUP) and NJIT (independent), where prebargaining faculty-administration relations were good. At some places, like Rider College (AAUP) and CMDNJ (AAUP), where prebargaining relations were very strained, relations have been improved, as bargaining has seemed to siphon off tension as faculty needs for participation have been fulfilled. At the state colleges (AFT), continuing union competition, difficult negotiations, individual leadership styles, and enrollment problems (all highly related factors) have created a continuing adversary situation. At Rutgers University, the relationships between the faculty and administration negotiators have become increasingly strained over the years. While the nature of the bargaining process has been somewhat contributory to deteriorating faculty-administration relations, the major effect of bargaining has been to reinforce growing faculty-administration strains deriving from administrative actions unrelated to bargaining. The tension derived primarily from efforts in recent years of the administration, spurred on by state authorities, to improve the efficiency of operations and services by centralizing authority in areas previously dealt with by the individual colleges. Whether one agrees or disagrees with the need to accomplish these objectives or the style with which they were accomplished, the consequence has been to threaten and diminish long-standing faculty authority within the colleges. Obviously, bargaining did not create the faculty tension deriving from these administrative actions, but it certainly served to reinforce faculty dissatisfaction. *One message from this experience is that under collective bargaining, organizational change is a much more complex task.*

e. In a study of six two and four year institutions in six states, Mortimer and Richardson (1977), came to the following conclusions:

i. At one study institution, a two year college, they found that "relationships among the internal constituencies of the institution were extremely poor. It is doubtful, however, that these relationships can be ascribed to the process of collective bargaining. Rather it would seem that the attitudes of the administration in approaching negotiations and in subsequently negotiating a strong contract have intensified the dissatisfaction that previously existed" (p. 90). The two institutions in their study achieving the least degree of accommodation to bargaining were those in which authoritarian administrative styles were carried over into negotiations, thus reinforcing prebargaining adversary relationships (p. 173).

ii. At another institution, Mortimer and Richardson (1977: 152), found that administrators with effective faculty relations prior to bargaining did not feel that bargaining had changed these relations. However, faculty union leaders felt otherwise.

iii. While the presidents at four of the six institutions under study were changing jobs in part because of collective bargaining tensions, the authors concluded that the inability of the presidents to adopt authoritarian styles to bargaining was partly the problem (p. 175).

iv. Adversary faculty-administration relationships developing during recognition campaigns or difficult contract negotiations carry over into other aspects of faculty-administrative relationships (p. 180).

v. "Other factors contributing to the adversarial tone are a consequence of faculty and administrative inexperience in making a collective bargaining agreement work" (p. 69).

vi. At one state college, Mortimer and Richardson concluded that "While collective bargaining cannot be given all or even most of the credit for the harmonious relationships which now exist within the college community, it has played an important role in the process" (p. 133).

(f) At Southwestern Massachusetts University (SMU), the initial relationship was extremely adversarial until a new president with a consultative rather than an authoritarian approach turned the situation around. The institution now characterizes itself as a model of contractual collegiality (Walker, Feldman, & Stone, 1976). Relation-

ships have also improved under bargaining at Rider College where difficult faculty-administration relationships led to unionization and subsequently to the first union strike in a private institution (Begin, Settle, & Alexander, 1975). In the opinion of the parties, the relationships there, while not perfect, have evolved to a much better level than prior to collective bargaining. "Before the onset of the faculty bargaining movement the discrepancies in faculty-administration perspectives at Rider College and the resulting tensions might have been resolved differently, i.e., the president, confronted with a serious lack of confidence by the faculty, might have been eventually forced to resign. But in the collective bargaining era, other alternatives for action by the faculty have apparently been substituted" (Begin, Settle, & Alexander, 1975: 125).

g. Collective bargaining offers faculty dissenting from administrative viewpoints a mechanism for venting overt dissatisfaction (Mortimer and Richardson, 1977). At Rutgers University, as well, a contract dispute over merit pay has provided an opportunity for the faculty to vent frustration with a wide range of administrative activities. Many faculty in the picket lines during the New Jersey State College strike in 1974 reported antiadministration feelings unrelated to the specific contract issues in dispute. The same was true at the Rider College strike in 1974 (Begin, Settle, & Alexander, 1975).

h. One aspect of collective bargaining that would seem to have some potential for straining faculty relationships is the grievance process, particularly where there are many grievances against departmental peers. However, most of the literature on faculty grievance resolution does not focus on the impact of the grievance process on institutional relationships. A study of Rutgers University concluded that while overall faculty-administration relationships did not appear to be severely altered due to the relatively small number of cases (seventy over five years), the confrontation among peers created by grievances was often bitter, since two-thirds of the grievances involved some level of negative peer review. The result has been a growing polarization among those directly involved in the process—the grievants, the AAUP counselors and negotiators, faculty in the affected departments, and the various levels of administration. Difficulties in recruiting and retaining grievance counselors for the AAUP was partially a product of the adversary nature of the process. The time required to process cases was another factor (Begin, 1978a).

The use of the grievance process for political purposes rather than due process tends to worsen relationships, although the development of such activity is usually the product of existing adversary relations. Political grievance activity was reported at CUNY, partly as a result

of competition between two unions (Newton, 1973: 64). For the same reason, the administration at the New Jersey State Colleges reported the existence of political grievances (Begin & Storholm, 1978). It was also reported that some grievances at SUNY were politically motivated (Satryb, 1974: 74). No such activity was found at Rutgers University, where there was neither union competition nor an adversary bargaining relationship (Begin, 1978a).

3. *The occupational and institutional scope of bargaining units contributes to adversary relationships.* Multi-institutional and multi-occupational bargaining units seem to have a greater potential for creating resentments when certain subsets of the bargaining units receive more favorable treatment. At CUNY, the creation of salary parity between two and four year institutions without a corresponding parity in respect to degree requirements was reported to have caused dissatisfaction in the senior institutions. As one CUNY faculty member indicated:

> My degree is a hard-won Ph.D. in Economics, ten years at Princeton including bachelor's, master's, and doctorate degrees. My publication record is good, and I teach a full load. And under the union contract a community college teacher with a "cheap" master's, one year beyond his bachelor's, from any two-bit teacher's college, will get approximately the same pay and benefits. In my opinion the outcome of the union contract is disgustingly unprofessional, even antiprofessional. (Kemerer & Baldridge, 1975: 74)

Of course, the two year college faculty would be likely to argue that the nature of the workloads dictates parity, the establishment of which resolves tensions long felt by two year college faculty.

At SUNY, the faculty at the four university centers (Buffalo, Binghamton, Albany, Stonybrook) have been reported to be unhappy with the leveling effects of their contract, in which the nonteaching professionals were perceived to have been better treated. The best indication of their dissatisfaction was their unsuccessful attempt to form a separate bargaining unit.

In the New Jersey State Colleges, the inability of the first bargaining agent (an NEA affiliate) to serve the needs of the librarians and administrators in the unit had the effect of turning over the bargaining agent in a very close election (Begin, Settle, & Alexander, 1975: 94−96). At Rutgers University, the addition of graduate research and teaching assistants to the faculty bargaining unit had a negative effect on faculty-administration relationships due to the difficult issues created by graduate student negotiations that were unresolvable at the institutional level. The state was reluctant to recognize the students

as employees for the purpose of medical insurance, and the lengthy debate substantially elongated negotiations, creating tension between the faculty and the administration.

So part of the tension that derives from bargaining is the result of bargaining unit construction, which combines heterogeneous occupations and institutions and makes it difficult for unions to achieve internal consensus across the subgroups.

4. *Except for strike data, little systematic information exists on the relative contribution of the different types of bargaining agents to adversary relationships.* Ten out of fifteen strikes to date at four year institutions have been at AAUP institutions, and none at NEA institutions. While the pattern partially reflects that the private institutions where the AAUP is the strongest have the right to strike under federal labor legislation, four of the five public strikes still occurred in AAUP bargaining units. It appears, therefore, that local conditions and not the type of bargaining agent were the major determinants of the strikes. In fact, a study of the strikes at Rider College (New Jersey) and the New Jersey State Colleges concluded that "the faculty still perceive the strike as the extreme and last effort to sensitize the administration to the faculty's position concerning participation in the decisionmaking process and the content of those decisions. At this point in time, faculty frustration not only has to have specific referents, i.e., concrete issues and/or persons, but the level of frustration has to be greatly heightened for strike activity to occur" (Begin, Settle, & Alexander, 1975:128). The strike at the Stevens Institute of Technology (New Jersey) in 1977 also fit this model.

SUMMARY

The review of the empirical research literature on the relationship between faculty bargaining and faculty reward systems provided a number of insights concerning the limits of that research and the findings on institutional change that it reports. Despite the massive amount of literature on the origins and consequences of faculty bargaining, a clear impression achieved from reviewing it is that many important conclusions are being drawn not from the output of systematic research but from partial and otherwise flawed evidence. Some of the more important caveats against which the current findings must be weighed are as follows:

1. The collective bargaining movement is still in its early stages and is characterized by a significant degree of instability and variety.

Accordingly, the results of cross-sectional research often tend to be sensitive to this instability. In depth, longitudinal research that not only balanced pre- and postbargaining states of institutional operation, but also monitored bargaining relationships continually, would contribute to a better understanding of faculty bargaining. Most unionized institutions, for example, did not have strong traditions of faculty participation prior to bargaining, so the effects of bargaining must be considered in that context and not some ideal prebargaining state of affairs.

2.   There is a heavy reliance on interviews or questionnaire surveys of the perceptions or opinions of the direct participants in the bargaining process and too little use of objective information.

3.   The most systematic research has dealt with the effects of unions on salaries, but other consequences of unions have not been balanced against economic outcomes in these studies.

4.   Studies often fail to control or at least recognize the possible effects of other forces for change in higher education, particularly affirmative action and market forces.

The failure to control for other environmental and organizational variables creating change in higher education is an important omission for at least two reasons. In the first place, the emergence of faculty collective bargaining is in an important way an adaptation of faculty as professionals to increasingly bureaucratized and centralized reward systems created by these other factors. Additionally, some of the initial research concluded that unions do not have major independent effects on higher education. Rather, the effect of unionism is to reinforce and accelerate the changes in the rationalization of policies and resources, authority distribution, and institutional relationships created by other forces for change. Accordingly, researchers need to be more sensitive to how faculty unionism fits into the total context of change in higher education.

Some of the other important problems and effects of faculty unionism illustrated by the literature review are as follows:

1.   At this time, the consequence of faculty bargaining strongly reflects prebargaining institutional conditions, an outcome that underlines the reactive nature of unions. In this vein, for example, while there are some troublesome signals on the effect of faculty unions on general faculty-administration relationships, the weight of the evidence thus far is that the basic nature of the bargaining process reflects underlying institutional relationships and in some extremely adversary situations has improved basic

faculty-administration relationships by channeling and resolving conflict.

2. Faculty influence has seemed to be enhanced at institutional and, for public institutions, at state levels. Under centralized bargaining in state systems, the influence of the faculty through local senates and local administrators has been diminished on some issues as the centralized bargaining structures have reinforced the movement of authority to the state level.

3. The operation of the grievance procedure seems to have the greatest potential for change within the department or school, the base of faculty authority. Grievances against peers contribute to colleague conflict. Additionally, the rationalization of policies and the improved external review of personnel decisions that the grievance procedure provides improves the ability of administrators to manage, but it is not clear that faculty authority is substantially reduced. Indeed, some authors concluded that the improved due process buttressed faculty authority.

4. Generally, faculty bargaining has not meant the end of traditional governance structures, although there is a trend toward more formalized interactions between collective bargaining processes and traditional governance processes. Since courts and administrative agencies find that senates are neither employer-dominated company unions nor mandatory subjects of negotiations, the nature of bargaining versus traditional governance interactions is in the hands of the parties.

5. Issues dealing with individual security (tenure provisions) and union security (agency shop provisions) have presented unions with some of the most difficult negotiating problems.

6. The relative economic effects of faculty unions fall within a range of 0–10 percent and tend to be largest in the earliest years of bargaining. While the effects of faculty unions on rank and occupational salary differentials are mixed, there is evidence of a major reduction in institutional differentials under bargaining. Faculty contracts contain merit provisions, but there is no systematic evidence on the impact of unions on the merit issue.

7. The effect of faculty unions on the quality of education has not been examined systematically. The absence of general agreement in the literature on how to conceptualize and measure effective education will no doubt complicate the establishment of a cause and effect relationship between bargaining and the educational and research output of institutions of higher education.

8. Finally, to conclude that faculty unionism primarily reinforces and accelerates inevitable changes created by other factors is not also to conclude that the accommodation between bargaining and higher education traditions cannot be accomplished better under some conditions than others. While there is little systematic association of the type of bargaining agent with bargaining outcomes affecting reward systems, administrative leadership style, union competition, bargaining unit structure, the type of institution, the state of prebargaining faculty participation, participant values about governance, and the nature of the bargaining relationship have been found to have an effect on how higher education problems get resolved through collective bargaining.

NOTES TO CHAPTER 12

1. This discussion is drawn from Begin (1978b).

2. In the private sector and in many public jurisdictions, issues have been divided into mandatory subjects of negotiations; permissive subjects of negotiations, which may not be negotiated to impasse; and illegal subjects. The purpose of these divisions is to separate managerial prerogatives, which an employer may negotiate, from those issues dealing with the terms and conditions of employment of employees, which must be negotiated.

3. The cases represented all the administrative or court decisions from four year institutions dealing with the scope of negotiations question. Most of the two year college scope decisions were also included, particularly if the cases dealt with governance issues or other issues not covered in other cases. All of the deliberations of the National Labor Relations Board for private institutions were also included in the analysis.

※   *Part V*

Some Implications for Policy

In this final chapter we seek to review a number of the external pressures on higher education that are currently affecting its academic productivity and adaptability to change. In this context, we suggest a number of policy alternatives and strategies that might employ the creative use of academic rewards. Explicit attention is paid to the fact that the monetary resources available to higher education for use in assigning rewards will probably be declining in the future.

Chapter 13

Adaptability to Change and Academic Productivity

William E. Becker, Jr., and
Darrell R. Lewis

Generally, in the realm of American higher education, interventions by legislators and boards of regents are feared by administrators and faculty alike. In the case of administrators this fear may be based on the belief that such intervention restricts their ability to institute change as it is needed. Faculty, on the other hand, typically view this intervention as an infringement fringement on their "academic freedom." Such intervention is also disdained simply because many faculty view themselves as self-ruling professionals who are unaccountable to anyone other than their peers. Yet, administrators and faculty alike are today facing a changing environment that increasingly involves external intervention, restrictions in financial resources, and other external shocks outside their control.

A host of external pressures are increasingly confronting higher education. Pressures for change are coming from (1) changing social demand for educational services in the forms of both enrollment sizes and compositions; (2) falling real resources available in the forms of declining tuition revenues, declining governmental support, and the debilitating effects of inflation; (3) increasing governmental regulations in the forms of new financial accounting, safety, and anti-bias rules and procedures; (4) expanding attitudes of staff egalitarianism in the forms of unionization; and (5) growing bureaucracy in the forms of administrative centralization, consolidation and formalized rules. Such pressures obviously have implications for an institution's academic productivity and adaptability to change. Depending on the institutional arrangements that have been imposed by outside author-

ities or developed in collaboration with faculty governance, there is little question that the administrator's ability to bring about change depends in part upon his or her ability to use positive and negative rewards effectively.

The collection of chapters in this volume represents an attempt to provide some quantitative data and qualitative judgments about the nature, extent, and likely effects of academic rewards in the context of these pressures on higher education today. In this final chapter we intend to review each of these pressures and to suggest a number of policy alternatives and strategies that might employ the creative use of academic rewards.

CHANGING DEMAND

The most dramatic change that administrators and faculty in higher education have to cope with now and in the foreseeable future is falling enrollments. Faculty, administrators, boards, and legislators are not accustomed to working in and managing an institution that is part of a declining industry. Yet this is an external pressure that must be attended to.

During the 1950s and 1960s, the percentage of high school graduates continuing their formal education increased dramatically. By 1970, 60 percent of all high school graduates went on to postsecondary institutions. This is roughly the same percentage that attended college at the turn of the century, but well above the percentage attending college in the 1920s and 1930s. However, the percentage of "birth cohorts" attending college has risen continuously since the turn of the century. Those who continued their education in the late 1960s represented about 50 percent of the population born around 1950. This percentage is well above any previous cohort percentage of college enrollments. For example, at the turn of the century, only about 7 percent of the people born around 1880 attended college. It is highly unlikely, however, that this growth in the percentage of given cohorts attending college will continue.

Given the facts that the post-World War II "baby boom" will have passed through colleges by 1981 and that the percentage of high school graduates attending colleges has fallen since 1970, there is little question that higher education is and will continue to be a declining industry. Changes in the composition of demand for higher education have likewise caused increasing problems for faculty and administrators. For example, increasing student and societal interest in such areas as adult and community education, vocational and technical education, and professional education, along with reciprocal

declines in demand for teacher and general education, have all caused problems of resource and faculty imbalances in higher education.

While forecasts of future enrollment trends have been publicized widely, the methods for bringing about change or coping with these types of changes in higher education have not been systematically considered, especially as they relate to faculty behavior. This may be the result of the fact that current faculty, administrators, and boards have always operated in a growth industry. They may be unable or unwilling to face the reality of the situation.

All academic institutions are dependent on students for operating revenue. Both public and private school budgets are directly tied to tuition receipts. Public school budgets are certainly dependent on legislative appropriations, and these are set, at least implicitly, by student enrollments. Consequently, a reduction in enrollments implies a reduction in budgets. Depending on the size of the budget cuts, designed or random institutional change will follow in direct proportion. The question is whether this change can be a "managed change" or whether by necessity it must be a haphazard change.

FINANCIAL PRESSURES

It is generally agreed that there has been a reduction in the real value of resources devoted to most higher educational institutions during the last few years. While the specific figures vary according to the activity, institution, years, or price deflator chosen, the general pattern has been clear. Although total money expenditures for higher education have increased substantially, the real value of expenditures per student or "per unit" of most other outputs has actually declined. For example, from data recently made available by the National Center for Education Statistics (1978: 114, 212, 224), it can be estimated that average expenditures per student in 1976 constant dollars for higher education fell from $2,333 in 1972 to $2,188 in 1976. Dollar expenditures often have not risen as rapidly as would have been necessary simply to combat rising costs and national inflation. As Bowen (Chapter 9) points out, although faculty compensation has been recently increasing at the rate of around 6.4 percent a year, the compensation of other groups in the economy has continued to grow at the rate of 7–8 percent a year.

A large part of the problem, of course, is the labor-intensive nature of higher education and the greater difficulty in achieving real gains in productivity in this industry as compared to most other less labor-intensive industries. It has been noted by a number of economists that in order to even maintain the real value of resources devoted to

higher education over the long run either (1) the rate of increase in educational expenditures must exceed the overall rate of increase in costs for the economy as a whole, or (2) new means for achieving real gains in labor productivity must be found and employed. We certainly concur in this assessment and would strongly point to the reward systems found in higher education today as one of the more potent means remaining for increasing productivity.

Inflation-induced financial pressures are compounded with the concurrent falling enrollments, tuition receipts, and government appropriations. As argued by Freeman (Chapter 4), the nonprofit nature of higher education institutions also compounds the problem, since there is no buffer or residual account that can be depleted as labor costs rise.

Such financial distress as we have described causes a number of direct and indirect results. If the financial pressures become strong enough, the results could lead to complete inflexibility and reduced productivity. In most cases, financial distress inevitably breeds some faculty tension and suspicion and often a considerable amount of vested interest and "turf" protection. The risk is that such stress may seriously undermine higher education's "sense of community" (i.e., a shared commitment to common goals and to working together in collegial governance) and "sense of excellence" (i.e., a shared commitment to excellence in scholarship and to working together in a meritocracy). In such circumstances, rational decisionmaking in the context of academic reward systems is significantly diminished. This, of course, leads in turn to a further decline in productivity and to additional financial pressure.

INCREASING GOVERNMENTAL REGULATIONS

Another development that may cripple an academic instituion's flexibility is the recent increase of external regulations. Most non-academic institutions have been living with the various forms of federalism for some time now. However, recent governmental regulations have affected the higher education scene as well. Legislation to protect the environment against pollution, new health and safety laws, minimum wage legislation, the application of affirmative action regulations, and many new accounting regulations have all tended to affect higher education in at least two significant ways: the nature of the traditional academic reward system has tended to be undermined, and operating costs have increased without producing anything like an offsetting rise in output.

It is generally agreed that the academic productivity of a university and the excellence of its faculty are heavily dependent upon the working arrangements that faculty find congenial and on a reward system according to individual merit as judged by colleagues in their respective disciplines or professions. Moreover, the conditions that faculty in major universities consider ideal for their work satisfaction and that affect their productivity are in sharp contrast to the ways business enterprises or governmental bureaucracies operate. Unfortunately, most governmental regulations today are predicated on industrial-governmental models of personnel practice and authority.

Most government compliance personnel, with backgrounds in business or government, cannot be expected to be interested in preserving and strengthening the faculty system of governance and rewards. Instead, as Lester (1974:122) and others have pointed out, "through the rather inflexible application of rules designed for industry model situations, their actions tend to weaken the faculty system and strengthen centralization of authority and control within the university."

As an example, consider government regulation to eliminate sex discrimination in pay. At many institutions, this has resulted in a civil-service-like system of compensation for university faculty, with each rank defined in terms of minimum standards of classroom time, committee assignments, or publications. In such cases, specified pay grades within the rank through which the faculty member moves according to length of time in rank may become the "objective" criterion of productivity. Yet time or load counts may have little to do with faculty or institutional excellence. Why, for example, should a faculty member strive for the better placement of students, increased student satisfaction or learning, or greater professional participation when the reward structure is simply dependent on time of service?

Similarly, consider the impact of many of the new formalized accounting schemes aimed at measuring faculty time allocation. While the intent may be laudable—increased accountability to reduce fraud—the application is often quite harmful. For example, most federal and state grants are now routinely requiring the measurement of the percentage of time faculty devote to a given project. The enforcement of this requirement has typically failed to take into account the fact that numerous studies have shown an average university faculty work week in excess of sixty hours. The assumption is apparently made that because a normal bureaucrat's work week is forty hours (or less), such must also be true in academia. Will the implied imposition of a forty hour work week in higher education advance or stifle the work ethic of the professoriate?

Applications of regulations—however well intentioned—can pose a threat to university methods and procedures for rewards and incentives for faculty. They may also lead to a reduction in productivity, while adding to the cost of operation. While outside pressures and regulations are exerted in the name of safety, antibias, and financial accountability, they often tend to weaken the very system that is expected to respond.

While the new generation of university regulators are enthusiastically applying rules and procedures from an industrial model, they have failed to recognize the consequences of these regulations even in industry. The growth rate of industrial productivity—output per unit of labor input—was cut by at least one-half a percentage point in 1975 as a consequence of such governmental regulations. That, at least, is the conclusion of a major new productivity study by Edward F. Denison at the Brookings Institution (1978). The application of such corrective requirements and bureaucratic reporting to higher education is surely having similar effects. In fact, the consequence may be even more severe in academia, since faculty are not accustomed to dealing with such restrictions and regulations.

To the extent that external regulations apply equally to all institutions, the output of all institutions will be affected roughly the same. However, institutions that can effectively minimize dealing directly with governments should have a comparative edge.

Given the financial difficulties that have already begun to press upon higher education institutions, especially as they continue to decline in the 1980s, the temptation to run to legislatures for more direct funding will be great. Administrators at land grant universities, for example, will be tempted to give up more of their "constitutional independence" to gain additional funds. Private schools will look increasingly to direct government subsidies for survival. In fact, private schools have been pushing for subsidies of one form or another for quite some time now. Unfortunately, most administrators are missing the probable cost of such direct subsidy. Increasing direct subsidy gives legislators and government bureaucrats increasing means to impose and enforce regulations that can cut institutional flexibility and restrict productivity gains.

Given that administrators, faced with survival fears, are or will be looking to more government subsidies for the needed funds, it is surprising that most of them desire this subsidy to be direct as opposed to a subsidy to students with matched tuition increases. Administrators may perceive direct subsidies to be to the institution's and to their own personal advantage. They may have more confidence in their own ability to "monopolize" legislative funding than in their

institution's ability to compete for subsidized students (and their tuition dollars). However, such reasoning typically overlooks the leverage the governmental unit gets on the institution. Direct subsidy usually provides the funding source (both state and federal) with the wherewithal to impose costly requirements and regulations.

EXPANDING EGALITARIANISM

In American higher education today, there are growing faculty attitudes that favor a more equal distribution of salaries and other rewards. Although, as Begin (Chapter 12) indicates, the recent advent of collective bargaining and unionization in higher education has resulted from a number of complex issues and causes ranging from legislative and other external intrusions on traditional faculty governance to inadequate salary allocations, a common appeal found within the circle of most union advocates has been the at least implicit call for greater "salary equity." In fact, the very nature of collective bargaining in the United States is controlled by the principle of majority rule and generally tends to be in conflict with a "star" faculty system and with large variances in salaries and other forms of academic rewards based on merit judgments. As Wollett (1973: 42) points out, "collective bargaining is essentially an egalitarian activity (wherein) . . . it emphasizes utilitarianism, standardization, and uniformity." Thus, a major question arises: If these values achieve primacy in higher education, what will be the effect on the quality and productivity of faculty effort?

Freeman (Chapter 4) has found from his work that academic salaries today may already be based more on "equitable" rather than market-oriented salary policies. There may be reason, therefore, to believe that screening and efficiency are, in fact, disliked by many of today's faculty (and administrators). If faculty are fearful of attempts by administrators to implement market- and productivity-based salary allocation schemes, there is a high probability that the faculty will unionize to preserve the status quo. Begin (Chapter 12) clearly suggests that such is likely.

Begin (Chapter 12), as well as Dornbusch (Chapter 3), point to the fact that a faculty union could be quite strong if organized and led by "star" faculty. Implementing a market-oriented strategy at an institution where the most prestigious departments happen to be in areas that are nonindustry or nongovernment related, will probably bring forth "stars" as union organizers.

The existence of a strong union does not necessarily imply that efficiency and market forces will be ignored. It does imply, however,

that administrators will be highly constrained if the faculty union is based on an egalitarian philosophy. Such a philosophy is, of course, contrary to a "discriminating" plan for faculty rewards based on individual merit and productivity.

To preserve or establish a reward system with merit pay and dollar allocations based on screening and market pressures, administrators will have to fight hard at the bargaining table. If they do not, the institution will lose much of its ability to simply preserve its rank and quality position in the hierarchy of higher education institutions. Institutions without an egalitarian-based faculty union have at least greater capability for pulling away from the institutions that do not have such resource allocation flexibility. If an institution wishes to forestall unionization and its concomitant inflexibility of resource use, a rational and accepted system of rewards (along with an active and effective system of faculty governance) would be one of its most influencial remedies.

GROWING BUREAUCRACIES

Higher education institutions, like most other forms of public service organizations, have undergone a phenomenal growth in size and complexity in the past twenty years. Endemic to such institutions and growth has been a parallel rise in bureaucracies. Similar to most other large and complex social systems, higher education has seen an increasing rise in administrative centralization, consolidation, and formalized rules. As a consequence of all this, the decisionmaking capacity of faculty and administrators alike in the governance and administration of higher education has been significantly affected.

The literature on problems of large complex systems is, of course, rich with illustrations of characteristics that tend to become manifest from such growth. We must recognize that the potential for increasing levels of alienation, declining access to decisionmakers, growth in costs of coordination and control, increasing challenges to basic value premises, increasing system rigidity, narrowing opportunities for innovation, and a declining overall performance of the system is present in today's large educational bureaucracies. If such events become real, it is obvious that academic productivity and educational services will suffer. It is equally obvious that faculty and administrators alike must guard against such institutional tendencies. Moreover, it should be clear from the chapters in this book that a solidly rationalized and carefully implemented academic rewards system can do much to obviate many of these bureaucratic tendencies.

FACULTY BEHAVIOR AND
INSTITUTIONAL CHANGE

As evident from the chapters by McKeachie (Chapter 1), Becker (Chapter 2), and Dornbusch (Chapter 3), there are differing views as to why individuals are in academe and what motivates them to be good teachers and researchers. From these three chapters, there is common agreement, however, that some type of faculty identification and reward system is necessary to maintain high productivity and adaptability to change. McKeachie stated that faculty have to be treated as individuals, with reward emphasis being placed on intrinsic factors. Becker, on the other hand, emphasized extrinsic rewards given intrinsic factors. Both McKeachie and Dornbusch emphasized the identification and rewarding of that which an individual does best. All three of these chapters, however, depend on the screening of individuals, something that Freeman (Chapter 4) and Becker (Chapter 2) both claim has not been fully occurring in today's higher education, especially in light of recent moves toward egalitarianism.

Given that higher education is a declining industry with increasing external constraints and expanding requirements, it is going to be extremely difficult to base any attempt at changing faculty behavior and productivity on an assumption of forthcoming resource increases from the outside. Rather, the immediate problem is likely to be maintaining given institutional quality and productivity levels as budgets are retrenched or diverted. Obviously, the temptation is greatest for institutions to meet decreasing budgets by following the precollege public school model—that is, first install a hiring freeze, and then as terminations occur, simply do not fill them. Then, if this method of cutback is not sufficient, follow a seniority rule for additional layoffs. At the same time, continue to give small but equal raises to all remaining faculty.

However, such a system of rewards and personnel policies will surely be short sighted in the long run. Flexibility will be gone, and academic productivity will surely decline. As Kirschling (Chapter 5) clearly points out, flexibility is a prerequisite for individual and institutional productivity in higher education. Appropriate reward system policies and procedures must be devised not only to maintain existing quality and productivity but to adapt to changing circumstances and to enhance future productivity as well.

Assuming that the goal of a department or school is to maintain the prestige and quality of its program(s) and department(s), then from the work of Cartter (1966a) and Roose and Anderson (1970)

we know this can be partially facilitated by maintaining a "stars" system. However, in applied areas which are open to competition from nonacademic industries (such as the health fields, economics, accounting, engineering, and other business and government related areas) this may be quite expensive if the declining academic institution attempts to compete with other growth sectors of the economy. At some nonacademic/academic salary differential, senior faculty in these applied areas will leave. As both Freeman (Chapter 4) and Cartter (1976: 184) indicate, experienced faculty do respond to market forces outside of higher education. The decline in relative salaries during the past few years has undoubtedly stimulated the outmigration of many senior professors to government and industry. As both Bowen (Chapter 9) and Freeman (Chapter 4) note, salary differentials are already substantial in many areas and they will surely widen in the future.

In market-sensitive areas, those academic institutions that can devise ways to keep their star salaries high relative to other academic institutions may be able to maintain their stars. That is, their stars' salaries may shrink relative to nonacademic salaries, but if their stars' salaries increase relative to salaries in other like academic institutions, their stars may feel relatively better off than stars in other academic institutions. Thus, the psychological factor of knowing that they are being treated better by their academic institution may be sufficient to keep these stars from jumping to nonacademic institutions.

In the case of star faculty who are not in areas that are directly applicable to nonacademic settings (such as artists, historians, classical scholars, and atmospheric scientists), faculty retention is obviously easier. In fact, a reverse strategy may be workable, but it may also be politically risky. Where stars are restricted to academe for employment, a unit may have a high probability of keeping these stars and at the same time keeping their salaries at or below those being paid to like faculty at other similar institutions. These faculty may not be "happy," but where else are they going to go in a declining industry? The only way they will be likely to receive an offer from another similar institution is if a senior faculty vacancy occurs through retirement or death. However, in a declining industry, the tendency is to replace expensive talent with cheaper talent. Such vacancies will tend to be filled by assistant professor appointments. In fact, many academic institutions have already imposed rules that restrict hiring to the assistant professor levels.

As McKeachie (Chapter 1) points out, however, "when you are rewarded for something that you previously did for fun, you are less likely to choose that activity when the reward is removed." It is

possible that faculty who do not receive salary increases in line with their counterparts at other like schools may stay with the institution but will cut back activities that they previously did for fun or for which they were rewarded in the 1960s but for which they no longer receive such rewards. Whether this will be research, teaching, or services to the institution is unclear. But given that it has been research in the past that has carried the heaviest pecuniary reward, as Tuckman (Chapter 8) demonstrates, it will probably be research that is cut back rather than teaching.

In the case of faculty who are tenured but are of less than star prestige, the thing to be emphasized across all departments is the screening of associate professors and full professors for salary increments and of associate professors for promotion to full professor stature. The salary scheme should give these individuals the expectation that incremental productivity will be matched with incremental salary gains. While internal peer review must be used to assess the value of individual faculty, an emphasis should also be placed on the comparison of professors in one department with another (either within the same institution or at another like institution). This type of merit scheme is financially possible in a declining industry provided the standard for merit pay consideration is sufficiently high so that only the top producers qualify. As indicated by Lewis and Kellogg (Chapter 6), such standards can be stated in terms of alternative proxy measures for teaching, research, and whatever else the institution deems important. Similar comparable "cumulative" standards can be established for promotion decisions.

For assistant professors, Astin and Bayer (Chapter 10) suggest that individual mentors may be needed to maximize the individual professor's productivity in accordance with institutional goals. This may be especially so for female faculty. Historically, the "academic mentor" system has been an informal working relationship between a senior and junior faculty member. To formalize this system may be difficult. However, required yearly reviews of assistant professors by a small team of senior faculty may be one way to assist assistant professors in learning what is expected of them. And as Dornbusch (Chapter 3) indicates, the specification of such performance criteria greatly facilitates both motivation and performance outcomes. The review team could also serve as an initial screen for salary determination. Their written review and proposed action for the assistant professor to follow could serve as the criteria for determining salary increments in subsequent years. Such a mentor review process should not lead to additional financial demand, but it may increase time pressures on some senior faculty.

It is important to note, as Becker (Chapter 2) suggests, that an increase in screening of faculty for promotion and merit pay need not add greatly to institutional cost. It need not necessitate an increase in salary budgets for the institution, but it will require some additional time from faculty for the screening process. However, it does imply a redistribution of funds from low producers to higher producers; thus, it is to the high producers' advantage to reallocate some of their time to screening. In addition, an increase in screening will result in an increase in output for the high producers. Unfortunately, Becker's analysis does not tell us how low producers will respond. They may or may not respond negatively or positively (or not at all).

An administrative need for flexibility, however, should not loose sight of ability to use a number of available nonmarket rewards and mechanisms. Freeman (Chapter 4), for example, indicates that the discretionary allocation of such items as honors and recognition, laboratory space, supplies, research and teaching assistants, and the like can all be effective as rewards in addition to salary increments. Becker's analysis (Chapter 2), however, calls into question whether nonpecuniary rewards will necessarily result in an increase in the output on which such rewards are granted.

With the decline in higher education, both Freeman (Chapter 4) and Bowen (Chapter 9) point out that the distribution of faculty by age is clearly getting older. This trend is likely to continue and could lead to possible stagnation, with fewer new ideas being developed and less dissemination of new ideas and concepts being taught in the classroom. Suggestively, departments and programs may want to target age profiles for their areas with deliberate strategies for the recruitment of younger faculty. As noted above, this may imply a policy that all retiring full professors be replaced by assistant professors. It may also imply the heavy allocation of pecuniary rewards to younger faculty and more nonpecuniary rewards to older faculty.

Tuckman's analysis (Chapter 8) would support such a strategy favoring younger faculty. He points out that faculty nearing retirement have few extrinsic incentives for publishing or teaching. In fact, his data indicate that faculty do tend to spend less time preparing for teaching and publishing their research as they age and approach retirement. Conversely, younger faculty have longer work lives with greater incentives for building their salary bases and tend to respond to discriminating merit systems.

In his review of this problem, Allan Cartter (1974: 305) has pointed out that if over the next ten years, the retirement age for college professors were lowered to age sixty-two from the present average of about sixty-seven, the number of openings each year

would increase by between 10 and 15 percent. This, of course, would greatly facilitate the entry of many new and younger professors. As part of an incentive strategy, the development of new annuity arrangements would do much to encourage many more voluntary early retirements. Some persons have also suggested that "tenure rights— so valuable in protecting academic freedom, but less defensible as a job-security privilege—be terminated after 25 years or at age 60, whichever is earlier" (Cartter, 1974: 305).

In recognition of these changing age profiles, gains in motivation and productivity may be facilitated by extending the promotion ladder beyond the full professor rank and by hiring new Ph.D.s below the assistant professor rank. It is obvious that as a greater percentage of faculty achieve full professor status, the variance in productivity for this rank will likewise increase. And, as documented by Freeman (Chapter 4), faculty of like rank tend to be treated equally within departments and colleges. Consequently, as Becker's work (Chapter 2) suggests, this will tend to reduce the output of high producers. However, the establishment of a higher rank—say a title of "university professor"—enables the identification of highly productive full professors. Such additional identification can facilitate the means by which administrators can reward outstanding scholars and teachers even in an egalitarian setting where those of equal rank get equal benefits.

As McKeachie (Chapter 1) notes, to change faculty behavior to enhance output, one can "examine the characteristics of desired faculty activities which can bring satisfaction and [create] situations in which these satisfactions can be found more readily." In short, one may produce gains in motivation and productivity by better matches among people, tasks, and rewards.

In the establishment of effective screening and of merit-based reward systems, the development of performance criteria is very important in influencing the performance of faculty. As Lewis and Kellogg (Chapter 6), Dornbusch (Chapter 3), and Doyle (Chapter 7) all point out, to influence behavior we need to work at specifying the criteria and insuring that we distribute resources and sanctions according to the review results. The empirical evidence from the chapters in this volume should convince even the most skeptical critic that one can measure and assess many of the various dimensions of teaching and research productivity in higher education. Qualitative evidence of such productivity can come from faculty publications, participation of faculty in professional meetings, special awards and other professional recognition, placement of students, number and amounts of grants awarded, student evaluation and learning, and most impor-

tantly, peer review. Appropriate performance criteria can be linked to such measures for individual faculty assessment.

Finally, as noted by Doyle (Chapter 7), there are a number of things that an institution or department can do to both enhance morale and, simultaneously, develop a better screening evaluation system. Certainly, the development of any screening or evaluation system must be done jointly with all the people who will be affected by it—faculty, administrators, students (when relevant to teaching), and maybe even trustees. Otherwise, the chances are good that it will be seen as an imposition to be resented. A second thing to insure is the provision of peer review and participation in the process. A third thing an institution or department can do to build a better system is to review that system regularly. Are the criteria consistent with departmental or institutional aims? Are there any parts of the system or process that are irrelevant or just not working? Are the procedures for collecting and interpreting performances still satisfactory?

To complement a thoughtful evaluation system, as pointed out by Doyle (Chapter 7), institutions should make sure that instructors have adequate resources to help them improve both their teaching and their research activities. In the context of teaching, at the very least, faculty should have easy access to well-publicized materials on instructional improvement. Many institutions provide their faculty with relatively easy access to instructional consultants or have offices that provide the instructional development services the faculty need. Such assistance is especially important in the development of staff improvement projects based on student evaluations and other forms of student feedback information.

CONCLUSION

In American higher education, a complex and diverse system of rewards has evolved as faculty and administrators have attempted to achieve control of those resources necessary for their adaptation to increasingly bureaucratic and financially pressured institutions. However, as many of the chapters in this volume indicate, the reward systems in higher education have not evolved identical patterns at all types of institutions. A part of this is clearly a function of different institutional aims and purposes; a part results from rapid change, faculty discontent, and the process of unionization; and a part comes from different traditions of faculty governance or administrative procedures and control. Whatever the pattern, however, the important point to note is that faculty review and screening for whatever purposes has always been and will always be a part of the various reward systems in higher education.

References

Aebi, Charles. 1972. The Application of Herzberg's Motivation-Hygiene Theory to College Educators Tested by Two Different Methodologies. Doctoral Dissertation, Ohio University.

Aigner, Dennis, and Clen Cain. 1977. Statistical Theories of Discrimination in the Labor Markets. *Industrial and Labor Relations Review* 30:175–87.

Allison, Paul D., and John A. Stewart. 1974. Productivity Difference Among Scientists: Evidence for Accumulative Advantage. *American Sociological Review* 39:596–606.

American Association of Higher Education. 1967. *Faculty Participation in Academic Governance.* Washington, D.C.

American Association of University Professors. 1960–1978. The Annual Reports of the Economic Status of the Profession. *AAUP Bulletin.*

_____ . 1971. Report of the Survey Subcommittee of Committee T. *AAUP Bulletin* 57:68–124.

_____ . 1972. Coping with Adversity: Report on the Economic Status of the Profession, 1971–72. *AAUP Bulletin* 58:178–243.

_____ . 1977. No Progress This Year: Report on the Economic Status of the Profession, 1976–77. *AAUP Bulletin* 63:146–73.

American Council on Education. 1977. *Accredited Institutions of Post-Secondary Education, 1976–77.* Washington, D.C.: Council on Post-Secondary Accreditation.

_____ . 1976–77. *A Fact Book of Higher Education.* Washington, D.C.

American Economic Association. 1969 *Index of Economic Journals* Volumes I–VIII. Homewood, Ill.: Irwin.

Andes, John. 1974. *Developing Trends in Content of Collective Bargaining Contracts in Higher Education.* Washington, D.C.: Academic Collective Bargaining Information Service.

Angell, George W. 1971. *Collective Negotiations in Upstate New York Community Colleges 1968–1971.* New York: State Public Relations Board.

Arrow, Kenneth. 1959. Toward a Theory of Price Adjustment. In M. Abramovitz, ed., *The Allocation of Resources.* Stanford: Stanford University Press.

Arrowsmith, William. 1967. The Future of Teaching. In Calvin B.T. Lee, ed., *Improving College Teaching.* Washington, D.C.: American Council on Education.

Asch, S.E. 1946. Forming Impressions of Personality. *Journal of Abnormal and Social Psychology* 41:258–90.

Astin, H.S. 1969. *The Woman Doctorate in America.* New York: Russell Sage Foundation.

_____ . 1978. Factors in Women's Scholarly Productivity. In H.S. Astin and W.Z. Hirsch, eds., *The Higher Education of Women.* New York: Praeger.

Astin, H.S., and A.E. Bayer. 1972. Sex Discrimination in Academe. *Educational Record* 53:101–18.

Astin, H.S.; M. Harway; and P. McNamara. 1976. *Sex Discrimination in Education: Access to Post-Secondary Education.* Final report to National Center for Education Statistics. Los Angeles: UCLA College of Education.

Atkinson, John W. 1977. Motivation for Achievement. In T. Blass, ed., *Personality Variables in Social Behavior.* Hillsdale, N.J.: Erlbaum Associates.

Bailey, Duncan, and Charles Schotta. 1972. Private and Social Rates of Return to Education of Academicians. *American Economic Review* 63:19–31.

Bailey, Stephen K. 1975. People Planning in Postsecondary Education: Human Resources Development. In James N. Nesmith, ed., *More for Less: Academic Planning with Faculty Without New Dollars.* New York: Society for College and University Planning.

Bain, George S. 1969. The Growth of White-Collar Unionism and Public Policy in Canada. *Relations Industrielle* 24:243.

Bain, Trevor. 1976. Collective Bargaining and Wages in Higher Education: The Case of CUNY (New York City). *Journal of Collective Negotiations in the Public Sector* 5:207–14.

Baker, B.O.; C.D. Hardyck; and L.F. Petronovick. 1966. Weak Measurement vs. Strong Statistics: An Empirical Critique of S.S. Steven's Proscriptions on Statistics. *Educational and Psychological Measurement* 26:291–309.

Baldridge, J. Victor; David V. Curtis; George Ecker; and Gary L. Riley. 1977. *Policy Making and Effective Leadership: A National Study of Academic Management.* San Francisco: Jossey-Bass.

Barbash, Jack. 1970. Academicians as Bargainers with the University. *Issues in Industrial Society* 1:22–28.

Bayer, A.E. 1970. *College and University Faculty: A Statistical Description.* Washington, D.C.: American Council on Education.

_____ . 1973. *Teaching Faculty in Academe: 1972–73.* Washington, D.C.: American Council on Education.

Bayer, A.E., and H.S. Astin. 1968. Sex Differences in Academic Rank and Salary Among Science Doctorates in Teaching. *The Journal of Human Resources* III:191–200.

_____ . 1975. Sex Differences in the Academic Reward System. *Science* 198:796–802.

Bayer, A.E., and J.E. Dutton. 1977. Career Age and Research-Professional Activities of Academic Scientists. *Journal of Higher Education* XLVIII:259–82.

Doyle, K.O., Jr., and R. Moen. 1978. Toward the Development of a Domain of Academic Motivation. *Journal of Educational Psychology* 70:231–36.

Doyle, K.O., Jr., and S.E. Whitely. 1974. Student Ratings as Criteria for Effective Teaching. *American Educational Research Journal* 11:259–74.

Dunham, R.E.; P.S. Wright; and M.O. Chandler. 1966. *Teaching Faculty in Universities and Four-Year Colleges.* Washington, D.C.: U.S. Office of Education.

Dunworth, John, and Rupert Cook. 1976. Budgetary Devolution as an Aid to University Efficiency. *Higher Education* 5:153–67.

Eble, Kenneth E. 1972. *Professors as Teachers.* San Francisco: Jossey-Bass.

Eckert, Ruth E., and John E. Stecklein. 1961. *Job Motivations and Satisfactions of College Teachers: A Study of Faculty Members in Minnesota Colleges.* Washington, D.C.: U.S. Government Printing Office.

Edgar, Earl. 1974. Collective Bargaining at Youngstown State University. Paper presented to Inter-University Council of Ohio State Universities, Spring.

Elliott, D.N. 1950. Characteristics and Relationships of Various Criteria for Effective Teaching. *Purdue University Studies in Higher Education* 70:5–61.

Evans, Michael K. 1969. *Macroeconomic Activity: Theory, Forecasting, and Control.* New York: Harper and Row.

Falcone, Michael A. 1975. *Collective Bargaining: Its Effects on Campus Governance.* Washington, D.C.: Academic Collective Bargaining Information Service, Special Report No. 16.

Farber, Stephen. 1977. The Earnings and Promotion of Women Faculty: Comment. *The American Economic Review* 67:199–217.

Fenker, Richard M. 1977. The Incentive Structure of a University. *Journal of Higher Education* 48:453–71.

Ferber, Marianne A. 1974. Professors, Performance and Rewards. *Industrial Relations* 13:69–77.

Ferber, Marianne A., and Betty Kordick. 1978. Sex Differentials in the Earnings of Ph.D.s. *Industrial and Labor Relations Review* 31:227–38.

Feuille, Peter, and James Blandin. 1974. Faculty Job Satisfaction and Bargaining Sentiments: A Case Study. *Academy of Management Journal* 17:678–92.

Finkin, Matthew W. 1976. The Arbitration of Faculty Status Disputes in Higher Education. *Southwestern Law Journal* 30:289–434.

Finkin, Matthew W.; Mertin C. Bernstein; Maryse Eymonerie; William Hammerle; W. Lee Hansen; T. Paul Schultz; and Peter O. Steiner. 1978. The Impact of Federal Retirement-Age Legislation on Higher Education: A Report of the Special Committee on Age Discrimination and Retirement. *AAUP Bulletin* 64:181–92.

Fisher, Franklin M. 1966. *The Identification Problem in Economics.* New York: McGraw-Hill.

Folger, J.K.; H.S. Astin; and A.E. Bayer. 1970. *Human Resources and Higher Education.* New York: Russell Sage Foundation.

Foster, Leo Leslie. 1976. Relationships Between University Faculty Satisfaction with Rewards and Attitudes Toward Collective Bargaining. University of Wisconsin. Unpublished paper.

Frank, Robert H. 1978. Family Location Constraints and the Geographic Distribution of Female Professionals. *Journal of Political Economy* 86: 117—30.

Freeman, Richard B. 1971. *Market for College-Trained Manpower.* Cambridge, Mass.: Harvard University Press.

_____. 1975a. Demand for Labor in a Nonprofit Market: University Faculty. In Daniel S. Hamermesh, ed., *Labor in the Public and Nonprofit Sectors.* Princeton: Princeton University Press.

_____. 1975b. Supply and Salary Adjustments to the Changing Science Manpower Market: Physics, 1948—1973. *American Economic Review* 65: 27—39.

_____. 1976. *The Over-Educated American.* New York: Academic Press.

_____. 1977a. The Decline in Economic Rewards to College. *Review of Economics and Statistics* 59: 18—29.

_____. 1977b. Employment Opportunities and Doctorate Manpower. Mimeograph Report to National Academy of Science. Washington, D.C.

_____. 1977c. The New Job Market for Black Academicians. *Industrial and Labor Relations Review* 3, No. 2 (January): 616—74.

French, John R.P., Jr.; R.D. Caplan; R.V. Harrison; and S.F. Pinneau, Jr. 1976. Job Demands and Worker Health: A Symposium. Paper presented at 84th Annual Convention of American Psychological Association, September.

French, John R.P., Jr.; C.J. Tupper; and E.F. Mueller. 1965. Work Load of University Professors. Ann Arbor: University of Michigan. Unpublished paper.

Frey, P. 1973. Student Ratings of Teachers: Validity of Several Rating Factors. *Science* 182: 83—85.

Fulton, Oliver. 1975. Rewards and Fairness: Academic Women in the United States. In Martin Trow, ed., *Teachers and Students: Aspects of American Higher Education.* New York: McGraw-Hill.

Fulton, Oliver, and M. Trow. 1974. Research Activity in American Higher Education. *Sociology of Education* 47: 29—73.

Furniss, W. Todd. 1977. Whatever Happened to Faith, Hope, and Charity? *The Chronicle of Higher Education* 14: 24.

Gagné, R.M. 1977. *Conditions of Learning.* 3rd ed. New York: Holt, Rinehart, Winston.

Garbarino, Joseph W. 1974. Creeping Unionism and the Faculty Labor Market. In Margaret S. Gordon, ed., *Higher Education and the Labor Market.* New York: McGraw-Hill.

_____. 1975a. *Faculty Bargaining: Change and Conflict.* New York: McGraw-Hill.

_____. 1975b. Faculty Union Activity in Higher Education—1974. *Industrial Relations* 14: 110—11.

Garbarino, Joseph W., and John Lawler. 1977. Faculty Union Activity in Higher Education—1976. *Industrial Relations* 16: 105—6.

_____. 1978. Faculty Union Activity in Higher Education—1977. *Industrial Relations* 17: 117—18.

Gershenfeld, Walter J., and Kenneth P. Mortimer. 1976. *Faculty Collective Bargaining Activity in Pennsylvania, The First Five Years (1970—1975).* Philadelphia: Center for Labor and Manpower Studies, Temple University, and Center for the Study of Higher Education, Pennsylvania State University.

Glass, G.V. 1974. Teacher Effectiveness. In H. Wahlberg, ed., *Evaluating Educational Performance*. Berkeley: McCutchan.

Goeres, Ernest R. 1977a. Consideration for Advancement on Salary Schedules. *Collective Bargaining Perspectives* 2.

_____. 1977b. Salary Schedules and Initial Placement of Personnel. *Collective Bargaining Perspectives* 2.

Gold, Lois Swirsky. 1974. Measuring Faculty Unionism: Quantity and Quality (Criticism and Comment). *Industrial Relations* 13: 325–31.

Goldberge, Arthur. 1964. *Econometric Theory*. New York: John Wiley.

Goldstein, A.P. 1971. *Psychotherapeutic Attraction*. Elmsford, N.Y.: Pergamon.

Gordon, Margaret S., ed. 1974. *Higher Education and the Labor Market*. New York: McGraw-Hill.

Gordon, Nancy M.; T.E. Morton; and I.C. Braden. 1974. Faculty Salaries: Is There Discrimination by Sex, Race, and Discipline? *American Economic Review* 64: 419–27.

Government Employee Relations Report No. 545. 1974. Washington, D.C.: Bureau of National Affairs, March 11.

Gronau, Reuben. 1977. Leisure, Home Production, and Work—The Theory of the Allocation of Time Revisited. *Journal of Political Economy* 85: 1099–1123.

Gronlund, N.E. 1976. *Measurement and Evaluation in Teaching*. New York: Macmillan.

Gross, Alan. 1977. Twilight in Academe: The Problem of the Aging Professoriate. *Phi Delta Kappan* 58: 752–55.

Guilford, J.P. 1954 *Psychometric Methods*. New York: McGraw-Hill.

Gustad, John W. 1960. *The Career Decisions of College Teachers*. Washington, D.C.: U.S. Department of Health, Education and Welfare.

_____. 1969. Man in the Middle: Conditions of Work of College and University Faculty Members. In Stanley Elam and Michael H. Moskow, eds., *Employment Relations in Higher Education*. Bloomington, Ind.: Phi Delta Kappa.

Haehn, James O. 1970. A Survey of Faculty and Administration Attitudes on Collective Bargaining. Report to the Academic Senate, California State Colleges, May.

Halstead, D. Kent. 1975. *Higher Education Prices and Price Indexes*. Washington, D.C.: U.S. Government Printing Office. Also Supplements 1975, 1976, and 1977.

Hammer, Tove Helland, and Samuel B. Bacharach. 1977. *Reward Systems and Power Distribution*. Ithaca, N.Y.: New York State School of Industrial and Labor Relations, Cornell University.

Hansen, W. Lee, and A.C. Kelley. 1973. Political Economics of Course Evaluations. *Journal of Economic Education* 5: 10–21.

Hansen, W. Lee, and Burton A. Weisbrod. 1972. Towards a General Theory of Awards, or Do Economists Need a Hall of Fame? *Journal of Political Economy* 80: 422–31.

Harmon, Lindsey B. 1965. *High School Ability Patterns: A Backyard Look from the Doctorate*. Washington, D.C.: Office of Scientific Personnel, National Academy of Science-National Research Council.

Hawkins, Robert G.; Lawrence S. Ritter; and Ingo Walter. 1973. What Economists Think of Their Journals. *Journal of Political Economy* 71:1017–32.

Heckman, James C., and Solomon Polachek. 1974. Empirical Evidence on the Functional Form of the Earnings-Schooling Relationship. *Journal of the American Statistical Association* 69:350–54.

Hedgepeth, Royster C. 1974. Consequences of Collective Bargaining in Higher Education. *Journal of Higher Education* 45:691–705.

Helson, H. 1959. Adaptation Level Theory. In S. Koch, ed., *Psychology: A Study of a Science*. New York: McGraw-Hill.

Herman, Edward E., and G.P. Skinner. 1975. A Survey of Faculty Attitudes Toward Collective Bargaining. *Industrial Relations Research Association Annual Proceedings* 28:266–77.

Hildebrand, M.; R.C; Wilson; and E.R. Dienst. 1971. *Evaluating University Teaching*. Berkeley: Center for Research and Development in Higher Education.

Hind, R.R.; S.M. Dornbusch; and W.R. Scott. 1974. A Theory of Evaluation Applied to a University Faculty. *Sociology of Education* 47:114–28.

Hodgkinson, H. 1974. Adult Development: Implications for Faculty and Administrators. *Educational Record* 55:263–74.

Hoenack, Stephen A. 1977. Direct and Incentive Planning Within a University. *Socio-Economic Planning Sciences* 11:191–204.

Hoenack, Stephen A., and Alfred L. Norman. 1974. Incentives and Resource Allocation in Universities. *Journal of Higher Education* 45:21–37.

Hoffman, Emily. 1976. Faculty Salaries: Is There Discrimination by Sex, Race and Discipline? Additional Evidence. *American Economic Review* 66:196–98.

Houthakker, H. 1952–53. Compensated Changes in Quantities and Qualities Consumed. *Review of Economic Studies* 19:155–64.

Johnson, George E., and Frank P. Stafford. 1974a. The Earnings and Promotion of Women Faculty. *American Economic Review* 64:901–903.

_____. 1974b. Lifetime Earnings in a Professional Labor Market: Academic Economists. *Journal of Political Economy* 82:549–70.

_____. 1977. The Earnings and Promotion of Women Faculty: Reply. *American Economic Review* 67:214–17.

Johnson, Mark D., and Kenneth P. Mortimer. 1977. *Faculty Bargaining and the Politics of Retrenchment in the Pennsylvania State Colleges 1971–1976*. University Park, Pa.: Center for the Study of Higher Education.

Julius, Daniel J. 1977. *Collective Bargaining in Higher Education: The First Decade*. Washington, D.C.: The American Association for Higher Education.

Juster, F. Thomas. 1975. *Education, Income and Human Behavior*. New York: McGraw-Hill.

Kamens, David, and Gian Sarup. 1978. Reward Systems, Faculty Alienation and Militancy: Academic Dilemmas in the Middle of the Academic Procession. *Research in Higher Education* 8:227–40.

Katz, David A. 1973. Faculty Salaries, Promotion, and Productivity at a Large University. *American Economic Review* 63:469–77.

_____. 1977. Tenure Ratios under Conditions of Positive or Negative Faculty Growth. *AAUP Bulletin* 63:301–303.

Kazlow, Carole, and Joseph Gianquinta. 1977. Tenure, Support of Collective Bargaining, and Unionism in Higher Education: Some Challenging Findings. *Research in Higher Education* 6:45–63.

Keast, William R., and John W. Macy, Jr. 1973. *Faculty Tenure: A Report and Recommendations by the Commission on Academic Tenure in Higher Education.* San Francisco: Jossey-Bass.

Kehrer, B.H. 1976. Factors Affecting the Incomes of Men and Women Physicians: An Exploratory Analysis. *The Journal of Human Resources* XI:526–45.

Kemerer, Frank R., and J. Victor Baldridge. 1975. *Unions on Campus.* San Francisco: Jossey-Bass.

King, Allan G. 1977. Is Occupational Segregation the Cause of Flatter Experience-Earnings Profiles of Women? *Journal of Human Resources* 12:541–49.

Kipps, Paul H. 1975. The Use of Course Evaluations to Influence Teaching and Research Activities. *Journal of Economic Education* 6:94–98.

Kirschling, Wayne R., and Robert Staaf. 1975. Efficiency and Productivity: A Behavioral View. *New Directions for Institutional Research* 2:61–90.

Klevmarken, Anders, and John M. Quigley. 1976. Age, Experience, Earnings, and Investments in Human Capital. *Journal of Political Economy* 84:47–72.

Koch, James V., and John F. Chizmar. 1973. The Influence of Teaching and Other Factors Upon Absolute Salaries and Salary Increments at Illinois State University. *Journal of Economic Education* 5:27–34.

———. 1976a. *The Economics of Affirmative Action.* Lexington, Mass.: D.C. Heath.

———. 1976b. Sex Discrimination and Affirmative Action in Faculty Salaies. *Economic Inquiry* 14:16–24.

Kuhn, Alfred. 1974. *The Logic of Social Systems.* San Francisco: Jossey-Bass.

Kulik, James A., and W.J. McKeachie. 1975. The Evaluation of Teachers in Higher Education. In Fred N. Kerlinger, ed., *Review of Research in Education.* Itaska, Ill.: F.E. Peacock.

Ladd, Everett Carll, Jr. 1978. The Economic Position of the American Professoriate. Paper prepared for delivery at a conference at the University of Southern California, January 25–27.

Ladd, Everett Carll, Jr., and S.M. Lipset. 1976. Sex Differences in Academe. *Chronicle of Higher Education* 12:18.

Lee, Barbara Ann. 1977. The Effect of Faculty Collective Bargaining on Academic Governance in Four-Year Colleges and Universities. Doctoral Dissertation, The Ohio State University.

Lenning, Oscar T. 1977. Previous Attempts to Structure Educational Outcomes and Outcome-Related Concepts: A Compilation and Review of the Literature. Boulder: National Center for Higher Education Management Systems.

Leslie, Larry L., and Teh-Wei Hu. 1977. The Financial Implications of Collective Bargaining. *Journal of Educational Finance* 3:32–53.

Lester, Richard A. 1974. *Antibias Regulation of Universities: Faculty Problems and Their Solution.* New York: McGraw-Hill.

———. 1977. Labor-Market Discrimination and Individualized Pay: The Complicated Case of University Faculty. In Industrial Relations Research Associ-

ation Series, *Equal Rights and Industrial Relations.* Princeton: Princeton University Press.

Levin, H.M. 1971. *Concepts of Economic Efficiency and Educational Production.* New York: National Bureau of Economic Research.

Levinson, Daniel J., et al. 1976. Periods in the Adult Development of Men: Ages 18 to 45. *The Counseling Psychologist* 6: 21—25.

Levy, Harold. 1975. *Academic Judgment and the Grievance Arbitration in Higher Education.* Washington, D.C.: Academic Collective Bargaining Information Service, Special Report No. 20.

Lewin, David. 1977. Public Sector Labor Relations: A Review Essay. In David Lewin, Peter Feuille, and Thomas A. Kochan, *Public Sector Labor Relations.* Glen Ridge, N.J.: Thomas Horton and Daughters.

Lewis, H. Gregg. 1963. *Unionism and Relative Wages in the United States.* Chicago: University of Chicago Press.

Light, Donald. 1974. Introduction: The Structure of the Academic Professions. *Sociology of Education* 47: 2—28.

Loeb, Jane, and M. Ferber. 1971. Sex as Predictive of Salary and Status on a University Faculty. *Journal of Educational Measurement* 8: 235—44.

Lovell, Michael C. 1973. The Production of Economic Knowledge. *Journal of Economic Literature* 9: 27—55.

Lowenthal, Marjorie F., and Lawrence Weiss. 1976. Intimacy and Crisis in Adulthood. *The Counseling Psychologist* 6: 10—15.

Lozier, G. Gregory, and Kenneth P. Mortimer. 1974. *Anatomy of a Collective Bargaining Election in Pennsylvania's State-Owned Colleges.* University Park, Pa.: Center for the Study of Higher Education.

Lussier, Virginia. 1974. *Albion College Votes "No Agent: " A Case Study.* Washington, D.C.: Academic Collective Bargaining Information Service, Special Report No. 7.

Madden, Janet F. 1973. *The Economics of Sex Discrimination.* Lexington, Mass.: Lexington Books.

Malkiel, B.G., and J.A. Malkiel. 1973. Male-Female Pay Differentials in Professional Employment. *American Economic Review* 63: 693—705.

Mannix, Thomas M. 1974. Community College Grievance Procedures: A Review of Contract Content in Ninety-Four Colleges. *Journal of the College and University Personnel Association* 25: 23—40.

_____ . 1977. Administration. In Daniel J. Julius, *Collective Bargaining in Higher Education: The First Decade.* Washington, D.C.: The American Association for Higher Education.

Marsh, John, and Frank P. Stafford. 1967. The Effects of Values on Pecuniary Behavior: The Case of Academicians. *American Sociological Review* 32: 740—54.

McKeachie, W.J. 1969. *Teaching Tips.* 6th ed. Lexington, Mass.: D.C. Heath.

_____ . 1977. A Modest Proposal. *Chronicle of Higher Education* 14: 21.

McKenzie, Richard B. 1972. The Economics of Reduced Faculty Teaching Loads. *Journal of Political Economy* 80: 617—19.

McLaughlin, Gerald W.; John C. Smart; and James R. Montgomery. 1978. Factors Which Comprise Salary. *Research in Higher Education* 8: 67—82.

Mead, George Herbert. 1934. *Mind, Self, and Society.* Chicago: University of Chicago Press.

Merton, Robert K. 1968. The Matthew Effect in Science. *Science* 189:58–63.

Metzger, W. 1973. Academic Tenure in America: A Historical Essay. In Commission on Academic Tenure in Higher Education, *Faculty Tenure.* San Francisco: Jossey-Bass.

Mincer, Jacob. 1974. *Schooling, Experience, and Earnings.* New York: National Bureau of Economic Research.

Mintz, Bernard, and Allen Golden. 1974. Faculty Collective Bargaining and the Arbitral Process. *The Journal of College and University Personnel Association* 25:33–39.

Miyamoto, S.F., and S.M. Dornbusch. 1956. A Test of Interactionist Hypotheses of Self-Conception. *The American Journal of Psychology* LXI:399–403.

Moen, R., and K.O. Doyle, Jr. 1977. Validation of the Academic Motivations Inventory. *Educational and Psychological Measurement* 37:509–12.

Moore, John W. 1971. *Attitudes Toward Collective Negotiations: Pennsylvania Community College Faculty.* University Park, Pa.: Center for the Study of Higher Education.

Moore, W.J. 1972. The Relative Quality of Economic Journals: A Suggested Rating System. *Western Economic Journal* 10:156–69.

Morgan, David R., and Richard C. Kearney. 1977. Collective Bargaining and Faculty Compensation: A Comparative Analysis. *Sociology of Education* 50:28–39.

Mortimer, Kenneth P. 1977. Recent Developments in Governance and Collective Bargaining. Speech given to Society for Professionals in Dispute Resolution, New York City, October 24.

Mortimer, Kenneth P., and G. Gregory Lozier. 1973. Contracts of Four Year Institutions. In E.D. Duryea, Robert S. Fisk, and associates, eds., *Faculty Unions and Collective Bargaining.* San Francisco: Jossey-Bass.

_____. 1974. Faculty Workload and Collective Bargaining. *New Directions for Institutional Research* 1:49–64.

Mortimer, Kenneth P., and Richard D. Richardson, Jr. 1977. *Governance in Institutions with Faculty Unions: Six Case Studies.* University Park, Pa.: Center for the Study of Higher Education.

Mortimer, Kenneth P., and Naomi Ross. 1975. *Faculty Voting Behavior in the Temple University Collective Bargaining Elections.* University Park, Pa.: Center for the Study of Higher Education.

Mortimer, Kenneth P.; Mark D. Johnson; and David A. Weiss. 1975. No Representation Victories in Faculty Collective Bargaining Elections. *Journal of the College and University Personnel Association* 26:34–43.

Moynihan, D. 1973. 'Peace'—Some Thoughts on the 1960s and 1970s. *The Public Interest* 32:3–12.

Mueller, E.F., and J.R.P. French, Jr. 1970. Relationship Between Uric Acid Level and Achievement Motivation. Washington, D.C.: U.S. Department of Health, Education, and Welfare. Research Report.

_____ . 1974. Uric Acid and Achievement. *Journal of Personality and Social Psychology* 30:336–40.

National Academy of Sciences. Annual *National Research Council Annual Survey of New Ph.D.s.* Washington, D.C.

National Center for Education Statistics. Annual. *Digest of Education Statistics.* Washington, D.C.: U.S. Government Printing Office.

_____ . Annual. *Projections of Education Statistics.* Washington, D.C.: U.S. Government Printing Office.

_____ . 1976a. *Financial Statistics of Institutions of Higher Education, Current Fund Revenues and Expenditures.* Washington, D.C.: U.S. Government Printing Office.

_____ . 1976b. *Higher Education: Salaries and Tenure of Instructional Faculty in Institutions of Higher Education, 1974–75.* Washington, D.C.: U.S. Government Printing Office.

_____ . 1976c. *Numbers of Employees in Institutions of Higher Education.* Washington, D.C.: U.S. Government Printing Office.

_____ . 1977. *Salaries, Tenure, and Fringe Benefits of Full-Time Instructional Faculty in Institutions of Higher Education, 1975–76.* Washington, D.C.: U.S. Government Printing Office.

_____ . 1978. *The Condition of Education: Statistical Report.* Washington, D.C.: U.S. Government Printing Office.

National Center for the Study of Collective Bargaining in Higher Education. 1975a. Dues Check-Off and Union Security Study. *Newsletter* 2:1–3.

_____ . 1975b. Merit Clauses in College Contracts. *Newsletter* 3:1–7.

_____ . 1977. Directory of Bargaining Agents and Contracts in Higher Education. New York: Baruch College.

National Education Association. Biennial Reports on faculty salaries under varying titles as follows: Salary Schedule Provisions or Salaries Paid in Degree-granting Institutions, 1953; Salaries Paid and Salary Practices in Universities, Colleges, and Junior Colleges, 1956 through 1964; Salaries in Higher Education or Salaries Paid and Salary-related Practices in Higher Education, 1966 through 1972. Washington, D.C.

_____ . 1964. *Teacher Supply and Demand.* Washington, D.C.: National Education Association Research Division.

_____ . 1965. *Salaries in Higher Education Continue to Grow.* Washington, D.C.: National Education Association Research Division.

Needham, Douglas. 1975. The Economics of Reduced Faculty Teaching Loads: Comment. *Journal of Political Economy* 83:219–23.

Neumann, Yoram. 1976, Structural Constraints, Power Perception, Research Performance and Rewards: An Organizational Perspective of University Graduate Departments. Ithaca, N.Y.: Cornell University.

New Jersey Public Employment Relations Commission. 1976. Findings in the Case Between AAUP and Rutgers University. Trenton, N.J.

Newton, David. 1973. CUNY—A Grievous Story. In James P. Begin, ed., *Academics at the Bargaining Table: Early Experience.* New Brunswick, N.J.: Institute of Management and Labor Relations, Rutgers University.

Niland, J. 1973. Where Have All the Ph.D.'s Been Going. Ithaca, N.Y.: Cornell University.

Oaxaca, R. 1974. Sex Discrimination in Wages. In O. Ashenfelter and A. Rees, eds., *Discrimination in Labor Markets.* Princeton: Princeton University Press.

Oberer, Walter E. 1969. Faculty Participation in Academic Decision Making. In *Employment Relations in Higher Education*, Bloomington, Ind.: Phi Delta Kappa.

O'Neill, J. 1971. *Resource Use in Higher Education.* Berkeley, Calif.: Carnegie Commission.

Perry, R.P.; R.R. Niemi; and K. Jones. 1974. Effect of Prior Teaching Evaluations and Lecture Presentation on Ratings of Teaching Performance. *Journal of Educational Psychology* 66:851–56.

Petersen, Stephen Haynes. 1976. Service as a Factor in Faculty Promotion and Tenure. Bloomington, Ind.: Indiana University. Unpublished Paper.

Petz, Donald C., and Frank M. Andres. 1966. *Scientists in Organizations.* New York: John Wiley & Sons.

Porter, R.C. 1965. A Growth Model Forecast of Faculty Size and Salaries in U.S. Higher Education. *Review of Economics and Statistics* 47:191–97.

Quandt, Richard. 1976. Some Quantitative Aspects of the Economics Journal Literature. *Journal of Political Economy* 84:714–55.

Reagan, Barbara B. 1975. Two Supply Curves for Economic Implications for Mobility and Career Attachment of Women. *American Economic Association* 65:100–107.

Reagan, Barbara B.; and B.J. Maynard. 1974. Sex Discrimination in Universities: An Approach through Internal Labor Market Analysis. *AAUP Bulletin* 60:13–21.

Rees, Albert. 1962. *The Economics of Trade Unions.* Chicago: University of Chicago Press.

Reskin, Barbara F. 1977. Scientific Productivity and the Reward Structure of Science. *American Sociological Review* 42:491–504.

Reuben, Elaine, and Leonore Hoffman, eds. 1975. *Unladylike and Unprofessional: Academic Women and Academic Unions.* New York: Modern Language Association Commission on the Status of Women.

Rich, Harvey E., and Pamela M. Jolicoeur. 1976. Faculty Work Role Expectations and Preferences. Paper presented at 1976 Meeting of the Pacific Sociological Association.

Roose, K.D., and C.J. Andersen. 1970. *A Rating of Graduate Programs.* Washington, D.C.: American Council on Education.

Rossman, Jack E. 1976. Teaching, Publication and Rewards at a Liberal Arts College. *Improving College and University Teaching* 24:238–40.

Saks, Daniel H. 1977. How Much Does a Department Chairperson Cost? *Journal of Human Resources* 12:535–39.

Satryb, Ronald. 1974. The Grievance Appeals Process within the State University of New York: A Descriptive Analysis. Doctoral Dissertations, University of Virginia.

Sawicki, Robert. 1975. The Unionization of Professors at the University of Delaware. Washington, D.C.: Academic Collective Bargaining Information Service, Special Report No. 13.

Schein, Edgar H. 1965. *Organizational Psychology.* Englewood Cliffs, N.J.: Prentice-Hall.

Schmeck, R.R.; F. Ribich; and N. Ramanaiah. 1977. Development of a Self-report Inventory for Assessing Individual Differences in Learning Processes. *Applied Psychological Measurement* 1:413–31.

Schneider, D.J. 1976. *Social Psychology.* Reading, Mass.: Addison-Wesley.

Seidman, Joel; Lane Kelley; and Alfred Edge. 1974. Faculty Attitudes and Choice of a Collective Bargaining Agency in Hawaii. *Industrial Relations* 13: 5–22.

Sharon, A.T. 1970. Eliminating Bias from Student Ratings of College Instructors. *Journal of Applied Psychology* 54:278–81.

Sheehy, Gail. 1976. *Passages.* New York: Dutton.

Shoup, Charles A. 1969. A Study of Faculty Collective Bargaining in Michigan Community Colleges. Doctoral Dissertations, Michigan State University.

Siegfried, John J., and Kenneth J. White. 1973a. Financial Rewards to Research and Teaching: A Case Study of Academic Economists. *American Economic Review* 63:309–15.

_____. 1973b. Teaching and Publishing as Determinants of Academic Salaries. *Journal of Economic Education* 4:90–99.

Simon, R.; S. Clark; and K. Galway. 1967. The Woman Ph.D.: A Recent Profile. *Social Problems* 15:221–36.

Skinner, B.F. 1968. *The Technology of Teaching.* New York: Appleton.

Smart, John C., and Gerald W. McLaughlin. 1978. Reward Structures of Academic Disciplines. *Research in Higher Education* 8:39–55.

Smith, Georgina. 1973. Faculty Women at the Bargaining Table. *AAUP Bulletin* 59:402–406.

Solmon, Lewis C. 1973. Women in Graduate Education: Clues and Puzzles Regarding Institutional Discrimination. *Research in Higher Education* 1:299–332.

Solomon, Henry, ed. 1977. The Growing Influence of Federal Regulations. *Educational Record* 58:270–89.

Sowell, T. 1975. *Affirmative Action Reconsidered. Was It Necessary in Academia?* Washington, D.C.: American Enterprise Institute for Public Policy Research.

Spriestersbach, D.C., and William J. Farrell. 1977. Impact of Federal Regulation at a University. *Science* 198:27–30.

Startup, R., and M. Gruneberg. 1976. The Rewards of Research. *Universities Quarterly* 30:227–38.

Stigler, George. 1950. *Employment and Compensation in Education.* New York: N.B.E.R.

Stiglitz, Joseph E. 1975. The Theory of "Screening," Education and the Distribution of Income. *American Economic Review* LXV:283–300.

Stone, Richard. 1965. A Model of the Educational System. *Minerva* (London) 3:172–86.

Strauss, Robert P. 1971. A Younger Economist's Views on the Market. *American Economic Review* 61:327–33.

Strober, Myra H., and A.O. Quester. 1977. The Earnings and Promotion of Women Faculty: Comment. *American Economic Review* 67:207–13.

Strong, S.R. 1968. Counseling: An Interpersonal Influence Process. *Journal of Counseling Psychology* 15:215–24.

Sullivan, A.M., and G.R. Skanes. 1974. Validity of Student Evaluation of Teaching and the Characteristics of Successful Instructors. *Journal of Educational Psychology* 66:584–90.

Tanur, Judith M., and R.L. Coser. 1978. Pockets of 'Poverty' in the Salaries of Academic Women. *AAUP Bulletin* 64:26–30.

Theil, H. 1952. Qualities, Prices, and Budget Enquiries. *Review of Economic Studies* 19:129–47.

Tinbergen, J., and H. Bos. 1965. *Econometric Models of Education.* Paris: O.E.C.D.

Tolles, N. Arnold, and Emanual Melichar. 1968. Studies of the Structure of Economists' Salaries and Income. *American Economic Review* 58:1–153.

Trent, James W., and A.M. Cohen. 1973. Research on Teaching in Higher Education. In Robert N.W. Travers, ed., *Second Handbook of Research on Teaching.* Chicago: Rand McNally College Publishing.

Trivett, David A. 1978. Compensation in Higher Education. *Research Currents* (ERIC and American Association for Higher Education), February-March.

Trow, Martin, ed. 1975. *Teachers and Students: Aspects of American Higher Education.* New York: McGraw-Hill.

Truax, C.B., and K.M. Mitchell. 1971. Research on Certain Therapist Interpersonal Skills in Relation to Process and Outcome. In Allen E. Bergin and L. Garfield, eds., *Handbook of Psychotherapy and Behavioral Change.* New York: Wiley.

Tuckman, Barbara and Howard. 1976. The Structure of Salaries at American Universities. *Journal of Higher Education* 47:51–64.

Tuckman, Howard P. 1976. *Publication, Teaching, and the Academic Reward Structure.* Lexington, Mass.: D.C. Heath.

Tuckman, Howard P., and Robert E. Hagemann. 1976. An Analysis of the Reward Structure in Two Disciplines. *Journal of Higher Education* 47:447–64.

Tuckman, Howard P., and Jack Leahey. 1975. What is an Article Worth. *Journal of Political Economy* 83:951–68.

Tuckman, Howard P.; James Gapinski; and Robert Hagemann. 1977. Faculty Skills and the Reward Structure in Academe: A Market Perspective. *American Economic Review* 67:692–702.

United States Bureau of the Census. 1963. *Occupational Characteristics.* Washington, D.C.: U.S. Government Printing Office.

_____. 1950, 1960, 1970. *Census of the Population.* Washington, D.C.: U.S. Government Printing Office.

_____. Annual. *Current Population Survey.* Washington, D.C.: U.S. Government Printing Office.

_____. Various. *Historical Statistics of the United States Statistical Abstract.* Washington, D.C.: U.S. Government Printing Office.

United States Department of Commerce. 1950–1971. *Survey of Current Business.* Washington, D.C.: U.S. Government Printing Office.

_____. 1977. *The National Income and Productivity Accounts.* Washington, D.C.: U.S. Government Printing Office.

United States Department of Labor. 1975, 1977. *Employment and Training Report of the President.* Washington, D.C.: U.S. Government Printing Office.

United States National Science Foundation. 1964a. *American Science Manpower.* Washington, D.C.: U.S. Government Printing Office.

_____. 1964b. *National Scientific Register.* Washington, D.C.: U.S. Government Printing Office.

_____. 1966. *Salaries and Selected Characteristics of United States Scientists.* Washington, D.C.

_____. 1968. *Support and Research Participation of Young and Senior Staff* (NSF 68–31). Washington, D.C.: U.S. Government Printing Office.

_____. 1970. *American Science Manpower.* Washington, D.C.: U.S. Government Printing Office.

_____. 1974. *Young and Senior Science and Engineering Faculty* (NSF 75–302). Washington, D.C.: U.S. Government Printing Office.

_____. 1976–1977. *Characteristics of Doctoral Scientists and Engineers in the United States.* Washington, D.C.: U.S. Government Printing Office.

United States Office of Education. 1957–58 through 1970–71. *Higher Education Salaries.* Washington, D.C.: U.S. Government Printing Office.

_____. 1972. *Digest of Educational Statistics.* Washington, D.C.: U.S. Government Printing Office.

_____. 1974–1977. *The Condition of Education.* Washington, D.C.: U.S; Government Printing Office.

_____. 1977. *Digest of Educational Statistics.* Washington, D.C.: U.S. Government Printing Office.

Uranowitz, S., and K.O. Doyle, Jr. 1978. Being Liked and Teaching: Effects and Bases of Personal Likability in College Instruction. *Research in Higher Education* 9:15–41.

Van Dyne, Larry. 1978. We No Longer Have Anything to Lose. *The Chronicle of Higher Education* 16:3–4.

Verderber, R.F. 1973. *The Challenge of Effective Speaking.* 2nd ed. Belmont, Calif.: Wadsworth.

Verry, Donald, and B. Davies. 1976. *University Costs and Outputs.* New York: Elsevier.

Vollmer, Howard M., and Donald L. Mills, eds. 1966. *Professionalization.* Englewood Cliffs, N.J.: Prentice-Hall.

Walker, Donald E.; David Feldman; and Greg Stone. 1976. Collegiality and Collective Bargaining: An Alternative Perspective. *Educational Record* 57:119–24.

Walker, J. Malcolm. 1976. Academic Governance: The End of 'Shared Authority.' Paper presented to Western Social Science Association, Tempee, Arizona, April.

Wallhaus, Robert A. 1975. *Measuring and Increasing Academic Productivity.* San Francisco: Jossey-Bass.

Weinberg, William M. 1976. Patterns of State-Institutional Relations Under Collective Bargaining. In Kenneth P. Mortimer, ed., *Faculty Bargaining, State Government, and Campus Autonomy.* Denver: Education Commission of the States.

Weinrich, John E. 1976. Appraising Faculty Performance for Merit Increases. *Improving College and University Teaching* 24:247–48.

Weisberger, June. 1976. *Faculty Grievance Arbitration in Higher Education.* Ithaca, N.Y.: Institute of Public Employment, Cornell University.

_____. 1977. Grievance Arbitration in Higher Education: Recent Experiences in the Arbitration of Faculty Status Disputes. Paper Presented at Fifth Annual Meeting of the Society of Professionals in Dispute Resolution, New York City, October 24.

Wherry, R.J. 1952. Control of Bias in Ratings. Department of the Army, The Adjutant General's Office, Personnel Research and Procedures Division, Personnel Research Branch.

White, Richard L. 1976. A Summary of the Research on the Impact of Collective Bargaining on the Governance of Higher Education. Paper prepared for Committee "T" of the American Association of University Professors.

Williams, Gareth; Tessa Blackstone; and David Metcalf. 1974. *The Academic Labor Market.* New York: Elsevier Scientific Publishing Company.

Wilson, D. and K.O. Doyle, Jr. 1975. Psychometric Characteristics of the Law School Evaluation Form. Minneapolis: University of Minnesota Measurement Services Center.

Wilson, R.C.; L. Woods; and J.G. Gaff. 1974. Social-Psychological Accessibility and Faculty-Student Interaction Beyond the Classroom. *Sociology of Education* 47:74–92.

Wollett, Donald H. 1973. Issues at Stake. In E.D. Duryea, Robert S. Fisk, and associates, eds., *Faculty Unions and Collective Bargaining.* San Francisco: Jossey-Bass.

Yuker, Harold E. 1974. *Faculty Workload: Facts, Myths, and Commentary.* Washington, D.C.: American Association for Higher Education.

Index

About the Editors

Darrell R. Lewis is an economist and associate dean of education at the University of Minnesota. His research interests have been in economic education and the economics of education with a current focus on higher education. He is the author or coauthor of numerous articles, monographs and books. His recent books include *Educational Games and Simulations in Economics, Current Issues of Economic Policy*, and *The Professor as Teacher: University Staff Development*.

William E. Becker, Jr. is associate professor of economics at Indiana University. His research interests are varied with numerous publications in the *American Economic Review, Journal of Finance, Journal of Human Resources, Journal of Economic Literature* and *Journal of Economic Education*. He has also authored *A Complement to Choice* and coauthored *Educational Games and Simulations in Economics*. He is currently a member of the American Economics Association's standing Committee on Economic Education and the Joint Council on Economic Education's Executive Committee.